The Knopf Collectors' Guides
to American Antiques

Robert Bishop & William C. Ketchum, Jr.
Series Consultants

A Chanticleer Press Edition

Glass Tableware, Bowls & Vases

Jane Shadel Spillman

With photographs by Raymond Errett

Alfred A. Knopf, New York

This is a Borzoi Book
Published by Alfred A. Knopf, Inc.

Copyright © 1982 by Chanticleer Press, Inc.
All rights reserved under International and Pan-American
Copyright Conventions. Published in the United States by
Alfred A. Knopf, Inc., New York, and simultaneously in
Canada by Random House of Canada Limited, Toronto.
Distributed by Random House, Inc., New York.

Prepared and produced by
Chanticleer Press, Inc., New York.

Color reproductions by Nievergelt Repro AG, Zurich, Switzerland.
Type set in Century Expanded by Dix Type Inc., Syracuse,
New York
Printed and bound by Kingsport Press, Kingsport, Tennessee.

First Printing

Library of Congress Catalog Number: 82-47849
ISBN: 0-394-71272-2

Contents

Acknowledgments

Many people have helped to make this book possible and assisted in its preparation. I am especially grateful to Dwight Lanmon, Director of The Corning Museum of Glass, who allowed us to use the museum's collection for the photographs; to Raymond Errett, who spent months photographing all the glassware in this guide; and to Patricia Driscoll and Nicholas Williams, who helped in the preparations for photography at the museum. Osna Fennar loaned examples of Carnival glass and Depression glass for Mr. Errett to photograph, and Harold Rothberg and Dallas Wurtzberger made their brilliant-cut pieces available to him. I also want to thank Robert Bishop and William C. Ketchum, Jr., who read the entire manuscript and made valuable suggestions. In Corning, special thanks go to Deborah Perry, who typed a large portion of the manuscript, often under pressure, and to my family who bore with the project very patiently. I owe special gratitude to Paul Steiner and his staff at Chanticleer. In particular, I want to thank Gudrun Buettner and Susan Costello, who developed the idea for this series; Carol Nehring, who supervised the art and layouts; Helga Lose and John Holliday, who saw the book through production; and most of all, Jane Opper, who with the help of Nancy Hornick edited and coordinated the project. Finally, my appreciation to Charles Elliott, Senior Editor at Alfred A. Knopf, for his editorial advice and support.

Picture Credits

All of the glassware in this book is from the collection of The Corning Museum of Glass, except for that in the following color plates: From Osna Fennar: 15, 34, 48, 51–52, 65–66, 69–70, 90–91, 96, 112, 144–145, 147, 151–152, 197, 212–213, 216–218, 247, 249, 251, 273, 277, 279, 285–289, 329, 334–335. From Harold Rothberg and Dallas Wurtzberger: 111, 207, 263–265. From anonymous collectors: 7, 12–13, 20 (right), 27, 45, 62, 157.

About the Author, Photographer, and Consultants

Jane Shadel Spillman

Curator of American Glass at The Corning Museum of Glass, author Jane Shadel Spillman is a leading authority on American antique glass and has lectured widely on the subject. She has written *American and European Pressed Glass in The Corning Museum of Glass* and *Glassmaking: America's First Industry*. Mrs. Spillman is also coauthor of *The Complete Cut & Engraved Glass of Corning, The Cut & Engraved Glass of Corning, 1868–1940*, and *M'Kee Victorian Glass: Five Complete Catalogs from 1859/60 to 1871*.

Raymond Errett

Photographer Raymond Errett is Conservator-Photographer at The Corning Museum of Glass, and has specialized in photographing glass for 20 years. His photographs have been featured in many national publications, and appear most recently in *Masterpieces of Glass* by Robert J. Charleston.

Robert Bishop

Director of the Museum of American Folk Art in New York City, consultant Robert Bishop is author of more than 40 books, among them *Treasures of American Folk Art*. He established the first master's degree program in folk art studies at New York University. Dr. Bishop is on the editorial boards of *Art & Antiques*, *Horizon Magazine*, and *Portfolio*.

William C. Ketchum, Jr.

Consultant and author of the Price Guide, William C. Ketchum, Jr., is on the faculty of The New School for Social Research and is a guest curator at the Museum of American Folk Art in New York City. He is also a consultant to the Sotheby Parke Bernet and Phillips galleries. Dr. Ketchum has written 17 books, including *A Treasury of American Bottles* and *The Catalog of American Antiques*, and is contributing editor of *Antique Monthly*.

Preface

Since earliest times, glass has been admired for its delicate yet enduring beauty. Ordinary utensils made of glass—tumblers, pitchers, and bowls—are often transformed into objects of art. Small wonder that glass collecting ranks as the third most popular field of collecting in the United States, surpassed only by coins and stamps. It appeals to all ages, budgets, and tastes. Glassware collections are as diverse as the numerous objects, colors, and glass types. Some people collect only certain shapes, such as butter dishes or decanters; others concentrate on a single color, particularly red or blue, or a decorative type, such as Carnival glass. Still other collectors focus on the products of one glasshouse or period. While many people simply enjoy the beauty of early American glass, some spend years researching the personal stories behind each piece or the history of a specific factory. Increasingly, American antique glass is being collected as an investment. Various collectors' clubs are scattered throughout the country, and antique glass shows and auctions take place practically year-round. Today, interest in collecting American antique glass is at its highest point since collecting in earnest began half a century ago.

This volume covers glass tableware, bowls, and vases made in the United States from Colonial days through World War II. Familiar tableware—wineglasses, sugar bowls, and plates—is included together with many pieces that are no longer fashionable, such as salt dishes, celery vases, spoon holders, and knife rests. Several kinds of glass—late 19th-century pressed, brilliant-cut, and Carnival—are still readily available. Glass objects of the 1930s and 1940s, especially Depression glass, are already avidly collected as the antiques of tomorrow. A companion volume covers antique American glass bottles, flasks, lamps, paperweights, and miscellaneous pieces, including doorknobs and dresser sets.

To help collectors recognize authentic antique tableware, bowls, and vases, this guide is organized by shape instead of by chronology, method of manufacture, or decorative style. The Hints for Collectors tell you what to look for and what to avoid, how to date different glassware, ways of estimating value, and how to recognize fakes. The Price Guide lists the currently accepted prices for all glass illustrated as well as the price range for matching glassware that is still available in sets. Some types of American antique glass are frequently no more expensive than quality modern tableware and are often substantially less. With this guide, a collector can select wisely and assemble a collection that is not only beautiful and distinctive but likely to increase in value.

A Simple Way to Identify Glass

Antique glass comes in a great variety of shapes with hundreds of patterns and designs. To guide collectors through this often bewildering array, we have chosen 350 representative examples of different types of antique tableware, bowls, and vases for full picture-and-text coverage. They include the most common shapes, patterns, and decorations, as well as a few rare historical pieces. The color plates and accompanying text are arranged in a visual sequence based on shape and decoration so that you can find an object without knowing its glass type, pattern name, manufacturer, or date.

Because it would be impossible to illustrate every decorative technique, pattern, and shape, this guide is also designed to help you identify and date glass tableware, bowls, and vases that are not shown. By using the tables and charts on glass types, pressed patterns, cut motifs, and decorative styles, you will be able to date and estimate the market value of hundreds of other pieces. The introductory essays on how glass is made, the history of the American glass industry, and changing decorative styles provide the necessary background for a basic understanding of American antique glassware. The table of American Glass Manufacturers offers a quick reference for the names of the major American manufacturers, their trademarks and signatures, factory locations, and dates of operation.

Experienced collectors already familiar with patterns, glass types, and manufacturers can refer to the Index directly. Using all of these tools, the beginning collector will find glass collecting easy, and the glass connoisseur will enjoy it more than ever before.

History of the American Glass Industry

The settlers who arrived in Jamestown, Virginia, a year after the establishment of the first English colony there in 1607 included a group of German and Polish glassblowers. The English Board of Trade had decided that glass production in the Colonies would be an ideal use for the abundant timber of the New World, especially since English forests, rapidly being destroyed, had to be conserved for shipbuilding. Despite plentiful fuel and sand, the chief requirements for glassmaking, the first attempt at production in the Colonies was a failure. Not only did the settlers face terrible hardships in the New World, but the English financiers lacked the necessary technical knowledge of the glass industry, and the imported glassblowers quarreled continuously. Moreover, the sheer distance of the markets to England made the venture impractical. Records indicate that samples of glass were sent back to England, yet only fragments from the glasshouse site remain of that first factory.

The First American Glasshouses

Although glasshouses were started in Salem, Massachusetts, New Amsterdam, New York, and Philadelphia in the mid-17th century, the colonists imported glass for their windows, wineglasses, and tableware into the early 18th century. The first successful glass factory in the Colonies was established by Caspar Wistar, a Philadelphia brass-button manufacturer who had emigrated from Germany. In 1739, Wistar imported German glassblowers to staff his factory in southern New Jersey. Official English policy at this time forbade all manufacture in the Colonies: America was supposed to produce only raw materials for factories in England and to provide a market for their finished goods. Defying this ruling, Wistar made bottles and window glass as well as some tableware. There are few records of Wistar's production; a few pieces inherited by Wistar's descendants indicate that bowls and candlesticks were made there. The search for American-made Wistar glass is complicated, however, by the fact that Wistar also imported and sold European glass.

The second successful glass entrepreneur in this country was Henry William Stiegel, who also came from Germany. Between 1763 and 1774 he built 3 glasshouses in Pennsylvania—the first at Elizabeth Furnace and 2 others at Manheim. Stiegel began producing fine tableware as well as bottles and window glass. Like Wistar, Stiegel imported workmen. Stiegel is supposed to have imitated German fashions in the glassware he made for his Pennsylvania Dutch neighbors (#40), and English styles for his customers in New York and Philadelphia (#133–134).

A third German, John Frederick Amelung, arrived with men and equipment to develop a large glass-factory complex in 1784 in Maryland. Backed by a group of merchants in Bremen, Amelung named the company the New Bremen Glassmanufactory. He produced the most sophisticated glass made in America up to that time, including goblets and tumblers (#41). Amelung made several signed and dated pieces for members of his family and for such important customers as Thomas Mifflin, the governor of Pennsylvania. Nearly 30 unsigned but very similar engraved pieces can now be attributed to this factory. Yet Amelung could not get Congress to pass protective tariffs and, like Wistar and Stiegel, found himself undersold by English competitors.

The War of 1812, when the English naval blockade cut off the supply of British-made goods, helped to free Americans from ruinous foreign competition. Nevertheless, of the 63 American glass factories started between 1790 and 1820, 34 failed after the war, when imported goods once again flooded the market. Despite this, glass production increased throughout the 19th century. The Boston Crown Glass Manufactory, organized in 1787 but opened in 1793, was the first successful factory in New England. At first, it too made mainly bottles and window glass, producing tableware (#39) only incidentally.

Midwestern Glasshouses

As settlers moved westward toward the end of the 18th century, they created a new market for manufactured goods, but glass was difficult to ship overland and only wealthy settlers could afford it. In the 1790s, 2 glass manufacturers started factories in the Pittsburgh area, which proved an ideal location because it permitted river transportation to the entire western frontier and because nearby coal deposits provided fuel. The glass industry spread down the Ohio River to western Virginia (later West Virginia) and, by 1825, to Kentucky and Ohio.

Pressed Glass Factories and Decorating Shops

In the East, the Boston Crown Glass Manufactory had expanded to 3 factories by 1818, and the New England Glass Company was organized across the Charles River from Boston. In the 1820s and 1830s, workmen from this factory started companies in New York City, Brooklyn, and Philadelphia. The New England Glass Company became one of the largest producers of pressed tableware (#25) and other decorative blown glass (#68, #121). Its output and reputation were rivaled only by the Bakewell factories (#106) in Pittsburgh and by the Boston & Sandwich Glass Company (#336), founded in 1825. Many scattered bottle and window glasshouses had also begun to flourish in southern New Jersey, upstate New York, New Hampshire, and Connecticut by the beginning of the 19th century. Toward the end of the century, there were more than 100 glass factories in the United States and almost as many glass-decorating shops, whose proprietors bought undecorated glassware and later sold it with cut or enameled designs.

20th-century Glass

Although the production of tableware was severely curtailed during World War I, after the war and in the 1930s factories mass-produced thousands of machine-made pieces in a new variety of tableware shapes and colors. In more recent decades, the revival of interest in handcrafts, such as woodworking, pottery, and weaving, spread to glass when the birth of the Studio Movement in 1962 encouraged individual glass artists and influenced design in large factories. For the first time, glassmaking was recognized as one of the fine arts. Our oldest industry had become our newest art.

Changing Decorative Styles

The first glassware used by the colonists was imported English, Venetian, and Dutch ware, and probably only a few wealthy individuals could afford such amenities. But by the early 18th century, English glassware was common in upper-class homes, especially in cities like Philadelphia, New York, and Boston. The earliest 18th-century glasses were heavy free-blown pieces made of England's best lead, or flint, glass. Toward the end of the century, glasses became lighter and such decorations as engraving and enameling became popular. Early American glassmakers like Stiegel, Amelung, and Wistar merely reflected the styles popular in England and Germany. There is no style unique to America for this earliest period.

Blown 3-mold Glass

It was not until the early 19th century, when glass was blown in full-size molds, that American glassware began to develop its own style and decoration. This first mold-blown glass is called blown 3-mold by collectors because someone erroneously thought that all the molds had only 3 parts. In fact, molds had 2, 3, 4, or even 5 parts, depending on the complexity of the piece. The earliest blown 3-mold patterns imitated cut-glass motifs, with geometric designs combining diamonds, squares, vertical ribs, and sunbursts. Tumblers (#45, #46), mugs (#55), decanters (#103), large and small pitchers (#81), serving dishes (#254), and sugar bowls (#131, #132) are the commonest shapes of this type, while stemware (#10) is rare. Slightly later designs feature simple floral and scroll motifs using ferns, flowers, and chains (#136). Most blown 3-mold pieces are of colorless glass and were made in New England. Some colorless and rare colored patterns may come from the early midwestern factories in Kent, Mantua, and Zanesville, Ohio. Blown 3-mold glass was a popular alternative to cut glass from about 1810 until about 1835, when it was gradually replaced by pressed glass.

Pressed Glass

The invention of the pressing machine in the 1820s was perhaps the most important contribution of the American industry to glass technology. Although the use of molds had increased efficiency, the pressing machine tripled the production of American tableware. In earlier free-blown and mold-blown glassware, the foot of an object had sometimes been made with a small handpress resembling an old-fashioned lemon squeezer. The pressing machine now made it possible to shape and decorate an entire object in a single operation that took only a few seconds. But in the earliest pressed pieces, contact with the cold metal mold produced an unattractive network of chill wrinkles on the surface. Soon the makers of pressed molds turned from imitations of cut glass to patterns with stippled backgrounds that covered the wrinkles. In the 1840s, the introduction of heated molds eliminated the chill marks and patterns became simpler. At first it was difficult to produce glasses with thin rims; perhaps this is why there are few drinking glasses among early pressed examples. As techniques improved and manufacturers found new glass formulas, they could produce thinner glass and a greater variety of shapes. By the late 1840s, pressed tableware was sold in matching sets, like china. Most sets were colorless and in fairly simple patterns. Handles were usually still applied by hand. Large objects like compotes, vases, and lamps could now be pressed in separate parts that were fused while hot, making it possible to produce

many shapes with fewer molds.

Although over 1500 pressed-glass patterns are known today, fewer than half can be attributed to a particular factory. Collectors call the earliest pressed glass of the 1830s lacy-pattern glass. It consists of intricate patterns with stippled backgrounds (#142, #143), and is usually heavier than later pressed glass. Pressed glass of the late 1840s and 1850s has simpler patterns composed of geometric designs combining circles, squares, and diamonds (#20, #23). In the 1860s and 1870s, hundreds of new pressed patterns were introduced, many in colored glass. They often featured realistic fruit or flower decoration (#31) or portraits of historical figures (#199, #200). The 1870s and 1880s saw a greater use of color and special effects such as frosting (#294), staining (#145), and acid-etching (#32). From the end of the 19th century until about 1915, pressed patterns imitated the latest expensive, brilliant-cut designs (#291).

Free-blown Glass
Despite the widespread use of pressed glass in the 19th century, blown glassware was always in demand. Styles hardly varied, except that the glass itself became lighter in the last quarter of the century. Possibly the only folk art form in American glass was made in the early 19th century by workmen on their own time between shifts in the bottle factories of New Jersey, New York, and New England. This glassware is often decorated with lily pads and threading (#123), and no 2 pieces are ever exactly alike.

Cut Glass and Engraved Glass
Cutting and engraving remained the most expensive forms of decoration throughout the 19th century. Cutting was done with steam-powered stone wheels. Most of the designs were copies of those popular in England, combining diamonds, fans, and panels (#54). From the 1820s to the 1840s, these designs were cut by the New England Glass Company in Massachusetts, by factories in New York City, and by Bakewell's glasshouses and other Pittsburgh firms. Engraving was even more highly specialized than cutting. Until late into the century, skilled engravers were rare in the United States, and engraved patterns were mainly composed of simple flowers or initials (#30), although occasional pieces displayed city views or hunting scenes (#21).

After the great exhibition of 1851 in London, when the Victorian idea of "good taste" changed, glass manufacturers began to seek new styles. Some glass of this period imitated other substances: mercury glass (#171) copied silver and opaque mottled glass resembled tortoiseshell. In the 1880s, other glassmakers created new heat-sensitive glass that could be partially shaded by reheating certain portions. Some of the most popular of these art-glass shades include Peachblow (#67), Amberina (#150), Burmese (#333), Agata (#191), and Wild Rose (#68). Other types of enameled decoration imitated fine porcelain (Royal Flemish, #182; Crown Milano, #181) or coral (Coralene, #350). These new trends, which required decoration of the entire surface, also fostered more elaborate glass-cutting patterns. Brilliant-cut glass, the term for this new style, was popular from about 1880 until 1915. Production was centered at the gigantic Libbey Company in Toledo, Ohio, at C. Dorflinger & Sons in White Mills, Pennsylvania, and at several cutting firms in Corning, New York. With the outbreak of World War I, raw materials became scarce, and many manufacturers turned from cutting to overall floral engraving (#33). Others used inexpensive pressed blanks on which a few flowers could be cut or engraved. In the 1920s and 1930s, stemware became much thinner and delicately cut patterns predominated.

Special Color Effects
At the turn of the century, Art Nouveau glass, originally a French style, became fashionable in the United States. The most prominent American Art Nouveau glassmakers were Louis C. Tiffany of Tiffany Glass & Decorating Company and Frederick Carder of Steuben Glass Works. Tiffany, the son of the owner of the famous New York jewelry store, imitated the iridescence found on ancient glass and experimented with new techniques, including layered glass like that used to make paperweights (#343), and Japanese designs. Frederick Carder, an Englishman, opened the Steuben Glass Works with financial support from T. G. Hawkes & Company, a local glass-cutting firm. Carder made all types of colored and fancy glassware, some of it similar to Tiffany's and some quite original (#344).

To capitalize on the demand for colored glass, the pressed glass factories added gilding or red and amber staining to some of their patterns. They sprayed other patterns with chemicals to make them iridescent, a technique that proved especially popular. The resulting purple, orange, and green iridescent glass manufactured between 1905 and 1920 is collected today as Carnival glass (#285–289).

Depression Glass
The glass of the 1920s reflected the austerity of postwar life. Tableware began to be pressed by automatic machines. Most of this glassware, now collected as Depression glass, was made in midwestern factories. Although some of the patterns are reminiscent of 19th-century designs (#249), many also reproduce the sharp corners and precise lines of Art Deco styles (#152). In the 1940s and 1950s, glassmaking was almost entirely confined to small-scale factories making quality tableware, such as Fostoria and Cambridge (#34), and to large corporations like Anchor-Hocking that turned out thousands of machine-made pieces (#69). Like Depression glass before it, this tableware of the 1940s and 1950s has now been discovered by collectors and enjoys new popularity.

How Glassware Is Made

Making glass is a complex process requiring skilled artisans and special ingredients. The basic raw material for glass is silica, usually in the form of sand. Other substances can be added to color or purify the glass, or to make it melt faster. Sometimes broken fragments, known as cullet, are also added to speed the melting process. This combination of raw materials is called a batch. Once all the ingredients have been mixed, the batch is shoveled into ceramic pots within a furnace and heated for about 24 hours at a temperature of 1000° F or more. When the glass reaches a nearly liquid, or molten, state, it is ready to be worked.

Until the 17th century, most glass was made with sand, and an alkali such as potash, soda, or lime was added to help it melt. In the 1670s, the English glass manufacturer George Ravenscroft substituted lead for soda and discovered that this produced a softer, more sparkling glass. Although lead glass could not be blown as thin as the earlier glass, it was ideally suited for cutting or engraving. Ravenscroft called this new product "flint glass" because the lead was refined from calcined flint. The greater the proportion of lead, the heavier and more brilliantly clear the glass. Flint glass became the English standard for tableware and was widely copied, especially in the United States. The term "flint glass" was used throughout the 19th century to indicate quality table glass made with lead, although flint was not an ingredient after the 18th century. In the 1860s, pressed glass manufacturers in the Midwest adopted a new nonlead glass formula made with lime for thinner glassware. Collectors usually refer to this type of glass as lime glass.

Glass Colors

Most silica contains iron impurities that give glass a natural green, brown, or aquamarine color. This type of glass was used in the 18th and 19th centuries to make bottles and the first American tumblers and mugs. The shades of green, brown, or aquamarine usually varied from light to dark, however, depending on the amount of iron impurities, the temperature of the furnace, and the length of time the glass was heated. This crude glass has always been the least expensive to manufacture and is still used today to make some bottles. Colorless glass, employed primarily for tableware and medicine bottles, requires purer sand and the addition of manganese as a decolorizer.

All types of glass can be artificially colored by adding metallic oxides. Instead of acting as a decolorizing agent, manganese added in greater amounts will produce light purple. Blues of various shades are achieved by adding cobalt or copper; yellow-green is formed with uranium. Red can be made by the addition of gold, copper, or, in modern times, the less expensive chemical, selenium. Pink glass is created by using less copper or gold, although this color is not often encountered in glass before the 19th century. Most foremen of glass factories in the 18th and 19th centuries carried notebooks with color recipes that were often closely guarded secrets. Many of these recipe books are now filed away in libraries and could still be followed if a manufacturer were willing to take the time and trouble.

Shaping Glass

There are 3 basic methods for forming glass shapes: free-blowing, mold-blowing, and pressing. For free-blown glass, a blower gathers a glob of molten glass from the pot onto one end of a hollow 4-to-6-foot blowpipe. He blows air into the other end of the blowpipe, forming a bubble. This bubble is rolled into a symmetrical form on a metal or stone slab, called a marver. Then it is tooled by hand into the desired shape—a pitcher, bowl, or vase—and smaller globs of molten glass, called gathers, are added as necessary for the handle, stem, or foot.

Glass-blowing requires a team of 3 to 5 people, headed by the gaffer, who carries out the principal shaping of the object. Assistants do the preliminary blowing and smoothing, bring the gaffer additional gathers of hot glass, supply him with tools, and do secondary shaping. When the lower part of the object is finished, an assistant brings a solid iron rod called the pontil or punty. This rod, which has a little molten glass on the end, is placed against the base of the object, to which it adheres, and the blowpipe is broken off. The gaffer then takes the rod and, using shears and other tools, trims and shapes the upper part and rim of the piece. Once the object is completely formed, the pontil rod is broken away, leaving a rough scar on the bottom called a pontil mark, which may be ground and polished later for a smoother bottom. During this complex process, the soft, cooling glass has a tendency to sag. To prevent the piece from sagging on one side, the gaffer must periodically reheat it at the furnace and turn the piece constantly while shaping it. When all shaping is completed, the object is gradually cooled, or annealed, in a special tunnel-shaped oven for up to 24 hours.

Mold-blown glass requires less handwork and is consequently more quickly made. The worker blows the molten glass into a metal mold to insure uniform shape and decoration. There are 2 basic types of molds: part-size pattern molds and full-size molds. A part-size pattern mold is a round, cuplike mold with 1 or 2 parts. The blower puts a hot gather of glass inside the mold and then expands it to impress the pattern on the outside of the object. When the piece is removed, it is expanded further and tooled into its final shape. In contrast, a full-size mold has 3, 4, or more hinged parts. The gather of glass is blown to its final size inside the mold, and needs only minor shaping for the neck or lip after removal.

For pressed pieces, molten glass is dropped directly into a metal mold and pressed with a plunger. As a result, the walls of pressed pieces are never as thin as blown examples. Pressing in the 19th century required 2 to 4 men, depending on how much hand-finishing was needed. The presser's principal task was to cut off the exact amount of molten glass needed to drop into the press: too much glass might give the object "fins" around the edges; too little glass would not fill the mold.

Twentieth-century machine-pressing is completely automated. The glass is melted in a temperature-controlled tank and fed directly into the mold. When the mold opens, a conveyor belt transports the piece to the annealing oven, from which it emerges completely formed and decorated. Semi-automated blowing machines were introduced in the 1890s for the production of bottles, containers, and tumblers. Fully automated glassblowing, however, was not perfected until the 1940s. Today many tableware manufacturers continue to produce machine-blown tumblers, but most other machine-made pieces are pressed.

Decorating Techniques

After the basic shape has been completed, by whatever method, the surface of the glass may be decorated by applying threads, chains, and other pieces of molten glass while the object is still *16* hot, or by cutting, engraving, or etching after the piece has annealed. In cutting, a stone wheel is used to cut away the surface of the glass. Engraving also cuts the surface, but with a finer edge, employing a smaller stone or copper wheel. The cutter positions his wheel on the far side of the object and looks through the glass to see his work. The engraver works with the wheel between himself and the object. Once completed, an engraved design can be polished to make it transparent; usually, however, it is left with a grayish, matt finish that causes the engraving to stand out.

Acid-etching is sometimes mistaken for engraving because it, too, may have a grayish, matt finish. The etched design is achieved with acid, which eats away at the surface. When examined under a magnifying glass, engraved designs have curved edges, while the edge of an acid-etched design cuts vertically into the surface of the glass. Etching was especially popular on tableware of the 1920s and 1930s. All 3 of these decorative techniques are more time-consuming and expensive to produce than molded or pressed decoration.

Colored decoration is also produced in several ways. The surface of the object can be enameled with a special paint, or enamel, made from powdered glass—a method used since Roman times. Gilt decoration can also be painted on the outside surface; this was an especially popular means of giving pressed glass a more expensive appearance. Using a more elaborate technique, an object is enclosed, or cased, with another layer or several layers of colored glass. Then a design may be cut, engraved, or etched through the casing to expose the original surface. Another, less expensive way to achieve the layered look is by staining the outside surface with chemicals, especially red or amber. Finally, colored glass itself can be shaded by reheating portions of the object, which causes these areas to change color. This method of decoration was fashionable in art glass of the 1880s and 1890s.

Parts of a Glass Object

Glassware is made in every shape and style imaginable. The main part of a piece is called the bowl (on stemware, vases, sugar bowls, and centerpieces) or the body (on pitchers, creamers, decanters, and tumblers). The area beneath the bowl or body is known as the base. Many objects also have a stem and a foot. Instead of a foot, some bowls and vases have a collarlike base. All free-blown or mold-blown glassware bears a pontil mark beneath the foot or base. This mark may be rough, polished, or

Creamer

pouring lip

rim

handle

body

stem

foot

Goblet

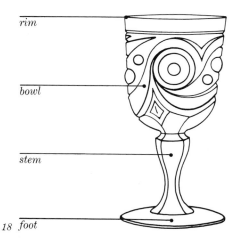

rim

bowl

stem

foot

covered by a cut design. Occasionally, the stem has a buttonlike or round knob, called the knop. Depending on its function, an object may have 1 or 2 handles, a pouring lip, or a cover. An especially elaborate or decorative knob on a cover is called a finial. Covered bowls, plates, and platters may have a flat shelflike rim, or flange, and some bowls have a high galleried rim to support a domed cover.

Sugar bowl

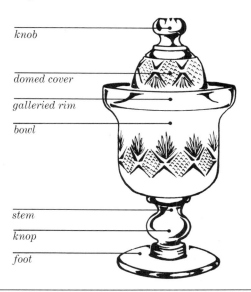

knob

domed cover

galleried rim

bowl

stem

knop

foot

Covered bowl

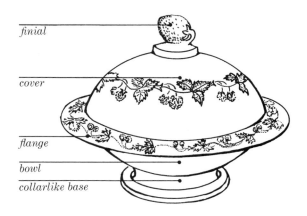

finial

cover

flange

bowl

collarlike base

Six Basic Glass Types

Free-blown
Look for a rough or polished pontil mark beneath the foot or base. On a cover, the pontil mark is located on the inside or on the top.

Blown in a Part-size Pattern Mold
If you can feel the contours of the pattern on the inside of the piece, the object is mold-blown. You should also be able to see or feel mold marks on the outside of the bowl or foot. If the pattern is smaller and sharper near the base and fainter and larger near the top, it was blown in a part-size pattern mold. This type of glassware often has ribs or diamonds of various sizes. The pontil mark is rough or polished.

Blown in a Full-size Pattern Mold
If the pattern is the same size everywhere on the piece, and you can feel the contours of the pattern on the inside of the object, it was blown in a full-size pattern mold. Most glassware of this type was made in the early 19th century and is called blown 3-mold glass. It usually has geometric patterns with squares, diamonds, vertical ribs, and sunbursts. Some late 19th-century pieces were also blown in full-size pattern molds. The pontil mark is rough, polished, or covered by a design.

Pressed
The pattern can only be felt on the outside; the inside should be completely smooth. Pressed edges are blunt, unlike the sharp edges of cut glass. You may be able to see or feel mold marks on the bowl or foot.

Cut
The edges of the design should be very sharp. Look for a polished pontil mark or a cut design beneath the base or foot. Cut glass is usually free-blown or mold-blown.

Engraved
Engraved designs are mainly monograms, flowers, leaves, or scenes. The engraving is usually grayish, but rarely it is polished and transparent. Engraving appears on free-blown glass and occasionally on pressed glass. Look for a polished pontil mark on free-blown pieces.

pontil mark on top or underneath

pontil mark underneath

pontil mark on top or underneath

small ribs

large ribs

large ribs

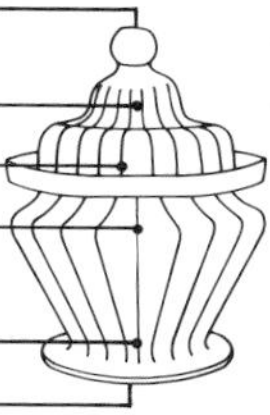

small ribs

pontil mark underneath

pontil mark on top or underneath

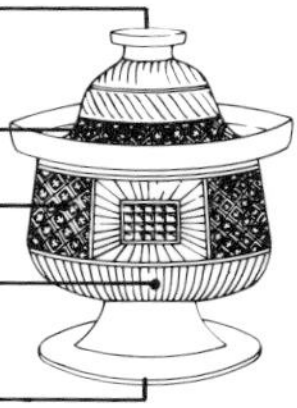

same size pattern overall

pontil mark underneath

smooth inside

pattern on outside

smooth inside

pattern on outside

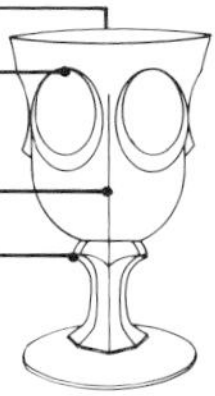

mold mark

blunt point

sharp scallop or point

cut notch

sharp edge

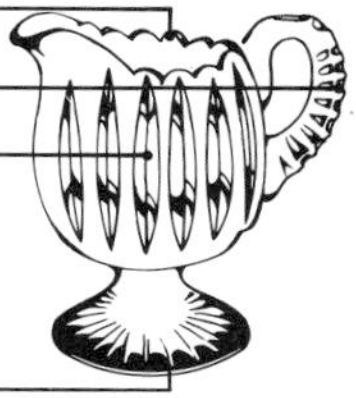

cut design underneath

monogram

wreath

pontil mark underneath

How to Use This Guide

Identifying and dating antique American glassware requires a combination of many skills. By following the simple steps outlined below, you will be able to date most of the objects that you find at antique shops, auctions, flea markets, yard sales, and perhaps even in your own attic.

Preparation
1. The 350 examples in this guide have been divided into 11 groups. The introductory essay preceding each group discusses guidelines for dating the range of objects in that section. Knowing these general hints at the start will save you time and prevent mistakes later.
2. Information-at-a-Glance explains the text headings and type of specific information under each category.
3. Before you begin to collect glass, you should know what factors influence price. Read the introduction to the Price Guide carefully.

Using the Visual Key
1. To identify a piece of glassware, first turn to the Visual Key. Select the shape within one group that most resembles your object, then turn to the entry numbers indicated above the shape.
2. Narrow your choice to a single color plate. Then read the Description and the Type and Dimensions sections. These categories specify the identifying characteristics of the type illustrated. If your example matches the general description, refer to the Locality and Period section to date your piece. The rest of the entry will explain where the object was made, whether it has matching glassware, its history, and collecting hints.
3. Look in the Price Guide under the entry number for the current market value of glass of this type. The price range for all items listed under Matching Glassware is also included, from the least to the most expensive.

Using Pattern or Design as Your Guide
If you identify the shape of your piece but cannot find the same pattern or design, check to see if the differences are included in the Description section under *Variations*. If they are covered, then all of the information in this entry and the Price Guide (except for Matching Glassware) applies to your object as well. If your design does not appear under *Variations*, check one of the following quick reference guides.
1. For pressed patterns:
Over 60 pressed patterns, including 22 not shown elsewhere in the book, are illustrated in the Pressed Pattern Guide. They are divided into 4 groups, according to period and style. If you find your exact pattern in this table and it also appears in a color plate, turn to the entry number indicated next to the pattern name. Check Matching Glassware; if your shape is listed, you will be able to date your piece based on the entry. The Price Guide indicates the price range that you can expect. If your pattern is illustrated in the Pressed Pattern Guide but does not appear elsewhere in the book, you can still determine its approximate value. From the same pattern group, select one that is illustrated in a color plate. In the Price Guide, the Matching Glassware for this illustrated entry will suggest a price range for your similar piece. For the best price estimate, select the same shape as yours in several comparable patterns, and use an average of their prices as your guide.

2. For cut motifs:

To help you recognize the most common cut designs, the Cut Motif Guide illustrates 16 basic cut motifs. The section "Cut Glass by Period" classifies all of the cut pieces in the guide by date: 19th-century cut glass (c. 1810–80), brilliant-cut glass (c. 1880–1915), and 20th-century cut glass (c. 1915–50). By checking the color plates indicated for each group, you should be able to identify the style of cutting on your piece with a specific period. You may determine an approximate value by reviewing the price ranges of similarly shaped objects with the same cutting style dating from the same period. It is important to remember, however, that the value of all cut glass is based on whether it can be attributed to a known firm and on the quality of the cutting.

3. For other types of decoration:

If you cannot find the decoration you are looking for on the correct shape, check the listing in the Index under one of the following categories: applied decoration, acid-etched, art, Art Nouveau, cased, enameled, engraved, gilt, and stained. Under each heading, you will find the shapes illustrated and their plate numbers. Once you can identify the type of decoration, you will be able to date your object.

Checking Specialized Information

Since many shapes and decorative styles are associated with a specific period, it is often possible to establish an approximate date by choosing either the shape or pattern that most closely resembles your object. To find more information, consult the Bibliography. Here, specialized books are arranged according to glass type.

Once you are familiar with the many glass types, you will find the Tips for Recognizing Glass Types and Styles a useful quick reference. This checklist summarizes distinguishing characteristics of different kinds of glassware, potential areas of confusion, and ways to recognize fakes.

Information-at-a-Glance

Each entry in this guide consists of a color plate and a descriptive text. At a glance, you can recognize the glass type you are looking for and, on the same page, find all the necessary facts for identifying and dating it. The entry number is repeated in the Price Guide and for cross-references throughout the book. Named patterns appear in captions.

Description

Each description covers the general shape of the object, its decoration, and important secondary features, such as a pouring lip, cover, or handle. Key identification features are italicized. Inscriptions or trademarks on the base of an object, which are not visible in the photograph, are also noted. (Important trademarks are illustrated in the table of American Glass Manufacturers.) The pontil marks on free-blown, mold-blown, and a few early pressed pieces are also described. All known colors of an object are indicated, as well as the kind of glass (transparent, opaque, opalescent, or iridescent). Clear glass is referred to as colorless. *Variations* notes differences in shape or pattern. Technical terms are defined in the Glossary.

Type and Dimensions

This section describes how the glass was made and decorated, and provides the dimensions of the type shown. Height is measured from the highest point and includes the cover or pouring lip. A dimension range is given for free-blown or mold-blown pieces, and for pressed glassware made by more than one factory, since sizes vary considerably. Because the lead content in early 19th-century glass is sometimes important in determining the place of origin or date of a piece, this information is also provided. In colorless examples, lead glass is generally clearer and heavier than nonlead glass. Ultraviolet light may be used to check the lead content of colorless glass: lead glass turns bluish. This information is not mentioned for Carnival glass and Depression glass, which never contain lead, nor for art, Art Nouveau, and other opaque, colored glass because the lead content is difficult to determine.

Locality and Period

This category indicates where glass of the type shown was made and the period of manufacture. If several companies produced the same type of glass, a general locality is given, and the company that made the glass illustrated is discussed in the Comment section. The table of American Glass Manufacturers provides more complete information on dates of operation.

Matching Glassware

Whenever the example illustrated was made as part of a matching set, the other tableware is listed here. This category does not apply to the variations. Objects that have similar decorative motifs but were not made as a set are also included. Cross-references are provided for matching pieces illustrated.

Comment

This section covers the history of the glass illustrated and information on decorative techniques, pattern names, and the popularity of the piece.

Hints for Collectors

Here you will find such collecting tips as how to identify and date glass of the type illustrated, what features to look for, what telltale signs to avoid, how to recognize reproductions, and whether glass of this type is a good investment.

Glass Tableware, Bowls & Vases

Visual Key

The glassware included in this guide has been divided into 11 groups. For each, a symbol appears on the left, along with a description of the range of shapes within that group. Drawings of representative objects included in the group are shown on the right. The plate numbers are indicated above each shape. Occasionally, similar objects appear in other groups. To help you find these pieces, their plate numbers have an asterisk (*). The group symbol is repeated on the opening page of the section concerning that group and again in the Price Guide.

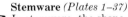

Stemware *(Plates 1–37)*
In stemware, the shape of the bowl and the length of the stem vary greatly. Many early wineglasses have a short stem, while late 19th- and early 20th-century wineglasses and goblets have a longer one. Most stemware was designed for beverages, but some forms were used to serve eggs, jelly, or sherbet.

Tumblers, Mugs, Tankards, and Cups *(Plates 38–69)*
These forms range from cylindrical to barrel-shaped or slightly conical. Mugs, tankards, and cups have handles; tumblers do not. Some cups also have a foot.

Pitchers, Jugs, Decanters, and Bar Bottles *(Plates 70–113)*
Pitchers always have a handle and a pouring lip. Although jugs also possess a handle, they may lack a pouring lip. Pitchers may be barrel-shaped, globular, or tall with a distinct waist. Most jugs are round to pear-shaped with a long neck. Decanters and bar bottles also have long necks but are usually more cylindrical. Decanters have a small flat lip and a glass stopper, while bar bottles have a heavy rounded lip and lack a stopper.

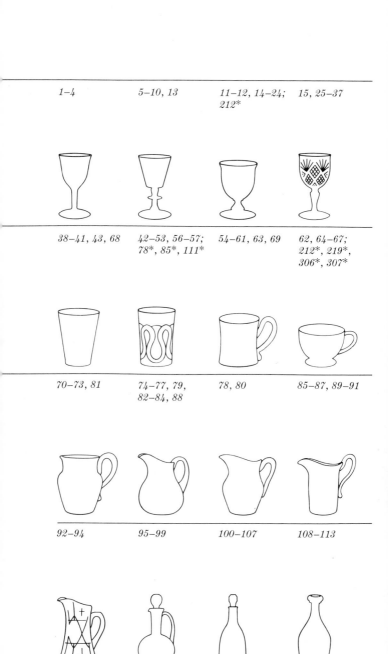

1–4   5–10, 13   11–12, 14–24; 212*   15, 25–37

38–41, 43, 68   42–53, 56–57; 78*, 85*, 111*   54–61, 63, 69   62, 64–67; 212*, 219*, 306*, 307*

70–73, 81   74–77, 79, 82–84, 88   78, 80   85–87, 89–91

92–94   95–99   100–107   108–113

Sugar Bowls and Creamers *(Plates 114–154)*
Sugar bowls and creamers come in many shapes—globes,
cylinders, and hexagons—with all types of decoration. Many
sugar bowls have handles and covers, but others do not.
Creamers, which resemble larger pitchers, have a pouring lip
and a handle. Both forms may have a foot and sometimes a stem.

Salt Dishes, Condiment Servers, and Small Table Accessories
(Plates 155–198)
These small table accessories include salt dishes, vinegar cruets,
pickle jars, biscuit boxes, and syrup jugs, as well as such novelty
items as toothpick holders, match holders, knife rests, and
napkin rings.

Plates *(Plates 199–219)*
Most plates are circular, although a few are oval, square, or
hexagonal. Those with cut designs and pressed patterns tend to
be elaborate, and often have a scalloped rim. In contrast, free-
blown plates with applied decoration are usually simple.

Covered Bowls and Butter Dishes *(Plates 220–247)*
Covered bowls and butter dishes were common in the 19th
century. Although some butter dishes have flat plates for the
base, most have bowls. Many covered bowls possess a shelflike
rim. Several are in animal shapes, such as ducks, roosters, fish,
or clams.

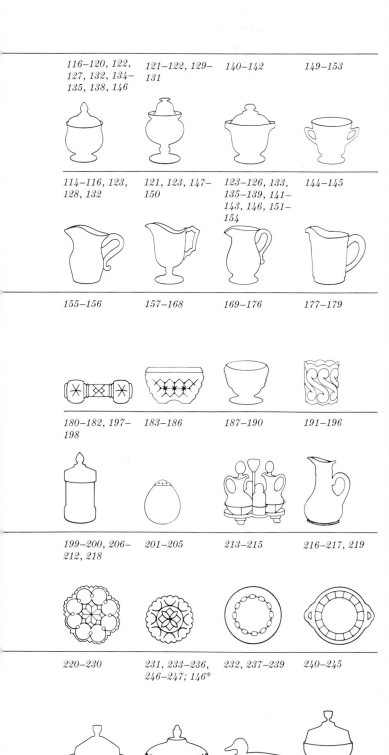

116–120, 122, 127, 132, 134–135, 138, 146

121–122, 129–131

140–142

149–153

114–116, 123, 128, 132

121, 123, 147–150

123–126, 133, 135–139, 141–143, 146, 151–154

144–145

155–156

157–168

169–176

177–179

180–182, 197–198

183–186

187–190

191–196

199–200, 206–212, 218

201–205

213–215

216–217, 219

220–230

231, 233–236, 246–247; 146*

232, 237–239

240–245

Bowls *(Plates 248–289)*
The classic bowl is a simple circular form, made in nearly every type of glass. However, some bowls are oval or rectangular. Many have scalloped or flaring rims. Some cut-glass examples are novelty shapes, such as acorns or leaves. Decoration varies greatly, and many bowls are elaborate. Celery dishes and trays are also included in this group.

Centerpieces *(Plates 290–313)*
Most of these large pieces have high stems or elaborate silver-plated frames. They include salvers, compotes, covered bowls on stands, punch bowls, epergnes, and bride's baskets.

Celery Vases, Spoon Holders, and Spill Holders
(Plates 314–323)
These pieces, which resemble vases, were common in the 19th century but are no longer used today. Celery vases are found in all types of glass; spoon holders and spill holders are primarily of pressed glass.

Vases *(Plates 324–350)*
These upright vases come in a greater variety of shapes, colors, and types of decoration than any other form. They are made in all types of glass.

248, 255

249–254, 266–269; 29*, 219*

256–260

261–265

270–272

273–278

279–289

290, 298–307

291–293

294–297

308–313

314–317, 320

318–319, 321

322–323; 146*

324, 326, 341–345, 349

325, 336–340

327–329

330–336

335, 346, 348–350

347–348

Stemware

Stemware can be broadly defined as drinking glasses with stems and feet. Most stemware was designed to hold alcoholic beverages or water. A few forms, such as jelly and sherbet glasses and eggcups, were used for solid foods.

In the late 18th and early 19th centuries, very few stemware shapes were made in free-blown and mold-blown glass, and our ancestors were not always particular about using a specific size or shape for a specific purpose. Eggcups and wineglasses, for example, were interchangeable: a glass-factory advertisement of about 1850 lists "egg or wine glasses" for sale. Large goblets (#12), which we might use as water goblets, were probably intended for wine, beer, or cider in the 19th century because water was not served at a meal. Medium-size glasses (#2, #4, #6, #7, #10) were intended for any type of wine including sherry. Only champagne was served in specially designed flute shapes (#13).

The advent of the pressing machine in the 1820s brought a revolution to glassmaking: glassware could be mass-produced in many shapes with the same pattern. For the first time, matching tableware sets were priced within reach of the middle class. American glass manufacturers and housewives began to assign distinct functions to different stemware. The number of sizes and shapes steadily increased throughout the 19th century. When brilliant-cut glass became popular around the turn of the century, it was marketed in sets with a different stemware shape for each course, including separate glasses for red and white wines. Manufacturers of pressed glass offered the same variety in sets that were less expensive. In reaction to this mass-produced ware, many glasshouses designed blown and engraved sets, but of course at a much higher price.

During the 1910s and 1920s, Art Nouveau stylists like Louis C. Tiffany designed sets of blown glass that were influenced by the shape and decoration of brightly colored Venetian glassware of the 19th century. This was the first time that Americans thought it proper to drink wine from colored glasses.

In dating stemware, there are several important points to remember. The more colorful a glass, the more likely it was produced in the latter part of the 19th or early 20th century. The longer the stem is in relation to the size of the bowl, the later the glass. Finally, heavy cut stemware was popular from about 1880 to 1915. Lighter-weight, thinner glasses with delicate cutting and engraving were preferred immediately before and after this period: 1860–80 and 1920–40.

Late blown wineglass

Description
Plain round-bottomed bowl with straight stem and circular foot. Thin walls. Pontil mark polished. Colorless.

Type and Dimensions
Free-blown bowl with drawn, tooled stem and foot. Lead glass. Height: 4½–5″. Rim diameter: 2¼–2½″.

Locality and Period
Throughout the United States; probably the Northeast. c. 1870–1900.

Comment
This type of glass was so common during the late 19th century that it could have been made in almost any glasshouse. Today it is more rare than either the cheaper pressed versions or the more expensive blown and cut glasses. By the end of the 19th century, a rough pontil mark was a sign of an unfinished glass: either a glass meant for cutting or engraving, or possibly one that was brought home from the factory before it was finished. This round-bottomed bowl is similar to other wineglasses from the 1870s and 1880s. Around the turn of the century, the stem began to lengthen in proportion to the bowl, and greater variety in bowl shapes became the rule (#34).

Hints for Collectors
Because blown wineglasses are not available in sets, they are not especially sought after. They are much less expensive than either pressed or cut stemware of the same period. Late 19th-century wineglasses are thinner than early 19th-century examples.

Early blown wineglass

Description
Plain conical bowl with straight stem and circular foot. Pontil mark rough. Color: *slightly grayish. Variations:* walls may be thin or thick.

Type and Dimensions
Free-blown bowl with drawn, tooled stem and foot. Lead or nonlead glass. Height: 5–5¼". Rim diameter: 2½–2¾".

Locality and Period
Massachusetts, Pennsylvania, and Maryland. c. 1790–1810.

Comment
The unusual shape of this glass is hard to pin down to a period. Its color resembles pieces from John Frederick Amelung's New Bremen Glassmanufactory in New Bremen, Maryland, but its shape is much rounder than most late 18th-century glasses of this size. The glass may have been made later than those from Amelung's factory. Very little is known about tableware from the earliest Philadelphia and Maryland glass factories, but it is possible that these houses were making nonlead glasses like the one illustrated. A factory at Germantown, Massachusetts, which operated for a brief period in the mid-18th century, also may have made glassware like this, but its products have not been documented.

Hints for Collectors
Plain glasses like this are a challenge to date and identify. Examine the quality of the glass, how it was made, and whether it has bubbles. Bubbles and an irregular shape are signs of poor workmanship. These elements are easy to overlook on a patterned glass, but they cannot be hidden on a plain one.

Description
Uneven trumpet-shaped bowl with molded vertical ribs. Short
straight stem and circular foot. Pontil mark rough. Transparent
glass bubbly throughout. Color: usually greenish or amber.
Variations: ribs may be swirled (#16); quality of glass varies
greatly.

Type and Dimensions
Bowl blown in vertically ribbed pattern mold. Stem and foot
drawn and tooled. Nonlead glass. Height: 4¾–5¼". Rim
diameter: 2¼–2½".

Locality and Period
Probably western Pennsylvania and Ohio. c. 1800–30.

Matching Glassware
Tumblers (#44), pitchers (#72), bar bottles (#113), creamers and
sugar bowls (#117), salts (#176), plates (#214), and bowls
(#274). Not made as set.

Comment
Judging from the bubbly glass, uneven shape and proportions,
most of these glasses were probably blown in a bottle factory.
The example illustrated is attributed to the Mantua Glass Works
in Mantua, Ohio, which operated from 1821 to 1829. Wineglasses
like these are much rarer than tumblers, bottles, pitchers, or
related decorated glassware. Perhaps the early settlers on the
western frontier preferred stronger spirits.

Hints for Collectors
Because midwestern blown glass is often greenish and bubbly,
even an expert may confuse it with Mexican glass of the 1920s
and 1930s. Look beneath the foot for wear marks, such as minute
scratches where the foot touches the table. However, on some
glasses even scratch marks are sometimes counterfeit.

Trumpet-shaped wineglass

Description
Trumpet-shaped bowl with thick stem and circular foot. Thin walls. Pontil mark rough or polished. Color: usually colorless; occasionally transparent greenish or amber. *Variations:* bowl may have cut, engraved, or enameled decoration, or molded ribs; rim of foot may be plain, or folded for added strength.

Type and Dimensions
Free-blown or mold-blown bowl. Applied or drawn stem and foot. Lead glass; rarely colored nonlead glass. Height: 4–4¾". Rim diameter: 2–2¼".

Locality and Period
Massachusetts, New York, New Jersey, Pennsylvania, and Maryland. c. 1780–1820.

Comment
The trumpet-shaped wineglass and the button-stem wineglass (#5) are the most common wineglass forms dating from the earliest period of American glass. Their small capacity suggests that our ancestors were not heavy wine drinkers. Americans were known for their consumption of distilled spirits, such as whiskey and rum; only in the cities did most people drink wine.

Hints for Collectors
Look for a smoothly ground and polished pontil mark on decorated wineglasses and a rough mark on plain ones. Decorated forms rarely have a rough pontil mark. If the pontil has been ground smooth and the bowl is not decorated, the glass is a later copy or possibly English. Most American collectors consider the English glass less valuable, but the price of both is generally the same. Plain wineglasses are seldom found in sets, although both plain and decorated glasses may have been sold that way originally.

5 Button-stem wineglass

Description
Bucket-shaped bowl with thick bottom. Thick walls. *Buttonlike knop on straight stem.* Circular foot. Pontil mark rough or polished. Color: usually colorless; occasionally transparent greenish or aquamarine. *Variations:* bowl may have cut, engraved, or enameled decoration (#6, #7).

Type and Dimensions
Free-blown or mold-blown bowl. Applied, tooled stem and knop. Applied, tooled foot. Lead glass or colored nonlead glass. Height: 3½–4¼". Rim diameter: 2–2¼".

Locality and Period
The Northeast and western Pennsylvania. England and continental Europe. c. 1800–40.

Comment
Collectors call these glasses button-stem wines because of the distinctive flat knop. They were also made in England and on the Continent, but American pieces are considered the most valuable by American collectors. The glasses will hold only 2 or 3 ounces. Although they may have been used as cordial glasses, today they are excellent for sherry.

Hints for Collectors
Do not hesitate to collect a set of slightly different-size wineglasses. Slight variations in size and proportion are typical of free-blown glass and add to its appeal. Colored nonlead glasses are usually Continental. If the pontil mark is ground smooth and polished, and the bowl is plain, the glass is probably English. Today it is unusual to find these glasses in sets.

Decorated button-stem wineglass

Description
Bucket-shaped bowl with thick bottom. Flowers and leaves enameled (left) *or engraved* (right). Thick walls. Straight stem with *buttonlike knop.* Circular foot. Pontil mark rough or polished. Color: *mostly colorless;* sometimes faint yellowish or greenish tinge. *Variations:* colors of enameled decoration vary; bowl may have molded ribs as seen on right.

Type and Dimensions
Free-blown bowl or mold-blown for ribs. Applied, tooled stem and knop. Applied, tooled foot. Nonlead glass. Height: 4–4½″. Rim diameter: 2–2½″.

Locality and Period
Continental Europe: probably Germany, Bohemia, and Switzerland; widely exported to the United States. c. 1800–40.

Matching Glassware
Set with engraved decanter.

Comment
Antique dealers often claim that this type of glassware was made by Henry William Stiegel's American Flint Glass Works in Manheim, Pennsylvania, during the 1770s. However, the distinctive bucket shape was not used until much later.

Hints for Collectors
Beware of any glass that is said to be Stiegel's, since the Stiegel factory never marked its glassware. An authentic piece from this glasshouse might sell for 50 times the price of these 19th-century wineglasses. Enameled glass was probably not made by Stiegel; the glasshouse "flowerer" mentioned in Stiegel's 1773 account book was an engraver. Mold-blown examples of the decorated wineglass are less common than free-blown ones.

Cut button-stem wineglass

Description
Bucket-shaped bowl with thick bottom and lines cut around bowl. Thick walls. Straight stem with *buttonlike knop.* Circular foot. Pontil mark polished. Colorless. *Variations:* cut lines may be panels (left), rays (center, right), circles, fans, diamonds, or combinations of these motifs. Thick bottom may be cut into panels (center and right).

Type and Dimensions
Free-blown bowl. Applied, tooled stem with added knop. Applied, tooled foot. Lead glass. Height: 3½–4½". Rim diameter: 2–2¼".

Locality and Period
Massachusetts, New York, New Jersey, and Pennsylvania. c. 1800–40.

Matching Glassware
Set with champagne glasses, tumblers, and decanters.

Comment
Cut button-stem wineglasses are harder to find than plain ones, although they were probably made by most tableware glasshouses during the early 19th century. Collectors generally associate these glasses with the Pittsburgh area, specifically with one of the Bakewell glasshouses, but they were widespread in the Northeast.

Hints for Collectors
Watch out for glasses with their rims ground down to remove chips. This repair changes the proportion of the cut design to plain areas on the bowl, making the wineglass less valuable. Although originally sold in matching sets, these glasses are more often found singly or in pairs. Some collectors assemble a set with one of each pattern.

Engraved Gravic wineglass

Description
Bucket-shaped bowl with large engraved iris design and small
flower wreaths on bowl and around foot. Thin walls. Straight
stem has buttonlike knop. Circular foot, with Gravic Glass
trademark of T.G. Hawkes. Pontil mark polished. *Colorless.*
Variations: several flower designs, including carnation,
chrysanthemum, aster, rose, and a general floral pattern; also
strawberry pattern. May have cut hobstar or sunburst
underneath foot.

Type and Dimensions
Free-blown bowl with applied, tooled stem, knop, and foot.
Stone-wheel engraved after annealing. Lead glass. Height:
5½–6″. Rim diameter: 2½–3″.

Locality and Period
T.G. Hawkes & Company, Corning, New York. c. 1903–30.

Matching Glassware
Set of tableware, including glasses and serving pieces.

Comment
Gravic Glass was a trademark registered by Hawkes in 1903 to
distinguish this cheaper line of stone-engraved ware, mostly
floral designs, from his brilliant-cut glass. In the 1920s Hawkes
produced the same Gravic patterns, but changed the name to
"satin engraved."

Hints for Collectors
Hawkes's Gravic Glass and the Tuthill Cut Glass Company's
similar floral and fruit engravings are the most sought-after
stone-engraved ware. Although many smaller firms did the same
kind of work, their glasses do not command as high a price. The
shape of this glass is virtually identical to earlier simple
wineglasses (#5, #7), but it came about 60 years later.

9 Cut water goblet

Description
Bucket-shaped bowl with cut vertical ribs around sides and 2 horizontal lines at middle. Engraved eagle and shield below rim on 1 side. Thin walls. Solid stem has flat buttonlike knop. Circular foot has cut sunburst underneath. Colorless. *Variations:* many patterns, including very small cut diamonds, cut and polished circles, and engraved flowers; may have cut hobstar underneath. Usually without eagle and shield.

Type and Dimensions
Free-blown bowl with applied, tooled stem and foot. Cut and copper-wheel engraved after annealing. Lead glass. Height: 6–6¼". Rim diameter: 3⅜–3½".

Locality and Period
Blank probably from Tiffin Glass Company, Tiffin, Ohio; possibly another Ohio firm. c. 1930–50. Cut by T.G. Hawkes & Company, Corning, New York. c. 1930–50; with seal, c. 1937–39.

Matching Glassware
Set with wine, champagne, sherry, and cordial glasses, and fingerbowls. *Without engraved eagle and shield.*

Comment
This cut pattern, called Venetian, is different from Hawkes's turn-of-the-century Venetian pattern with cut hobstars and ovals. In the late 1930s, President Franklin D. Roosevelt ordered a set of this crystal for the White House before a visit from the King and Queen of England. The presidential seal, an eagle and shield, was engraved on the pattern in 1937.

Hints for Collectors
Glasses from the White House turn up from time to time. In the 19th century it was common for presidential families to sell to the public the glass, china, and furniture of previous administrations.

Venetian pattern

Blown 3-mold wineglass

Description
Barrel-shaped bowl with molded geometric pattern of diamonds and vertical ribs. Thick walls. Straight stem has flat buttonlike knop. Circular, slightly domed foot. Pontil mark rough. *Colorless. Variations:* shape of bowl sometimes more trumpetlike; many patterns, mostly combining squares, diamonds, ribs, waffling, and sunbursts.

Type and Dimensions
Bowl blown in full-size mold for pattern and shape, then tooled into final form. Applied, tooled stem and foot. Lead glass. Height: 3¾–4″. Rim diameter: 1¾–2″.

Locality and Period
New England: probably Boston & Sandwich Glass Company, Sandwich, Massachusetts; and New England Glass Company, Cambridge, Massachusetts. Possibly New York City, Philadelphia, and New Jersey. c. 1815–35.

Matching Glassware
Tumblers in 2 sizes, goblets, and miniature decanters. Not made as set.

Comment
Wineglasses with blown 3-mold bowls are much less common than plain or cut examples. Similar glasses were made in nonlead glass at the royal factory in Portugal in the 19th century, but few of these glasses reached this country.

Hints for Collectors
The Metropolitan Museum of Art in New York City has sold reproductions of these glasses for several years. Reproductions have the same pattern as the glass illustrated, but are always marked "MMA." Reproductions are more conical and about 3⅛″ high.

Depression goblet

Description
Oval bowl has *overall pressed diamond pattern* and plain rim with 3 horizontal rings below. Thick walls. Straight stem with round knop. *Square foot* has sunburst underneath. Color: transparent pink, light green, or colorless; rarely transparent red or dark blue.

Type and Dimensions
Machine-pressed in mold for pattern and shape. Height: 5½″. Rim diameter: 3¼″.

Locality and Period
Hocking Glass Company, Lancaster, Ohio. c. 1935–37.

Matching Glassware
Large set with plates and bowls in several sizes, serving dishes, pitchers, tumblers, wine and sherbet glasses, salt and pepper shakers, sugar bowl, creamer, cups, saucers, and butter dish.

Comment
The Miss America pattern shown is a copy of the Waterford line by T.G. Hawkes & Company, Hunt Glass Company, and other 1930s cut glass firms. This 10-ounce goblet is a good example of machine-made Depression glass inspired by the more expensive cut pieces.

Hints for Collectors
Depression glass will more likely turn up at flea markets or specialized Depression glass shops than in antique stores. Except for rare shapes and colors, this glass is still very affordable. Colorless pieces are the most common and least expensive, followed by pink or green examples; red or blue glasses are the most valuable. Both the matching butter dish and the salt and pepper shakers have been reproduced and may be difficult to distinguish from originals.

Miss America pattern

Description
Trumpet-shaped bowl. Short stem with buttonlike knop. *Square foot* with rosette design underneath. Colorless. *Variations:* bowl round to trumpet-shaped; plain circular foot with rough pontil mark, or square foot with polished surfaces and no rosette; rarely engraved scenes or monograms.

Type and Dimensions
Free-blown bowl and applied, hand-pressed foot. Lead glass. Height: 5–5½″. Rim diameter: 2¾–3″.

Locality and Period
Boston area: Boston Crown Glass Manufactory; Thomas Cains's South Boston Flint Glass Works; New England Glass Company, Cambridge. c. 1800–20. England. c. 1790–1820.

Comment
This glass is in a European style of the late 18th century. The English name "rummer" may be a corruption of the German *roemer*, meaning "wineglass," or perhaps the glass was originally used for drinking rum. In England, however, rum was considered a lower-class drink. Since these glasses are stylish, it is more likely that they were used for wine.

Hints for Collectors
Most European rummers are decorated with engraved pictures, simple monograms, or cut panels; they are rarely transparent dark blue or green. American glasses are always colorless and usually plain. Similar glasses with square feet and made of nonlead glass are probably German or Bohemian. Because the rummer shape has not been very popular with American collectors, undecorated glasses are relatively inexpensive for such an early period.

13 Flute champagne glass

Description
Trumpet-shaped bowl with straight stem and circular foot. 2 flat buttonlike knops on stem. Bowl may be plain (left) or decorated with cut panels (right). Pontil mark rough or polished. Colorless. *Variations:* cut decoration may be more elaborate.

Type and Dimensions
Free-blown bowl with applied, tooled stem and foot. Lead glass. Height: 6½–7″. Rim diameter: 2¼–2½″.

Locality and Period
Massachusetts, New York, New Jersey, and Pennsylvania. England. c. 1800–30.

Comment
These flute, or trumpet-shaped, glasses are a very old form, dating back to the Middle Ages. In early 19th-century America, they were used to serve champagne, which was a new drink at that time. By the 1880s, however, saucer-shaped champagne glasses (#28) had become the rage, and flute shapes were no longer made. The plain glass illustrated here was used as a measure, indicated by the lines scratched at the 1- and 2-ounce levels by some previous owner. The glass will comfortably hold 2 ounces.

Hints for Collectors
Popular in England as well as the United States, the 2 versions of this glass are nearly impossible to distinguish. A plain glass with a rough pontil mark, like the one illustrated, is always American. The cut example bearing a polished pontil mark could be either English or American. As a rule, glasses with a better finish and more elaborate decoration were made in England.

14 Firing glass

Description
Trumpet-shaped bowl with heavy short stem and heavy circular foot. Bowl rarely may have crudely engraved monogram or Masonic decoration, as seen here, usually compass and architect's T square combined with sun, moon, olive branches, and all-seeing eye. Motto "SIELENTIO DE FIEDE" on 1 side and engraved circle below lip. Thick walls. Pontil mark rough. Colorless. *Variations:* often lacks engraving.

Type and Dimensions
Free-blown bowl with drawn, tooled stem and foot. Nonlead glass. Copper-wheel engraved after annealing. Height: 4–4½". Rim diameter: 2⅜–2¾".

Locality and Period
Germany, Bohemia, and England; widely exported to the United States. c. 1780–1820.

Comment
Glasses with this shape are called firing glasses because of their use in private clubs and drinking societies. When club members wished to show approval of a speech or join in a toast, they thumped the foot of the glass on the table. A crescendo of knocks sounded like gunfire. Early collectors attributed these glasses to Amelung's factory in Maryland, but it seems unlikely that any were made there.

Hints for Collectors
Many of the earliest American Masonic lodges, such as the one George Washington belonged to in Virginia, owned sets of firing glasses. Although engraved glasses today are scarce, the more common plain ones are relatively inexpensive. The glass illustrated here has an air bubble in the stem, a decorative feature that sometimes increases the value of a piece.

Depression stemware

Description
Bowl conical (left), cup-shaped with wide ribs (center), or trumpet-shaped with panels (right). All have pressed pattern of stylized flowers or scrolls. Stem, when present, straight with knop at top, or short. Circular foot flat or domed. Transparent glass. Color: *Rose Cameo pattern (left) green only;* Mayfair (center) colorless, light blue, pink, green, or yellow; Patrician (right) pink, green, amber, or yellow. *Variations:* many patterns; occasionally geometric.

Type and Dimensions
Machine-pressed for pattern and shape. Height (left): 5⅛"; rim diameter: 3¾". Height (center): 4"; rim diameter: 2½". Height (right): 5¼"; rim diameter: 3¹⁄₁₆".

Locality and Period
Ohio: Rose Cameo at Belmont Tumbler Company, Bellaire, c. 1931; Mayfair at Hocking Glass Company, Lancaster, c. 1931–37; Patrician at Federal Glass Company, Columbus, c. 1933–37.

Matching Glassware
Rose Cameo: set with bowls, salad plates, sherbet glasses, and tumblers. Mayfair: large set with pitcher (#70), bowls (#273), tumblers, and other tableware. Patrician: set with tumblers, sugar bowl and creamer (#151), and other tableware.

Comment
Mayfair is one of the most popular Depression-glass patterns among collectors, and pink the least expensive color.

Hints for Collectors
Beware of green, blue, or pink reproductions of the small whiskey tumblers in Mayfair. Originals were made in paler green or blue, and rarely in pink. New glasses are also thicker and the rose has a single, rather than double, stem.

Rose Cameo, Mayfair, and Patrician patterns

Trumpet-shaped jelly glass

Description
Trumpet-shaped bowl with molded swirls, curved slightly at rim.
Round knop between bowl and tooled foot. Pontil mark rough or
polished. Color: colorless or grayish. *Variations:* bowl may be
plain; sometimes lacks knop.

Type and Dimensions
Blown in vertically ribbed pattern mold and then swirled.
Applied knop and foot. Lead glass. Height: 4–4½″. Rim
diameter: 2½–3″.

Locality and Period
Massachusetts and Pennsylvania. England. c. 1790–1810.

Comment
Jelly glasses were originally used to serve a puddinglike dessert.
They were not intended as drinking glasses, although their shape
is similar to English ale glasses of the same period. Today some
collectors use these glasses for sherry. The English glass is much
more common than the American form, possibly because the
shape was going out of fashion by the 1820s, when the American
glass industry had begun to prosper.

Hints for Collectors
Because fewer people collect jelly glasses, they are less
expensive than English wineglasses of the same period.
Reproductions are uncommon. Most glasses from antique shops
are English; American examples are rare. If the pontil mark is
polished, the glass is English; if rough, it may be American and
will be more expensive. The 2 types are virtually impossible to
distinguish when the pontil mark is rough.

Early geometric-style pressed tumbler

Description
Conical glass with pressed diamond pattern around sides. Thick walls. Flat circular foot. Colorless. *Variations:* other patterns include Thumbprint, (#297, #298), Excelsior, Huber, and Colonial (#22); these patterns usually colorless; rarely opalescent white, transparent blue, purple, or yellow.

Type and Dimensions
Pressed in mold for pattern and shape. Lead glass. Height: 4–4½". Rim diameter: 3½–3⅝".

Locality and Period
Bakewell, Pears & Company, Pittsburgh, and other western Pennsylvania firms. c. 1850–70.

Matching Glassware
Set with butter dish, covered compote, and salver.

Comment
These footed tumblers somewhat resemble wineglasses but lack a true stem. They were probably meant for whiskey or other alcoholic drinks. They are certainly heavy enough for tavern use, although they may also have been popular in the home. This pattern is called Victoria.

Hints for Collectors
Footed tumblers have not been reproduced very often, making them a good choice for collectors. Because they are so sturdy, it is rare to find a chipped glass. They can be used fairly safely in the home, as long as ordinary care is taken. Generally, tumblers of this type are not as expensive as other drinking glasses.

Victoria pattern

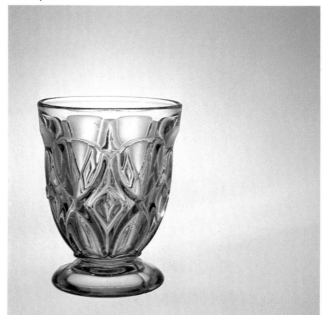

Early geometric-style pressed ale glass

Description
Heavy conical bowl with pressed pattern of ovals below rim and vertical fluting around sides. Thick walls. Circular foot. Colorless. *Variations:* several faceted patterns, including Ashburton (#20) and Huber.

Type and Dimensions
Pressed in mold for pattern and shape. Lead glass. Height: 6½–6¾″. Rim diameter: 3–3¼″.

Locality and Period
Bakewell, Pears & Company, Pittsburgh; possibly other midwestern companies. c. 1870–80.

Matching Glassware
Set with goblets and compote.

Comment
Ale glasses like the one shown were only made in pressed glass. They were primarily manufactured for use in public bars or restaurants, which accounts for their heavy weight. A Bakewell, Pears & Company catalogue of about 1875 referred to this ale glass as the Brooklyn pattern. The origin of the name is not known; however, it was common for companies to name a series of glasses after places, like the Cincinnati and New Orleans patterns of M'Kee & Brothers of Pittsburgh.

Hints for Collectors
Although these glasses are attributed to Bakewell, Pears & Company, they are not especially popular among collectors, perhaps because of their awkward shape. They have never been reproduced and are therefore a safe choice for beginners. Occasionally they may be confused with early 20th-century soda fountain glasses. Check the height; soda glasses have the same shape but are considerably larger.

Brooklyn pattern

19 Centennial pilsner

Description
Tall narrow bowl tapers toward bottom. *10 pressed panels around bowl*, with 1 star on each side; 1 inscribed "1876," the other has "1776" at center. Thick walls. Short paneled stem flares at base. Circular foot. Colorless.

Type and Dimensions
Pressed in mold for pattern and shape. Nonlead glass. Height: 7¼". Rim diameter: 2¾".

Locality and Period
Central Glass Company, Wheeling, West Virginia. c. 1875–76.

Matching Glassware
Beer mugs. Not made as set.

Comment
Many glass souvenirs were produced to commemorate the nation's Centennial in 1876. Some were made on the grounds of the Centennial Exhibition in Philadelphia by Gillinder & Sons, which built a factory for that purpose and sold thousands of pressed-glass souvenirs. However, many other companies around the country also made and sold souvenirs. This Centennial pilsner and its matching beer mug were patented by John Oesterling and Julius Palme of the Central Glass Company, April 11, 1876. The patent describes it as a pilsner; it was undoubtedly used for beer, even though its capacity is fairly modest. The ale glass (#18) is the more standard size for beer and ale.

Hints for Collectors
Since the Bicentennial in 1976, there has been a great surge of interest in items made and marketed 100 years ago. Over the last 5 years all of this glassware has greatly increased in price. The pilsner and beer mug are rare and not often seen in antique shops.

Description
Elongated bowl with overall pressed diamonds or geometric pattern. Straight stem swells slightly at base of bowl or near circular foot. Pontil mark polished, when present. Color: usually colorless; occasionally opalescent white, transparent green, blue, purple, or yellow. *Variations:* patterns mostly geometric.

Type and Dimensions
Pressed in mold for pattern and shape. Lead glass. Height: 5–5¼″. Rim diameter: 1⅞–2″.

Locality and Period
Massachusetts: Boston & Sandwich Glass Company, Sandwich; New England Glass Company, Cambridge. Pittsburgh: James B. Lyon & Company; Bakewell, Pears & Company; and other glasshouses. c. 1848–70.

Matching Glassware
Ashburton: set with stemware (#23), tumblers, mugs, sugar bowl, creamer (#126), decanters, pitchers, bar bottles (#109), eggcups, and serving pieces. Diamond Point: set with most tableware shapes including salver (#293).

Comment
Pressed-pattern jelly glasses are rarer than wineglasses from the mid-19th century. Most jelly glasses were free-blown or mold-blown. The glasses illustrated are Sharp Diamond (left), called Diamond Point by collectors, and Ashburton (right).

Hints for Collectors
The Ashburton jelly glass illustrated has a smoothly ground pontil mark because the entire glass was fire-polished to remove mold marks, making the piece look more like expensive cut glass. Most jelly glasses were not fire-polished, yet it is a desirable feature on early pressed glass.

Diamond Point and Ashburton patterns

Red-stained and engraved goblet

Description
Oval bowl with flat polished rim. *Engraved scene on 1 side* and scroll decoration on other. Thick walls. *Paneled stem with multifaceted knop.* Circular foot polished underneath. *Colorless glass stained red;* rarely red or amber casing. *Variations:* usually scenes of hunting, deer and dogs, or trailing vines; also American landmarks, such as the Battle Monument in Baltimore (illustrated here), New Orleans harbor, and the White House. Circles or ovals may replace scrolls. Foot may have cut petals or large scallops.

Type and Dimensions
Free-blown, tooled bowl with applied, tooled stem and foot. Ground and polished top rim and foot. Stained red or cased after annealing. Copper-wheel engraved through color. Nonlead glass. Height: 5½–5⅝". Rim diameter: 2¼–2⅜".

Locality and Period
New England Glass Company, Cambridge, Massachusetts; Brooklyn Flint Glass Works, Brooklyn, New York. Bohemia. c. 1850–70.

Comment
Both the New England and Brooklyn companies advertised Bohemian-style glassware, which combines engraved decoration with color. Yet the nonlead content and ground and polished rims suggest that these glasses were probably imported from Europe. Simpler goblets similar to the one illustrated came in sets with decanters and wineglasses.

Hints for Collectors
Similar glasses are still being made in Czechoslovakia today, but in modern examples, the red stain is quite thin and often scratched, and the engraving is shallower and less detailed.

Early geometric-style pressed goblet

Description
Heavy bell-shaped bowl with pressed row of large circles. Thick walls. Straight stem has collar at top. Circular foot shows 3 mold lines. Pontil mark rough. Color: colorless or opalescent white. *Variations:* decoration varies from geometric designs to elaborate floral or figure patterns; these also rarely transparent blue, purple, or yellow.

Type and Dimensions
Pressed in mold for pattern and shape. Lead glass. Height: 6–6½″. Rim diameter: 2¼–2½″.

Locality and Period
Massachusetts: Boston & Sandwich Glass Company, Sandwich, and New England Glass Company, Cambridge. Western Pennsylvania: Curling, Robertson & Company, Pittsburgh, and others. c. 1850–70.

Matching Glassware
Set with ale and champagne glasses, footed tumbler, and sugar bowl.

Comment
Modern collectors call this pattern Colonial, but it bears no resemblance to pre-Revolutionary glassware, which was made before the pressing machine was invented. The pontil mark indicates that the piece was fire-polished to remove mold marks.

Hints for Collectors
The simple geometric pattern and heavy glass on this example are typical of the 1850s and 1860s. Some patterns of this period were made in a full range of tableware, but the pattern illustrated came in very few shapes, indicating that it was not popular. Colored glasses are rare and command a higher price than colorless ones. The opalescent white may appear bluish.

Colonial pattern

Early geometric-style pressed eggcup

Description
Heavy shallow bowl with round bottom. *Pressed pattern of diamonds, circles, or facets*, or combinations of these. Thick walls. *Very short stem.* Circular foot. Color: rarely colorless; transparent yellow, blue, or purple. *Variations:* many different designs, mostly geometric. Stem varies as illustrated.

Type and Dimensions
Pressed in mold for pattern and shape. Lead or nonlead glass. Height: 3½–4″. Rim diameter: 2¼–2½″.

Locality and Period
Massachusetts, western Pennsylvania, West Virginia, and Ohio. c. 1850–70.

Matching Glassware
Set with glasses and serving pieces in Waffle and Thumbprint (center) and Ashburton (right, #20, #109, #126).

Comment
Eggcups appear only in pressed glass of the middle and late 19th century. They are sometimes confused with open salt dishes because of their similar size. The Palace pattern (center), called Waffle and Thumbprint by collectors, appeared in the 1869 catalogue of the New England Glass Company and an 1856 advertisement of Curling, Robertson & Company of Pittsburgh. It was probably also made by other manufacturers. The Divided Diamond pattern (left) cannot be attributed to a particular factory, but dates to the same period. The Ashburton pattern (right) was made by several factories.

Hints for Collectors
Geometric patterns were much less common during the last decades of the 19th century, when more realistic patterns became popular. Eggcups have never been reproduced.

Divided Diamond, Waffle and Thumbprint, and Ashburton patterns

Early geometric-style pressed eggcup or wineglass

Description
Round-bottomed bowl with pressed honeycomb pattern. Thin walls. *Short straight stem* is paneled. Circular foot has 3 mold lines. Color: usually colorless; rarely transparent yellow, blue, or amber; opaque green and white; or opalescent white. *Variations:* 2 different kinds of honeycomb patterns, covering various amounts of bowl; also engraved (#102).

Type and Dimensions
Pressed in mold for pattern and shape. Lead or nonlead glass. Height: 4–4⅛″. Rim diameter: 2¾–2⅞″.

Locality and Period
New England and New York. c. 1850–80. The Midwest. c. 1860–1900.

Matching Glassware
One of largest sets known, with glasses of all sizes, decanter (#102), bar bottle, pitcher, sugar bowl, creamer, butter dish, spoon holder, compote, and string holder.

Comment
Honeycomb is one of the most popular patterns ever produced. The New England Glass Company of Cambridge, Massachusetts, made 2 pressed versions: New York, with a plain upper third of the bowl; and Vernon, with an overall honeycomb. James B. Lyon & Company of Pittsburgh marketed the same 2 variations under the names "New York" and "Cincinnati."

Hints for Collectors
This shape is confusing because it is rather large for an eggcup and has a shorter stem than most wineglasses. According to early advertisements, it was meant for both purposes. Beware of nonlead reproductions that can be confused with midwestern glasses made in the 1890s.

Honeycomb pattern

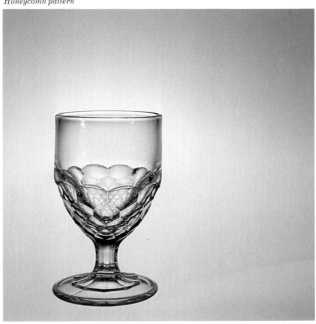

25 Early geometric-style pressed goblet

Description
Round-bottomed bowl with pressed comet design. Thick walls. *Baluster-shaped stem* has panels. Flat circular foot with 3 mold lines. Colorless. *Variations:* at least 2 pressed comet designs, including the one illustrated and Horn of Plenty (#56).

Type and Dimensions
Pressed in mold for pattern and shape. Lead glass. Height: 6¼–6½″. Rim diameter: 3–3¼″.

Locality and Period
Massachusetts: probably Boston & Sandwich Glass Company and Cape Cod Glass Company, Sandwich; and New England Glass Company, Cambridge. c. 1850–70.

Matching Glassware
Set with water pitcher, wineglasses, tumblers, and mugs.

Comment
This early patterned glass was probably used for water; glasses of this size are listed in New England catalogues as goblets. Smaller glasses were used for wine (#24, #26). The Cape Cod Glass Company marketed a comet pattern in 1869, which may have been this one. M'Kee & Brothers of Pittsburgh sold a different comet pattern, which collectors now call Horn of Plenty. The pattern illustrated is known as Comet.

Hints for Collectors
If you order this pattern by mail, be sure to specify which pressed pattern you want. There are at least 2 pressed comet patterns and 1 cut pattern.

Comet pattern

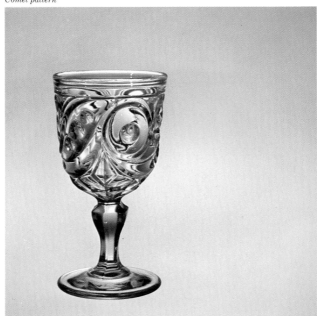

Early geometric-style pressed wineglass

Description
Heavy conical bowl has pressed stylized pineapple design alternating with tulips. Thick walls. Straight paneled stem. Circular foot has 3 mold lines. *Colorless. Variations:* hundreds of patterns, including circles, panels, diamonds of many sizes, and flowers and fruit; foot may lack mold marks.

Type and Dimensions
Pressed in mold for pattern and shape. Lead glass. Height: 5–5¼". Rim diameter: 2¼–2½".

Locality and Period
Massachusetts: probably Boston & Sandwich Glass Company, Sandwich; New England Glass Company, Cambridge; and several other factories in area. c. 1850–70.

Matching Glassware
Set with drinking glasses, decanter, bar bottle, pitchers in various sizes, sugar bowl, compote, and bowls.

Comment
It is still possible to collect a whole table setting of New England Pineapple. Like all patterned glass of the 1850s and 1860s, this is flint glass, which has a low to medium lead content and is consequently both heavy and very clear.

Hints for Collectors
Antique dealers often charge more for the earlier flint glass than the later, lighter-weight lime glass (#24, #31). New England Pineapple was a favorite in the 1930s and 1940s, and is now hard to find. Both the goblet and wineglass have been reproduced. These reproductions are lighter in weight and will probably show less wear; they were never fire-polished and always have mold marks.

New England Pineapple pattern

Brilliant-cut cordial or liqueur glass

Description
Round or trumpet-shaped bowl with cut pattern of hobstars, crosshatching, diamonds, and fans. *Thick walls at base, thinner toward rim.* Stem straight (left, right) or baluster-shaped (center) with notched cutting. Circular foot has cut hobstar (center) or sunburst (left, right) underneath. Color: colorless; occasionally cased with transparent red, blue, green, or yellow. *Variations:* arrangement of motifs varies; stem may lack cutting.

Type and Dimensions
Free-blown bowl with applied or drawn stem. Applied, tooled foot. Cut after annealing. Lead glass. Height (left): 4⅛–4½"; rim diameter: 2–2⅛". Height (center): 4½–4⅝"; rim diameter: 2–2⅛". Height (right): 3½–3⅝"; rim diameter: 1⅝–1¾".

Locality and Period
Throughout the United States. c. 1890–1915.

Matching Glassware
Set with decanter and cordial glasses; also large stemware set with wine and champagne glasses, goblets, and finger bowls.

Comment
The trumpet-shaped glass is a traditional 20th-century form for sherry, although sherry glasses are normally larger. The small capacity of the glasses illustrated suggests they were originally used for cordials. Today a round bowl for cordials is more common.

Hints for Collectors
Cut stemware of this period is always thicker toward the base to strengthen the glass for cutting, and very thin near the rim for a finer drinking edge. Glasses made after 1910 are more uniform in thickness. These glasses are fairly common and have never been reproduced.

Brilliant-cut saucer champagne glass

Description
Shallow saucer-shaped bowl, thinner and flaring slightly at rim.
Deeply cut hobstar design between miter cuts. *Hollow hourglass
stem opens to bowl;* with flutes and notch cutting. Circular foot
has cut sunburst underneath. Colorless. *Variations:* hundreds of
patterns, usually combinations of hobstars and diamonds;
occasionally simple panels. Stem may be solid; foot may have cut
hobstar underneath.

Type and Dimensions
Free-blown bowl with drawn, tooled stem and applied, tooled
foot. Cut after annealing. Lead glass. Height: 4½–5″. Rim
diameter: 3⅝–4″.

Locality and Period
Throughout the United States. c. 1890–1910.

Matching Glassware
Large set with stemware in several sizes, finger bowls, and
plates.

Comment
The glass illustrated here was cut by J. Hoare & Company of
Corning, New York, around 1900. The saucer-shaped champagne
glass replaced the flute champagne glass (#13) in the 1880s. A
hollow stem was added around 1900.

Hints for Collectors
Hollow-stemmed glasses are particularly fragile since they lack
the additional support of solid stems. Intact examples may be
hard to find. Look for cracks or glued pieces. These glasses are
often stained by sugar or wine that has dried inside the hollow
stem. Although it is sometimes possible to remove them with
extensive soaking, such stains decrease the value.

Description

7-piece set: (below, left to right) champagne and white-wine glasses, finger bowl and underplate; (opposite) goblet, red-wine and cordial glasses. *All pieces have overall cut star pattern.* Stemware has round bowl; thick walls at base, thinning toward rim. Straight *stem cut in panels, with multifaceted knop. Cut sunburst underneath circular foot.* Finger bowl and matching underplate uniformly thick; plate with scalloped edge, bowl with plain rim. Color: colorless; *only white-wine glass cased* in red, green, amber, and rarely blue. *Variations:* several hundred cut patterns combining different cut motifs, such as stars, hobstars, strawberry-diamonds, fans, pinwheels, and other intricate designs; foot may have cut hobstar underneath. Sometimes acid-stamped trademark or paper label.

Type and Dimensions

Free-blown bowl with drawn stem and applied, tooled knop and foot. Cut after annealing (white-wine glass cased with color, then pattern cut through). Lead glass. Goblet height: 6¼–6⅜″; rim diameter: 3⅛–3¼″. Red- and white-wine height: 5¼–5⅜″; rim diameter: 2⅞–3″. Cordial height: 4½–4⅝″; rim diameter: 2–2⅛″. Champagne height: 5–5⅛″; rim diameter: 3⅜–3½″. Finger bowl height: 4½–4¾″; rim diameter: 5¹⁄₁₆–5⅛″. Underplate diameter: 7¹⁄₁₆–7⅛″.

Locality and Period

Corning, New York: T.G. Hawkes & Company and J. Hoare & Company. C. Dorflinger & Sons, White Mills, Pennsylvania. Possibly other factories. c. 1882–1915.

Matching Glassware

Set with sherry glasses, serving pieces, and salt (#159); tumblers after 1900.

Russian pattern

Comment

The pattern illustrated was the first in the new brilliant-cut style and was widely admired and copied. It was patented in 1882 by Philip MacDonald, a cutter for T.G. Hawkes & Company. After the Russian ambassador in Washington and the American ambassador in Moscow ordered sets in 1883 and 1884, the pattern became known as Russian. President Benjamin Harrison ordered a large set of several hundred pieces for the White House in 1886. With additions, the set was used until the late 1930s, when President Franklin D. Roosevelt replaced it with a simpler pattern designed by Hawkes, known as the Venetian pattern (#9). The Russian pattern for the White House set was initially ordered from the Hawkes company, but some reorders also went to the Dorflinger firm. This glassware was always expensive because of its elaborate cutting. The place setting shown here was cut by Hawkes in the 1880s.

Hints for Collectors

The earliest brilliant-cut glass, made between 1882 and 1900, is not marked. It is worth seeking because both plain, uncut blanks and cut ware are usually of higher quality than much of the post-1900 cut glass. Cased pieces, or what many collectors call "colored cut to clear" glass, are rarer and consequently much more expensive. Except for white-wine glasses, which often had colored casing, cased pieces such as bowls and vases were usually special orders. Pressed copies in the Daisy and Button pattern (#261) are also extremely popular and still being made.

Engraved goblet

Description
Bucket-shaped (left) *or round* (right) *bowl with engraved flower wreath encircling initial and cut facets at bottom. Thin walls.* Straight stem has cut panels. Circular foot. Pontil mark polished. *Colorless. Variations:* 2 or 3 initials or short name (#119); stem may lack panels.

Type and Dimensions
Free-blown bowl with drawn stem and tooled foot. Copper-wheel engraved after annealing. Lead glass. Height: 5½–6″. Rim diameter: 3–3¼″.

Locality and Period
Massachusetts, New York, New Jersey, and Pennsylvania. c. 1865–85.

Matching Glassware
Complete tableware set with drinking glasses of all sizes, celery vase, compote, and cheese dish.

Comment
Simple engraved glasses became popular after the Civil War and were often purchased in large sets. The goblet with an engraved "N" shown here was part of a set made at the Boston & Sandwich Glass Company in 1869 for the Reverend C.S. Nutter upon his retirement from the Methodist Church in Sandwich, Massachusetts.

Hints for Collectors
Pressed-glass copies with similar engraving were originally much cheaper than blown goblets, but are more expensive today. To make sure a glass is blown, look for the pontil mark, which in this period was always polished. Pressed glass is usually thicker, and the engraving is shallower and more crudely done.

31 Realistic-style pressed goblet

Description
Round-bottomed bowl with pressed design of bleeding heart flowers around sides. Thin walls. Straight stem has knop at base. Circular foot with 3 mold lines. Colorless. *Variations:* 20–30 different floral and fruit patterns from the 1870s and 1880s, such as Rose-in-Snow, Rose Sprig, Wildflower (#49), Stippled Forget-Me-Not, Dahlia, Lily-of-the-Valley, Beaded Tulip, Primrose, Flower Pot, and Clematis.

Type and Dimensions
Pressed in mold for pattern and shape. Nonlead glass. Height: 6⅜–6½". Rim diameter: 3⅛–3¼".

Locality and Period
Pittsburgh: King, Son & Company's Cascade Glass Works, c. 1870–90; United States Glass Company, c. 1891–1900.

Matching Glassware
Set with wine and cordial glasses, tumblers, mugs, eggcups, pitcher, creamer, sugar bowl, bowls, butter dish, cake plate, covered compotes, plates, platter, relish dish, salt, spoon holder (#318), and celery vase.

Comment
This pattern appears in the 1875 catalogue of King, Son & Company, the only firm known to have made it. Although it was called Floral Ware in the catalogue, collectors today refer to the pattern as Bleeding Heart because it depicts that flower.

Hints for Collectors
Although this pattern was made perhaps 10 years after the early geometric-style goblet (#25), it is the same shape. Not until the end of the century did stemware shapes begin to change. Shape is often helpful in dating glasses.

Bleeding Heart pattern

Locke Art wineglass

Description
Oval bowl with etched flowers and leaves around sides. Very thin walls. Stem has double knop and cut panels. Circular foot. Pontil mark polished. Color: usually colorless; rarely cased in transparent orange, green, or blue. Signed "Locke Art" or "J. Locke" underneath foot or on bowl. *Variations:* stem shape varies considerably, including several knopped types and some lacking knop and panels.

Type and Dimensions
Free-blown bowl with applied, tooled stem and foot. Acid-etched after annealing. Lead glass. Height: 5¾–5⅞". Rim diameter: 2½–2⅝".

Locality and Period
Blank probably made in Pittsburgh factory. Acid-etched by Locke Art Company, Mount Oliver, Pennsylvania. c. 1900–20.

Matching Glassware
Many stemware shapes, pitchers, and bowls. Not made as set.

Comment
Joseph Locke, an English engraver and cameo carver, developed several art-glass colors, such as Amberina (#332) and Pomona (#259), at the New England Glass Company in the 1880s. When the New England firm moved to Toledo, Ohio, Locke started his own company and developed acid-etched art glass. He also became artistic director of the new United States Glass Company.

Hints for Collectors
Locke's acid-etched glass is not well known and consequently not as expensive as most art glass. Look for the signature, which may be either underneath the foot or worked into the design of the bowl. The design on Locke pieces is of a much higher quality than that on machine-etched stemware (#34).

Description
Baluster-shaped (left) *or bell-shaped* (right) *bowl with engraved floral and scroll pattern.* Thin delicate walls. Straight stem tapers toward base. Circular foot has matching pattern. *No pontil mark.* Colorless. *Variations:* shape of bowl and stem varies as shown; engraving mostly stylized flowers, leaves and stems, and/or scroll designs. Foot may have trademark.

Type and Dimensions
Free-blown bowl with applied, tooled stem and foot. Copper-wheel engraved after annealing. Lead glass. Height (left): 8¾–9¼"; rim diameter: 3¼–3½". Height (right): 5¾–6¼"; rim diameter: 3¼–3½".

Locality and Period
Corning, New York: T.G. Hawkes & Company and Hunt Glass Company. Pairpoint Corporation, New Bedford, Massachusetts; Libbey Glass Company, Toledo, Ohio; and others. c. 1920–40.

Matching Glassware
Set with wine, champagne, sherbet, liqueur, cordial, and iced tea glasses, and dessert plates.

Comment
These elaborately engraved glasses are typical of stemware of the 1920s and 1930s after heavy brilliant-cut ware was out of fashion. Both glasses illustrated were made by T.G. Hawkes & Company and are marked "HAWKES" underneath the foot. Similar stemware was made at other glasshouses and imported from Europe. European versions are difficult to identify.

Hints for Collectors
Glassware of this period is just beginning to be collected, and it is still possible to assemble a complete set.

Mold-blown 1930s stemware

Description
Conical bowl with elaborate etched floral and leaf pattern (center, right) *or scroll pattern* (left); sometimes with vertical panels (left, right). *Thin walls.* Stem straight, with gentle swelling in middle and 2 knops, at top and bottom; or baluster-shaped with 4 petals near base. *Flat circular foot.* Color: usually colorless; occasionally transparent pale green, yellow, or pink. *Variations:* rarely engraved decoration; stem may be swirled; stem may have additional knop at center or only 1 knop.

Type and Dimensions
Mold-blown bowl; pressed stem and foot. Joined while hot, then annealed. Acid-etched after annealing. Lead or nonlead glass. Height (left): 5½–5⅝″; rim diameter: 4–4⅛″. Height (center): 7¾–7⅞″; rim diameter: 3⅝–3¾″. Height (right): 4⅞–5″; rim diameter: 4³⁄₁₆–4¼″.

Locality and Period
Ohio: Cambridge Glass Company, Cambridge; A.H. Heisey & Company, Newark. Fostoria Glass Company, Moundsville, West Virginia. Bryce Brothers, Mt. Pleasant, Pennsylvania. c. 1925–45.

Matching Glassware
Set with stemware, iced tea glasses, and plates (7″).

Comment
Most glassware factories of this period offered a range of shapes and a separate range of etched patterns that could be ordered. The examples shown are from Cambridge Glass, the 2 colorless pieces in the Rosepoint pattern and the green in pattern No. 732.

Hints for Collectors
This mold-blown stemware originally sold at a higher price than the pressed Depression glass. Today both cost about the same.

Rosepoint and No. 732 patterns

Spanish threaded wineglass

Description
Oval bowl has evenly spaced pattern of molded bubbles and horizontal threading around lower bowl. Thin walls. *Slender baluster stem* with 2 knops at top. Circular foot. Pontil mark polished. Color: transparent green, blue, amber, or colorless; with colorless, black, or green threading. *Variations:* bowl usually bucket-shaped. Foot may have trademark.

Type and Dimensions
Bowl blown in bubble-patterned mold. Applied, tooled threading, stem, and foot. Height: 8⅜–8½". Rim diameter: 3¼–3½".

Locality and Period
Steuben Glass Works, Corning, New York. c. 1920–33.

Matching Glassware
Set with champagne glasses, goblets, finger bowls, plates, and large bowl.

Comment
Steuben's bubbly, threaded Spanish glassware was popular in the 1920s for its handmade and antique look. The Consolidated Lamp & Glass Company of Coraopolis, Pennsylvania, marketed a much cheaper version in the 1920s called Catalonian glass, which was probably also mold-blown.

Hints for Collectors
Although superficially similar, Catalonian glass is thicker, clumsier, and crudely colored. Most Steuben glasses are marked "STEUBEN" underneath the foot. But even without a trademark, the appearance of these glasses is distinctive.

36 Cased goblet and wineglass

Description
Shallow, round (left, right) or bell-shaped (center) bowl with
engraved floral designs or cut panels around sides. Thin walls.
Long slender stem with 1–2 knops under bowl. Circular foot.
Pontil mark polished. Color: *colorless, cased* in blue, red, yellow,
green, purple, or black. *Variations:* 50–75 different patterns,
usually engraved flowers and scrolls or simple cut designs.
Buttonlike or round cut knop; foot may have engraving.

Type and Dimensions
Free-blown bowl with applied or drawn stem, and applied, tooled
foot. Cased with color; cut or copper-wheel engraved after
annealing. Lead glass. Height (left): 7¾–7⅞"; rim diameter:
4–4½". Height (center): 9¾–9⅞"; rim diameter: 4–4½". Height
(right): 5¾–5⅞"; rim diameter: 3–3½".

Locality and Period
Corning, New York: Steuben Glass Works, c. 1920–33; and
H.P. Sinclaire & Company, c. 1920–29. Libbey Glass Company,
Toledo, Ohio. c. 1920–39. Pairpoint Corporation, New Bedford,
Massachusetts. c. 1920–30.

Matching Glassware
Large set with stemware, finger bowls, and salad plates.

Comment
The unusually long stems and comparatively short bowls are
typical of 20th-century stemware. The thin glass and simple cut
patterns also distinguish these glasses from 19th-century pieces.

Hints for Collectors
Glasses from Steuben, Libbey, and Sinclaire are usually marked
underneath the foot. Pairpoint glasses may have a paper label.
Several midwestern factories produced similar glasses, but these
are of lighter weight and have pressed stems.

Tiffany white-wine glass

Description
Shallow, round ribbed bowl with long hollow stem and circular foot. Acid-etched "L.C.T. Favrile" underneath foot. Pontil mark polished. Color: *opalescent pink bowl with transparent green stem. Variations: shapes and colors vary greatly among different sets;* many opaque and transparent colors, including iridescent gold and blue.

Type and Dimensions
Bowl and stem blown in separate vertically ribbed molds. Applied, tooled stem and foot. Height: 8–8⅛″. Rim diameter: 3–3⅛″.

Locality and Period
Tiffany Glass & Decorating Company, Corona, New York. c. 1915–24.

Matching Glassware
Stemware set with red-wine, sherry, cordial, and champagne glasses, goblets, and tumblers; finger bowl. Salt dips (#170), punch bowls (#305), and vases (#343); not made as set.

Comment
Louis Comfort Tiffany's stemware is not as well known to collectors as his iridescent vases and stained-glass windows and lamps. But it is usually of fine quality and much less expensive.

Hints for Collectors
Genuine Tiffany glass is almost always marked "L.C.T. Favrile" or, more rarely, "L.C. Tiffany" or just "Favrile." Tiffany coined the term "Favrile" to designate handmade glass. Some glasses also bear a stock number. It is important to be familiar with the different Tiffany forms and colors or to buy from an experienced dealer because counterfeit Tiffany trademarks are sometimes put on pieces by unscrupulous sellers.

Tumblers, Mugs, Tankards, and Cups

Tumblers, mugs, and tankards are basically cylindrical forms, while cups are often more rounded. Although there is no real difference between a mug and a tankard, collectors usually call only a very large mug a tankard.

Large mugs and tankards (#60, #63) were the earliest forms made in the United States. During the 18th century in Europe and America, these glasses were commonly used to serve ale, beer, cider, and perry, a cider made from pears. In this country, tumblers were used by German-Americans and made at Amelung's glasshouse in New Bremen, Maryland, and possibly also at Stiegel's factory in Manheim, Pennsylvania (#40, #41). Many tumblers, large mugs, and tankards originally had covers to keep flies out of the beverage. However, few covers have survived. The simple tumbler persisted in free-blown and mold-blown glass into the 19th century, but the larger tumblers, tankards, and mugs gradually became less common.

The development of the glass-pressing machine in the 1820s led to more variations in shape, pattern, and function. Catalogues of the 1860s from pressed glass firms, such as the New England Glass Company and M'Kee & Brothers, show a great variety of beer mugs and ale glasses, which were probably intended for use in taverns rather than homes.

Glass cups were rare in the 18th and 19th centuries and usually of blown glass. The difference between mugs and cups is slight. Cups are usually smaller than mugs and may have a foot. Glass cups were probably more whimsical than functional. Delicately handled cups (#62, #64) were used to serve such "ladies' drinks" as lemonade or sweet wine. Modern collectors call the pressed mugs "handled whiskeys," although catalogues of the period refer to them as lemonade glasses.

In the late 19th century, 2 new handled forms were introduced: the tall, cylindrical lemonade glass (#58) and the small, round punch cup (#67). Both of these types were made in art glass, especially by such famous houses as the Boston & Sandwich Glass Company and the New England Glass Works. Small art-glass tumblers (#68) were occasionally made, but they are less common. Cut-glass punch cups made around the turn of the century were imitated in pressed glass, usually in similar patterns. Punch cups with matching punch bowls are still made and are sold by thrift shops and variety stores.

After the turn of the century, tall tumblers (#53), used for iced tea and highballs, were introduced in cut glass and in the cheaper pressed glass. The tall tumbler is still common today, although many of the other forms, like the lemonade glasses, have disappeared.

Tumblers have not changed much over the past 200 years, so it is seldom possible to date them by shape or size. Decoration is probably the best guide for dating these glasses. The blown 3-mold pattern was made only from 1815 to 1835. Pressed tumblers did not appear until about 1845; the earliest pressed patterns were usually geometric and were followed by realistic designs. Geometric patterns reappeared in pressed glass at the turn of the century, but these later geometric patterns, made with lime glass, are thinner and of lighter weight than early pressed examples made with lead glass.

Blown bottle-glass tumbler

Description
Bubbly cylindrical glass. Thin walls become thick at base. Pontil mark rough. Color: transparent amber, brown, or green.
Variations: may be conical; with threaded decoration (#61).

Type and Dimensions
Free-blown, then tooled into shape. Applied threading. Nonlead glass. Height: 3¼–3½″. Rim diameter: 2¾–3″.

Locality and Period
New Hampshire, Connecticut, New York, and New Jersey. c. 1840–75.

Comment
The tumbler illustrated is attributed to one of 4 factories that operated in Stoddard, New Hampshire, from 1842 to 1873. All of these houses produced mainly bottles, hence the dark color of their glassware. Similar tumblers were undoubtedly made in bottle glasshouses in New England, New Jersey, and New York. In the 1920s and 1930s, when collectors were interested in identifying glass from early factories, it was possible to visit the area where a factory had been located, talk to people, and get from them glasses that their fathers or grandfathers had made at the local factory. It is on this hearsay that most attributions to bottle and window glasshouses were made.

Hints for Collectors
Free-blown simple ware like this tumbler is impossible to identify with a specific glasshouse on the basis of shape and style, but occasionally it has some family origin; yet, even this is tenuous. Because each free-blown piece was the original creation of a glassblower, the proportions and shape depended upon whim as well as skill. No 2 blown tumblers are ever exactly alike. Bottle-glass tumblers are rare.

Blown tumbler

Description
Conical glass with thick flat bottom and plain rim. Pontil mark rough. Color: usually colorless or slightly grayish; sometimes transparent amber, green, or aquamarine. *Variations:* many tumblers are more cylindrical; some with cut or enameled flowers or leaves.

Type and Dimensions
Free-blown, then tooled into shape. Lead or nonlead glass. Height: 5–5½″. Rim diameter: 4–4½″.

Locality and Period
Massachusetts, New Jersey, Pennsylvania, and Maryland. c. 1785–1830.

Comment
The glass illustrated, which is nonlead, is the same shape and grayish color as several tumblers from Amelung's New Bremen Glassmanufactory in Maryland, and may have been made there. This basic shape, however, was popular throughout the first quarter of the 19th century, especially in glass factories far from urban centers. Tumblers similar to it appear in advertisements of the Boston Crown Glass Manufactory from 1815 to 1816, but the Boston glasses were undoubtedly colorless lead glass.

Hints for Collectors
Plain tumblers are often undervalued by antique collectors because they lack a pattern and cannot be attributed to a particular glasshouse or given a specific date. They are excellent pieces for beginning collectors and make an attractive set with a plain pitcher or decanter.

Description
Conical glass slightly flaring at rim. *Enameled decoration of birds, hearts, and flowers* in white, yellow, red, blue, and green; enameled inscription reads, "My Love You Like Me Do" (left); "We Too Will Be True" (right). Thin walls. Pontil mark rough. Colorless. *Variations:* a few other inscriptions, mostly in German.

Type and Dimensions
Free-blown, then tooled into shape. Enameled after annealing. Nonlead glass. Height: 4–4¼″. Rim diameter: 3–3¼″.

Locality and Period
Possibly Henry William Stiegel's American Flint Glass Works, Manheim, Pennsylvania. c. 1770–74. Germany, Bohemia, and Switzerland. c. 1760–1800.

Comment
This glass was common in southern Germany, Bohemia, and Switzerland toward the end of the 18th century. But the English inscriptions, probably translations of German sayings, suggest that the glass was made at Stiegel's factory. The glass could also have been made abroad for export to the Pennsylvania Dutch community.

Hints for Collectors
Fewer than a dozen of these glasses with English inscriptions are known, most in museum collections. It is possible, however, that others will be found. Glasses with German inscriptions are probably from Germany. These glasses were fairly common imports and are relatively easy to find today. Reproductions are still being made in Czechoslovakia for sale in gift shops; these glasses bear no inscription and look quite new.

Amelung tumbler

Description
Conical glass with thick flat base. *Engraved initials within wreath or garland, with crown above* on 1 side; engraved scene with house, grass, trees, and ducks on opposite side. *Thick walls. Pontil mark rough. Transparent, slightly grayish glass. Variations: engraved pattern and monogram unique on each piece.* Most tumblers originally had matching lid. May be engraved "New Bremen Glassmanufactory" on side.

Type and Dimensions
Free-blown, then tooled into shape. Copper-wheel engraved after annealing. Nonlead glass. Height: 7⅞". Rim diameter: 5⅞".

Locality and Period
John Frederick Amelung's New Bremen Glassmanufactory, New Bremen, Maryland. c. 1785–95.

Comment
More is known about Amelung glass than almost any other 18th-century American glass type. Although this glass is not marked, the type of engraving leaves no doubt about its origin. Personal monograms or inscriptions inside a floral wreath or garland with a crown above are an Amelung characteristic and a common convention in 18th-century German-style engraving. The glass illustrated here belonged to the family of George and Meta Repold, explaining the "GMR."

Hints for Collectors
Amelung glasses were undoubtedly sold in sets that included wineglasses and probably some other pieces. Fewer glasses are attributed to Amelung's factory today than 25 years ago because of considerable research since the 1950s. Only 30 examples can be reliably attributed to Amelung's glasshouse, 6 of which have turned up in the past 20 years.

Paneled bar tumbler

Description
Conical glass with 6 or 8 pressed panels around sides. Color: transparent white, blue, green, amber, purple, or colorless. *Variations:* panel shape and number may vary, as seen here.

Type and Dimensions
Pressed in mold for pattern and shape. Usually nonlead, but occasionally lead glass. Height: 3–4″. Rim diameter: 2⅜–3½″.

Locality and Period
Western Pennsylvania, West Virginia, and Ohio. c. 1850–80.

Comment
These common bar tumblers were made for use in commercial establishments. They appeared in the 1875 catalogue of Bakewell, Pears & Company in Pittsburgh. But several pages of similar tumblers were also listed in the catalogues of M'Kee & Brothers of Pittsburgh in the 1860s and 1870s. This type of bar tumbler was a staple product of every glasshouse in the Midwest, although possibly a few were made in the East. Most midwestern examples are made of nonlead glass, a fact that can help in establishing their date and origin.

Hints for Collectors
If these tumblers could be definitely attributed to the Bakewell glasshouse, they would command a much higher price. But this identification is impossible because the glasses were never marked. Do not be misled into paying a premium Bakewell price. This type of tumbler has never been popular enough among collectors to be reproduced.

43 Pennsylvania Dutch engraved tumbler

Description
Conical glass with engraved stylized scrolls or flowers. Thin walls. *Pontil mark rough, with grayish ring.* Colorless. *Variations:* 12–14 vertical panels around lower body below engraving (left); engraved tulips and/or birds in Pennsylvania Dutch style (right).

Type and Dimensions
Free-blown or mold-blown for panels. Copper-wheel engraved after annealing. Nonlead glass. Height: 4⅝–6″. Rim diameter: 3¾–5¾″.

Locality and Period
Germany, Bohemia, and Switzerland. c. 1790–1840.

Matching Glassware
Mugs, tankards, compote, and decanter. Not made as set.

Comment
The traditional Pennsylvania Dutch motifs illustrated are of German origin. All glasses like this were once thought to be made by Stiegel in Manheim, Pennsylvania, but there is no evidence that glass of this type was ever made in this country. It was probably imported from Europe, much of it made expressly for German-Americans like the Pennsylvania Dutch.

Hints for Collectors
Glasses like this were not made by Stiegel. Examine the pontil mark; nearly all tumblers and mugs with this type of engraving have a ring of rough grayish glass around the rough pontil scar. This is a sure indication of European origin. Both types of tumblers illustrated were reproduced in the 1920s in Europe and by the Pairpoint Corporation in New Bedford, Massachusetts. Beware of glasses that are heavier and lack the characteristic pontil mark.

Early midwestern ribbed tumbler

Description
Conical glass with slightly depressed base. *Closely spaced molded, swirled ribs* (left) *or broken-swirl ribs* (right). Thin walls. Pontil mark rough. Color: transparent green, amber, or colorless.

Type and Dimensions
Blown in vertically ribbed mold, then swirled and expanded. Second set of ribs superimposed on swirls by redipping in same mold. Nonlead glass. Height: 4½–5⁹⁄₁₆″. Rim diameter: 4¾–4⅜″.

Locality and Period
Western Pennsylvania and Ohio. c. 1800–40.

Matching Glassware
Wineglasses, pitchers (#72), bar bottles (#113), sugar bowls, creamers, salts (#176), plates (#214), and bowls (#274). Not made as set.

Comment
Swirled and broken-swirl ribbing are especially associated with glass from Ohio. The double ribbing, or broken-swirl pattern, was made only in midwestern factories.

Hints for Collectors
Broken-swirl ribbing is particularly desirable because it is rarer than swirled ribbing. For this reason, broken-swirl glasses are often more expensive. Nearly identical tumblers with swirled ribs were made in Mexico in the 1920s and 1930s but not with broken swirls. Mexican glass usually has many tiny bubbles. Ohio examples will have fewer bubbles, if any.

45 Blown 3-mold tumbler

Description
Conical or cylindrical glass. Molded geometric pattern of vertical ribs, sunbursts, and fields of diamonds. Thin walls. Pontil mark rough. Color: usually colorless; rarely transparent blue or purple. *Variations:* great variety in size, shape, and pattern.

Type and Dimensions
Blown in full-size mold for pattern and shape, then tooled into final form. Lead glass. Height (left): 5–6″; rim diameter: 4¼–4½″. Height (right): 3—3½″; rim diameter: 3½–4″.

Locality and Period
New England. c. 1820–35.

Matching Glassware
Decanters, pitchers, wineglasses, inkwells, small lamps, peg lamps, toy bowls, toy decanters, and toy pitchers. Not made as set.

Comment
Large glasses like the one on the left were named flip glasses by collectors from the mistaken belief that they were used to serve a warm drink known as flip. Preparing a hot beverage in a thin-walled tumbler would certainly have led to breakage. Probably cold ale or beer was served in these large glasses. This originally German design became popular during the 18th century. The large shape was not made after about 1830 and seldom appears in pressed glass.

Hints for Collectors
The Metropolitan Museum of Art in New York City has reproduced flip glasses for the past 10 years in both colored and colorless glass, all of which bear the "MMA" inscription on the base.

Blown 3-mold tumbler

Description
Conical or barrel-shaped glass. Molded geometric pattern of
vertical and diagonal ribs, sunbursts, and fields of diamonds in
various combinations. Thin walls. Pontil mark rough. Color:
usually colorless; rarely transparent blue or purple. *Variations:* 3
shapes including cylinder (not shown); many different sizes and
patterns (#45); rarely with colored rim, as seen on right.

Type and Dimensions
Blown in full-size mold for pattern and shape, then tooled into
final form. Applied threading on rim (right only). Lead glass.
Height: 3½–4". Rim diameter: 2⅞–3¼".

Locality and Period
New England. c. 1820–35.

Matching Glassware
Left and center with decanters, pitchers, creamers, and sugar
bowls. Not made as set.

Comment
The barrel-shaped glass on the left is less common than the
cylinder or cone.

Hints for Collectors
Tumblers like the one in the center have been reproduced for the
past 15 years by The Metropolitan Museum of Art in New York
City. Like most of its reproductions, these tumblers are marked
"MMA" on the mold. To determine whether a piece is mold-blown
or pressed, feel the inside of the glass. A pressed piece will be
smooth on the inside, but on mold-blown glass you can feel the
pattern. This is because air pressure from blowing makes the
glass inside follow the impressions in the mold. A pressed glass,
however, takes on the smooth contour of the plunger used to
press the glass into the mold.

Rock-crystal whiskey glass

Description
Cylindrical glass flaring at rim, with thick base ground and polished. *Engraved, polished thistle pattern around sides. Thick walls become thin at rim.* Colorless. *Variations:* several hundred patterns, mostly floral and fruit designs; sometimes cut pattern. Rim may be straight; base may be acid-stamped: "J. HOARE & CO./1853/CORNING."

Type and Dimensions
Free-blown, then tooled into shape. Deeply copper-wheel engraved after annealing, then polished. Lead glass. Height: 2¼–2½". Rim diameter: 2¼–2½".

Locality and Period
Throughout the United States. c. 1895–1910.

Comment
The glass illustrated was made in the factory of J. Hoare & Company of Corning, New York. It is typical of the so-called polished rock-crystal style of engraving, which was popular for at least 2 decades beginning in the 1890s. It differs from ordinary matt engraving in which the glass is left unpolished and the engraved portion appears frosted-gray. Rock crystal is uniformly crystal-clear, inspiring its name. Some rock-crystal patterns came in a set of stemware with a matching decanter, unlike the example shown.

Hints for Collectors
Unlike the small pressed whisky taster (#50), these glasses are large enough to hold a more substantial drink. They were probably used for "neat spirits" (straight alcohol, without the addition of water or fruit juice), which became fashionable around the turn of the century. Although early and late rock-crystal ware are nearly identical, the earlier glass is heavier.

Depression tumbler

Description
Cylindrical glass with overall pressed geometric pattern of honeycomb (left) or vertical panels below horizontal bands (right). Color: honeycomb in transparent pink or green; paneled in colorless, transparent green, or sometimes pink or cobalt-blue; rarely purple. *Variations:* many geometric patterns include hobnails, vertical ribs, and diamonds; rim flared.

Type and Dimensions
Machine-pressed in mold for pattern and shape. Height (left): 3¾"; rim diameter: 2¾". Height (right): 4¼"; rim diameter: 3⅛".

Locality and Period
Hex Optic (left) at Jeannette Glass Company, Jeannette, Pennsylvania. c. 1928–32. New Century (right) at Hazel-Atlas Glass Company, Wheeling, West Virginia. c. 1930–35.

Matching Glassware
Large set of tableware in both patterns. Hex Optic (left) also with ice bucket; New Century (right) with wineglasses, cocktail pitcher, and ashtray.

Comment
In Depression glass, tumblers are much more common than stemware. Perhaps the footed tumblers (#15) were a stemware substitute, since they are at least as common as cylindrical ones. Since Prohibition was in effect countrywide until 1933, and locally much later, it is not surprising that few patterns offer decanters or wineglasses, but nearly all have tumblers and iced tea glasses. The patterns illustrated are Hex Optic, or Honeycomb (left), and New Century (right).

Hints for Collectors
Dark colors like the purple illustrated and cobalt-blue are rarer and more expensive than light green and pink.

Hex Optic and New Century patterns

Realistic-style pressed tumbler

Description
Cylindrical glass with pressed floral design around middle; double band of raised diamonds below rim; single diamond band at base. Thin walls. Color: transparent light blue, light and dark amber, light green, or colorless. *Variations:* many different fruit and floral patterns, such as Blackberry (#138), Baltimore Pear, Beaded Grape, Medallion, and Strawberry (#244).

Type and Dimensions
Pressed in mold for pattern and shape. Nonlead glass. Height: 4–4¼″. Rim diameter: 3–3¼″.

Locality and Period
Pittsburgh: Adams & Company, c. 1875–91; United States Glass Company and possibly others, c. 1891–1900.

Matching Glassware
Large set with stemware, pitcher, salt and pepper shakers, creamer (#148), sugar bowl, butter dish, celery vase, spoon holder, compote, round and square bowls (#256), platters, trays, and cake plate on stand. Not all pieces in all colors.

Comment
Adams & Company marketed the Wildflower pattern in the 1870s and probably made it for the next 20 years until the firm merged with the United States Glass Company in 1891. The pattern was reissued later by the United States Glass Company, but may have also been made in another factory.

Hints for Collectors
Because this was a popular pattern for many years, it was made in a great variety of tableware shapes and colors. Most colors have been reproduced. Be very wary when purchasing anything in this pattern. The differences between reproductions and original examples are subtle and require handling both types.

Wildflower pattern

Pressed whiskey taster

Description
Small cylindrical glass with pressed leaf design around sides.
Colors: opaque white; opalescent white; transparent yellow, blue, purple, and green. *Variations:* embossed design may be in vertical panels of varying widths; rarely with enameled floral decoration below rim as illustrated.

Type and Dimensions
Pressed in mold for pattern and shape. Lead glass. Height: 1¾″. Rim diameter: 1″.

Locality and Period
New England: probably Boston & Sandwich Glass Company, Sandwich, Massachusetts. c. 1850–70.

Comment
The exact function of these small tumblers is not known. They are commonly called whiskey tasters, but their capacity is so small that it seems highly unlikely that they were ever used to hold alcohol. These were probably toys.

Hints for Collectors
Tasters in many colors and 3 or 4 patterns are relatively common. Those with extra enameled decoration are very rare and command a much higher price. A small quantity of pressed glass of all shapes was decorated with gilt or enamel after pressing, usually to special order. This decoration is seldom found today in good condition. These glasses are too small for any modern use except as jigger glasses and have not been reproduced.

51 Carnival water and whiskey tumblers

Description
Cylindrical glass with pressed design of grapes and leaves around sides, horizontal cable below rim, and thumbprintlike circular depressions near base. Thick walls. *Opaque glass with iridescent finish.* Color: orange, purple, green, light or medium blue, or light green. *Variations:* may lack thumbprints and cables; some marked "N" on base.

Type and Dimensions
Pressed in mold for pattern and shape. Iridescent finish sprayed on before annealing. Height (left): 4–4⅛″; rim diameter: 3–3⅛″. Height (right): 2¼–2⅜″; rim diameter: 2¼–2⅜″.

Locality and Period
West Virginia: Northwood Glass Company, Wheeling; Fenton Art Glass Company, Williamstown. Ohio: Imperial Glass Company, Bellaire; Millersburg Glass Company, Millersburg. c. 1905–20.

Matching Glassware
Large set with tableware, decanter, pitcher, bowl (#288), punch bowl, and miscellaneous pieces such as humidor and dresser set. All shapes not made in all colors.

Comment
The illustrated Grape and Cable with Thumbprint pattern by Northwood is one of many grape designs found on Carnival glass. Some firms had more than one grape pattern. Northwood's was the most popular and therefore is the one most common today.

Hints for Collectors
Even without a trademark, this pattern by Northwood is unmistakable. Fenton produced a variation of Northwood's Grape and Cable pattern, but no other company used the thumbprint motif around the base.

Grape and Cable with Thumbprint pattern

52 Gold-decorated pressed tumbler

Description
Cylindrical glass has pressed loop pattern around sides; lower loops with diamond pattern. *Gilded on band below rim and on upper loops.* Pressed sunburst underneath base. Colorless. *Variations:* sometimes ruby-stained (#145) instead of gilded.

Type and Dimensions
Pressed in mold for pattern and shape. Gilding applied after annealing and fired on. Nonlead glass. Height: 4–4⅛". Rim diameter: 2⅞–3".

Locality and Period
Pittsburgh: George Duncan & Sons and United States Glass Company; other firms. c. 1890–1915.

Matching Glassware
Set with goblets, plates (8"), covered sugar bowl and creamer, butter dish, spoon holder, toothpick holder, pickle dish, compotes (6", 7", 8"), celery tray, and syrup jug.

Comment
Colorless pressed glass with gilded or ruby-stained decoration was very common around the turn of the century (#223). The tumbler illustrated here is in the New Jersey pattern, introduced by George Duncan & Sons of Pittsburgh around 1890 and continued by the United States Glass Company after their merger of 1891. The pattern appeared in catalogues as part of the states series (#57) until 1915.

Hints for Collectors
Late pressed-glass patterns like New Jersey are still relatively inexpensive and, because they were mass-produced, easier to find than the earlier pressed patterns. This is an imitation cut pattern; both the softness of the rounded edges and the light weight make it easy to distinguish from cut tumblers.

New Jersey pattern

Brilliant-cut highball tumbler

Description
Cylindrical glass with elaborate cut pattern and plain rim; center motifs are pinwheel (left), and hobstar and fan (right). Flat base has cut hobstar underneath. *Thick walls become thin at edge.* Colorless. *Variations:* shape cylindrical to slightly flaring at rim, as illustrated; more than 500 patterns, including star and fan combined with diamonds, hobstars, and other cut motifs.

Type and Dimensions
Free-blown, then tooled into shape. Cut after annealing. Lead glass. Height: 5–5½". Rim diameter: 2½–3½".

Locality and Period
Throughout the United States. c. 1900–15.

Matching Glassware
Set with wine, champagne, and cordial glasses, goblets, decanter, and pitcher.

Comment
Although collectors often call this an iced tea glass, in turn-of-the-century catalogues it was listed as a highball glass. This was a new form in that period for a new drink. Teddy Roosevelt is the first president to have ordered highball glasses for the White House; he requested the Russian pattern (#29).

Hints for Collectors
The glass illustrated on the left is marked "Fry," indicating it was blown and cut by H.C. Fry Glass Company of Rochester, Pennsylvania, one of the better-known cutting shops. The unmarked glass is a gift to The Corning Museum of Glass, given in 1964 by the daughter of A.L. Blackmer, the owner of a cutting shop in New Bedford, Massachusetts. It is of equal or better quality than the Fry version. Yet, as in most cases, the marked glass commands a higher price in an antique shop.

54 Bakewell-type cut mug

Description
Cylindrical glass with smoothly polished base. Vertical panels on lower half and alternating *cut strawberry-diamonds and fans around upper half.* Thick walls. Ear-shaped handle crimped at base. *Colorless. Variations:* several patterns include strawberry-diamonds combined with fans, arches, or circles.

Type and Dimensions
Free-blown, then tooled into shape. Applied, tooled handle. Cut after annealing. Lead glass. Height: 3¼–3½". Rim diameter: 2¾–3".

Locality and Period
Western Pennsylvania and West Virginia. Possibly Philadelphia, Boston, and New York. c. 1820–50.

Comment
This type of mug is rare and not found as often as similar-looking tumblers. Its small capacity indicates that it was probably used for whiskey instead of beer or ale. Collectors often refer to this design as Bakewell-type glassware because many identical tumblers were made in Bakewell's factories. In 1825, Bakewell, Page & Bakewell advertised a similar tumbler with an opaque white sulphide base bearing the portrait of an American statesman. These glasses are even rarer than the mug.

Hints for Collectors
When buying pieces with handles, check carefully for small cracks at the points where the handle is attached to the glass. These cracks are usually a fault in manufacturing caused by the difference in temperatures between body and handle when the handle was applied. It remains a weak point in the finished mug and decreases the sturdiness of the glass.

Blown 3-mold mug

Description
Cylindrical glass. Molded geometric patterns of diagonal ribs, sunbursts, and fields of diamonds. Thin walls. Ear-shaped handle crimped at base. Pontil mark rough. Color: usually colorless; rarely transparent blue or purple. *Variations:* patterns may differ in arrangement of geometric motifs.

Type and Dimensions
Blown in full-size mold for pattern and shape. Applied, tooled handle. Lead glass. Height: 2⅞–3″. Rim diameter: 2½–3″.

Locality and Period
New England and Philadelphia. c. 1815–35.

Matching Glassware
Tumblers, bowls, and salt. Not made as set.

Comment
The small size of this mug indicates that it was used for whiskey or other strong spirits rather than for beer or ale. Possibly it was a lemonade glass (#64). Blown 3-mold glasses are all relatively lightweight and fragile, so it is likely that they were used in homes rather than in taverns.

Hints for Collectors
Like the lemonade glass (#64), this is a very rare form of blown 3-mold glass. Wineglasses (#10) and tumblers (#46) are both relatively common shapes. Tumblers, pitchers, and sugar bowls in this pattern were reproduced in New Jersey factories in the 1930s, mostly in colored glass. However, reproductions of the mug are not known.

Early geometric-style pressed tumbler and mug

Description
Cylindrical shape. Pressed swirled cometlike pattern of diamonds and circles; plain rim. Thick walls. Ear-shaped handle on mug crimped at base. Polished pontil mark on mug; no mark on tumbler. *Colorless. Variations:* mostly simple and abstract designs, such as diamonds, ovals, or circles.

Type and Dimensions
Tumbler and mug pressed in mold for pattern and shape. Handle applied on mug. Lead glass. Height: 3–3⅛″. Rim diameter: 2½–2⅝″.

Locality and Period
M'Kee & Brothers, Pittsburgh; possibly Boston & Sandwich Glass Company, Sandwich, Massachusetts. c. 1860–70.

Matching Glassware
Large set with goblets, wine, champagne, and jelly glasses, decanter, pitcher, bar bottle, eggcups, table set (#146), celery vase, plates, footed bowl, compote, and lamp.

Comment
Collectors call this pattern Horn of Plenty, although it appears in M'Kee catalogues of 1860 and 1864 as the Comet pattern. Some authorities contend that the name was inspired by Halley's comet, which made a dramatic appearance in 1835. Yet it is unlikely that the event inspired glassmakers 25 years later. Both the mug and tumbler were reproduced in the 1930s.

Hints for Collectors
The name "Comet" was used for several different glass patterns during the middle to late 19th century. Another pressed tumbler made about the same time by a New England factory bears a different comet design (#25). Libbey Glass Company also made a cut comet design around 1900.

Horn of Plenty pattern

57 Late 19th-century pressed tumbler and mug

Description
Cylindrical glasses with pressed peacock-feather pattern around sides. Smooth rim and flat base. Thin walls. C-shaped handle on mug. *Colorless. Variations:* about 20 different abstract patterns in states series; pattern illustrated is Georgia; others include grape clusters for California and swirl pattern for Indiana.

Type and Dimensions
Pressed in mold for pattern and shape. Nonlead glass. Height: 3½–3¾″. Base diameter: 2¼–2¾″.

Locality and Period
United States Glass Company, Pittsburgh. c. 1895–1910.

Matching Glassware
Set with pitcher, bowls, cruet and syrup jug (#194), sugar bowl, creamer, butter dish, spoon holder, cake plate, and lamp.

Comment
The Georgia pattern shown was advertised in 1902 as part of the states series, which was produced by the United States Glass Company, a consortium of midwestern factories that merged in 1891. The patterns bear no relationship to the states themselves; the names were used mainly as a selling device.

Hints for Collectors
Even if you do not recognize the pattern, you can easily tell that this tumbler and mug were produced later than the cometlike pressed mug and tumbler (#56). On the later examples, the glass is thinner and not as glossy. The handle of the mug is pressed as part of the mold rather than applied separately after pressing. Later examples are also lightweight and less sturdy. Only since the 1960s have later patterns like this one attracted collectors.

Georgia pattern

Description
Tall cylindrical glass. Engraved floral pattern around upper body and horizontal threading around lower body. Thin walls. Handle attached near base. Pontil mark polished. Colorless, with light cranberry-red, yellow, blue-green, or green threading; or amber with amber threading. *Variations:* engraved initials instead of flowers; may lack engraving; threading from base to rim. Crackly decoration may replace flowers on upper half.

Type and Dimensions
Free-blown body, tooled into shape. Applied threading and handle. Copper-wheel engraved after annealing. Lead glass. Height: 5½–6″. Rim diameter: 2¼–2⅜″.

Locality and Period
Massachusetts: probably Boston & Sandwich Glass Company, Sandwich; possibly New England Glass Company, Cambridge. c. 1875–88.

Matching Glassware
Set with pitcher.

Comment
This tall glass first appeared in the 1870s, when lemonade graduated from a "ladies' drink" to become universally popular. The glasses illustrated are usually attributed to the Boston & Sandwich Glass Company, but glasses in this size and shape have also been found in Pomona glass (#259), which was made exclusively by the New England Glass Company. The decoration on Pomona glasses is usually different.

Hints for Collectors
Single glasses like these turn up fairly frequently at reasonable prices, usually with light cranberry-red threading. Other colors are less common. This form has never been reproduced.

59 Double-handled mug

Description
Cylindrical mug with folded rim and round foot. *Thick walls.*
Monogram engraved inside wreath opposite elaborate double,
twisted handle. Pontil mark rough. *Colorless. Variations:*
usually single handle with or without engraving; sometimes floral
design rather than initials. Rim usually not folded.

Type and Dimensions
Free-blown, then tooled into shape. Applied, tooled base and
handle. Copper-wheel engraved after annealing. Lead glass.
Height: 5½–6″. Rim diameter: 3¼–3½″.

Locality and Period
The Northeast: probably Massachusetts, New York, and
Pennsylvania. c. 1800–35.

Comment
Most large mugs of this type are made of nonlead glass rather
than the lead glass of this example. The twisted handle is
unusual in American glass and very desirable. The engraved
initials are typical of early 19th-century glass.

Hints for Collectors
Although it is seldom possible to identify the original owner of a
monogrammed glass, it is a challenge to try. Ask the antique
dealer whether any family history is associated with the glass.
Engravings are often interesting documents of American social
history and customs.

Early tankard

Description
Cylindrical mug with horizontal threading around sides. Thin walls. *Straplike handle has thumb rest and crimped base. Base of mug slightly depressed.* Pontil mark rough. Color: transparent green or amber. *Variations:* more barrel-shaped (#63).

Type and Dimensions
Free-blown, then tooled into shape. Applied threading; applied, tooled handle. Nonlead glass. Height 6–7″. Rim diameter: 3½–4½″.

Locality and Period
Probably Caspar Wistar's Wistarburgh Glassworks or another southern New Jersey factory. c. 1750–1820. Possibly Germany. c. 1750–1800.

Comment
This tankard's form and decoration are decidedly 18th-century European. Since American glassware styles lagged somewhat behind European fashions, this mug may have been made here in the early 19th century. The 18th-century strap handle and thumb rest are rarely found after 1810, when handles became simpler.

Hints for Collectors
Early tankards are rare and consequently expensive. They are most likely to be found at auction sales of collections established in the 1920s and 1930s. It is difficult to distinguish German and American glass of this period. Caspar Wistar, a German immigrant, may have introduced the style. Either glass type is valuable, but in this country an American example will command a higher price.

61 Free-blown mug

Description
Cylindrical mug with horizontal threading around upper body.
Thick rim and walls. Irregular ear-shaped handle crimped at
base. Pontil mark rough. *Bubbly glass.* Color: transparent
aquamarine, greenish-amber, or brown. *Variations:* sometimes
barrel-shaped (#63); some have round foot; may lack threading.
Rarely handle or foot of another color.

Type and Dimensions
Free-blown, then tooled into shape. Applied handle and
threading. Nonlead glass. Height: 2½–4″. Rim diameter:
2¼–3″.

Locality and Period
New England, New York, and New Jersey. c. 1820–50.

Comment
The colors of the glass indicate that this mug was made in a
bottle or window glasshouse. Frequently, examples may have
bubbly glass, an uneven rim, or other irregularities. Yet they are
usually very sturdy.

Hints for Collectors
Glasses and mugs in free-blown bottle glass are much less
common than sugar bowls or pitchers of a similar style.
Consequently, they are usually more expensive. All early mugs
are rare, but those made of green and brown bottle glass are
especially valuable. Do not confuse these early pieces with
crudely engraved greenish, bubbly glassware. The engraved
examples are 20th-century imports from Czechoslovakia.

Free-blown lemonade or punch cup

Description
Cylindrical bowl with ear-shaped handle, short stem, and circular foot. Thin walls. Pontil mark, when present, rough or polished. Colorless. *Variations:* may have engraved decoration.

Type and Dimensions
Free-blown bowl, tooled into shape. Applied, tooled stem, foot, and handle. Lead or nonlead glass. Height: 3–3½". Rim diameter: 2–2¼".

Locality and Period
Throughout the United States. c. 1830–80.

Comment
Plain glasses like this one are difficult to narrow down to a specific glasshouse or date. Lemonade cups were popular for a long time during the 19th century. As a rule, women did not drink spirits or strong wine. Etiquette and custom demanded that the "gentle sex" drink lemonade, very mild wine, or mild punch.

Hints for Collectors
The glass illustrated has several features that mark it as a late example. The nonlead glass content suggests that it was probably made after 1864. There is no pontil mark, indicating that it was held for finishing in a snap case, a clawlike tool developed in the 1860s that holds the glass without leaving a mark. This development is useful for dating blown glass made before or after 1860. Finally, the way the handle is applied is a late style. If you compare this cup with earlier mold-blown punch cups (#55, #64), you will see that the top of the handle of the earlier glass is folded over and that the tail of the handle has a more obvious crimp. Lacking all of these features makes this later free-blown glass much less valuable.

Beer mug

Description
Barrel-shaped mug with wide, straplike C-shaped handle. Pontil mark rough. *Slightly bubbly glass.* Color: transparent purple, light or dark amber, light or medium green; *rarely colorless.* *Variations:* some early mugs are cylindrical rather than barrel-shaped; many in both shapes have horizontal threading (#60).

Type and Dimensions
Free-blown body, tooled into shape. Applied, tooled handle. Nonlead glass. Height: 4–6″. Rim diameter: 3–3¾″.

Locality and Period
Probably New Jersey; possibly Pennsylvania. Germany. c. 1750–1800.

Comment
The barrel shape is a typical 18th-century form but particularly difficult to attribute to a specific glasshouse. American mugs are always colored because they were made in bottle and window glasshouses that only used colored glass. German mugs are sometimes colorless.

Hints for Collectors
German mugs in this shape nearly always have engraved or enameled decoration. They were formerly attributed to Stiegel's glasshouse, but this now seems doubtful. Be wary of any mug offered as Stiegel's; it will be much more expensive and probably German.

Blown 3-mold punch cup

Description
Globe-shaped bowl. Molded herringbone pattern composed of vertical and diagonal ribs plus fields of diamonds on lower bowl and circular foot. Thin walls. Ear-shaped handle crimped at base. Pontil mark rough. Color: usually colorless; rarely transparent blue or purple. *Variations:* bowl varies from cylindrical to globular, as shown; several geometric patterns include sunbursts, waffling, or various kinds of ribbing.

Type and Dimensions
Blown in full-size mold for pattern and shape. Lower part tooled to form foot. Applied handle. Lead glass. Height: 2½–3". Rim diameter: 2¼–2½".

Locality and Period
New England and Philadelphia. c. 1815–35.

Matching Glassware
Wineglasses, tumblers, bowls, salts, sugar bowls, and inkwells. Not made as set.

Comment
This form is very rare in blown 3-mold glass. The blower probably used a mold meant for a tumbler or salt dish (#173). Although the cup might have been used to serve punch, the smaller size was probably for lemonade or some other "ladies' drink." Punch in the late 18th and early 19th centuries was a potent, hot rum or whiskey drink consumed mostly by men. The term "punch" comes from the Hindi word for 5, *pāc*, because it had 5 ingredients, including spirits and sugar.

Hints for Collectors
This early form of blown 3-mold has never been reproduced. Because it is rare and usually hard to find, the glass is much more expensive than most other tumblers of this period.

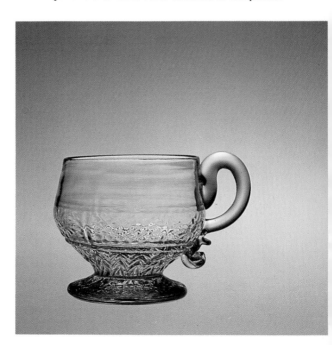

Carnival punch cup

Description
Circular cup has pressed arch-and-hobstar pattern alternating with raised diamonds and smaller hobstars. Thick walls. 6-pointed star pressed on base. C-shaped handle with ribs. *Opaque glass with iridescent finish.* Color: orange-amber, green, or purple.

Type and Dimensions
Pressed in mold for pattern and shape. Iridescent finish sprayed on before annealing. Height: 2¼–2⅜″. Rim diameter: 3¼–3⅜″.

Locality and Period
Ohio: Imperial Glass Company, Bellaire; Millersburg Glass Company, Millersburg. West Virginia: Fenton Art Glass Company, Williamstown; Northwood Glass Company, Wheeling. c. 1905–20.

Matching Glassware
Set with tumblers, punch bowl, large and small creamers, pitcher, fruit bowl with stand, and serving bowl with metal holder. All shapes not made in all colors.

Comment
The imitation cut-glass pattern illustrated was made by Imperial Glass, a company responsible for most of the imitation cut-glass patterns in Carnival glass. Collectors call the pattern Fashion, but Imperial referred to it simply as No. 204½. All glass factories gave their patterns numbers, and many patterns were never given names. The iridescent orange-amber color illustrated was one of Imperial's "sunset hues," which collectors now call marigold.

Hints for Collectors
Purple or green punch cups in the Fashion pattern are rare and much more expensive than the color illustrated.

Fashion pattern

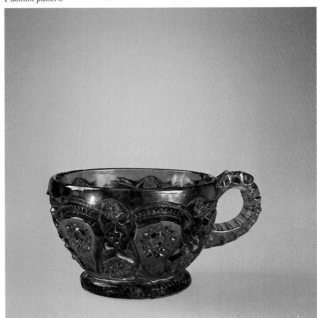

Depression punch cup

Description
Circular cup with circular foot and C-shaped handle. Color: transparent dark red. Variations: shape may be square or cylindrical; sometimes overall bubble pattern (#335).

Type and Dimensions
Machine-pressed in mold for pattern and shape. Height: 2⅜″. Rim diameter: 3¼″.

Locality and Period
Anchor-Hocking Glass Corporation, Lancaster, Ohio. c. 1939–65.

Matching Glassware
Set with tumblers, goblets, saucers, plates, bowls, covered sugar bowl, creamer, pitcher, compotes, punch bowl, and vases (#335).

Comment
Anchor-Hocking called this red glass Royal Ruby. Similar transparent red glass was made by several other Depression glass firms in several patterns, but most of these are relatively ornate and easy to distinguish from Anchor-Hocking's plain or bubble pattern.

Hints for Collectors
In 1977, Anchor-Hocking reissued several Royal Ruby shapes, among them tumblers, punch cups, and square bowls. All of these reissues are lighter in weight than the original pieces and marked with the company trademark (the originals never had a trademark).

Royal Ruby line

Wheeling Peachblow punch cup

Description
Cylindrical cup, slightly rounded at top and base. Thin walls.
Circular handle. Pontil mark polished. Color: *opaque white lining
with outer layer of yellow glass at base, shading to coral near
rim;* matt finish. *Variations:* with or without amber trim on
handle.

Type and Dimensions
Free-blown and cased. Applied handle. Partially reheated to
develop shading. Acid-treated after annealing for matt finish.
Height: 2⅜–2⅝″. Rim diameter: 2¾–3″.

Locality and Period
Hobbs, Brockunier & Company, Wheeling, West Virginia.
c. 1886–90.

Matching Glassware
Pitchers, bowls, vases (#345), sugar bowls, creamers, and
cruets. Not made as set.

Comment
Unlike the Mt. Washington and New England Peachblow
glassware (#280, #68), Wheeling Peachblow always has a
transparent layer of glass that has an opaque white lining.
Hobbs, Brockunier & Company produced Peachblow under a
license from the New England Glass Works. Basically, it is
Amberina glass (#150) with a white lining.

Hints for Collectors
Reproductions of many different shapes in Peachblow glass were
made in the 1960s by Imperial Glass Company of Bellaire, Ohio,
but the coloring is usually whiter than on originals. Another
Peachblow is being made by Pilgrim Glass Corporation in
Ceredo, West Virginia, but lacks the white lining.

New England Peachblow tumbler

Description
Cylindrical tumbler. Thin walls. *Opaque white near base, becoming pink on upper body.* Pontil mark polished.

Type and Dimensions
Free-blown, then tooled into shape. Partially reheated to develop pink shading. Height: 3½–4″. Rim diameter: 2½–2¾″.

Locality and Period
New England Glass Works, Cambridge, Massachusetts. c. 1886–88.

Matching Glassware
Bowls, vases, and toothpick holders (#179); rarely punch cups. Not made as set.

Comment
Wild Rose was patented in 1886 by the New England Glass Works during the craze for Peachblow glass, which lasted about 5 years. Collectors often call this type of glass New England Peachblow to distinguish it from Wheeling Peachblow (#67, #345) by Hobbs, Brockunier & Company, and Mt. Washington Glass Works' Peachblow (#280), which are slightly different in color. Glasses with similar coloring were also made in Europe during this period.

Hints for Collectors
All 3 types of Peachblow are rare and expensive. But the colors of each type are sufficiently distinctive to tell one kind from another. New England Peachblow may have a diamond-shaped paper label with "WILD ROSE/N.E.G.W." on the base. Like most trademarks, a label increases the value of a piece. Reproductions of New England Peachblow were made in Italy around 1970 in a variety of shapes. But these copies usually have rough pontil marks and a slightly grayish cast.

Wild Rose line

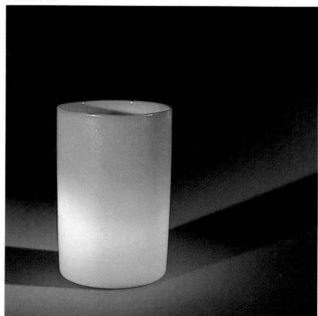

Depression mug

Description
Cylindrical mug with slight swelling near base and C-shaped handle. Thick walls. Mug illustrated on right has pressed dots on handle and around base, and "Tom & Jerry" in Old English script with scrolls on side. Base marked "MCK" (right) and "OVENWARE FIREKING 26" (left). Color: opaque white, light green, black, and ivory; red lettering. *Variations:* "Tom & Jerry" may be in block letters.

Type and Dimensions
Pressed in mold for pattern and shape. Decal applied after annealing. Height (left): 3¼"; rim diameter: 3¼". Height (right): 3⅜"; rim diameter: 2⅞".

Locality and Period
Plain mug at Anchor-Hocking Glass Corporation, Lancaster, Ohio. c. 1941–59. Tom & Jerry mug at McKee Glass Company, Jeannette, Pennsylvania. c. 1935–55.

Matching Glassware
Punch bowl set in Tom & Jerry with bowl and 4–6 mugs.

Comment
Tom & Jerry punch mugs were made to serve Tom and Jerry, a hot eggnoglike punch that was drunk at Christmastime. They were extremely popular, judging by the quantity of mugs remaining today.

Hints for Collectors
This opaque glass is one of the least popular types of Depression glass. It was used for a large variety of kitchenware, including custard cups, pie plates, and loaf pans. Most examples are still available and very inexpensive. Because of the comparatively recent date, there is no need to worry about reproductions.

Pitchers, Jugs, Decanters, and Bar Bottles

Pitchers, jugs, decanters, and bar bottles are pouring and storing utensils for all types of liquids, including wine, cider, and strong spirits, as well as water and milk, which did not become common table beverages until the second half of the 19th century. Containers of all sizes—from half pint to half gallon—were used on both sideboard and table from the Colonial period onward.

Pitchers are among the earliest forms of tableware. The very first pitchers and jugs were probably made from gourds and other dried vegetables long before the techniques of firing clay or blowing glass were known. Today pitchers and jugs can be found in the cheapest Staffordshire pottery or the finest porcelain and glass or the most magnificent silver and pewter. Classic shapes such as the globe- (#79), barrel- (#71), and pear-shaped (#80) pitchers were made in ceramic and metal as well as in glass during the 18th and 19th centuries. Cylindrical forms (#86, #87) and corset-shaped pitchers (#92, #94) are found principally in glass, rarely in other materials. Because of the wide variation, it is impossible to date pitchers by their shape. Instead, decorative techniques or the method of manufacture offer the best clues to dating.

Decanters and bar bottles are nearly always made of glass. They are virtually identical in shape but have different types of lips. The decanter has a small flat lip, and the inside of the neck is always ground to fit a matching ground stopper for an airtight seal that prevents evaporation. A bar bottle has a heavy rounded lip, and its neck is not ground, since a cork was probably used instead of a glass stopper. Both forms came in all colors throughout the 19th century, although colorless examples are by far the most common. Decoration varies from cut, engraved, and molded designs to pressed patterns. Shape is less variable and often serves as a guide in dating.

Tapered (#101) and globe-shaped (#105, #106) decanters of the early 19th century were followed by barrel-shaped (#103) or cylindrical (#107) forms in the mid-19th century. Decanters with handles, called decanter jugs, became popular in the late 19th and early 20th centuries. Decanters that are square in cross section were made in blown 3-mold glass in the 1820s and in cut glass around 1900. During the 1920s and 1930s, the tantalus set was introduced: a locking wooden frame for 2 or 3 square-shaped decanters. This design was especially popular during Prohibition. Bar bottles were probably used in inns, taverns, and other public drinking places, while carefully finished decanters were intended for home use. Water bottles, still another variation with broad necks and spreading mouths, are found primarily in the late 19th century. Like bar bottles, they never have stoppers.

Pitchers and decanters were often sold with matching drinking glasses—pitchers with tumblers and decanters with matching wine or cordial glasses as well as whiskey tumblers. These matching sets are yet another indication that both forms were used primarily at home.

70 Depression pitcher

Description
Barrel-shaped body bulges below pouring lip. Pressed pattern of vertical ribs interspersed with stylized rose bouquets on sides. Square handle. Flat base. Color: transparent light blue or pink; rarely transparent light green, yellow, or colorless. *Variations:* many floral patterns, such as Rose Cameo or Patrician (#15).

Type and Dimensions
Machine-pressed in mold for pattern and shape. Height: 5⅞″. Base diameter: 3¾″.

Locality and Period
Hocking Glass Company, Lancaster, Ohio. c. 1931–37. Other patterns by midwestern firms such as Federal, Hazel-Atlas, Macbeth-Evans, Jeannette, and Indiana. c. 1925–40.

Matching Glassware
Large set with wineglasses (#15), cordials, cocktail glasses, goblets, footed tumblers, bowls (#273), butter dish, covered candy dish, divided celery dishes (9″, 10″), covered sugar bowl, creamer, cups, saucers, decanter, pitchers (8″, 8½″), plates, platters, salt and pepper shakers, vase, and numerous serving dishes. Not all shapes in all colors.

Comment
Mayfair, also called Open Rose, is among the 3 most popular Depression-glass patterns, with the widest range of pieces.

Hints for Collectors
Blue Mayfair pieces are more expensive than pink, and the rare yellow and green command the highest prices in all Depression glass. The whiskey tumbler is the only shape in this set that has been reproduced. Only the pink resembles original examples, but reproductions are heavier, and the rose has a single stem.

Mayfair pattern

71 Engraved pitcher

Description
Barrel-shaped pitcher with 12 panels around narrow base. *Engraved leaf design* below rim, and flowers and leaves below shoulder. *Thin walls.* Small pouring lip. *Hollow ear-shaped handle crimped at depressed base.* Pontil mark rough. Colorless. *Variations:* engraving may be absent; panels are rare.

Type and Dimensions
Free-blown or blown in mold for panels. Tooled into shape. Pinched pouring lip. Applied handle. Copper-wheel engraved after annealing. Lead glass. Height: 5¼–6″. Base diameter: 3–3¼″.

Locality and Period
Probably western Pennsylvania. c. 1820–50.

Matching Glassware
Celery vases and occasionally sugar bowls. Not made as set.

Comment
All glassware of this type has been found around Pittsburgh. The paneled design is originally English. A few sugar bowls have similar molded panels and the addition of a lacy-patterned pressed base, which helps to date them to the second quarter of the 19th century. Sugar bowls without the pressed base may be slightly earlier.

Hints for Collectors
A polished pontil was not necessary on 18th-century bottles and decanters with a pushed-in, or depressed, base since the pontil was raised from the table. By the 19th century a polished pontil, even on a piece had depressed base, was a sign of quality, especially when a piece had further decoration, like the engraved pitcher shown here. The rough pontil is therefore unusual.

Early midwestern ribbed pitcher

Description
Barrel-shaped pitcher bulges below lip and narrows toward base. *Molded diagonal swirls around body.* Thin walls. *Small pouring lip.* Flattened ear-shaped handle slightly crimped at depressed base. Pontil mark rough. Color: transparent greenish, aquamarine, or amber. *Variations:* body sometimes more rounded; sometimes molded in broken swirl pattern (#44).

Type and Dimensions
Blown in ribbed mold, then swirled and expanded. Pinched pouring lip. Applied handle. Nonlead glass. Height: 6½–7″. Base diameter: 3–3½″.

Locality and Period
Ohio: probably Zanesville, Mantua, or Kent. Western Pennsylvania. c. 1820–40.

Matching Glassware
Tumblers (#44), bar bottles (#113), sugar bowls and creamers, salts (#176), plates (#214), and bowls (#274). Not made as set.

Comment
This type of swirled ribbing is exclusively associated with the early bottle and window glasshouses in Ohio and western Pennsylvania. But unless signed, it is usually impossible to differentiate the products of the various glasshouses of the Ohio River basin. Ribbing is one of the oldest decorative motifs; it appears on Roman glass around the 1st century B.C., soon after the invention of the blowpipe. Ribbing is also found on Venetian ware of the 15th century and on 18th-century English pieces.

Hints for Collectors
Mexican glassware of the 1920s and 1930s looks very much like midwestern glassware of this type. Although the colors are nearly identical, Mexican glass is usually very bubbly.

Free-blown pitcher

Description
Barrel-shaped pitcher with horizontal threading around neck.
Thick walls. *Small pouring lip.* Ear-shaped handle crimped at
depressed base. Pontil mark rough. Color: transparent
aquamarine, green, brown, or amber. *Variations:* shape ranges
from bulbous to cylindrical; some lack threading; many have
circular foot.

Type and Dimensions
Free-blown, then tooled into shape. Pinched pouring lip. Applied
handle and threading. Nonlead glass. Height: 8–9″. Base
diameter: 3½–4½″.

Locality and Period
New England, New York, and New Jersey. c. 1820–50.

Comment
The pitcher illustrated was purchased by the glass authority
George McKearin from a resident of Vernon, New York. It is
attributed to the Mt. Vernon Glass Company, which operated
from about 1810 to 1844, solely because this factory was in the
immediate vicinity. But the attribution is uncertain. The range of
colors indicates that this pitcher was made in a bottle or window
glasshouse and not in a tableware factory.

Hints for Collectors
Free-blown pieces like this pitcher vary according to the whim
and degree of skill of the blower. It is this individual character
that gives these pieces their charm. This type of free-blown glass
is rare and may be impossible to assemble in sets, but an
assorted collection of plain pieces and pieces with threading make
an attractive group.

Description
Slender pear-shaped pitcher with horizontal threading around elongated neck, and crossed lily-pad decoration on lower body. Thin walls. Small pouring lip. Ear-shaped handle slightly crimped at base. Circular crimped foot. Pontil mark rough. Color: transparent green, aquamarine, light amber, or dark amber; very dark amber appears opaque. Variations: lily pads may be swirled (#122) or straight (#123). Some pitchers lack foot.

Type and Dimensions
Free-blown, then tooled into shape. Applied, tooled handle, foot, and threading. Pinched pouring lip. Lily pads tooled from added gather of glass. Nonlead glass. Height: 7–8″. Foot diameter: 3–4″.

Locality and Period
Vermont, New Hampshire, Massachusetts, Connecticut, upstate New York, and southern New Jersey. c. 1820–60.

Matching Glassware
Sugar bowls (#122), creamers (#123), bowls, and compotes. Not made as set.

Comment
The lily-pad decoration is unique to American glassware, although a simpler, applied lily-pad decoration was used in Germany. It was probably brought to the United States and developed by the many immigrant German glassblowers. The pitcher illustrated is attributed to a mid-19th-century factory in Lockport or Lancaster, New York.

Hints for Collectors
The crossed lily-pad decoration is both rare and extremely expensive. Few reproductions of the crossed lily pads exist; those made in the 1940s imitate the straight or swirled style.

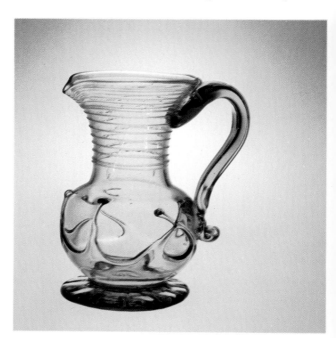

75 Johnson lily-pad pitcher

Description
Pear-shaped pitcher with folded rim. Horizontal threading around neck, and lily-pad decoration swirled toward right on lower body. Small pouring lip. Ear-shaped handle crimped at base. Circular foot. Pontil mark rough. Color: transparent green, aquamarine, or light amber; dark green or reddish amber may appear opaque or black. *Variations:* body cylindrical to globular; lily pad may be swirled, crossed (#74), straight (#123), or a combination of 2 of these. Some pitchers lack foot.

Type and Dimensions
Free-blown, then tooled into shape. Applied, tooled handle, foot, and threading. Pinched pouring lip. Lily pads tooled from added gather of glass. Nonlead glass. Height: 7–8″. Foot diameter: 3–4″.

Locality and Period
New Hampshire, New York, and New Jersey. c. 1846–70.

Matching Glassware
Sugar bowls (#122), creamers (#123), bowls, and compotes. Not made as set.

Comment
This piece is attributed to Matt Johnson, a blower who worked at 2 factories, in Redwood and Harrisburg, New York, in the 1830s. He worked at factories in Stoddard and Keene, New Hampshire, from 1846 to 1870. Like most glassblowers of the 19th century, Johnson went wherever work was available.

Hints for Collectors
The double lily pad illustrated, which consists of a curved and a straight pad, is an unusual variation. The dark reddish-amber pieces are probably from the Weeks & Gilson factory at Stoddard and the lighter ones from New York or Keene.

76 Spanish Lace pitcher

Description
Globe-shaped pitcher has overall raised opalescent white design of flowers and leaves against colored background. *Square mouth with opalescent white ruffled rim* and small pouring lip. Colorless C-shaped handle thicker at base. Pontil mark polished. Color: transparent red, light blue, or light yellow—all with opalescent white design. *Variations:* raised designs include hobnails (#77), coin-dot circles, vertical ribs, and lacy scrolls.

Type and Dimensions
Blown in mold for pattern, then tooled into shape and reheated to develop opalescent color. Tooled rim, lip, and neck. Applied handle. Nonlead glass. Height: 8–9″. Base diameter: 3½–4″.

Locality and Period
Hobbs, Brockunier & Company, Wheeling, West Virginia; possibly others in West Virginia or Ohio. c. 1885–1900.

Matching Glassware
Water set with tumblers; other pitchers, bowls, butter dish, cruet, syrup jug, celery vase, spoon holder, vase, and lamp.

Comment
Shaded or partly colored glassware was extremely popular in the 1880s and 1890s. In some cases, the shading extends from base to rim, as in Amberina (#332), Wheeling (#345) and New England (#68) Peachblows, and Burmese (#333). On this opalescent glass, the raised design has the second color. Collectors often call this type of glass Spanish Lace, although the name really applies to only one of the many patterns.

Hints for Collectors
This heat-sensitive glassware is less expensive than Amberina, Burmese, and other shaded ware. Beware of the many 20th-century reproductions of Spanish Lace.

77 Frances Ware pitcher

Description
Globe-shaped pitcher of *frosted glass with overall evenly spaced hobnails. Amber stain on square neck and rim.* Colorless C-shaped handle. Circular base rests on hobnails. Pontil mark rough. Matt finish. *Variations:* occasionally lacks hobnails.

Type and Dimensions
Blown in mold for hobnail pattern, then tooled into shape. Applied handle. Acid-treated after annealing for matt finish. Neck and rim stained amber. Height: 8–8½". Diameter: 6½–7".

Locality and Period
Hobbs, Brockunier & Company, Wheeling, West Virginia. c. 1885–90.

Matching Glassware
Set with other pitchers in several sizes, large and small tumblers, finger bowls, serving bowl and tray.

Comment
Frances Ware is the name given this combination of matt, or satin, finish and amber staining. It is still another version of the art glass that became popular in the 1880s. The finish was probably inspired by the New England Glass Works' popular Pomona art glass, which is also frosted and stained glass.

Hints for Collectors
Frances Ware is not as well known as Pomona (#259) or Crown Milano (#181, #310) art glass. But because this type of glass was made by only one firm and in limited quantities, its value will probably increase in the future. Today it is relatively common and reasonably priced.

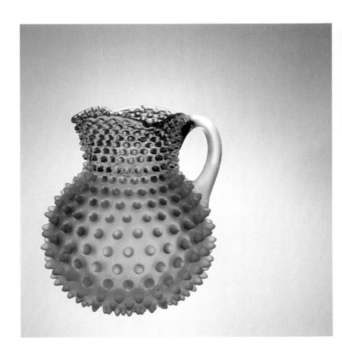

78 Brilliant-cut water set

Description
Set of cylindrical tumblers and barrel-shaped pitcher. *Cut pattern of strawberry-diamonds above vertical panels.* Pitcher has cut panels with notched edges on neck, deeply scalloped rim, and notched ear-shaped handle. Cut sunburst on base of both forms. Colorless. *Variations:* patterns mostly cut hobstars, diamonds, fans, panels, and other motifs of the period; sometimes acid-stamped trademark on base. Pitchers may be corset-shaped (#92, #94).

Type and Dimensions
Free-blown, then tooled into shape. Applied handle. Cut after annealing. Lead glass. Pitcher height: 8–8½″; base diameter: 4–4½″. Tumbler height: 4–4½″; base diameter: 3–3¼″.

Locality and Period
Throughout the United States. c. 1900–15.

Matching Glassware
Set with wine, champagne, sherry and cordial glasses, goblets, decanter, bowls, and vase.

Comment
The water set illustrated bears the trademark of H. P. Sinclaire & Company of Corning—the "s" within a laurel wreath. However, many similar sets are unmarked and thus difficult to attribute to any particular factory. Water sets were common around the turn of the century. They were made in late 19th-century pressed-glass patterns (#85) as well as in cut glass and some of the colorful art glasses (#76). Occasionally they are found with matching trays, although trays are more common in pressed glass.
Cut-glass water sets were made in many patterns and can be found in the catalogues of most cutting shops around the turn of

the century. The sets were not used exclusively for water but also for punch or lemonade. The tumblers could be used for serving whiskey. It is likely that such sets were also brought to the table to serve beverages to guests at between-meal gatherings. Water sets were more common than sets of decanters and matching wine and cordial glasses, possibly because there were areas of the country where the consumption of alcohol was frowned upon. This was especially true in the southeastern United States, where organizations like the Women's Christian Temperance Union and the Methodist Church were influential.

Hints for Collectors
Look for an acid-stamped trademark underneath these tumblers and near the base of the handle on this pitcher. Marked sets are always more valuable than unmarked ones. To determine the quality of a piece, look first at the quality of the blank. It should be free of bubbles or other flaws, as well as symmetrically shaped and clearly transparent. If the glass is grayish or has a yellowish or greenish tinge, the blank is probably inferior. To determine the skill of the cutter, look at various elements in the pattern to make sure all the lines meet as they should. It is especially easy to check deep miter cuts, which often separate the various motifs in cut patterns. Miter cuts that do not come together exactly at a point in every instance indicate poor workmanship and poor quality control within a shop. It is also important to look for modern retouching on the edge of a piece to salvage a cracked or broken area. If the pattern runs up into the scalloped rim, the piece has been cut down since its original manufacture and should not command as high a price.

79 Brilliant-cut pitcher

Description
Globe-shaped pitcher with cut pattern of strawberry-diamonds and fans below neck. Vertical panels with dotted lines cut around neck. Thick walls. Scalloped, high pouring lip. Notched ear-shaped handle. Cut sunburst on base. Color: *usually colorless*, rarely cased with transparent red, blue, green, or yellow. *Variations:* hundreds of patterns combining strawberry-diamonds with hobstars, pinwheels, notches, and other motifs; occasionally cut hobstar on base.

Type and Dimensions
Free-blown, with tooled lip. Applied, tooled handle. Cut after annealing. Lead glass. Height: 8–8½". Diameter: 6–6¼".

Locality and Period
Throughout the United States. c. 1880–1900.

Matching Glassware
Set with tumblers, goblets, wine and cordial glasses, bowls, compote, sugar bowl and creamer, decanter, salt, and vase.

Comment
This pitcher was made by C. Dorflinger & Sons of White Mills, Pennsylvania. The Irish or English strawberry-diamond and fan motifs came to America around 1800, reaching the greatest popularity from 1815 to 1835.

Hints for Collectors
Do not confuse this pitcher with an early 19th-century example cut with the same motifs. The pitcher illustrated is more globe-than barrel-shaped, and the attachment of the handle varies significantly. Before the Civil War, the handle was attached at the top, then curved down and crimped at the base. After the 1880s, the handle was attached first at the base and curved up. The earlier crimped handle is more valuable.

Description

Pear-shaped pitcher with cut horizontal ribs (stepcuts) underneath lip and around neck. 3 sections of cut block diamonds around lower body separated by vertical panels with square panels above and below. High pouring lip. Scalloped rim. Heavy ear-shaped handle. Flat base with cut sunburst. Colorless. *Variations:* mostly geometric patterns including circles and diamonds of various sizes.

Type and Dimensions

Free-blown, then shaped. Applied, tooled handle. Cut after annealing. Lead glass. Height: 8–9″. Base diameter: 3½–4″.

Locality and Period

New York City, New Jersey, Philadelphia, Pittsburgh, and possibly Boston. England. c. 1820–40.

Matching Glassware

Probably tumblers; possibly mugs, decanters, celery vases, oval bowls, and compotes. Not made as set.

Comment

This type of cutting resembles Anglo-Irish styles of the same period. Cut glass was advertised by several Pittsburgh firms, the largest being Benjamin Bakewell's. It was also made at the New England Glass Company in Cambridge, Massachusetts; New York Glass Works and Brooklyn Flint Glass Works in New York City; Jersey Glass Company in Jersey City, New Jersey; and Kensington Glass Company, Philadelphia. It is impossible to attribute a particular cut pattern to one company.

Hints for Collectors

Early 19th-century cut glass is not as popular and often less expensive than cut glass made 40 to 50 years later. Although the earlier patterns are not as elaborate, the quality is the same.

Blown 3-mold pitcher

Description
Barrel-shaped pitcher with horizontal rings below wide rim; 2 rows of molded Gothic arches around body. Medallion encloses "GIN" inscription underneath ear-shaped handle with crimped base. Thin walls. Small pouring lip. *Flat base has pressed sunburst.* Pontil mark rough. Colorless. *Variations:* may be cylindrical; pattern usually geometric waffles, ribs, and sunbursts (#46, #55, #64); rarely inscribed.

Type and Dimensions
Blown in mold for pattern and shape. Tooled pouring lip and neck. Applied, tooled handle. Lead glass. Height: 6½–7″. Base diameter: 4–4¼″.

Locality and Period
Massachusetts: Boston & Sandwich Glass Company, Sandwich, and New England Glass Company, Cambridge. c. 1820–35.

Matching Glassware
Decanter (#103). Not made as set.

Comment
This pitcher is especially rare because it was blown in a decanter mold (#103). Decanters with silver labels that hung by a chain around the neck were popular among those who could afford these extras. Others bought molded decanters with "GIN," "RUM," or "WINE" embossed on the front. In the example illustrated, the blower shaped the pitcher in a decanter mold with the "GIN" inscription, but covered the inscription with the pitcher handle.

Hints for Collectors
Whimsies or mistakes like this pitcher are usually one of a kind and command premium prices even if damaged. The pitcher shown here bears a crack where it was broken and repaired.

Description
Pear-shaped pitcher with evenly spaced rows of vertical cleats below waist. Thick walls. *High pouring lip* with horizontal ribs underneath. Ear-shaped handle crimped at base. Circular base rests on cleats. Color: colorless; rarely transparent light purple. *Variations:* several patterns, including Bull's Eye and Curtain.

Type and Dimensions
Blown in mold for pattern, then tooled into shape. Applied, tooled handle. Lead glass. Height: 9–10″. Base diameter: 3½–4½″.

Locality and Period
Probably New England Glass Company, Cambridge, Massachusetts. c. 1870–90.

Matching Glassware
Lamp chimneys and bar bottles in pattern illustrated; bar bottles in Bull's Eye pattern. Not made as set.

Comment
This pitcher somewhat resembles pressed examples (#86–88). Mold-blown glass is less common in the late 19th century and usually has less variety of patterns and shapes than pressed glass. The pitcher illustrated is one of the few late 19th-century examples known.

Hints for Collectors
There are few matching mold-blown pieces for this pitcher, which may partly explain why this pattern has not been popular. Even though it is older than Carnival or Depression glass, this sturdy, well-proportioned pitcher is often less expensive. It is an excellent choice for a beginning collector.

83 Beehive pitcher

Description
Pear-shaped pitcher with beehivelike rings around body. Heavy thick walls. *High pouring lip.* Ear-shaped handle crimped at base. Circular foot. Pontil mark rough or polished. Colorless. *Variations:* number of rings may vary.

Type and Dimensions
Free-blown, then tooled into shape. Tooled rings and lip. Applied, tooled handle and foot. Lead glass. Height: 8–9″. Base diameter: 3–4″.

Locality and Period
Probably Boston & Sandwich Glass Company, Sandwich, Massachusetts. c. 1830–60.

Matching Glassware
Sugar bowl and creamer set; also lamp. Not made as set with pitcher.

Comment
Beehive decoration appears on only a few pieces; some have been fairly reliably attributed to the Boston & Sandwich Glass Company. Although only one creamer and matching sugar bowl are known, it seems probable that others were made.

Hints for Collectors
Most pieces of this type are very reasonably priced, considering their age and rarity. Although no glasses were made to match this pitcher, any blown glasses of the same period will go with it.

Pillar-molded pitcher

Description
Heavy pear-shaped pitcher with raised vertical ribs extending from underneath base to rim. Wide pouring lip. Ear-shaped handle crimped at depressed base. Pontil mark polished. Color: transparent light or dark blue, light or dark purple, amber, colorless, or opaque white; very dark colors may appear opaque. Rarely, contrasting white stripes on each rib, as shown here. *Variations:* rarely, vertical threads of colored glass on each pillar; occasionally twisted.

Type and Dimensions
Blown in ribbed mold for pattern and shape. Extra glass applied on each rib to form stripes. Tooled pouring lip. Applied, tooled handle and applied threading. Lead or nonlead glass. Height: 9–10″. Base diameter: 3–3½″.

Locality and Period
Western Pennsylvania and West Virginia. c. 1840–70.

Matching Glassware
Celery vases, bar bottles (#110), footed bowls (#300), vases (#340), small bowls (#276), cruets, molasses cans, and candlesticks. Not made as set.

Comment
Pillar-molded glass is said to have been used on steamboats that traveled the Ohio River from Pittsburgh to New Orleans, although this has never been documented. These pitchers are heavy enough for use in a public bar or a steamboat saloon.

Hints for Collectors
Because pillar-molded glass is very popular with collectors, it is relatively expensive compared with free-blown ware of the same period. Yet it is cheaper than rare pieces of art or cut glass. Pillar-molded glass was made only in the United States.

Description
Set with pitcher and 2–12 tumblers. *Rectangular pitcher with pressed wide vertical ribs and narrow horizontal ribs;* scalloped edges; high pouring lip; squared-off handle; and 4 paw-shaped feet. Cylindrical tumblers with matching rib pattern. Color: opalescent yellow, blue, or colorless. *Variations:* many opalescent patterns, both geometric (#228) and floral.

Type and Dimensions
Pressed in mold for pattern and shape. Nonlead glass. Pitcher height: 8″; base diameter: 3″. Tumbler height: 4″; rim diameter: 3⅛″.

Locality and Period
Northwood Glass Company, Indiana, Pennsylvania; c. 1897–98; Northwood Glass Company, Wheeling, West Virginia; c. 1901–1905.

Matching Glassware
Set with sugar bowl, creamer, butter dish, spoon holder, footed dishes in individual and serving sizes, salt and pepper shakers, cruets and water set tray.

Comment
Alaska is a typical turn-of-the-century pattern both because of its angular shapes (all matching pieces except the tumblers illustrated are square) and because of its combination of opalescent and transparent colors. The manufacturer was probably copying the more expensive mold-blown opalescent ware that was popular during the same period (#76). All of the square or rectangular pieces in this pattern have 4 paw feet, inspiring some collectors to call the pattern Lion's Leg. However, the tumblers lack this distinctive feature and are not as easily recognized as the other pieces in the pattern.

Alaska pattern

Harry Northwood, founder of Northwood Glass Company, came from a notable glassmaking family located in Stourbridge, England. He moved to the United States in the late 1880s and worked in several different glasshouses in the Midwest before starting his own factory in Pennsylvania in 1897. He sold the factory in 1898 and went back to England for a short period, but later returned to the United States and purchased the defunct Hobbs, Brockunier & Company glasshouse in West Virginia, where he opened his second glasshouse. Northwood was an inventive manager, and his first factory produced a tremendous range of colors and techniques, including opalescent pressed glass, pink slag (#154), custard glass (#230), and other colorless and colored pressed glass in many patterns. Sometimes Northwood produced the same pattern in opalescent, Carnival, and ordinary pressed glass. He had made some of this glass in the various factories he managed before 1897, and continued to make the same lines in Wheeling, adding the production of Carnival glass after 1905. Many of Northwood's pieces are marked "N" or "N" enclosed in a circle. A large number of turn-of-the-century pressed patterns, like the one illustrated here, as well as many patterns in custard and Carnival glass have no stemware, only tumblers in 2 or 3 sizes and punch cups. This may have been an attempt to appeal to consumers of modest means, who did not ordinarily drink wine at the table and who could not afford the more expensive cut and art glasses.

Hints for Collectors
Blue is considered to be the most desirable color in this pattern and is consequently the most expensive, followed by yellow. This pattern has never been reproduced and is still very inexpensive.

Late 19th-century pressed pitcher

Description
Hexagonal pitcher with *6 Gothic arches around body; 3 with classically draped woman alternating with 3 Daisy and Button patterned arches.* Thick walls. High pouring lip has leaf underneath. Rectangular handle and 4 feet have barklike pattern. Colorless. *Variations:* may have flat collarlike base instead of feet; female figure in several poses, sometimes crouching.

Type and Dimensions
Pressed in mold for pattern and shape. Nonlead glass. Height: 9¼". Base diameter: 4".

Locality and Period
Gillinder & Sons, Philadelphia. c. 1882–90.

Matching Glassware
Large set with goblets, plates, butter dish, covered compotes in several sizes, creamer, sugar bowl, celery vase, sauce dish, and spoon holder.

Comment
This Classic pattern was introduced in the 1880s and is typical of the late 19th century, with its mixture of motifs drawn from a variety of sources. The classically draped female figure and the arches are inspired by the Gothic Revival of the mid-19th century. The Daisy and Button motif is a pressed version of the brilliant-cut Russian pattern (#29). The barklike effect on the feet and handle is similar to the textured surface on the covered duck and hen dishes (#238, #239). In later examples, a sturdier collarlike base replaces the feet.

Hints for Collectors
This pattern is especially popular and more expensive than most pressed pitchers, but so far it has never been reproduced.

Classic pattern

Late 19th-century pressed pitcher

Description
Cylindrical pitcher with *portrait of Admiral George Dewey enclosed in wreath on 1 side.* On opposite side, list of about 10 ships from Battle of Manila Bay. In between, figures of sailors and marines and inscription, "You may fire when ready, Gridley." Row of beads below rim and mortar shells around base. High pouring lip. Thick walls. Ear-shaped handle. Circular foot. Colorless. *Variations:* cannonballs may replace mortar shells.

Type and Dimensions
Pressed in mold for pattern and shape. Nonlead glass. Height: 8¾". Base diameter: 4".

Locality and Period
Beatty-Brady Glass Company, Dunkirk, Indiana. c. 1898–1900.

Matching Glassware
Set with tumblers.

Comment
This glass was patented in 1898, after Admiral George Dewey's squadron defeated the Spanish in the Battle of Manila Bay in the Philippine Islands on May 1, and marked the end of the Spanish-American War. Dewey became a hero overnight and was briefly spoken of as a presidential candidate. Collectors call this pattern Dewey-Gridley.

Hints for Collectors
Commemorative pieces like this pitcher and the Garfield and Grant plates (#199, #200) have become increasingly popular since the American Bicentennial. They are now harder to find and will probably continue to increase in value.

Dewey-Gridley pattern

Description
Pear-shaped pitcher has pressed stippled drapery pattern with floral design below waist. Thin walls. *High pouring lip.* Ear-shaped handle crimped at base. Circular foot has panels where it joins body. Colorless.

Type and Dimensions
Pressed in mold for pattern and shape. Tooled lip. Applied, tooled handle. Nonlead glass. Height: 10–10¼″. Foot diameter: 3½–3¾″.

Locality and Period
Pittsburgh area; possibly Adams & Company. c. 1870–85.

Matching Glassware
Large set with goblets, memorial plates (#200), bowls, butter dish, cake plate on stand, compotes, sugar bowl, creamer, honey dish, oval pickle dish, sauce dish, and spoon holder.

Comment
This pattern is called Garfield Drape by collectors, named after the memorial plate that has similar drape decoration around the rim (#200). Following the assassination of President James A. Garfield in 1881, the Adams firm advertised a Garfield plate to commemorate his death and to boost sales. This pattern has never been especially popular with collectors.

Hints for Collectors
The applied, rather than pressed, handle on this pitcher is unusual for this period. There is no pontil mark because the pitcher was held in a snap case for tooling. The snap case began to replace the pontil rod around 1870.

Garfield Drape pattern

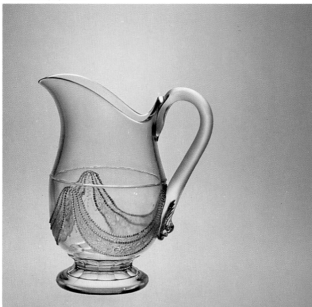

89 Realistic-style pressed pitcher

Description
Cylindrical pitcher with pressed double flowering vine superimposed on narrow vertical ribbing. Thin walls. *High pouring lip.* Ear-shaped handle crimped at base. Pontil mark polished. Color: colorless; transparent blue, white, or amber; opalescent white. *Variations:* sometimes single vine, leaves, or other flower design on ribs; ribs may be coarse or fine.

Type and Dimensions
Pressed in mold for pattern and shape. Tooled, shaped lip and applied, tooled handle. Lead or nonlead glass. Height: 8–8¼″. Base diameter: 4–4¼″.

Locality and Period
M'Kee & Brothers, Pittsburgh; Boston & Sandwich Glass Company, Sandwich, Massachusetts; and others. c. 1864–75.

Matching Glassware
Large set with stemware, tumblers, castor set (#189), decanter, sugar bowl, creamer, butter dish, celery vase, spoon holder (#319), salt, bowls, plates, cake stand, and lamp.

Comment
Like many pressed patterns, Bellflower was once associated exclusively with the Boston & Sandwich Glass Company. However, it also appears as Ribbed Leaf in an 1864 M'Kee catalogue and was probably made by several other firms, judging from the number of variations.

Hints for Collectors
A complete set of Bellflower can be assembled without much effort, but is usually expensive. Because it was made by more than one firm, there are both lead and nonlead examples, which often vary in quality. This pattern has been reproduced.

Bellflower pattern

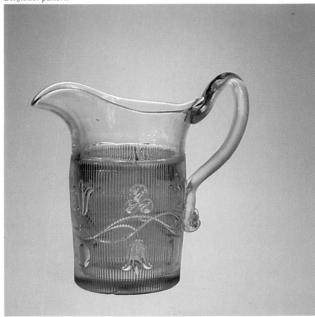

90 Depression water pitcher

Description
Cylindrical pitcher narrows at base. *Pressed honeycomb pattern on lower body; unpatterned upper body* with ring below rim. *Arched ice lip.* C-shaped handle. Circular base has thick edge. Color: transparent deep red, green, pink, amber, or colorless.

Type and Dimensions
Machine-pressed in mold for pattern and shape. Height: 8½″. Base diameter: 4¾″.

Locality and Period
Hocking Glass Company and, later, Anchor-Hocking Glass Corporation, Lancaster, Ohio. Similar patterns by midwestern firms such as Federal, Jeannette, Indiana, Paden City, and Hazel-Atlas. c. 1930–50.

Matching Glassware
Set with tumblers in 5 sizes, including iced tea and whiskey tumblers; also decanter, sherbet glasses, and underplates.

Comment
The Hocking Georgian pattern illustrated has been produced since the 1930s. Another Georgian pattern made in green and colorless glass by the Federal Glass Company is lighter in weight and lacier, resembling Mayfair (#70). The ice lip on this pitcher, made to catch ice cubes, was a popular feature in the 1930s, when refrigerators and ice cubes became more common.

Hints for Collectors
The Georgian pattern is not popular among collectors, perhaps because it comes in a limited range of shapes. Anchor-Hocking is still producing the matching tumblers today in colorless glass, using the same molds, and it is virtually impossible to tell these apart from originals.

Georgian pattern

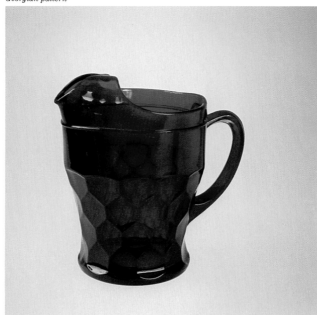

91 Carnival pitcher

Description
Cylindrical pitcher with overall pressed barklike pattern and plain band below rim. Small pouring lip. Ear-shaped handle. Pressed sunburst on base. Color: *transparent orange-amber with iridescent finish.*

Type and Dimensions
Pressed in mold for pattern and shape. Iridescent finish sprayed on before annealing. Height: 8⅝–9⅛". Base diameter: 4¼–4¾".

Locality and Period
West Virginia: Fenton Art Glass Company, Williamstown; Northwood Glass Company, Wheeling. Ohio: Imperial Glass Company, Bellaire; Millersburg Glass Company, Millersburg. Possibly others. c. 1905–20.

Matching Glassware
Water set with tumblers.

Comment
The Treebark pattern illustrated is one of the few Carnival patterns that has never been identified with one of the 4 major producers of Carnival glass. The limited range of shapes and single color indicate that it may have been produced by a firm that normally made plainer pressed glass and was perhaps experimenting with Carnival glass. Collectors call this iridescent amber color marigold.

Hints for Collectors
This pattern has never been reproduced and it is rare since relatively little was made. Most reproductions of Carnival glass were made in the 1950s by the Fenton Art Glass and Imperial Glass companies. Unlike original examples, they are marked "IG" or "F" on the base. In some instances, these initials may have been removed to disguise a reproduction.

Treebark pattern

Corset-shaped brilliant-cut pitcher

Description
Heavy corset-shaped pitcher with cut geometric pattern of sunbursts and X's. Scalloped rim. *Thick walls.* High pouring lip has notched prism cuts. Ear-shaped handle cut in horizontal rings and notches. Flat base has cut sunburst. Colorless. *Variations:* many cut motifs, mostly hobstars, pinwheels, diamonds, and sunbursts and X's shown here; occasionally cut hobstar on base.

Type and Dimensions
Free-blown, then tooled into shape. Applied handle. Cut after annealing. Lead glass. Height: 9–10″. Base diameter: 4–4½″.

Locality and Period
Throughout the United States. c. 1895–1915.

Matching Glassware
Set with tumblers.

Comment
The pitcher illustrated was cut at Dithridge & Company in Cambridge, Massachusetts, but is not marked because the Dithridge firm did not use a trademark. It was handed down in the Dithridge family from one generation to the next.

Hints for Collectors
Unsigned standard pitchers like this one are still relatively inexpensive because they are fairly common and easy to find. Innumerable vases (#327) and pitchers have the so-called corset shape. The pattern is a typical turn-of-the-century style, combining many cut motifs over most of the surface. The notches on the handle are also characteristic of brilliant-cut glass.

93 Pitcher-form brilliant-cut vase

Description
Narrow corset-shaped pitcher with high pouring lip and serrated rim. Cut rows of vertical lines around sides alternating with vertical rows of hobstars, hobstars becoming larger as base flares. Ear-shaped handle cut in notches. Cut hobstar on base. Colorless. *Variations:* many different motifs, including hobstars, pinwheels, diamonds, miter cuts, and strawberry-diamonds.

Type and Dimensions
Free-blown, then tooled into shape. Applied handle. Cut after annealing. Lead glass. Height: 14½–14¾″. Base diameter: 6–6¼″.

Locality and Period
Throughout the United States. c. 1900–20.

Comment
This pitcher was cut at the Ideal Cut Glass Company of Canastota, New York, for the Norton Company of Worcester, Massachusetts, and descended in the Norton family. The carefully cut, intricate design was intended to show off the possibilities of the Norton cutting wheels. The shape is common for the period, but the piece's extreme height makes its use as a pitcher impractical. Filled, it was both too heavy and too awkward to pour from; it was probably intended as a vase or merely to be shown off on a sideboard.

Hints for Collectors
Most of these pieces are unmarked and there is usually no way to identify the cutting shop or the cutter. However, the high quality is unmistakable, and a similar pitcher would be a good buy regardless of the lack of a trademark.

94 Brilliant-cut pitcher

Description
Cylindrical pitcher flares slightly at bottom. *Notched prism cutting around lower body; large hobstars below scalloped rim.* Thick walls. Small pouring lip. Heavy ear-shaped handle wider at base. Cut sunburst on base. Pontil mark polished. Color: colorless; rarely overlaid with transparent red, blue, or green. *Variations:* many patterns with hobstars, pinwheels, diamonds, or strawberry-diamonds; may lack prism cutting; occasionally cut hobstar on base.

Type and Dimensions
Free-blown, then tooled into shape. Applied handle. Cut after annealing. Lead glass. Height: 9–9¼". Base diameter: 6–6¼".

Locality and Period
Throughout the United States. c. 1900–14.

Matching Glassware
Set with tumblers of various sizes, cordial glasses, whiskey and cordial jugs, and probably decanter.

Comment
The Hindoo pattern was cut by J. Hoare & Company of Corning, New York, and bears the acid-stamped circular trademark "J. HOARE & CO./1853/CORNING" on the base. The Hoare company adopted this trademark around 1895, when many other glass-cutting firms were also registering trademarks. The date 1853 refers to the year the founder, John Hoare, emigrated from England to the United States.

Hints for Collectors
Cut-glass patterns are often identified by numbers instead of names. Without a trademark or number, it is difficult to identify either the pattern or the cutting firm. A trademark rarely affects quality, yet marked pieces are considered more valuable.

Hindoo pattern

Crackle-glass champagne pitcher

Description
Pear-shaped pitcher with overall layer of crackled glass. Fluted
rim has wide pouring lip. *Side pocket opens into body underneath
handle.* Ropelike design around neck twisted on 1 side to form
handle. Flat circular base. Pontil mark rough. Colorless.

Type and Dimensions
Free-blown, then rolled in crushed glass while still warm for
crackle effect. Pocket formed by blower. Applied handle. Tooled
lip and neck. Lead and nonlead glass. Height: 11–12″. Base
diameter: 3–4″.

Locality and Period
Boston & Sandwich Glass Company, Sandwich, Massachusetts.
c. 1870–85. Bohemia. c. 1875–1910. England. c. 1875–1900.

Comment
Pitchers with a side pocket were popular in the 1870s and 1880s.
The compartment, or pocket, was designed to hold ice to chill the
champagne. They are found only in blown glass since the pocket
could not be made with the plunger of a hand press. The surface
on this piece is meant to imitate cracked ice, an effect which
could also be achieved with a pattern mold or by plunging hot
glass, molded or blown, into water.

Hints for Collectors
Until recently most pitchers like the one illustrated were
attributed to the Boston & Sandwich Glass Company. However,
a catalogue of Bohemian glassmakers from about 1910 illustrates
the same form. English cutting firms also made similar pitchers.
Lead glass is American or English, while lighter-weight, nonlead
examples are probably Bohemian.

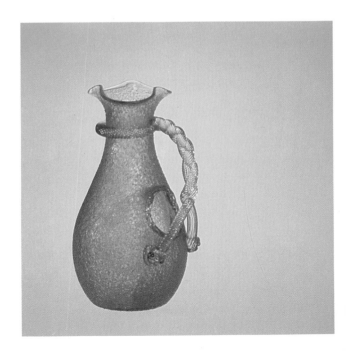

Description
Globe-shaped body with long cylindrical neck and small pouring lip. *6 pressed vertical cables* around lower body; silver fleur-de-lis decoration between ribs. C-shaped handle and flat circular base. Spherical stopper. Color: transparent red, dark and light blue, amber, or colorless; stopper usually colorless. *Variations:* stopper may be fan-shaped; decoration gilded instead of silver; scrolls may replace fleur-de-lis pattern.

Type and Dimensions
Bottle and stopper machine-pressed in separate molds for pattern and shape. Lip and upper neck hand-finished. Ground neck and stopper shaft. Applied handle. Silver-decorated after annealing. Height: 8½". Base diameter: 2¼".

Locality and Period
New Martinsville Glass Manufacturing Company, New Martinsville, Virginia. c. 1936–39. Similar patterns by Federal, Anchor-Hocking, Jeannette, Indiana, and Macbeth-Evans. c. 1925–40.

Matching Glassware
Large set with tumblers, pitchers, plates, bowls, butter dish, creamer, sugar bowl, and many serving dishes.

Comment
Strictly speaking, this is not Depression glass since it is hand-finished and was more expensive than most glass of that type. However, it is of the same period and often of interest to Depression-glass collectors. The pattern illustrated was advertised as Radiance by the New Martinsville firm.

Hints for Collectors
This piece is quite expensive for 1930s glassware, and the dark red illustrated is the rarest and most expensive color.

Radiance pattern

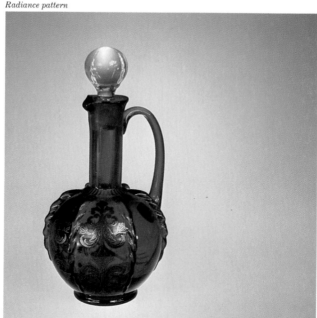

Description
Pear-shaped jug with long ground neck and high pouring lip. *Raised pillars swirl to right, with engraved decoration of birds, flowers, and bees.* Ear-shaped handle extends from neck to shoulder. Foot has 8 scallops. Acid-stamped "S" in laurel wreath on base. Pontil mark polished. Solid cone-shaped stopper has floral pattern and ground shank. Colorless. *Variations:* pillars sometimes straight instead of swirled; engraving mostly floral.

Type and Dimensions
Free-blown and tooled bottle and stopper. Ground neck and stopper shaft. Applied handle and foot. Cut and copper-wheel engraved pillars; cut foot. Lead glass. Height: 13¼". Base diameter: 3".

Locality and Period
H. P. Sinclaire & Company, Corning, New York. c. 1904–28.

Matching Glassware
Set with stemware and finger bowls with underplates.

Comment
This decanter with a handle is often referred to as a claret jug in glass catalogues. It is probably an early design made in the style of English rock crystal of the 1880s (#98). This polished engraving represents some of the highest-quality rock crystal. The pattern, called Birds, Bees, and Flowers, was expensive. This decanter sold for $350, according to a 1920 catalogue.

Hints for Collectors
The Sinclaire trademark is one of the most sought after. Some rock-crystal stemware sold in the United States is English, made by the 2 major firms, Thomas Webb & Sons and Stevens & Williams Company. It is usually signed by the engraver on the foot or within the design.

Birds, Bees, and Flowers pattern

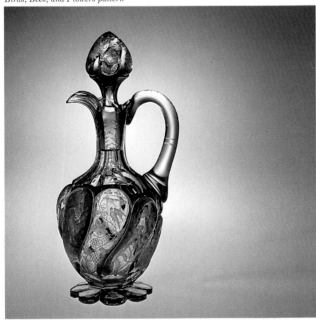

98 Rock-crystal decanter

Description
Globe-shaped jug with *row of raised ovals around shoulder and indented flower-and-leaf engraving on body and neck. Thick walls.* Wide flaring lip has row of ovals and small pouring spout. Neck bulges slightly before shoulder. Nearly square solid handle extends from neck to shoulder, with cut circles. Cut sunburst on base. Stopper on long paneled shaft has glass or silver ball. Colorless. *Variations:* several floral or naturalistic engraved patterns; sometimes marked on base or beneath handle.

Type and Dimensions
Blown in mold for pattern, then tooled into shape. Mold-blown stopper. Applied, cut handle; ground neck and stopper shaft. Copper-wheel engraved, cut, and polished after annealing. Lead glass. Height: 11–11½". Base diameter: 3–4".

Locality and Period
Libbey Glass Company, Toledo, Ohio. Eastern firms, such as J. Hoare & Company, Corning, New York, and Mt. Washington Glass Company, New Bedford, Massachusetts. c. 1895–1915.

Comment
The rock-crystal engraving style was introduced to America from England in 1886 and became especially popular after 1893, following an exhibit at the Chicago World's Fair by J. Hoare & Company. In 1904, Libbey Glass Company presented rock-crystal glassware at the St. Louis World's Fair.

Hints for Collectors
Originally the term "rock crystal" denoted a very expensive line of glass with raised panels (#97) and elaborate polished engraving. As prices increased, the term was applied more loosely to any polished engraving.

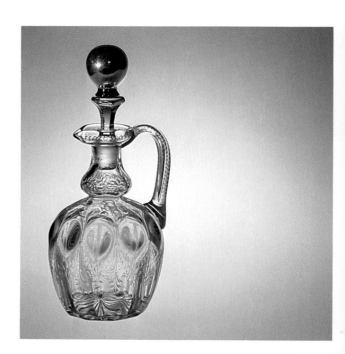

Description
Cylindrical jug with *pressed swirl-and-diamond pattern* on shoulder and swirls around neck. Engraved fern fronds and "C. M. Finch" on lower body. Thick C-shaped handle extends from top of shoulder to mid-body. Slightly depressed base has dimple. *Locking metal cap with keyhole fits over inner cork and* rests on flat lip. Cap stamped "Pat. Appl. for." Colorless. *Variations:* some jugs lack inscription.

Type and Dimensions
Pressed from bottom for pattern and shape, including handle, then tooled shut. Copper-wheel engraved after annealing. Nonlead glass. Height: 8½–8¾". Base diameter: 5–5¼".

Locality and Period
Pittsburgh: King, Son & Company's Cascade Glass Works; possibly United States Glass Company. c. 1891–1900.

Comment
This design was patented by the King firm in 1891. The pattern was used only for this jug. The unusual locking metal cap was probably intended to keep certain members of the household, possibly servants, out of the whiskey supply. It is an unusual precaution for this period, although locks became more common in the 1920s during Prohibition.

Hints for Collectors
No other locking jug designs are known, so they cannot have been too popular. Although these jugs are rare, pressed glass of the late 19th century is inexpensive compared with cut or engraved, blown examples. The pressing technique used here was common for decanters and bottles after 1890, and it leaves a dimple, rather than a pontil mark, on the base.

Brilliant-cut 20th-century decanter

Description
Cylindrical body has neck of nearly equal length. Overall cut pattern of hobstars and strawberry-diamonds on body. Thick walls. Faceted lip. Neck cut into vertical panels that continue on matching stopper. Polished flat base has sunburst. Colorless. *Variations:* body sometimes barrel- or square-shaped; several geometric patterns, including diamonds, circles, flutes, hobstars, and pinwheels.

Type and Dimensions
Free-blown body and stopper, both tooled into shape. Ground neck and stopper shaft. Cut after annealing. Lead glass. Height: 10–12″. Base diameter: 2½–3″.

Locality and Period
Throughout the United States. c. 1900–25.

Matching Glassware
Whiskey tumblers. Not made as set.

Comment
The decanter illustrated is by the Majestic Cut Glass Company of Elmira, New York, which operated for about 15 years in the early 20th century. Like many other American firms, Majestic used quality Belgian blanks imported from the Cristalleries de Val St. Lambert or bought blanks from the Pairpoint Corporation in Massachusetts. They did not use trademarks.

Hints for Collectors
The shape of this decanter is not found before 1900 and is obviously influenced by the shape of a liquor bottle. It was probably intended for whiskey rather than wine. Cut glass in an unnamed pattern, and by a little-known company, is still relatively inexpensive, often costing little more than a modern piece by a quality glasshouse.

Early cut and engraved decanter

Description
Tapered bottle with cut panels (right) *or honeycomb pattern* (left) *around neck* and cut vertical ribbing above flat base. Engraved drapery (left) or tiny stars (right) on body. Thin walls. Pontil mark polished. Faceted oval stopper. Colorless. *Variations:* many engraved patterns with stars and drapery.

Type and Dimensions
Free-blown bottle and stopper, both tooled into shape. Ground neck and stopper shank. Cut and copper-wheel engraved after annealing. Nonlead glass. Height: 9½–10¾". Base diameter: 3–3½".

Locality and Period
Bohemia and Germany; widely exported to the United States. c. 1790–1803.

Matching Glassware
Set with wine, flute champagne, and firing glasses, tumblers, and mugs. Often made for traveling liquor case.

Comment
Early collectors attributed these decanters, like most quality engraved ware, to the Amelung factory in New Bremen, Maryland. However, excavators at the factory site have not found fragments of this pattern. Only about half of Amelung's pieces are signed, and none bear this type of decoration. A manuscript of unknown German and Bohemian glass patterns entitled "Gardiner's Island Catalogue," at the Winterthur Museum in Delaware, is filled with decanters, tumblers, and stemware in this and similar patterns.

Hints for Collectors
Many antique stores still sell these decanters as Amelung glass, so caution is advised.

Description
Barrel-shaped (left, center) or tapered (right) bottle with *pressed honeycomb pattern*. Flat lip on decanter (left, right); round bar lip on bitters bottle (center). Thin walls. Flat base. Matching stopper on decanter; bitters bottle has cork stopper with metal and glass top. Color: colorless; later ware rarely transparent yellow, blue, amber, light green, or opaque white. *Variations:* shape varies as shown; 3 honeycomb patterns. Area above honeycomb may be plain, paneled, or engraved.

Type and Dimensions
Bottle and stopper pressed for pattern and shape. Neck shaped after pressing and ground on decanter. Copper-wheel engraved after annealing. Lead or nonlead glass. Decanter height: 9–10″; base diameter: 3–4″. Bitters height: 6–7″; base diameter: 2½–3″.

Locality and Period
New England. c. 1850–80. The Midwest. 1860–1900.

Matching Glassware
Large set with wine and cordial glasses, tumblers, goblets, pitcher, eggcups (#24), jelly glasses, sugar bowl and creamer, butter dish, spoon holder, compote, and string holder.

Comment
The pattern that covers only the lower body (left, center) is often called New York, while the overall honeycomb (right) is known as Vernon. Both variations were made by New England Glass Company and James B. Lyon & Company.

Hints for Collectors
The Honeycomb pattern was made for a longer period and by more factories than any other pattern. Colored pieces are usually more expensive.

Honeycomb pattern

Blown 3-mold labeled decanter

Description
Barrel-shaped bottle has *2 rows of molded arches around body, with medallion at front and ring at shoulder.* Flat neck rim. Pontil mark rough. *Hollow, flattened spherical stopper with pattern of diagonal ribs.* Colorless. *Variations:* pint or quart size; medallion in front blank or inscribed "CHERRY," "WHISKEY," "RUM" (right), "BRANDY," "WINE," or "GIN" (upside down at left, right side up at center).

Type and Dimensions
Bottle and stopper blown in mold for pattern and shape. Neck and stopper shaft ground. Lead glass. Height (quart): 9–10"; base diameter: 4–4½". Height (pint): 8–9"; base diameter: 3–3½".

Locality and Period
Massachusetts: Boston & Sandwich Glass Company, Sandwich, and New England Glass Company, Cambridge. c. 1825–40.

Matching Glassware
Serving pitcher (#81). Not made as set.

Comment
These mold-blown decanters were designed originally to imitate more expensive cut-glass decanters. Gradually, designers stopped using the cut-glass patterns and produced curvilinear patterns like the one illustrated. The molded label made it unnecessary to use the silver decanter labels, which were in style at the time.

Hints for Collectors
On one of the decanters illustrated, the workmen were careless and as a result "GIN" appears upside down and backwards. Mistakes like this are rare, however. They are usually sought after by collectors because they give a handmade charm.

Chain-decorated decanter

Description
Globe-shaped bottle has 4 chains around body and long neck.
Flat circular lip. Depressed base. Pontil mark rough. Hollow
stopper has mercury ring air trap at widest point. Colorless.
Variations: stopper may have chain; sometimes circular foot.

Type and Dimensions
Free-blown bottle, tooled into shape. Applied threading pinched
together at intervals to form chain. Tooled lip. Free-blown
stopper with horizontal, pinched-in air trap forming mercury
ring. Roughly ground neck and stopper shank. Lead glass.
Height: 9–10″. Base diameter: 3¼–3½″.

Locality and Period
Boston area: probably Thomas Cains's South Boston Flint Glass
Works and Phoenix Glass Works, c. 1812–35; and New England
Glass Company, c. 1818–35.

Matching Glassware
Pitchers, sugar bowls, creamers (#125), plates (#215), bowls,
lamps, and candlesticks. Not made as set.

Comment
This chain, or guilloche, decoration, which dates back to
Venetian glass of the 16th century, was popular in England for
nearly 2 centuries. Both the chains on the bottle and the mercury
ring air trap on the stopper are associated with the 2 factories
founded by Thomas Cains. However, the decanter could also
have been produced by the New England Glass Company.

Hints for Collectors
Both Old Sturbridge Village in Sturbridge, Massachusetts, and
the Museum of Fine Arts in Boston sell reproductions of chain-
decorated ware. Initials "osv" or "mfa" are scratched on the base
of copies.

Triple-ring decanter

Description
Globe-shaped bottle with long neck encircled by 3 tripartite rings. Thin walls. Flat circular lip and foot. Pontil mark rough. Hollow spherical *stopper with mercury ring air trap* inside at middle. Colorless. *Variations:* some bottles lack foot.

Type and Dimensions
Free-blown bottle with applied foot and neck rings. Free-blown stopper with horizontal, pinched-in air trap forming mercury ring. Ground neck and stopper shaft. Lead glass. Height: 9–10″. Base diameter: 2¾–3″.

Locality and Period
Boston area: Thomas Cains's South Boston Flint Glass Works and Phoenix Glass Works, c. 1812–35; and New England Glass Company, c. 1818–35.

Matching Glassware
Sugar bowl (#120) and milk pitcher. Not made as set.

Comment
This wine decanter was probably used with early blown wineglasses (#2, #4). It might have once had a silver ticket or label around its neck. Neck rings were common devices in England, intended to make a full decanter easier to hold and pour. Most American decanters and bar bottles bear these rings.

Hints for Collectors
Because more globe-shaped decanters were made in the East, they are easier to find there than in the Midwest. Plain midwestern decanters are often more barrel-shaped. Despite their age, these decanters are not very expensive today.

Bakewell-type cut decanter

Description
Globe-shaped bottle with 3 evenly spaced rings around long neck. Cut strawberry-diamond and *rising-sun* pattern around body; *cut panels* around base and shoulders. Thick walls. Wide flat lip. Circular foot. Pontil mark polished. Spherical stopper with cut circles around sides and cut sunburst on top. Colorless. *Variations:* cylindrical or barrel-shaped body; usually fans instead of rising sun; panels may be absent.

Type and Dimensions
Free-blown bottle and stopper, both tooled into shape. Tooled neck and applied, tooled rings. Applied foot. Ground neck and stopper shaft. Cut after annealing. Lead glass. Height: 11–11¼″. Base diameter: 3–3¼″.

Locality and Period
Bakewell, Page & Bakewell, Pittsburgh; also cutting shops throughout the Northeast. c. 1825–35.

Matching Glassware
Set with tumblers, mugs, wineglasses, celery vase, sugar bowl, creamer, and compote.

Comment
This particular decanter was presented to Henry Clay Fry of Rochester, Pennsylvania, by the Bakewell family at the opening of Fry's glass factory in 1867. Similar patterns were also cut in a number of other shops.

Hints for Collectors
The strawberry-diamond is the most common motif on cut glass from about 1810 to 1850. It is usually combined with fans or occasionally a rising sun, a torchlike motif, a waffle pattern, or diamonds of several sizes. These motifs were used by almost all the cutting shops of this period.

Engraved and cut decanter

Description
Cylindrical bottle with 3 evenly spaced rings around long neck. Cut panels around base and shoulders; engraved floral decoration around body. Thick walls. Wide flat lip. Pontil mark polished. Circular hollow stopper has cut sunburst on flat top. Colorless.

Type and Dimensions
Free-blown bottle and stopper, both tooled into shape. Applied, tooled rings and tooled lip. Ground neck and stopper shaft. Cut and copper-wheel engraved after annealing. Lead glass. Height: 9–9½″. Base diameter: 3–3½″.

Locality and Period
New England Glass Company, Cambridge, Massachusetts. c. 1850–60.

Matching Glassware
Set with goblets, tumblers, bowls, and compote.

Comment
The decanter illustrated is one of a pair made for John H. Leighton and bears his name on a lower panel. Leighton succeeded his father as supervisor of the New England Glass Company from 1851 until the 1870s. His own son, in turn, later became one of the firm's better engravers.

Hints for Collectors
Engraved pieces that can be associated with a particular glasshouse are rare. But sometimes even antique dealers do not recognize a name and will sell a piece inexpensively. In this case, the quality of the glass alone would make it worth purchasing, whether the origin could be recognized or not. However, it is always interesting to research a piece's history.

108 Engraved bar bottle

Description
Barrel-shaped bottle has engraved design of eagle holding arrows and branch, with stars above and "WINE" in shield below. *Heavy thick lip. Neck with 3 heavy rings.* Flat base. Pontil mark polished. Colorless. *Variations:* rarely engraved as shown.

Type and Dimensions
Free-blown with applied lip and rings. Copper-wheel engraved after annealing. Lead glass. Height: 9–10″. Base diameter: 3–3½″.

Locality and Period
Throughout the United States. c. 1815–35.

Comment
This bar bottle was used for serving and not for storage like most decanters. The tight-fitting stopper on decanters prevents evaporation over a long period. Bar bottles lack stoppers and usually have a heavy lip that is never ground inside. The bottles were probably filled, used, and washed in an evening, but it is not known whether they were used in bars and taverns or in homes. The American eagle was a popular patriotic symbol during this post-Revolutionary period and also appears on china, silver, and furniture.

Hints for Collectors
The engraving on this bar bottle makes it particularly valuable. Patriotic themes in American engraved glass are rare and always command a much higher price than engraved flowers and leaves. This bar bottle was probably made during or shortly after the War of 1812.

Description

Barrel-shaped bottle with pressed pattern of ovals. Heavy thick walls. *Heavy thick lip* and long neck. Color: usually colorless; rarely transparent yellow, amber, blue, or purple. *Variations:* hundreds of abstract patterns include Thumbprint, New York, Excelsior, and Huber. Rarely floral patterns.

Type and Dimensions

Pressed in mold for pattern and shape. Neck and lip tooled; gather added for lip. Lead and nonlead glass. Height: 9–9¼". Base diameter: 3–3¼".

Locality and Period

Massachusetts: Boston & Sandwich Glass Company, Sandwich; New England Glass Company, Cambridge. Pittsburgh area: Bakewell, Pears & Company and other firms. c. 1848–70.

Matching Glassware

Set with pitcher, decanter, celery vase, spoon holder, sugar bowl, creamer (#126), eggcup, (#23), jelly glass (#20), tumblers, mugs, honey and sauce dishes.

Comment

This Ashburton pattern is one of the earliest still available in sets. Unlike the decanter, the bar bottle has a heavy lip and the neck is not ground on the inside for a stopper.

Hints for Collectors

Pressed bar bottles are often less expensive than decanters because people mistake them for decanters without stoppers. Originally most had a patented cork stopper. Rare colored glass is more valuable than colorless bottles.

Ashburton pattern

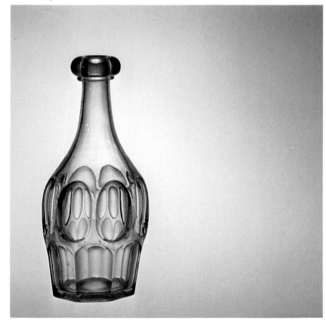

110 Pillar-molded bar bottle

Description
Conical bottle with heavy, molded vertical pillars from center of base to neck. Thick walls. *Heavy thick lip* with 1 ring just below and 1 heavy ring at neck base. Pontil mark rough. Color: transparent blue, purple, amber, or colorless; opaque white. *Variations:* proportion of neck to body variable. Rarely, vertical threads of colored glass on each pillar; occasionally twisted (#84).

Type and Dimensions
Blown in deeply ribbed mold, then shaped. Applied, tooled lip and neck rings. Lead glass. Height: 6½–8″. Base diameter: 4–5″.

Locality and Period
Western Pennsylvania and West Virginia. c. 1850–70.

Matching Glassware
Pitchers (#84), cruets, celery vases, vases (#340), punch bowls (#300), and bowls (#276). Not made as set.

Comment
This heavy glass is sometimes called steamboat glass because of the belief it was used on Ohio River steamboats. More likely, this sturdy ware was made to withstand rough use in taverns and inns. The unusual shape of this bar bottle is found only in pillar-molded glass, and is associated exclusively with factories in the Midwest.

Hints for Collectors
These bar bottles often had a pewter jigger top with a capacity of about 1 ounce. The caps were unique to pillar-molded bottles. Many, however, were lost over time, and today a covered bottle is unusual. Colors are usually intense in pillar-molded glass. Unlike molded swirled-rib glass, pillar-molded glass was not made in Mexico.

Brilliant-cut water bottle and tumbler

Description
Set with water bottle and tumbler. *Globe-shaped bottle with flaring wide mouth. Overall cut pattern of large hexagons* (hobnails) on body; notched prism cutting on neck with 2 groups of horizontal rings. *Cylindrical tumbler has matching pattern* with smooth band below rim. Both with cut sunburst on base. Colorless. *Variations:* mostly geometric patterns, including combinations of hobstars, diamonds, fans, and intersecting lines. Bottle often more rounded, with less flat base.

Type and Dimensions
Free-blown bottle and tumbler; tooled into shape. Cut after annealing. Lead glass. Bottle height: 7¼–7½"; base diameter: 5–5¼". Tumbler height: 3⅝–3⅞"; rim diameter: 3–3¼".

Locality and Period
Throughout the United States. c. 1890–1920.

Matching Glassware
Set with wine, cordial, sherry, and champagne glasses, goblets, decanter, finger bowls, plates, and bowls.

Comment
The Hobnail pattern illustrated is one of the earliest and simplest designs of the brilliant-cut period. This water bottle appeared in the 1890 catalogue of T. G. Hawkes & Company of Corning, New York.

Hints for Collectors
Unlike decanters, the neck of a water bottle is not ground and the lip is usually flaring. Similar bottles may have a collar around the shoulder and a matching tumbler that fits upside down over the neck to rest on the collar. This type of set, called a tumble-up, was meant for bedside use and made in pressed and cut glass.

Hobnail pattern

Description
Globe-shaped bottle with neck flaring slightly at rim. *Overall pressed pattern of closely spaced horizontal ribs.* Flat base. Color: transparent light and dark green, pink, colorless; or green with matt finish. *Variations:* usually matching mushroom-shaped stopper with flat panels around sides.

Type and Dimensions
Machine-pressed in mold for pattern and shape. Height: 8⅞". Base diameter: 4¼".

Locality and Period
Hocking Glass Company, Lancaster, Ohio. c. 1930–40. Similar patterns by midwestern firms, such as Federal, Macbeth-Evans, Indiana, Jeannette, and Hazel-Atlas. c. 1925–40.

Matching Glassware
Set with tumblers (5 oz.), wide-mouthed bottle, and covered water pitcher.

Comment
This pattern is called Circle by some collectors. The matching pitcher and tumblers also have horizontal ribs, but with vertical panels above and below. They are more common than the decanter illustrated or the iced tea server, which is marked "FRIGIDAIRE ICE TEA SERVER" on the base, an inscription commissioned by the Frigidaire Company.

Hints for Collectors
When refrigerators gradually changed the way of life of American housewives, glass companies found a whole new market in making utensils like square butter dishes (#247), iced tea servers, and bottles that fit inside the refrigerator and held beverages and leftovers—the 1920s and 1930s equivalents of plastic containers. The matching iced tea server is a find.

Circle pattern

Early midwestern ribbed bar bottle

Description
Globe-shaped bottle with molded diagonal swirls from base to neck. Round lip. Slightly depressed base. Pontil mark rough. Color: transparent light or dark amber or aquamarine. *Variations:* may be more cylindrical.

Type and Dimensions
Blown in vertically ribbed mold, then swirled and expanded. Applied, tooled lip. Nonlead glass. Height: 8–9″. Base diameter: 3–3½″.

Locality and Period
Ohio: Mantua, Zanesville, and Kent. Western Pennsylvania. c. 1820–40.

Matching Glassware
Salts (#176), tumblers (#44), sugar bowls, creamers, pitchers (#72), bowls (#274), and plates (#214). Not made as set.

Comment
We do not know exactly how these bottles were used on the western frontier. They may have been popular at inns or taverns for serving whiskey, the standard men's drink in those times. Perhaps they served as containers that were taken to a store or tavern and filled with a supply of strong spirits. A cork, or even the proverbial corncob, probably served as a stopper.

Hints for Collectors
Ohio swirled bar bottles are very popular with collectors of midwestern glass and are therefore expensive. Light green examples are the most common. The lack of sharp edges makes these bar bottles stronger than most decanters. The ribbing also serves to strengthen as well as decorate. They are rarely found in the East, suggesting use on the western frontier. Similar Mexican bottles usually have bubbly glass.

Sugar Bowls and Creamers

Today sugar bowls and creamers are among the most common glassware to appear together on the table. Yet they were not always bought in pairs. During the 18th century, most colonists used molasses, honey, maple sugar, or maple syrup as sweeteners. Only the wealthy used sugar, which was imported from the West Indies. Lumps of sugar were served in the sugar bowl and removed with special tongs. (Sugar spoons did not become common until the 19th century.) Cream was used for tea as well as coffee, although many colonists considered tea unpatriotic after 1776.

The earliest 18th-century sugar bowls are free-blown globe-shaped forms with matching covers. German-style sugar bowls of this period, such as those made by Wistar and Amelung, have handles, but those bowls attributed to Stiegel (#134) and made in the English style do not. Most early sugar bowls are small because sugar was so expensive. Some larger bowls that appear to be for sugar may have been used to serve sweetmeats. Early creamers (#115) were also small but were rarely part of a matching set, although they sometimes bear the same decoration as sugar bowls.

By the early 19th century, sugar bowls and creamers began to appear in pairs, but not many examples survive today. Few sets were made in blown 3-mold glass (#132) and early pressed glass (#142). In the mid-19th century, matching sugar bowls and creamers were the rule rather than the exception in pressed, blown, cut, or engraved tableware.

During the mid-19th century, pressed glass manufacturers introduced 4-piece table sets in many patterns, consisting of a sugar bowl, creamer, spoon holder, and butter dish, also called a covered nappy (#146). If the pattern was successful, more pieces were added. Carnival glass, produced by pressed glass factories from 1905 to 1920, also came in a range of patterns. These iridescent pieces are usually similar in shape to those made in other pressed glass. Art-glass sugar bowl and creamer pairs (#150) from the late 19th century are rare because art glass was more decorative than functional. Depression glass manufacturers of the 1930s and 1940s produced a wide variety of sugar bowls and creamers (#151, #152) in large inexpensive sets with matching plates, tumblers, goblets, and serving dishes.

Although both the sugar bowl and creamer were made in a variety of shapes from the 18th century onward, the presence of handles, covers, and rims on sugar bowls can aid in dating. Early 19th-century pressed sugar bowls lack handles, perhaps because they were difficult to press. Free-blown pieces from the same period often had handles. In the mid-19th century, handles almost disappeared altogether, not reappearing until the turn of the century. Covers and rims also reflected changing styles. In 18th-century sugar bowls, the cover rests either on a thread of glass placed on the outside of the bowl, just below the rim, or on the rim itself. By the early 19th century, galleried rims had become fashionable and covers sat on this wide inside rim. In later 19th-century pressed sugar bowls, the cover rests on a ledge inside the bowl. By the turn of the century, covers became optional.

Description
Cylindrical pitcher with molded vertical ribs and folded rim. Thin walls. Ear-shaped handle crimped at base. Pontil mark rough. Color: transparent purple, blue, or light or dark amber. *Variations:* body may be slightly rounder; 8–12 vertical ribs.

Type and Dimensions
Blown in 12-ribbed pattern mold. Expanded and shaped after removal. Tooled lip and applied, tooled handle. Lead glass. Height: 4½–5″. Base diameter: 2–3″.

Locality and Period
Western Pennsylvania: possibly Bakewell, Page & Bakewell, Pittsburgh. Wheeling, West Virginia. c. 1815–45.

Matching Glassware
Sugar bowl, possibly made as set. Celery vases and pitchers; not made as set.

Comment
This 12-ribbed design is confined mainly to glasshouses in western Pennsylvania. Sugar bowls and creamers in purple and blue are usually attributed to the well-known Bakewell factory, but they could have been made at any of the factories in Pittsburgh or Wheeling. The 12-ribbed mold was not used in any of the early Ohio factories.

Hints for Collectors
Counting the ribs in an object is tedious but it helps in pinning down its origin. Mexican pieces, which come in the same colors and pattern, often have more ribs that are more closely spaced.

Simple creamer

Description
Cylindrical pitcher has thick rim and base. Ear-shaped handle
crimped at base. *Pontil mark rough.* Color: *usually colorless;*
occasionally transparent aquamarine or greenish; rarely blue or
purple. *Variations:* body more pear-shaped; sometimes with
applied foot; rarely with engraved decoration such as drapes
and flowers.

Type and Dimensions
Free-blown, with tooled spout and applied, tooled handle. Lead
or nonlead glass. Height: 3¾–4″. Base diameter: 2¼–2¾″.

Locality and Period
Eastern United States. England. c. 1810–40.

Matching Glassware
Rarely, set with sugar bowl.

Comment
This is the simplest type of creamer made. Today it is seldom
found with its matching sugar bowl. Similar wares from England
were blown during this period, but they usually have a polished
pontil mark.

Hints for Collectors
Both Colonial Williamsburg and The Metropolitan Museum of
Art in New York City have marketed creamers similar to this,
although the Williamsburg example has a foot and is more
baluster-shaped, and the Metropolitan Museum piece is signed
"MMA" on the foot. Either reproduction could fool an unwary
beginner. Both have been on the market about 20 years.

Early midwestern sugar bowl and creamer

Description
Bowl with wide shoulder narrows at base. Galleried rim holds double-domed cover with folded rim and round knob on top. Creamer is cylindrical with narrow neck; ear-shaped handle. Both pieces have thin walls. Pontil marks rough. Color: transparent aquamarine, brilliant blue, amber, or purple; *never colorless. Variations:* either may have a circular foot.

Type and Dimensions
Free-blown bowl, cover, and creamer; tooled into shape. Nonlead glass. Bowl height: 7–7¼"; rim diameter: 4⅞–5⅛". Creamer height: 4¾–5"; base diameter: 2¼–2½".

Locality and Period
Ohio: Kent, Zanesville, and Mantua. Western Pennsylvania. c. 1815–35.

Comment
Early midwestern sugar bowls are noted for their high galleried rims, which were intended to keep their double-domed lids from slipping. Creamers are less distinctive because they are similar to eastern or English creamers of the same period. Often the creamers are impossible to place unless found with their matching sugar bowls.

Hints for Collectors
Glass from these early factories is rare and expensive. Sugar bowls and creamers often turn up without their mates. Because no 2 blown pieces are exactly alike, it is always difficult to make a suitable match. These pieces are so highly prized by collectors of midwestern glass, however, that no one should hesitate to buy even a lone example (providing it has been authenticated, of course).

Early midwestern ribbed sugar bowl

Description
Bowl with wide shoulder narrows at base. Galleried rim holds double-domed cover with folded rim and round knob on top. Circular foot. *Molded pattern of vertical ribs* on bowl and cover. Pontil marks rough on foot and cover. Color: transparent amber, blue, aquamarine, or purple; *never colorless. Variations:* sometimes lacks foot.

Type and Dimensions
Bowl and cover blown in 24-ribbed pattern mold. Tooled foot. Nonlead glass. Height: 6¼–6½″. Rim diameter: 5⅛–5⅜″.

Locality and Period
Ohio: Kent, Zanesville, and Mantua. Western Pennsylvania. c. 1815–35.

Matching Glassware
Rarely, set with creamer.

Comment
Any glass from the early Ohio factories is rare. The bowl shown here is attributed to the Zanesville glasshouse, which was known to use a 24-ribbed mold, but since molds were often sold from factory to factory, this could have been made by another midwestern firm.

Hints for Collectors
The early midwestern sugar bowl is easy to recognize with its galleried rim—a standard feature between 1825 and 1850 but not found in the 18th century. Look for this distinctive shape and you cannot confuse it with Mexican glass in the same pattern and colors.

Simple sugar bowl

Description
Globe-shaped bowl has galleried rim and domed cover with flat buttonlike knob. *Thick walls.* Circular foot with *rough pontil mark.* Color: transparent aquamarine, amber, green, or brown. *Variations:* shape sometimes more cylindrical. Some have stem or flat base.

Type and Dimensions
Free-blown bowl, tooled into shape. Applied, tooled foot. Cover blown and shaped separately. Nonlead glass. Height: 5¼–7″. Rim diameter: 3½–4½″.

Locality and Period
New England, New York, and New Jersey. c. 1820–50.

Matching Glassware
Rarely creamer. Not sold as set.

Comment
The bowl illustrated is attributed to a bottle and window glass factory located in Lockport, New York. Sugar bowls and creamers of this type were made in many bottle and window glass factories either for company sale or as gifts for relatives and friends. Some reproductions made in the 1920s and 1930s are difficult to distinguish from originals, even for experienced collectors.

Hints for Collectors
The shape, cover, and galleried rim are all typical of 19th-century sugar bowls. Both the quality of the glass and the workmanship on free-blown examples such as this vary greatly, and some pieces are more attractive than others. Examine a piece carefully before buying.

119 Engraved sugar bowl

Description
Globe-shaped bowl with engraved leaf wreath and inscription on 1 side. Galleried rim supports domed cover with conical faceted knob. Circular foot. Pontil mark polished. *Colorless. Variations:* initials rather than names are also common.

Type and Dimensions
Free-blown bowl and cover, tooled into shape. Applied, tooled foot. Copper-wheel engraved after annealing. Lead glass. Height: 7¼–7½". Rim diameter: 3–4½".

Locality and Period
Massachusetts: Boston & Sandwich Glass Company, Sandwich; New England Glass Company, Cambridge. c. 1865–88.

Matching Glassware
Set with wine, liquor, and champagne glasses, goblets, finger bowls, creamer, butter dish, serving dishes, and compote.

Comment
Engraving of this type is mostly associated with the 2 largest tableware factories in New England, although it was probably done at several glasshouses. It appears on sugar bowls in a catalogue of the Boston & Sandwich Glass Company of about 1870. Glassworkers at the New England Glass Company often made engraved pieces, which descended as heirlooms in their families. But as with most free-blown glass, there is no trademark.

Hints for Collectors
Since this glass is later and plainer than pre-Civil War cut glass or pressed pieces, it has only recently interested collectors. It is reasonably priced and a good choice for beginners. Look the bowl over carefully before making a purchase since quality varies considerably. The glass should be free from bubbles and flaws.

Triple-ring sugar bowl

Description
Cylindrical bowl has group of 3 horizontal rings around middle and near base. Galleried rim supports tall domed lid with 3 rings and flat knob with cut sunburst. Thick walls. Circular foot. Pontil mark rough. Color: usually colorless, rarely transparent dark blue. *Variations:* number and placement of rings vary; knob may be plain.

Type and Dimensions
Free-blown bowl and lid, both with applied, tooled rings. Applied, tooled foot and knob. Cut after annealing. Lead glass. Height: 8⅜–8½". Rim diameter: 5–5⅛".

Locality and Period
Boston area: Thomas Cains's South Boston Flint Glass Works and Phoenix Glass Works, c. 1812–35; New England Glass Company, c. 1818–35.

Matching Glassware
Decanters (#105) and milk pitchers. Not made as set.

Comment
Triple-ring decoration, like the chain (#125) and the mercury ring (stopper on #105), is most often associated with the Englishman Thomas Cains, who managed the South Boston Flint Glass Works and later owned and operated Phoenix Glass Works. This applied decoration is an English style that does not seem to have spread to the Midwest.

Hints for Collectors
The products of the glasshouses associated with Thomas Cains are not well known outside New England and are often undervalued by dealers.

Gadrooned sugar bowl and creamer

Description
*Both heavy circular forms have rings around waist and swirls
on gadrooned lower body;* multiple rings on stem; flat circular
foot. *Sugar bowl has galleried rim* and domed cover with swirls;
conical knob rests on 2 rings. Creamer is plain above waist, with
threading around high pouring lip; ear-shaped handle crimped at
base. Pontil marks polished. Color: usually colorless; rarely
aquamarine. *Variations:* several different pear shapes (#124).

Type and Dimensions
Free-blown forms with extra pattern-mold gather of glass
applied and tooled on lower body. Tooled spout. Applied, tooled
rings, stem, and foot. Colorless lead glass or colored nonlead
glass. Bowl height: 5¾–6″; rim diameter: 3–3½″. Creamer
height: 4¾–5″; base diameter: 2½–2¾″.

Locality and Period
Massachusetts: New England Glass Company, Cambridge;
Boston & Sandwich Glass Company, Sandwich; Thomas Cains's
South Boston Flint Glass Works, Boston. New Jersey.
c. 1820–40.

Matching Glassware
Celery vases and candlesticks. Not made as set.

Comment
Most gadrooned decoration was made between 1820 and 1860.
The set illustrated was created in 1838 by William Leighton, a
glassblower at the New England Glass Company, for his brother.

Hints for Collectors
Pieces associated with a known family, such as this pair, rarely
come on the market. The galleried rim is typical of this period
and the gadrooning is characteristic of New England glass.

Lily-pad sugar bowl

Description
Globe-shaped bowl has lily-pad decoration around body and galleried rim. Thin walls. *Funnel-shaped or circular foot.* Pontil mark rough. Matching *domed cover* has folded or plain rim, flat or round knob, and rough pontil mark. Color: transparent green, aquamarine, or dark or light amber; very dark amber and green appear opaque. *Variations:* many lily-pad decorations, including straight (opposite left), swirled (below left, opposite right), or crossed (#74). Bowl may have circular handles; sometimes short or high stem with or without knop.

Type and Dimensions
Free-blown forms, tooled into shape. Applied, tooled stem and foot. Lily pads tooled from added gather of glass. Nonlead glass. Height: 6½–8½″. Rim diameter: 4–4½″.

Locality and Period
New Hampshire, Vermont, Massachusetts, Connecticut, upstate New York, and southern New Jersey. c. 1820–60.

Matching Glassware
Rarely creamers (#123), pitchers (#74, #75), bowls, and compotes. Not made as set.

Comment
These sugar bowls, along with similar creamers and pitchers, are the closest that American glass has come to folk art. Each glassblower created his own design. Although a blower might have made many sugar bowls, it is unlikely that any 2 would be exactly alike. These pieces come in the typical shades of bottle glass, colored by various iron ore impurities. They were probably made by a blower at the end of a shift, or on company time if the factory was not busy. Frequently the pieces were designed as gifts for relatives or friends, but they were also sold in the

company stores. They were probably used primarily in country homes, where not much other table glassware was available because of its high price and the difficulties of transportation to rural areas. On rare occasions when pressed-glass pieces were available in country stores, they were more expensive than the blown pieces from local factories. And conversely, in towns and cities, especially cities like Boston and Pittsburgh where large tableware factories were in operation, housewives probably found pressed ware inexpensive, while blown glass from a bottle factory was more expensive and usually unavailable. The high-stemmed sugar bowl illustrated was originally purchased by a young woman traveling west with her family on the Erie Canal in New York. She settled upstate and probably acquired the sugar bowl directly from one of the window glass factories in the area where she lived or through which she had passed.

Hints for Collectors

Sugar bowls with lily-pad decoration are always very expensive and should only be purchased from a dealer who regularly handles early American glass. Matching creamers of a slightly different color are rare and were usually sold separately. Unfortunately, the many reproductions made between 1930 and 1960 by the Clevenger brothers at a small factory in New Jersey are nearly impossible to distinguish from authentic pieces. Other reproductions are still being made by another southern New Jersey factory, but these examples are usually heavier and thicker.

Description
Cylindrical or pear-shaped *pitcher may be plain* (below right) *or have horizontal threading* (below left), *lily-pad decoration* (opposite left), *and/or marvered swirls* (opposite right). Pinched pouring lip. Ear-shaped handle crimped at base. Circular foot. Pontil mark rough. Color: transparent green, aquamarine, or various shades of amber; very dark amber appears opaque. *Variations:* thickness of walls varies; slight shape differences, including flat base or long stem; handle elaborate or plain. Threading may be external in same color, or marvered swirls in white or contrasting color. Lily-pad decoration may be straight (#122), swirled (#122), or crossed (#74).

Type and Dimensions
Free-blown forms, tooled into shape. Tooled spout. Applied, tooled handle, stem, and foot. Lily pads tooled from added gather of glass; threading added and may be marvered. Nonlead glass. Height: 4–6½″. Base diameter: 2¼–3″.

Locality and Period
New Hampshire, Vermont, Massachusetts, Connecticut, upstate New York, and southern New Jersey. c. 1820–60.

Matching Glassware
Rarely sugar bowls (#122), pitchers (#74, #75), bowls, and compotes. Not made as set.

Comment
Among glassblowers in Germany, it was a tradition at the end of each shift to use the remaining glass in the pot to make whatever they pleased. Since most of the early glassblowers in the United States were German, this tradition was brought here in the 18th century. Collectors of American glass have always assumed that glassblowers used the time to make presents for family and

friends, but some glasshouse records indicate that the men could make free-blown tableware to sell if they wished. The lure of an extra source of income explains why so many of the free-blown pieces were made.

Most of the glassblowers in the United States tended to be itinerant workers—another German tradition. And as long as the glassblowers were skilled, they were always in demand. If work slackened at one factory, it was usually easy for a good blower to move on to another. (Pay was by the piece, not by the week.) In this way, the style of free-blown, tooled glass spread from the early southern New Jersey factories to bottle and window glasshouses in New York and New England during the 19th century. Whimsical or one-of-a-kind pieces like those illustrated reached a peak of popularity between 1840 and 1860, when similar pieces could be found all over the East.

Hints for Collectors

Decorative techniques like threading and marvered swirls are also found in English and German glassware of the period, but the combinations here are uniquely American. The lily-pad decoration was made only in the United States. Be cautious when buying this expensive glass. A substantial number of reproductions were made between the 1930s and 1960s that are difficult to distinguish from authentic examples. Several museums are also currently producing reproductions, but most museum pieces are marked with initials.

Looped creamer

Description
Pear-shaped pitcher with alternating loops of white and colored glass on upper body and gadrooning below. High pouring lip; ear-shaped handle crimped at base; short stem with multiple rings; circular foot. Pontil mark rough. Color: transparent aquamarine, various shades of green or amber, or colorless; very dark amber and green appear opaque. *Variations:* shape may be more globular. Stem or foot may be absent. *Gadrooned examples are rare and always have a foot* (#121).

Type and Dimensions
Free-blown, with tooled spout. Applied, tooled, marvered loops. Extra gather of glass applied and tooled around lower body. Applied, tooled handle, stem, and foot. Nonlead glass. Height: 7½–8″. Base diameter: 3½–4″.

Locality and Period
Southern New Jersey, New York, and New England. c. 1820–60.

Matching Glassware
Mugs, pitchers, flasks, sugar bowls, compotes, and vases (#337, #338). Not made as set.

Comment
The creamer illustrated descended in the family of a blower from the Bridgeton Glassworks in Bridgeton, New Jersey.

Hints for Collectors
Looped creamers like this were made during a 40-year period, but the style hardly changed. As a result, it is often hard to date these pitchers. A number of reproductions were produced by small New Jersey factories in the 1920s and 1930s, so it is wise to buy from a knowledgeable dealer. Looped creamers and sugar bowls are quite rare and expensive.

Chain-decorated creamer

Description
Slender pear-shaped pitcher with single chain below waist.
Heavy ear-shaped handle crimped at base. Circular foot has rough pontil mark. Color: colorless; rarely transparent deep blue. *Variations:* shape varies from cylindrical to globular, sometimes without waist.

Type and Dimensions
Free-blown, with tooled spout. Applied, tooled chain, handle, and foot. Lead glass. Height: 4¼–5″. Base diameter: 2¾–3¼″.

Locality and Period
Boston area: Thomas Cains's South Boston Flint Glass Works and Phoenix Glass Works, c. 1812–35; New England Glass Company, c. 1818–35.

Matching Glassware
Sugar bowls, bowls, plates (#215), pitchers, decanters (#104), lamps, and candlesticks. Not made as set.

Comment
Chain-decorated glassware is usually attributed to the Boston factories associated with the Englishman Thomas Cains, but it may also have been made in glasshouses in the Cambridge, Massachusetts, area. The chain design is an old Venetian decorative motif that later became popular in England. In this country, it is found on pressed and mold-blown glass as well as on free-blown pieces.

Hints for Collectors
English glass of this type and period is not commonly available in the United States. Most pieces found here are quite rare and probably American.

126 Early geometric-style pressed creamer

Description
Barrel-shaped pitcher with pressed pattern of ovals. High pouring lip. Ear-shaped handle crimped at base. Circular foot with mold marks. Pontil mark polished. Color: colorless; rarely opalescent white, opaque white, transparent yellow or purple. *Variations:* several different patterns, mostly geometric.

Type and Dimensions
Pressed in mold for pattern and shape. Lip fire-polished to remove mold marks. Applied, tooled handle. Lead glass. Height: 6–6½". Base diameter: 3–3¼".

Locality and Period
Massachusetts: New England Glass Company, Cambridge; Boston & Sandwich Glass Company, Sandwich. Pittsburgh: Bakewell, Pears & Company; probably others in Pittsburgh area. c. 1848–70.

Matching Glassware
Set with sugar bowl, jelly glasses (#20), eggcups (#23), tumblers, mugs, decanter, bar bottle (#109), pitcher, celery vase, spoon holder, and honey and sauce dishes.

Comment
Ashburton is one of the most popular and long-lived patterns of American glass. The name appears in advertisements for the Boston & Sandwich Glass Company as early as 1848, in an 1869 catalogue of the New England Glass Company, and in an 1875 catalogue of Bakewell, Pears & Company.

Hints for Collectors
The Ashburton pattern may be easily confused with the cut glass it imitates (#127). Look for mold marks, which are usually visible on the foot, even after fire-polishing. Handles, when present, are always applied except on beer mugs.

Ashburton pattern

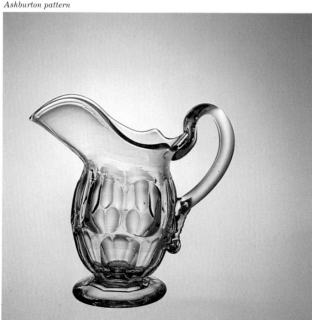

127 Cut sugar bowl

Description
Heavy globe-shaped bowl with 2 rows of *shieldlike cut facets* and galleried rim. Bell-shaped cover has cut facets around dome and flat buttonlike knob. Circular foot. Pontil marks polished. *Colorless. Variations:* facets usually circular, oval, or hexagonal.

Type and Dimensions
Free-blown bowl and cover, both tooled into shape. Applied, tooled foot. Cut after annealing. Lead glass. Height: 5¾–6″. Rim diameter: 4½–5″.

Locality and Period
Massachusetts: probably Thomas Cains's South Boston Flint Glass Works and Phoenix Glass Works, Boston; New England Glass Company, Cambridge; Boston & Sandwich Glass Company, Sandwich. c. 1812–40.

Matching Glassware
Rarely creamer. Occasionally made as set.

Comment
Simple cut facets are rare in early 19th-century glass. The galleried rim and bell-shaped cover are typical of sugar bowls of the 1820s and 1830s (#121).

Hints for Collectors
The creamer for this sugar bowl is rare. Sugar bowls of this period were always covered but seldom had handles, unlike those of the later 19th century. Because they are free-blown, no 2 examples are alike. The chances of replacing a broken cover or of finding a compatible creamer are slight.

128 Bakewell-type cut creamer

Description
Barrel-shaped pitcher with step-cutting under lip and below serrated rim. *Cut strawberry-diamond and fan motifs on lower body*, with flat panels cut above and below. Ear-shaped handle. Flat circular base. Pontil mark polished. Colorless. *Variations:* other decorations include circular panels and diamonds.

Type and Dimensions
Free-blown bowl, tooled into shape. Applied, tooled handle and tooled lip. Cut after annealing. Lead glass. Height: 6¼–6¾″. Base diameter: 4–4½″.

Locality and Period
Bakewell, Page & Bakewell, Pittsburgh; New England Glass Company, Cambridge, Massachusetts; Jersey Glass Company, Jersey City, New Jersey; probably Brooklyn Flint Glass Works, Brooklyn, New York; and other factories in New York City and Philadelphia. c. 1810–40.

Matching Glassware
Set with sugar bowl, tumblers, mugs, wineglasses, goblets, celery vase, compote, decanter, and pitcher. Also sold singly.

Comment
This decoration was originally English. American examples are most often attributed to the Bakewell, Page & Bakewell factory, which cut many variations of this pattern. But the pitcher illustrated was handed down in the family of a glasscutter who worked at the Union Glass Company in Philadelphia and at a factory in New York City, which indicates the strawberry-diamond motif was more widespread than is recognized.

Hints for Collectors
Creamers in this pattern are not as common as the larger water pitchers. English examples are rare and often more elaborate.

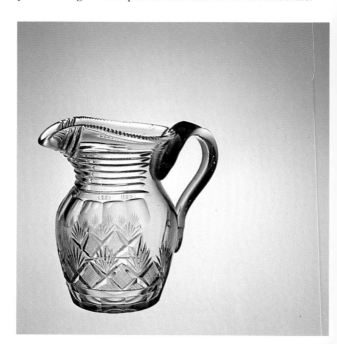

Bakewell-type cut sugar bowl

Description
Cylindrical bowl with galleried rim. *Cut strawberry-diamonds and fans* on bowl and on bell-shaped cover with round knob. Cut sunburst on knob. Thick walls. High stem has hollow round knop. Flat circular foot. Pontil mark polished. *Colorless.* *Variations:* bowl more globular; strawberry-diamonds combined with arches or roundels; lid knob may be plain.

Type and Dimensions
Free-blown bowl and cover, both tooled into shape. Applied, tooled stem and foot. Cut after annealing. Usually lead glass; rarely nonlead. Height: 8⅞–9″. Rim diameter: 4–4½″.

Locality and Period
Pittsburgh; possibly the Northeast. c. 1815–35.

Matching Glassware
Rarely creamer; decanters, celery vases, pitchers, tumblers, and wineglasses. Sold both in sets and singly.

Comment
The strawberry-diamond cut, one of the most common motifs in pressed and cut ware, remained popular until the end of the 19th century. This originally English pattern first appears in American catalogues of the 1880s. Both Presidents James Monroe and Andrew Jackson are believed to have used a variation of this Bakewell pattern in the White House during the 1820s and 1830s. Neither set exists today.

Hints for Collectors
Decanters and celery vases in this pattern are easy to find, but sugar bowls are less common, especially those with a high stem. Imported English pieces are rare and usually heavier and more elaborately cut.

130 Engraved sugar bowl

Description
Globe-shaped *bowl with galleried rim and engraved berry-and-leaf pattern.* Bell-shaped cover with leaf wreath design and flat buttonlike knob. High stem has round knop. Circular foot. Pontil mark rough. Color: colorless; rarely pale green. *Variations:* several engraved decorations, mostly floral or fruit designs.

Type and Dimensions
Free-blown bowl and cover, both tooled into shape. Applied, tooled foot. Copper-wheel engraved after annealing. Lead glass. Height: 7–7¼". Rim diameter: 3¾–4".

Locality and Period
Pittsburgh area: probably Bakewell, Page & Bakewell and John Robinson & Sons. c. 1815–35.

Matching Glassware
Creamers, decanters, pitchers, celery vases, and compotes. Not made as set.

Comment
Engraved sugar bowls, decanters, and pitchers in this shape and style are usually attributed to the Pittsburgh area because they are often found there. Northeastern pieces of the period usually have applied and tooled decoration or, occasionally, cut decoration rather than engraving.

Hints for Collectors
Sugar bowls and creamers with this type of engraving are not often found in pairs, but enough survive to assemble nearly matching sets. There are no known reproductions or imitations. These engraved pieces are more expensive than the plain blown glass of the same period.

Blown 3-mold sugar bowl

Description
Bucket-shaped bowl has *molded geometric pattern of sunbursts and waffling within squares, with vertical ribs below.* Galleried rim supports matching domed cover with flat buttonlike knob. Circular, ribbed domed foot with folded rim. Pontil marks rough on bowl and cover. Color: colorless; rarely transparent blue or purple. *Variations:* 25–30 patterns combining squares, diamonds, ribs, waffling, and sunbursts. Foot may lack dome.

Type and Dimensions
Bowl and cover blown in separate full-size molds for pattern and shape. Applied, tooled foot blown in vertically ribbed mold and expanded. Lead glass. Height: 5½–6½". Rim diameter: 3¾–4¼".

Locality and Period
Massachusetts: Boston & Sandwich Glass Company, Sandwich; New England Glass Company, Cambridge. c. 1825–35.

Matching Glassware
Mugs, tumblers, decanters, bowls, creamers, and inkwells. Not made as set.

Comment
Blown 3-mold sugar bowls are more common than creamers and come in more patterns. Few were made in matching patterns.

Hints for Collectors
Blown 3-mold glass was reproduced in the 1920s and 1930s in New Jersey glasshouses. Some of these reproductions were so clumsily manufactured, and in such uncharacteristic colors, that they are easy to spot. Others were expertly crafted and found their way into several museum collections. Beware of any blown 3-mold piece in unusual colors, such as amber or green. There are no reproductions of the rare sugar bowl shown.

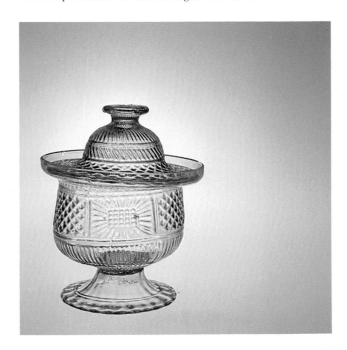

132 Midwestern blown 3-mold sugar bowl and creamer

Description
Both forms have *molded pattern of diamonds and squares with vertical ribs*. Globe-shaped bowl with galleried rim and circular foot; *domed cover* with rib pattern and large round knob. Globe-shaped creamer with high waist and flat bottom; ear-shaped handle crimped at base. Pontil marks rough. Color: colorless; rarely transparent blue or purple. *Variations:* many patterns, mostly geometric, with ribs, diamonds, squares, and sunbursts.

Type and Dimensions
Bowl and creamer blown in separate full-size molds for pattern, then tooled into shape. Cover blown in 16-ribbed mold and then shaped. Lead glass. Bowl height: 6–6½"; rim diameter: 3¾–4¼". Creamer height: 4–4½"; base diameter: 2¾–3¼".

Locality and Period
Probably Ohio: Zanesville, Kent, and Mantua. c. 1815–30.

Comment
Both this pattern and the purple color are extremely rare. Most blown 3-mold glass is colorless and was made in New England factories. However, the shape and rim of this sugar bowl are distinctly midwestern. Some Ohio factories made glass of this type, but the mold has never been traced to any particular firm.

Hints for Collectors
Because colored blown 3-mold glass is rare and highly prized, many of the reproductions are colored. Be suspicious of any colored blown 3-mold glass until you have handled many examples. Today, of course, the chances of finding an original colored piece are slight. Reproductions—as long as they are sold as such—are reasonably priced and quite attractive.

133 Stiegel-type creamer

Description
Pear-shaped pitcher has molded diamond pattern. Ear-shaped *handle crimped at base.* Plain circular foot. Pontil mark rough. Color: colorless, transparent purple, blue, green, or opaque white. *Variations:* some creamers are plain.

Type and Dimensions
Blown in diamond-patterned mold with 15 diamonds in each row. Expanded and shaped after removal. (Plain creamer free-blown). Applied foot and handle. Lead glass. Height: 3½–3¾″. Base diameter: 2–2½″.

Locality and Period
Possibly Henry William Stiegel's American Flint Glass Works, Manheim, Pennsylvania. c. 1770–74. England. c. 1760–90.

Matching Glassware
Sugar bowls (#134) and pitchers. Not made as set.

Comment
Henry William Stiegel is probably the most colorful figure in early American glassmaking. He came to Pennsylvania from Germany as a young man, went to work for an iron founder, married his employer's daughter, and inherited the business. Stiegel, known as Baron Stiegel because of his extravagant ways, used the profits from his iron furnace to start his glass business. After 9 years, he went bankrupt and served a term in debtors prison. It is said that he became a schoolmaster after the Revolutionary War.

Hints for Collectors
Stiegel-type glassware is rare and expensive, especially if it can be traced to a Pennsylvania family. An English creamer of the same color and type bought in England would cost much less. Green creamers are the least common and the most expensive.

134 Stiegel-type sugar bowl

Description
Bucket-shaped bowl has molded diamond pattern and folded rim. *Small circular foot.* Pontil mark rough. Matching cover has flanged rim; pointed knob with swirled ribbing. Color: colorless, transparent deep blue, or opaque white. *Variations:* some covered bowls plain.

Type and Dimensions
Bowl and cover blown in diamond-patterned mold with 16 diamonds in each row. Expanded and shaped after removal. Applied, tooled foot and knob. Blue examples are either mold-blown or free-blown; colorless examples mold-blown only; white examples free-blown only. Lead glass. Height: 6–7". Rim diameter: 4–4½".

Locality and Period
Possibly Henry William Stiegel's American Flint Glass Works, Manheim, Pennsylvania. c. 1770–74. England. c. 1760–90.

Matching Glassware
Creamers (#133) and pitchers. Not made as set.

Comment
Since there are no signed pieces, it is difficult to attribute glassware to Stiegel's factory. The sugar bowl illustrated and the somewhat similar creamer (#133) are nearly indistinguishable from English glass of the same period and style. The many pieces found in eastern Pennsylvania in this 18th-century shape and these colors once led researchers to believe all of this glass was made by Stiegel. Today they are more skeptical.

Hints for Collectors
Stiegel-type glass is both rare and very expensive. But it is occasionally found by major dealers.

135 Midwestern diamond-patterned sugar bowl and creamer

Description

Globe-shaped sugar bowl has galleried rim and matching double-domed cover with round ribbed knob. Globe-shaped creamer has irregular smooth rim and ear-shaped handle crimped at base. *Molded diamond pattern* on both; *scalloped feet.* Pontil marks rough. Color: transparent blue, amber, or greenish-aquamarine; rarely purple. *Variations:* foot may be absent.

Type and Dimensions

Bowl, cover, and creamer blown in diamond-patterned molds with 10 diamonds in each row. Expanded and shaped after removal. Applied feet and creamer handle. Lead or nonlead glass. Bowl height: 6⅞–7⅛"; rim diameter: 5–5¼". Creamer height: 5–5¼"; base diameter: 2⅜–2½".

Locality and Period

Ohio: Kent, Zanesville, and Mantua. Western Pennsylvania. c. 1815–35.

Comment

The pair illustrated is probably from the Zanesville factory, which used a 10-diamond mold. However, molds were often sold by one factory to another, so the attribution is not certain. A well-matched pair like the examples illustrated is rare.

Hints for Collectors

This particular shade of blue is often confused with Mexican glass of the 1920s and 1930s. However, Mexican sugar bowls do not have the galleried rims and high domed lids of authentic midwestern pieces. Be suspicious of any sugar bowl that does not have these features. The creamers are, unfortunately, less distinctive.

136 Blown 3-mold creamer

Description
Pear-shaped pitcher with *raised trefoil decoration at waist and ribbing below.* Ear-shaped handle crimped at base. Circular foot. Pontil mark rough. Color: usually colorless; rarely transparent blue. *Variations:* several patterns, mostly geometric, combining ribs, diamonds, waffling, sunbursts, and squares.

Type and Dimensions
Blown in full-size mold for pattern, then tooled into shape. Applied handle. Lead glass. Height: 5–6″. Base diameter: 3–3½″.

Locality and Period
Massachusetts: Boston & Sandwich Glass Company, Sandwich; New England Glass Company, Cambridge. c. 1825–35.

Matching Glassware
Pint-size decanters. Not made as set.

Comment
The earliest pieces blown in full-size molds had geometric patterns (#131, #132) and were probably an imitation of cut-glass designs. However, many glassmakers soon discovered that different patterns were possible, and a variety of designs became popular.

Hints for Collectors
A similar pattern has been reproduced on decanters and tumblers for The Metropolitan Museum of Art in New York City by the Imperial Glass Company of Bellaire, Ohio. The reproductions are marked "MMA" in the mold.

137 Late lacy-pattern pressed creamer

Description
Barrel-shaped pitcher has *pressed pattern of overlapping scales around body, and heart motif with stippling under lip.* Single ring around middle. Heavy thick walls. Handle has 2 opposite curves. Smooth circular foot. Color: usually colorless; rarely opaque white.

Type and Dimensions
Pressed in mold for pattern and shape. Lead glass. Height: 4½–4¾". Base diameter: 2¾–3".

Locality and Period
Massachusetts: Boston & Sandwich Glass Company, Sandwich, or New England Glass Company, Cambridge. c. 1840–60.

Comment
This piece was formerly considered an early lacy pattern because of its similarity to those ornate designs (#142, #143). Although it has some stippling, the later date indicates that it is transitional between lacy and patterned glass of the mid-19th century (#126). Only creamers were made in this pattern; there is no other matching glassware.

Hints for Collectors
This is the most common and least expensive of the early pressed creamers and an excellent choice for beginning collectors. It has never been reproduced, and most examples are in good condition because of their heavy thick glass. White examples are rarer and more valuable.

138 Realistic-style pressed sugar bowl and creamer

Description
Both forms *bucket-shaped, with raised pattern of blackberries and leaves* and plain circular foot. Sugar bowl has berry cluster for each handle and berry knob on matching cover. Creamer has high pouring lip and plain handle. Color: opaque white or colorless. *Variations:* many fruit and floral patterns.

Type and Dimensions
Bowl, cover, and creamer pressed in separate molds for pattern and shape. Bowl height: 6¾"; rim diameter: 4⅛". Creamer height: 4⅞⁄₁₆"; base diameter: 2⅞".

Locality and Period
Hobbs, Brockunier & Company, Wheeling, West Virginia. c. 1870–80.

Matching Glassware
Set with goblets, eggcups, bowls in several sizes, water pitcher, spoon holder, celery vase, butter dish, compote, and salt.

Comment
The Blackberry pattern, one of several designs by William Leighton, became in 1870 one of the first patented glass patterns. Similar berry-pattern sugar bowl and creamer sets, usually on high stems, were made in the 1880s and 1890s.

Hints for Collectors
Opaque white glass, called milk glass, is difficult to collect because it has been reproduced by several companies. During the 1940s, reproductions of the Blackberry pattern were made in both white and colorless glass in Ohio and West Virginia. The early examples are dense opaque white, while reproductions are a shinier pearly white with thinner walls. The differences may be even less apparent if the glass was made by Westmoreland, which in many cases has simply been reusing its old molds.

Blackberry pattern

Enameled art-glass creamer

Description
Globe-shaped pitcher has *enameled floral decoration* on sides.
Silver-plated rim, pouring lip, attached handle, and cover; silver
unit fits into bowl rim. Thin walls. Circular base. Color: opaque
white with blue and pink enameling. *Variations:* several
enameled designs, usually floral or leaf patterns. Decoration on
silver rim may be geometric.

Type and Dimensions
Bowl blown in full-size mold for shape. Enameled after
annealing. Acid-treated for matt finish. Applied metal rim and
handle. Height: 5–5½″. Base diameter: 3½–4″.

Locality and Period
Possibly Smith Brothers Decorating Shop or Mt. Washington
Glass Company, New Bedford, Massachusetts; or midwestern
firm. c. 1875–1900.

Matching Glassware
Set with sugar bowl.

Comment
Glassware with metal rims was popular only in the last quarter
of the 19th century. It was a practical design since the same mold
could serve for both the sugar bowl and creamer with different
metal fittings. Glassware in this period was often intended to
imitate china. Decorating shops like the Smith Brothers in New
Bedford enameled both glassware and porcelain in the same
styles, if not the same pattern.

Hints for Collectors
Glass of this type is relatively inexpensive since it is just coming
to the attention of collectors. It is never marked, however, so it
is usually impossible to identify the manufacturer. These pieces
have not been reproduced.

140 Late lacy-pattern pressed sugar bowl

Description
Hexagonal bowl with 6 panels of 2 pressed Gothic arch designs.
Galleried rim. Circular foot. *Matching hexagonal domed cover*
has plain knob on circular platform. Color: transparent yellow,
deep blue, purple, turquoise, green, or colorless; opaque light
blue. *Variations:* 2 patterns illustrated; center bowl has slightly
coarser design and scalloped foot.

Type and Dimensions
Bowl and cover pressed in separate molds for pattern and shape.
Lead glass. Height: 5¼–5½″. Rim diameter: 4¾–5″.

Locality and Period
Massachusetts: Boston & Sandwich Glass Company, Sandwich;
New England Glass Company, Cambridge. Possibly midwestern
firm. c. 1840–60.

Comment
The design on these sugar bowls appears to be transitional
between the earliest lacy patterns (#142, #143) and the simple
mid-century designs (#126). The sugar bowls shown came in
more colors than most pressed pieces of this period. The shape
resembles early lacy glass, but it is not stippled. The Gothic arch
motif was never made in a set of matching glassware.

Hints for Collectors
This design has never been reproduced. The high galleried rim
and corners are very easily chipped. Watch for a slightly lower
rim, which would indicate that the piece has been ground down
to remove chips.

141 Late lacy-pattern pressed sugar bowl and creamer

Description
Both forms have pressed C-scroll and stippled pattern on panels, and diamond-and-dot pattern on circular foot. *Hexagonal sugar bowl* has galleried rim and *matching domed cover* with hexagonal knob. *Hexagonal creamer* has different scroll pattern, high pouring lip, and ear-shaped handle. Color: transparent yellow or blue, or opaque light blue. *Variations:* scroll pattern varies slightly.

Type and Dimensions
Bowl, cover, and creamer pressed in separate molds for pattern and shape. Lead glass. Bowl height: 5¾–6"; rim diameter: 4¾–5". Creamer height: 5¼–5½"; base diameter: 2¾–3".

Locality and Period
Massachusetts: New England Glass Company, Cambridge; Boston & Sandwich Glass Company, Sandwich. The Midwest: Curling, Robertson & Company, Pittsburgh, and other midwestern firms. c. 1848–70.

Comment
The California pattern first appeared in an advertisement of Curling, Robertson & Company in the 1850s. A slightly different scroll design was used in the 1869 catalogue of the New England Glass Company. It probably originated about 1848–50, around the time of the California gold rush expeditions, inspiring the pattern name. The pattern on the sugar bowl always differs slightly from its matching creamer.

Hints for Collectors
This is one of the few early sugar-bowl-and-creamer sets, and its pattern has never been reproduced. It is still relatively easy to find in colorless glass; colored examples are much rarer.

California pattern

Lacy-pattern pressed sugar bowl and creamer

Description
Both hexagonal forms have pressed pattern of diamonds in shields and acanthus leaves against stippled background. Bowl has galleried rim with leaf pattern and *matching domed cover* with flowerlike knob. Creamer has high pouring lip and thick handle with 3 knobs. Both have circular foot with serrated edge. Color: colorless; rarely opalescent bluish-white. *Variations:* plain rim.

Type and Dimensions
Bowl, cover, and creamer pressed in separate molds for pattern and shape. Lead glass. Bowl height: 6″; rim diameter: 4¾″. Creamer height: 4⅜″; base diameter 2⁹⁄₁₆″.

Locality and Period
Massachusetts: probably Boston & Sandwich Glass Company, Sandwich, or New England Glass Company, Cambridge. c. 1827–45.

Comment
Elaborate patterns like this one are called lacy patterns. They were made for only 20 years, before simpler designs became popular. These intricate patterns were often used to disguise the cloudy surface that resulted when hot glass was poured into a cool iron mold. Heating the mold enabled glassmakers to produce a clearer glass.

Hints for Collectors
This is the only early lacy pattern with a sugar bowl and creamer. No other forms were made in the pattern. In some, the glass appears rough and almost experimental when compared with later examples. These pieces are both rare and expensive. The pattern has never been reproduced. Look for chips on the galleried rim of the sugar bowl. This damage lessens the value.

Lacy-pattern pressed creamer

Description
Barrel-shaped pitcher with *overall pressed geometric pattern featuring chain and beads around middle;* abstract design above chain and alternating Gothic arches and wheat sheaves below. Thick walls. Stippling below serrated rim and on ear-shaped handle. Circular foot has serrated edge. Color: colorless; rarely opaque light blue. *Variations:* 2 additional patterns include peacock feathers above chain instead of abstract design and baskets of flowers instead of arches.

Type and Dimensions
Pressed in mold for pattern and shape. Lead glass. Height: 4¼". Base diameter: 2½".

Locality and Period
New England: Boston & Sandwich Glass Company, Sandwich, Massachusetts; New England Glass Company, Cambridge, Massachusetts; or Providence Flint Glass Company, Providence, Rhode Island. Possibly the Midwest. c. 1827–40.

Comment
Fragments of the pattern illustrated have been found at the site of the Boston & Sandwich Glass Company. However, the broken glass may have been cullet, bought from another firm to be melted down and used as raw material. Two variations are also from New England, but the creamer with the basket of flowers was made in the Midwest.

Hints for Collectors
Early lacy-pattern pressed glass is unlike the glass of any other country and has never been reproduced. However, it is expensive. Colored pieces cost several times as much as colorless ones because they are rare and more attractive.

Carnival milk pitcher

Description
Cylindrical pitcher with overall pressed chair-caning pattern and octagonal medallions with stars around sides. High pouring lip. Notched ear-shaped handle. Flat base. Color: transparent pale amber or rarely transparent purple, both with *iridescent surface;* or colorless. *Variations:* handle rarely different color.

Type and Dimensions
Pressed in mold for pattern and shape. Iridescent finish sprayed on before annealing. Height: 5¼". Base diameter: 3½".

Locality and Period
Ohio: Imperial Glass Company, Bellaire; Millersburg Glass Company, Millersburg. West Virginia: Fenton Art Glass Company, Williamstown; Northwood Glass Company, Wheeling. c. 1905–20.

Matching Glassware
Large set with wineglasses, goblets, mugs, tumblers, cups and saucers, covered sugar bowl, creamer, round bowls in several sizes, square bowl, compotes in 3 sizes, cruets, decanter, pickle dish, water pitcher, salt and pepper shakers, spoon holder, butter dish, and lamp. In colorless glass only, also table set, water set, and 2-handled celery vase.

Comment
Collectors call the pattern illustrated Star Medallion or occasionally Cane and Star Medallion. The pitcher shown here was made by the Imperial Glass Company, which specialized in imitation cut patterns in Carnival glass.

Hints for Collectors
This milk pitcher is slightly larger than a creamer and much smaller than a water pitcher. Milk pitchers were made only in late 19th-century pressed glass and are rare.

Star Medallion pattern

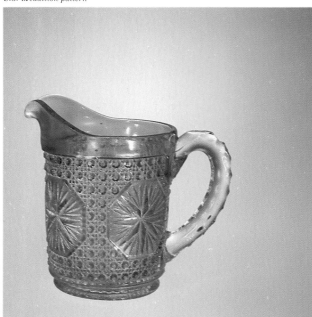

Red-stained milk pitcher

Description
Cylindrical pitcher with red-stained upper body. Row of pressed upside-down hearts around base, with quatrefoil design inside each heart. Ear-shaped handle. Pressed sunburst on base. Color: colorless, stained red. *Variations:* dates and names of places or people may be lightly engraved through stain.

Type and Dimensions
Pressed in mold for pattern and shape. Tooled rim and pouring lip. Applied handle. Red-stained after annealing. Height: 3⅞–4⅛". Base diameter: 2¼–2½".

Locality and Period
The Midwest. c. 1890–1915.

Matching Glassware
Set with tumblers, mugs, custard cups, sugar bowl, creamer, water pitcher, toothpick holder, and salt and pepper shakers.

Comment
Red-stained glass like this was very popular in the last decade of the 19th century and through the first half of the 20th century. The pattern illustrated, called Heart Band by collectors, was made by M'Kee & Brothers of Jeannette, Pennsylvania, from about 1897 to 1912. The pitcher was probably stained at the M'Kee factory, although some pieces may have been sold to smaller decorating shops for staining and initialing. The hand finishing on this pitcher is unusual for this period.

Hints for Collectors
Unlike the more popular red-stained patterns, such as Ruby Thumbprint, Kings Crown, and Red Block, this pattern has never been reproduced. Reproductions are fairly easy to detect, since stained glass made in the 1930s and later was not fired, and the stain comes off.

Heart Band pattern

146 Early geometric-style pressed table set

Description
4-piece set: spoon holder, butter dish, sugar bowl and creamer. *Overall pressed cometlike pattern of large circles with swirling tails.* Butter dish and sugar bowl have matching covers. Butter dish with finial of George Washington's head; sugar bowl with faceted conical knob. Creamer with ear-shaped handle. Color: colorless; rarely transparent yellow, blue, or purple. *Variations:* rarely George Washington finial; usually like sugar bowl knob illustrated.

Type and Dimensions
Each piece pressed in mold for pattern and shape. Free-blown, applied handle of creamer. Lead or nonlead glass. Spoon holder height: 4½–4¾"; rim diameter: 3⅜–3½". Butter dish height: 4⅞–5"; rim diameter: 6⅛–6⅜". Sugar bowl height: 7¼–7½"; rim diameter: 4½–4⅝". Creamer height: 6⅞–7⅛"; base diameter: 3⅜–3½".

Locality and Period
M'Kee & Brothers, Pittsburgh. Possibly Massachusetts: Boston & Sandwich Glass Company and Cape Cod Glass Company, Sandwich; New England Glass Company, Cambridge. c. 1860–70.

Matching Glassware
Large set with wine, champagne, and jelly glasses, goblets, mugs, tumblers (#56), eggcups, small plates, compotes on high and low stems, decanter, bar bottle, large pitcher, celery vase, and lamp.

Comment
This pattern has been collected since the 1930s, when collectors named it Horn of Plenty. It is found in a greater variety of shapes and sizes than most pressed-glass patterns. The design

Horn of Plenty pattern

appears as the Comet pattern in an 1860 catalogue of M'Kee & Brothers, but many collectors feel certain that it was also made at Sandwich. A price list of the Cape Cod Glass Company names glassware in the Comet pattern, but since none is illustrated, one cannot be certain that this is the same pattern. At least one other pressed pattern has cometlike motifs (#25). The pieces illustrated are a complete table set, which was a popular way to market pressed glass. Catalogues from the 1860s to the end of the 19th century are full of groupings of these 4 objects, which were basic to a table setting. Presumably, if a housewife liked the table set, she might buy other pieces to go with it. This particular merchandising practice does not seem to have been applied to other types of glass. The butter dish illustrated is the only shape in this pattern with a George Washington motif. Most butter dishes, or covered nappies, in this pattern have the same finial as the one on the sugar bowl. Only colorless butter dishes and a few transparent yellow examples have this unusual finial. As with most pressed patterns of this period, colored pieces are not often found, and we cannot assume they were produced in sets. Only occasionally does a single piece in transparent yellow, blue, or purple turn up. The 1850s and 1860s seem to have been a period when manufacturers of pressed glass were still experimenting with color. In the 1870s colored sets became more common.

Hints for Collectors
Reproductions of the 1930s made in nonlead glass are often difficult to distinguish, although they are lighter in weight than originals. Unusual shapes or whimsies in this pattern, such as tumblers with an added pouring lip, were also made in the 1930s.

Description.
Oval creamer has vertical rows of pressed strawberry-diamonds alternating with rows of pointed rectangular panels. High pouring lip. *Angular handle. Short stem has ridge at middle. Circular foot.* Color: colorless; rarely transparent amber or yellow; very rarely transparent blue.

Type and Dimensions
Pressed in mold for pattern and shape. Nonlead glass. Height: 6¼–6½". Base diameter: 3½–3¾".

Locality and Period
Pittsburgh: Bryce, Walker & Company, c. 1876–91; United States Glass Company, c. 1891–1907.

Matching Glassware
Large set with sugar bowl, tumblers, mugs, goblets, cordials, oval bowls in several sizes, round bowl, plates, cake plate, butter dish, castor bottles, celery vase, covered and uncovered compotes in several sizes, compote with dolphin stem, marmalade jar, pickle dish, relish dish, sauce dish, footed salt, spoon holder, pitcher, and syrup pitcher.

Comment
This pattern is popular with collectors, probably because it comes in so many forms. It was originally patented as the Imperial pattern, but later the name was changed to Maltese Cross because covered pieces have knobs in the form of a Maltese cross. The name "Jacob's Ladder" was adopted by collectors in the 1930s and refers to the ladderlike design.

Hints for Collectors
Most of the colorless glassware in this pattern is widely available and inexpensive. However, colored examples and the compote with a dolphin stem are very rare and high priced.

Jacob's Ladder or Maltese Cross pattern

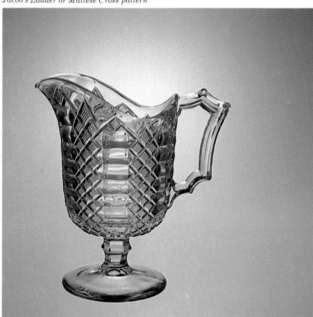

Realistic-style pressed creamer

Description
Cylindrical pitcher has pressed floral pattern and ribbing around lower bowl. Scallop-shell design around pouring lip and diamond pattern below rim and on stem. *Square handle.* Circular foot is ribbed underneath. Color: transparent pale blue, pale amber, pale green, or colorless. *Variations:* several hundred patterns, many with realistic fruit and floral designs or highly stylized designs. Rim or foot may be smooth or scalloped.

Type and Dimensions
Pressed in mold for pattern and shape. Nonlead glass. Height: 5⅜–5½". Base diameter: 3–3¼".

Locality and Period
Pittsburgh: Adams & Company, c. 1875–91; United States Glass Company and others, c. 1891–1900.

Matching Glassware
Large set with sugar bowl, stemware, tumblers (#49), pitcher, butter dish, spoon holder, celery vase, cake plate, compote, platter, oblong relish dish, salt and pepper shakers, open salt tray, and bowls (#256). Only goblets and plates in all colors.

Comment
Adams & Company originated the Wildflower pattern illustrated, which was reissued by the United States Glass Company. Wildflower is a typical floral pattern of the 1870s.

Hints for Collectors
This pattern is one of the most often reproduced, and 19th-century originals are difficult to distinguish from 20th-century copies. Look for signs of wear to confirm age. The blue creamer illustrated differs slightly from the standard and may be either a contemporary copy or a 20th-century reproduction.

Wildflower pattern

Brilliant-cut sugar bowl and creamer

Description
Both forms *cut vertically with sharp prisms*. Serrated rim.
Thick heavy glass. Ringed stem and circular foot with cut
sunburst underneath. Circular sugar bowl has 2 notched handles.
Circular creamer has narrower body with identical notched
handle and high pouring lip. Color: colorless; rarely cased in
transparent red or green. *Variations:* many motifs and shapes,
including hobstars, strawberry-diamonds and fans, and others;
occasionally high pedestal foot.

Type and Dimensions
Bowl and creamer free-blown, then tooled into shape. Tooled
spout. Applied, tooled stem and handles. Cut after annealing.
Lead glass. Bowl height: 4¼–4½"; rim diameter: 3¾–4¼".
Creamer height: 4–4¼"; base diameter: 3¼–3½".

Locality and Period
Throughout the Northeast. c. 1900–15.

Comment
The set illustrated was handed down in the family of a cutter
who worked at a small shop in Wellsboro, Pennsylvania, which
was a branch of J. Hoare & Company of Corning, New York,
around 1915. But this common pattern and shape could have
been made in any number of small cutting shops around the
country at the turn of the century.

Hints for Collectors
Look for an acid-etched trademark on brilliant-cut glass. On
pieces with handles, the mark may be on the side, near the
attachment of the handle. Otherwise, check the edge of the base.
These marks are very faint and may require using a strong light.
The trademark of a major firm will increase the value of a piece.

Amberina sugar bowl and creamer

Description
Both forms have *shallow bowls* with faint vertical ribs at base; circular foot with ribs radiating from hollow knopped stem. Sugar bowl has 2 delicate ear-shaped handles. Creamer has 1 handle and small pouring lip. "Libbey" in script enclosed in circle acid-etched near polished pontil mark. Color: transparent *red around rim, becoming amber at bowl base;* amber stem becomes red at foot. *Variations:* several patterns include overall diamonds, swirls, and circles (#220).

Type and Dimensions
Bowl and creamer blown in same ribbed mold, then tooled into shape. Tooled spout. Applied, tooled handles, stems, and feet. Partially reheated to develop shading. Bowl and creamer height: 4½–4¾". Rim diameter: 4¼–4¾".

Locality and Period
Massachusetts: New England Glass Works, Cambridge, c. 1883–88; Mt. Washington Glass Company, New Bedford, c. 1883–95. Libbey Glass Company, Toledo, Ohio. c. 1917.

Matching Glassware
Bowls, tumblers, punch cups, butter and cheese dishes (#220), toothpick holders, cruets, pitchers, vases (#332), baskets, and centerpieces (#261). Not made as set.

Comment
This distinctive shaded glass, known as Amberina, is actually amber glass that has been partially reheated to develop red color on only part of the glass.

Hints for Collectors
Amberina was widely imitated, but few copies are signed. Floral designs are found only on Bohemian and English copies. American copies are in harsher colors and modern shapes.

Description
Conical bowls with pressed scroll pattern and zigzags and dots below rim. Circular, slightly domed foot. Sugar bowl has 2 ear-shaped handles; creamer has 1 handle and small pouring lip. Color: transparent green, pink, amber, or colorless. *Variations:* sugar bowl may have matching cover with round knob. Other lacy-scroll patterns include Madrid (#218), Bowknot, Cameo, and Cherry Blossom.

Type and Dimensions
Machine-pressed in separate molds for pattern and shape. Bowl and creamer height: 3½″. Rim diameter: 3¾″.

Locality and Period
Federal Glass Company, Columbus, Ohio. c. 1933–37. Similar patterns by Jeannette, Hazel-Atlas, Anchor-Hocking, Indiana, Paden City, Fenton, Macbeth-Evans, and other midwestern firms. c.1925–40.

Matching Glassware
Large set with tumblers in 4 sizes, footed tumblers (#15), sherbet glasses, cups and saucers, bowls in 4 sizes, oval vegetable bowl, plates in 4 sizes, grill plate, oval platter, covered butter dish, covered cookie jar, salt and pepper shakers, covered sugar bowl, and pitchers in 2 sizes.

Comment
The Patrician pattern illustrated, also called Spoke by some collectors, is a typical lacy-scroll Depression-glass pattern. A good many continued in production well into the 1940s.

Hints for Collectors
Because sugar bowl covers are easily broken, it is hard to find an intact bowl and cover in this pattern. For this reason, the cover alone is worth about 4 times the cost of a sugar bowl.

Patrician pattern

Depression sugar bowl and creamer

Description
Conical bowls with pressed horizontal ribs and circular, slightly domed foot. Sugar bowl has 2 square handles; creamer has 1 handle and slightly high pouring lip. Color: transparent blue or purple; colorless; rarely transparent pink. *Variations:* sugar bowl may have flat metal cover with round knob. Other patterns include Ruba Rombic, Newport Tea Room, and Pyramid.

Type and Dimensions
Machine-pressed in separate molds for pattern and shape. Bowl and creamer height: 3″. Rim diameter: 3¾″.

Locality and Period
Hazel-Atlas Glass Company, Wheeling, West Virginia.
c. 1934–42. Similar patterns by Jeannette, Federal, Anchor-Hocking, Indiana, Paden City, Fenton, Macbeth-Evans, and other midwestern firms. c. 1926-40.

Matching Glassware
Large set with tumblers in 4 sizes, sherbet glasses, bowls in 6 sizes, covered butter dish, covered cheese dish with wooden board, plates in 5 sizes, platters (10″, 12″), cups and saucers, salt and pepper shakers, custard cups, and ashtray.

Comment
The Moderntone pattern by Hazel-Atlas, called Wedding Ring by some collectors, reflects the influence of Art Deco styles of the late 1920s and 1930s. Art Deco was introduced at a Parisian exhibition of decorative arts in 1925 and had its greatest influence on handmade glass, silver, ceramics, and furniture.

Hints for Collectors
The Moderntone in the blue illustrated is especially sought after. Pink and colorless examples are rarer but less expensive because of a lesser demand.

Moderntone pattern

153 Enameled sugar bowl and creamer

Description
Matching *pressed oval bowls on 2 feet, with enameled floral decoration* on 2 sides and scalloped rim; rope design on sides extends from rim to base of foot. Sugar bowl lacks cover. Creamer has high pouring lip and plain handle, ribbed where attached to body. Color: opaque white with naturalistic enameled design, or marbled purple. *Variations:* fruit instead of flowers.

Type and Dimensions
Pressed in separate molds for pattern and shape. Enameled after annealing. Nonlead glass. Bowl height: 5″; width: 4¼″. Creamer height: 5½″; width: 4¼″.

Locality and Period
Probably Challinor, Taylor & Company, Ltd., Tarentum, Pennsylvania. c. 1870–90.

Comment
This combination of enameled and pressed glass is rare except on opaque white glass, where it was probably meant to imitate porcelain. Enameling is also found on opaque white blown glass for a ceramic effect. Challinor, Taylor & Company specialized in opaque white glass, called milk glass, and marbled glass (#339), called slag by collectors. The examples illustrated appeared in this company's catalogue in marbled glass.

Hints for Collectors
The enameling on these pieces may be worn from years of use, so be sure to examine the decoration carefully. Sugar bowls were often made without covers in the last decade of the 19th century. Check inside the rim of a bowl for a lip; if one is present, the bowl originally had a cover. If the cover is missing, the value is significantly reduced.

Pink slag creamer

Description
Bucket-shaped bowl *with raised scroll and floral pattern and 4 ribbed feet.* Rim has large and small scallops, largest forming pouring lip. Ear-shaped handle has beaded decoration. Color: *marbled pink and white,* cream-white, or opalescent blue and yellow.

Type and Dimensions
Pressed in mold for pattern and shape. Height: 4¾". Width: 3¾".

Locality and Period
Northwood Glass Company, Indiana, Pennsylvania, and later, Wheeling, West Virginia. c. 1898–1919.

Matching Glassware
Set with sugar bowl, butter dish, toothpick holder, water set, large pitcher, tumblers, and bowls in several sizes.

Comment
Collectors call this pattern Inverted Fan and Feather. It was made in pink slag glass as well as in cream-white custard glass, opalescent glass, and rarely iridescent Carnival glass. The Northwood firm referred to this mixture of colored and white glass as mosaic glass.

Hints for Collectors
Pink slag is a valuable and rare collectible. The creamer shown is quite expensive in spite of the fact that a scallop is broken from the rim. Pink slag toothpick holders and tumblers were reproduced by the St. Clair Glass Company in Elwood, Indiana, several years ago, but their glass is characteristically much darker. Other colors of marbled glass are being reproduced by the Imperial Glass Company in Bellaire, Ohio.

Inverted Fan and Feather pattern

Salt Dishes, Condiment Servers, and Small Table Accessories

Most of the small containers in this group were used to serve seasonings and condiments. They include salt dishes, oil and vinegar cruets, pickle jars, and syrup jugs. Other novelties that were popular on the 19th-century table are toothpick holders, cracker jars, knife rests, and napkin rings.

Today salt and pepper are commonly used together, although originally salt was served alone. It was not until the late 19th century that pepper joined salt at the table. The first salts were open dishes intended for communal use. People took generous pinches of salt, using their fingers. The earliest American salts were small, circular free-blown or mold-blown dishes, which hardly changed in shape or pattern until the early 1820s when pressed glass competitors introduced oval and rectangular forms (#161–162). Mold-blown salts are more common than free-blown ones. Both were made in colorless and colored glass. Unlike tumblers, salt dishes were rarely made in bottle and window glass factories. Only a few American blown salts have cut decoration (#159–160).

There are hundreds of pressed patterns, many in lacy designs similar to the patterns of larger lacy dishes (#166–167) and some in the geometric and realistic styles common in the mid-19th century. Most pressed patterns are distinctly American and were later borrowed by European manufacturers. Some salt patterns were made to match other tableware in the late 19th century.

Individual salt dishes began to replace communal salts in the last quarter of the 19th century. By this time, etiquette required the use of small spoons, rather than the fingers. Individual salt dishes, or dips, were made only in a few cut-glass patterns and pressed-glass imitations, usually with vertical ribs (#157). Salt shakers came into use around the same time and have remained fashionable ever since. They vary little in size, but display many patterns and colors in both transparent and opaque glass, including art glass (#184) and Depression glass (#186).

A host of other serving containers for condiments and seasonings often accompanied salt dishes on the table. Castor sets—metal frames with 3 to 6 bottles for oil, vinegar, pepper, mustard, and other spices—were popular from the late 18th to the early 20th centuries (#187–190). The bottles were made of mold-blown, cut, or pressed glass, in unique designs or in patterns that matched other tableware. Separate cruets for oil and vinegar were also sold without the frames (#191). Syrup jugs for molasses or cane syrup date from the 1850s to the early 1900s. The earliest jugs often had patented metal lid-and-spout combinations to minimize dripping (#192–194). Pickle jars were made in cut, pressed, and art glass (#198). By the 1880s and 1890s, manufacturers advertised fancy silver-plated frames, especially for decorative art glass (#179–182). To counter these elaborate pieces, pressed glass manufacturers offered a variety of candy dishes and jars in the less expensive iridescent Carnival glass (#197). By the Depression-glass era, the number of shapes for condiment dishes and candy jars steadily increased.

Toward the end of the 19th century, toothpick holders (#177), along with napkin rings (#155) and knife rests (#156), also found a place on the table. These and other Victorian novelties, like match holders (#178), are found mostly in pressed glass, except for knife rests, which are generally cut glass.

Pressed napkin ring

Description
Octagonal loop stands at right angle to flat octagonal base.
Pressed sunburst on base. *Colorless. Variations:* a few patterns,
mostly imitations of brilliant-cut motifs, including diamonds and
hobstars.

Type and Dimensions
Pressed in mold for pattern and shape. Nonlead glass. Height:
2–2⅛″. Base diameter: 2–2⅛″.

Locality and Period
Probably United States Glass Company, Pittsburgh; also Ohio
firms. c. 1890–1910.

Comment
Napkin rings were extremely popular in the last 2 decades of the
19th century. Most were made in silver or silver plate with
simple designs similar to this glass example or with figural
patterns. Glass napkin rings are much less common not only
because fewer were made, but because they were easily broken
and not as many have survived. Silver is also more likely to be
treasured and passed on.

Hints for Collectors
Despite their present scarcity, napkin rings are not particularly
expensive. They were made in either brilliant-cut glass or
pressed imitations and do not appear in free-blown, mold-blown,
or art glass. Neither pressed nor cut patterns were made to
match other forms of tableware. But they were a common
feature of table settings during this period and are sought after
by collectors of Victorian glass.

Brilliant-cut knife rest

Description
Heavy dumbbell shape with cut diamonds, pinwheels, and other geometric patterns on ends. Band of cut diamonds at middle, and rings near balls. *Colorless. Variations:* several geometric cut patterns, mostly hobstars, diamonds, and facets.

Type and Dimensions
Free-blown, then tooled into shape. Cut after annealing. Lead glass. Length: 5–5½". Ball diameter: ¾–1".

Locality and Period
Throughout the United States. c. 1890–1920.

Comment
Knife rests like this were made in nearly every American cut glass shop in the late 19th and early 20th centuries. Unlike other cut tableware, few knife rests have trademarks. A great variety of patterns were cut on the same basic dumbbell shape. Most of the well-known tableware patterns could not be adapted for knife rests because of the form's unusual size and shape. The rests were used by the principal carver and server at the table or on the sideboard, so only 1 or 2 were usually needed at a meal.

Hints for Collectors
Knife rests appear mainly in cut glass, although a few were made in pressed glass in patterns imitating the cut ones. The most common pattern is the lapidary cut in which each end of the knife rest is covered with triangular facets. The same design was used for decanter and perfume-bottle stoppers. Neither cut-glass knife rests nor pressed imitations are very expensive today.

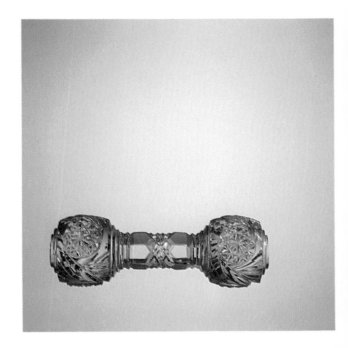

Pressed individual salt

Description
Rectangular bowl (left) *with cut corners and 4 feet, and pressed diamond pattern on bottom. Circular bowl* (right) *with overall pressed vertical prism pattern*, superimposed stars around bowl, and sunburst on flat base. Thick walls. Colorless. *Variations:* bowl may be square; diamonds or vertical ribs may replace vertical prisms.

Type and Dimensions
Pressed in mold for pattern and shape. Nonlead glass. Height (left): ⅞–1″; length: 1½–1⅝″. Height (right): 1–1⅛″; base diameter: 1¼–1⅜″.

Locality and Period
Throughout the United States. c. 1870–1940.

Comment
Individual salt dips for the dining table gradually came into use after the mid-19th century. They began to appear in pressed glass catalogues of the 1860s, although they were still outnumbered by communal salts. About this time, mold-blown salt shakers were introduced. By the 1890s, shakers far outnumbered the open style, probably because they were easier to use. Individual salts were made in cut, art, and Art Nouveau glass (#170), and less often in the pressed glass shown. The pressed patterns are usually simple and often imitate cut designs.

Hints for Collectors
Individual salts are usually very inexpensive in both cut and pressed glass, since the demand for them is limited. Art glass and Art Nouveau examples are generally higher priced, reflecting the popularity of Tiffany and Steuben glassware in any form or imitation.

Blown 3-mold salt

Description
Rectangular bowl bulges slightly at ends. *Waffle pattern on sides and diagonal ribs on ends.* Thick walls. *Flat polished rim has vertical ribs. Oval base has impressed sunburst pattern.* Color: colorless; rarely transparent purple. *Variations:* bowl may be circular or oval. 5–6 different combinations of diamonds, vertical ribs, and fans.

Type and Dimensions
Blown in full-size mold for pattern and shape. Rim ground and polished after annealing. Lead glass. Height: 1½–1⅝″. Length: 3⅛–3¼″.

Locality and Period
Massachusetts: New England Glass Company, Cambridge; possibly Thomas Cains's South Boston Flint Glass Company, Boston. c. 1815–25.

Matching Glassware
Oval and rectangular dishes (6–10″). Not made as set.

Comment
All blown 3-mold salts are rare, but this early style is quite inexpensive for blown 3-mold glass. The oval and rectangular dishes are probably the most difficult to find and command the highest prices.

Hints for Collectors
Glass of this type can easily be confused with colorless pressed glass of similar weight or with later blown 3-mold salts. Look for a smoothly ground, polished rim on early blown 3-mold pieces. Pressed glass usually has a scalloped rim; later blown 3-mold salts have a folded rim and are usually of thinner glass.

Brilliant-cut salt

Description
Cradle-shaped bowl with rectangular mouth has *overall cut pattern of stars within diamonds.* Thick walls. Rim smooth and polished, with fine notches. 4 notched corners. Raised arch in base. Colorless. *Variations:* other motifs include vertical prism cuts alone or combined with diamonds. Bowl may be oval; base may lack arch.

Type and Dimensions
Free-blown, then tooled into shape. Cut after annealing. Lead glass. Height: 1⅝–1¾". Rim length: 3–3⅛".

Locality and Period
Corning, New York: T. G. Hawkes & Company and J. Hoare & Company. C. Dorflinger & Sons, White Mills, Pennsylvania. c. 1882–95.

Matching Glassware
Set with stemware (#29), bowls, and vases; tumblers after 1900.

Comment
The Russian pattern shown here was made by many different cutting shops, but the shape of this salt suggests that it was made in one of the 3 shops listed. The absence of a trademark, however, makes it impossible to identify which one. Trademarks were not used on cut glass before 1890, and some companies never used them. C. Dorflinger & Sons, one of the largest cutting firms, used paper labels only.

Hints for Collectors
Open, or master, salts like this are rare in brilliant-cut glass because the communal style was considered old-fashioned by the time brilliant-cut glass became popular in the late 19th century. In spite of their rarity, these salts are not expensive.

Russian pattern

Bakewell-type cut salt

Description
Oval bowl with cut pattern of alternating strawberry-diamonds and fans. Thick walls. Flat polished rim has tiny notches. *Oval base with sunburst.* Colorless. *Variations:* arrangement of strawberry-diamonds and fans varies. Rim may lack notches.

Type and Dimensions
Free-blown, then tooled into shape. Cut after annealing. Rim ground and polished. Lead glass. Height: 1½–1⅝″. Length: 3¾–3⅞″.

Locality and Period
The Northeast. Possibly England. c. 1820–40.

Comment
Throughout the 19th century, cut glass was a status symbol that only the wealthy could afford. The development of blown 3-mold glass, and then pressed glass, brought the same patterns within reach of the middle classes. Pieces with the very popular strawberry-diamond and fan designs are often called Bakewell-type glassware because many objects with similar motifs were cut at the Bakewell factories in Pittsburgh. But the designs were also cut in factories throughout the Northeast.

Hints for Collectors
Although these salts are scarcer than blown 3-mold salts, they are usually not as expensive. Early cut salts of the 1820s and 1840s are easy to distinguish from later examples of the 1890s (#159). The patterns on early pieces are simpler and the glass is usually thicker. Glass cut in the strawberry-diamond motif has sharper edges than glass blown in molds.

161 Lacy-pattern pressed salt

Description
Oval dish with deeply scalloped rim and oval base. *Pressed pattern of curving peacock feathers around sides.* Thin walls. 8-pointed star pressed on base. Color: transparent light greenish-aquamarine, cobalt blue, or colorless; opalescent grayish-white or white; rarely opaque purple. *Variations:* 12 patterns, mostly slight variations in feather design. Base may have double trefoil and beaded pattern, with serrated or beaded edge, or smooth edge with 8-pointed star or sunburst.

Type and Dimensions
Pressed in mold for pattern and shape. Lead glass. Height: 1½–1⅝″. Length: 3½–3⅝″.

Locality and Period
New England: probably Boston & Sandwich Glass Company, Sandwich, Massachusetts. c. 1830–45.

Matching Glassware
Large plates and toddy plates (#210), bowls, sugar bowls, creamers, mustard jars, trays (#257), and rare footed compote. Not made as set.

Comment
The peacock-feather motif was a popular design in American households of the mid-19th century. Most tableware with this design was not sold in sets, however, since the idea of matching pressed pieces had not yet become common.

Hints for Collectors
All varieties of this salt are rare and expensive. Colorless examples will probably be slightly less expensive than colored ones, which are generally preferred by collectors.

Rectangular pressed salt

Description
Shallow rectangular bowl with sharp cut corners; sides narrowing toward rectangular base. *Horizontal ridge* around middle and below *scalloped notched rim.* Thin walls. *Base has pressed waffle pattern.* Color: transparent blue, light or dark amber, purple, or colorless.

Type and Dimensions
Pressed in mold for pattern and shape. Lead or nonlead glass. Height: 1½–1⅝″. Rim length: 3–3⅛″.

Locality and Period
The Northeast. Possibly England or Scandinavia. c. 1850–60.

Matching Glassware
Bowls (5″, 7″) with waffle or sunburst on base. Rarely, rectangular dish (12″) in transparent green. Not made as set.

Comment
This salt and its companion dish are unlike any other examples of American pressed glass. The pattern is much simpler than others of this period. The origin of these pieces is something of a mystery, although the simple style indicates that they may be English or Scandinavian. But since a large number of these salts are found in the United States, they could be American. The wooden model of a bowl in this design was found in Sandwich, Massachusetts, several years ago, along with models of other pressed-glass pieces. All were supposed to have been models for the Sandwich factory moldmakers.

Hints for Collectors
All of these pieces except the large rectangular dish are relatively common and quite inexpensive. Most are found in the cheaper colorless glass.

163 Stag's-head pressed salt

Description
Cradle shape curving upward into scrolls at each end. Raised stag's-head design on each side between 2 C-scrolls; stippled background. Hollow rectangular base flares toward bottom; has sunburst pattern and ribbed decoration around edges. Color: transparent amber or blue, opalescent grayish-white, or colorless; rarely light green. *Variations:* may lack stippling and ribs; may have waffle design on base.

Type and Dimensions
Pressed in mold for pattern and shape. Nonlead glass. Height: 1⅝–1¾". Length: 3–3⅛".

Locality and Period
England. Europe: probably Denmark and Sweden; possibly France and Germany. Widely exported to the United States. c. 1850–70.

Comment
For a long time these salts were thought to be American. Recently, however, authorities have discovered their true origin as European because they are shown in factory catalogues from several European glasshouses.

Hints for Collectors
Scandinavian salts are relatively common in the United States and a wise purchase for collections that are not limited to American glass. Colorless salts are more available and usually less expensive than colored examples.

Scallop-shell pressed salt

Description
Cradle shape curving upward into scrolls at each end; 4 scroll-shaped feet. *Scallop shell in center of each side with stippled arc* below and plain panel around base. Thin walls. Base has diamond pattern. Color: opalescent white, transparent purplish-blue or medium amber, or colorless. *Variations:* hairpin design may replace scrolls; may have waffle pattern on base.

Type and Dimensions
Pressed in mold for pattern and shape. Lead glass. Height: 1⅝–1¾". Length: 3⅛–3¼".

Locality and Period
New England. France. c. 1830–50.

Comment
Salts like this one with a diamond-pattern base and scrolls on the sides are probably French. As a general rule, French pressed glassware is more ornate than American lacy-pattern pressed glass and the designs often stand out in higher relief. Some French glass of this type, although it appears to be pressed, is actually mold-blown. If the pattern can be felt on the inside of the object, it is probably French and not American. Salts with a hairpin design and waffled base are American. Both French and American designs are easier to find in colorless glass. Colored examples like the one illustrated are rare and expensive.

Hints for Collectors
Continental pressed glass is often of very high quality and sometimes better made than American pressed glass. But it is not much appreciated in this country; no matter how rare or beautiful, Continental glass usually is less expensive than American work.

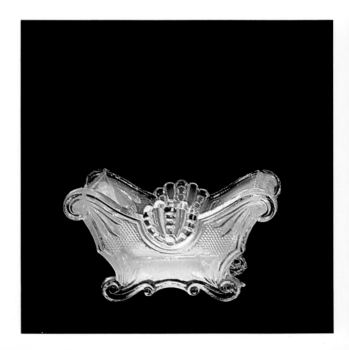

165

Boat-shaped pressed salt

Description
Paddle-wheel-steamer shape with "LAFAYET" on each wheel and
"B. & S. GLASS CO." on stern. Oval base. Thick walls. Color:
transparent light, medium, or dark blue, opaque white,
opalescent white, or colorless. *Variations:* several base
variations, including plain, with "SANDWICH" inscription, with
scroll, or sunburst design. Stern may have 2 windows instead of
lettering. Similar salt has plain wheels and "J. ROBINSON & SONS/
PITTSBURGH" or just "PITTSBURGH" on stern. Another, shaped
more like a rowboat, lacks paddle wheels and lettering.

Type and Dimensions
Pressed in mold for pattern and shape. Lead glass. Height:
1½–1⅝". Length: 3½–3⅝".

Locality and Period
Boston & Sandwich Glass Company, Sandwich, Massachusetts.
John Robinson & Sons, Pittsburgh. c. 1830–45.

Comment
The salt illustrated is among the very few objects bearing the
famous Boston & Sandwich Glass Company name. For many
years, collectors thought that the pattern was a commemorative
of Lafayette, the French officer and Revolutionary War hero, in
honor of his triumphant return to America in 1825. But since the
pressing machine was not perfected until several years later, it is
more likely that the inscription refers to a steamer by that name,
which traveled the East Coast in the decades after 1825.

Hints for Collectors
All versions and colors of these salts are rare and quite
expensive. The Pittsburgh design, which may have been copied
from the Sandwich company, is the rarest of all.

Lacy-pattern pressed salt

Description
Rectangular box on 4 feet has Gothic arches alternating with
hearts on sides and stars on ends. Stippled background. Thin
walls. *Rim notched, flaring slightly.* Plain rectangular base.
Color: transparent medium blue or light purple, semitransparent
grayish-white, opalescent blue, or colorless. *Variations:* ends
may have 1 or 2 stars. Base may have 3 slightly different
sunburst patterns. Stars may replace hearts; others have arches
only; those without hearts may lack stippling.

Type and Dimensions
Pressed in mold for pattern and shape. Lead glass. Height:
1¾–1⅞″. Length: 2¾–2⅞″.

Locality and Period
Massachusetts: perhaps Boston & Sandwich Glass Company,
Sandwich, and New England Glass Company, Cambridge.
c. 1830–45.

Matching Glassware
Sugar bowls in several styles (#140), creamers, shallow bowls,
plates, and rarely jewelry caskets. Not made as set.

Comment
The Gothic arch motif derives originally from medieval
architecture, which saw a revival in the mid-19th century in both
England and the United States. Only in American pressed glass
are the heart and Gothic arch motifs combined.

Hints for Collectors
All varieties of this salt are rare but colorless versions are
slightly easier to find. The Gothic arch motif appears on French
pressed-glass goblets and tumblers in a variety of colors,
including opaque reddish-brown and black, 2 colors never found
in American pressed glass.

Lacy-pattern pressed salt

Description
Rectangular box on 4 feet has scroll design on all sides against stippled background. Row of alternating ovals and diamonds around rim. Thick walls. Smooth oval knobs around edge of flat base with scroll design. Color: transparent light green, blue-green, yellow-green, amber, or blue; colorless or opaque olive-green. *Variations:* S-scroll instead of C-scroll; either design may lack stippling. Base may have sunburst.

Type and Dimensions
Pressed in mold for pattern and shape. Lead or nonlead glass. Height: 1¾–1⅞". Length: 2¾–2⅞".

Locality and Period
Boston & Sandwich Glass Company, Sandwich, Massachusetts. New York: Mt. Vernon Glass Works, Mt. Vernon; Saratoga Glass Works, Saratoga. c. 1830–45.

Comment
Fragments of scroll-pattern glass have been found at only 3 factory sites, indicating that this design was made in all 3 places. But these glass fragments, called cullet, could also have been bought from another factory, to be melted down into new glass. The Sandwich company probably made the lead-glass version of this salt with the same glass it used for its tableware, while both of the New York bottle glasshouses made the nonlead version.

Hints for Collectors
Unlike most pressed salt patterns, this one is equally valuable in both lead and nonlead. Colorless examples are relatively common and inexpensive for lacy-pattern salts. Dark colors are the rarest.

Floral-pattern pressed salt

Description
Rectangular box on 4 feet has bowl of flowers on each side and alternating scallops and points around rim. Thin walls. Flat base inscribed "N. E. GLASS COMPANY BOSTON." Color: transparent light green, opalescent white, opaque white, or colorless. *Variations:* base with "JERSEY GLASS CO. NR. N. YORK" inscription or with sunburst only; sides with fruit instead of flowers.

Type and Dimensions
Pressed in mold for pattern and shape. Lead glass. Height: 2–2⅛". Length: 2⅞–3".

Locality and Period
New England Glass Company, Cambridge, Massachusetts. Jersey Glass Company, Jersey City, New Jersey. c. 1830–50.

Comment
Salts bearing the name of a company are exceptional in pressed glass. This is the only marked piece known from the Jersey Glass Company, although the firm was in operation for over 30 years. Since the older and larger New England Glass Company marked a few other pieces, it is likely that the New Jersey firm copied the original New England design. There is no way to determine the origin of the unmarked variation; it could have been made by either firm or another company altogether.

Hints for Collectors
These salts are highly prized, primarily because of their rare inscription. Many may be chipped or cracked, however, especially around the rim. The unmarked version and the salt from the New England Glass Company are the easiest to find and usually the least expensive. Those bearing the Jersey Glass Company name are the rarest.

169 Crown pressed salt

Description
Circular crownlike cup with 12 scallops around rim and 6 on foot. Thick walls. Color: transparent amber or blue-green, opalescent white, or colorless; rarely transparent purple. *Variations:* rim may have added diamond cutting, sometimes with band of gilt decoration.

Type and Dimensions
Pressed in mold for pattern and shape. Nonlead glass. Height: 2⅜–2½". Rim diameter: 3½–3⅝".

Locality and Period
M'Kee & Brothers, Pittsburgh, Pennsylvania; possibly other Pittsburgh firms. France and Belgium. c. 1855–75.

Comment
Variations with cut or gilt decoration are European and were probably made during the same period as the American examples. Despite their more elaborate designs, these European versions are usually much less expensive than those from Pittsburgh. M'Kee catalogues of 1860, 1864, and 1868 call these Imperial salts, probably because of their crownlike shape. The variation has an added cut motif; such embellishment of pressed objects with cutting is unusual in America but common in France.

Hints for Collectors
Many collectors of American glass prefer the early lacy-pattern salts (#161, #166) to these plainer ones. As a result, pressed salts like the example illustrated are often much less expensive. Since the glass is heavy, it does not chip easily and usually can be found in good condition.

Tiffany salt dip

Description
Bulb-shaped bowl with flaring rim narrows to thick circular foot; 6 molded ribs around body. Pontil mark polished. Paper label underneath foot reads "TIFFANY/FAVRILE/REGISTERED TRADEMARK" with "LCT" scratched on glass. Color: *iridescent* gold, blue, or silver. *Variations:* shading ranges from deep blue to completely gold or silver with blue visible only at pontil mark; occasionally lacks trademark.

Type and Dimensions
Blown in ribbed mold, then tooled into shape. Iridescent finish sprayed on before annealing. Height: 1¾–1⅞". Rim diameter: 2¼–2⅜".

Locality and Period
Tiffany Glass & Decorating Company, Corona, New York. c. 1893–1910.

Matching Glassware
Set of 6 individual salt dips. Stemware (#37), tumblers, bowls, punch bowls (#304), vases (#343), and other decorative pieces. Not made as set.

Comment
Individual salt dips became popular in the 1890s, although the style appears in pressed glass as early as the 1860s. Communal salts vastly outnumbered the individual style, however, until the last decade of the century.

Hints for Collectors
Salt dips like the one illustrated were allotted to each diner, and occasionally shared by 2 diners, at fashionable tables. They were often sold with tiny silver salt spoons, which are more easily found today than the salts themselves. Like all Tiffany glass, the salt shown here is expensive.

171 Mercury-glass salt

Description
Circular goblet shape with round feet and rim. *Thin double walls.* Color: colorless with *silvery mercury coating on interior* (left); *rarely with colored casing* in transparent red (right), blue, or green, and cut in simple geometric pattern. *Cork stopper* on base inscribed "NEGC." *Variations:* cork may lack inscription.

Type and Dimensions
Free-blown, then tooled into double-walled form. Interior lined with mercury; sealed with cork to protect mercury coating from air. Cased in transparent layer (right) and cut through. Lead glass. Height: 3¼–3½". Rim diameter: 3–3⅛".

Locality and Period
Cambridge, Massachusetts: New England Glass Company and Boston Silver Glass Company. c. 1855–70.

Matching Glassware
Small vases, mantle garnitures, and doorknobs. Not made as set.

Comment
Mercury glass was patented in London in 1853 and in the United States in 1855 by the Boston Silver Glass Company. It was an inexpensive nontarnishing substitute for silver.

Hints for Collectors
Cased examples like the red salt illustrated are much rarer than plain ones. Similar mercury salts were also made in Europe, but Continental examples are made of lighter nonlead glass and often have enameled decoration. Most English pieces are stamped "Thompson" or "Varnish Patent" on the corks. American salts command the highest prices.

Goblet pressed salt

Description
Hexagonal goblet shape, with 6 plain panels around sides.
Thick flat rim. Thin walls. Short hexagonal stem and flat
hexagonal foot. Color: transparent purple, light yellow, blue, or
colorless. *Variations:* some heavier, with rounded rim and
circular foot.

Type and Dimensions
Pressed in mold for pattern and shape. Lead or nonlead glass.
Height: 2¾–2⅞". Rim diameter: 2¾–2⅞".

Locality and Period
New England and the Midwest. c. 1850–70.

Comment
This is an open salt intended for communal use. Like most plain
pieces, it is hard to identify with a particular glasshouse.
Probably a number of factories used the same popular design.
Matching tableware was not as common during the mid-19th
century as in modern glassware. This simple pattern would have
blended easily with the variety of pottery and glass at a table
setting.

Hints for Collectors
Salts like the one illustrated are a good starting point for a
beginning collector because they are relatively available and
inexpensive. Goblet-shaped salts have never been reproduced, so
there is no danger of buying an imitation. Colored examples are
less common and are usually considered more desirable.

173 Blown 3-mold salt

Description
Conical shape with galleried rim, narrowing toward thick round foot. Pattern of sunbursts, ribs, and waffling around sides and plain band bulging below rim. Thin walls. Pontil mark rough. Color: transparent purple or colorless; rarely cobalt-blue. *Variations:* several patterns, all different arrangements of same motifs.

Type and Dimensions
Blown in full-size mold for pattern, then tooled into shape. Tooled foot. Lead glass. Height: 2–2¼". Rim diameter: 2½–2¾".

Locality and Period
Massachusetts and Pennsylvania. c. 1820–35.

Matching Glassware
Pitchers, decanters, sugar bowls, shallow bowls, and celery vases. Not made as set.

Comment
This salt was obviously made in a small tumbler mold, since it has the basic tumbler shape. The blower constricted the base and then flattened it to form the foot. The foot cannot be mold-blown because the air pressure in a mold is not great enough to force the glass through the small opening for the foot. For the same reason, handles on blown 3-mold glass are always applied.

Hints for Collectors
Colored blown 3-mold glass salts are more common than larger pieces. A number of reproductions, however, mostly in colored glass, were made in the 1930s by several small New Jersey factories. The reproductions are very difficult to tell from originals, even for experienced collectors. Unusual colors or examples that are obviously new-looking should be avoided.

Free-blown salt

Description
Irregular circular cup with crimped foot. Rarely, horizontal rings around bowl as shown. *Thick walls.* Pontil mark rough. Color: transparent cobalt-blue, amber, green, or brown. *Variations:* usually lacks rings; some with applied horizontal threading.

Type and Dimensions
Free-blown, then tooled into shape. Applied, tooled foot. Nonlead glass. Height: 2–2⅛″. Rim diameter: 2¼–2¾″.

Locality and Period
Southern New Jersey, New York, and southern New England. c. 1800–50.

Comment
These salts can be traced to bottle glasshouses because of their thick heavy glass. They vary a great deal in quality as well as in shape and design, depending on the skill of the blower and on the quality of the batch of molten glass. Pieces like this frequently contain bubbles or bits of unmelted raw material called stones. Imperfect examples were probably never sold by a tableware factory.

Hints for Collectors
Free-blown salts often have a great deal of charm, although they are sometimes of uneven quality or lopsided. Beware of very bubbly glass, however; it may be a 20th-century copy. Many reproductions were made in the 1930s in New Jersey.

Stiegel-type salt

Description
Conical bowl has waist near middle, narrowing below. *Overall diamond pattern.* Thin walls. Short stem and circular foot. Pontil mark rough. Color: transparent green, blue, purple, or colorless. *Variations:* foot with scalloped edge.

Type and Dimensions
Blown in diamond mold for pattern, then expanded and shaped. Applied, tooled foot. Lead or nonlead glass. Height: 2¾–2⅞″. Rim diameter: 2½–2⅝″.

Locality and Period
Probably Henry William Stiegel's American Flint Glass Works, Manheim, Pennsylvania. c. 1770–73. England. c. 1760–1800.

Matching Glassware
Pitchers, flasks, sugar bowls, and creamers. Not made as set.

Comment
Stiegel glass often imitates English styles of the late 18th century. But because no pieces are marked, they can never be positively attributed to Stiegel. In England, this shape was used to serve either salt or punch, a popular alcoholic drink. English collectors call these bonnet cups, possibly because their shape resembles an upturned bonnet.

Hints for Collectors
It is often impossible to distinguish English and American versions of this salt. Early 19th-century midwestern pieces (#176) are also very similar to Stiegel-type salts, although only midwestern examples may have a swirled rib pattern. Price varies according to color. Colorless examples are the least expensive; green is the rarest hue and most costly, while blue and purple are slightly more common.

Early midwestern ribbed salt

Description
Cup has waist near middle, narrowing below. *Swirled diagonal ribs* (left) or *broken-swirl ribs* (right). Thin walls. *Rim smooth, never folded.* Short stem and circular foot. Pontil mark rough. Color: transparent light or dark amber, aquamarine, or pale green; rarely blue or purple. *Never colorless. Variations:* diamond pattern instead of swirls; foot with scalloped edge.

Type and Dimensions
Blown in vertically ribbed mold, then swirled and expanded. Second set of ribs superimposed on swirls by redipping glass in same mold. Lead or nonlead glass. Height: 2¾–2⅞″. Rim diameter: 2¾–2⅞″.

Locality and Period
Western Pennsylvania and West Virginia. Ohio: Zanesville, Mantua, and Kent. c. 1815–35.

Matching Glassware
Tumblers (#44), pitchers (#72), bar bottles (#113), sugar bowls, creamers, bowls (#274), and plates (#214). Not made as set.

Comment
Glass of this type is usually attributed to Ohio, but could also have been made in Pittsburgh or Wheeling, West Virginia. This type of decoration and these colors were not used in the East.

Hints for Collectors
These salts are easy to confuse with Mexican examples made in the 1930s. Be suspicious if a glass has a folded rim, many small bubbles, and few signs of wear. Only American examples have broken-swirl ribbing. Diamond-pattern examples are the rarest, and pieces with swirled ribbing the most common.

Description
Cylindrical shape with pressed pattern. Barrel design (left) has thick stem and circular foot; 1 Cupid figure on each side. S-repeat pattern (right) has large and small scallops on rim and scalloped base. Color: Barrel (left) transparent blue or amber. S-repeat (right) transparent amber, blue, green, purple, or colorless; rarely stained red. *Variations:* many fanciful patterns (left) such as coal scuttles, animals, umbrellas, and hats; sometimes gilt decoration (right).

Type and Dimensions
Pressed in mold for pattern and shape. Nonlead glass. Height (left): 3⅞–4"; rim diameter: 2¾–2⅞". Height (right): 2⅜–2½"; rim diameter: 2–2⅛".

Locality and Period
Barrel: the Midwest. c. 1870–85. S-repeat: United States Glass Company, Pittsburgh. c. 1890–1910.

Matching Glassware
S-repeat: large set with stemware, pitchers, bowls, plates, sugar bowl, creamer, cruets, and other serving pieces.

Comment
Glass toothpick holders (right) appeared at the very end of the 19th century. The fact that they were made in only the most inexpensive pressed glass suggests that, in some refined circles, the use of toothpicks was not considered proper at the table. These containers resemble match holders (left), but the whimsical designs on match holders rarely matched other tableware. The toothpick pattern is called S-repeat.

Hints for Collectors
Toothpick holders have only begun to interest collectors in the past 10 years. They are still easily found and quite inexpensive.

S-repeat pattern

Pressed match holder

Description
Cylindrical shape with pressed pattern. Woven basket design (left) has 2 handles and figure of bird at side; saddle design (right) covers body and rim. Both with flat bases. Color: transparent blue, purple, yellow, green, or light or dark amber. *Variations:* many fanciful patterns, such as coal scuttles, animals, umbrellas, and hats.

Type and Dimensions
Pressed in mold for pattern and shape. Nonlead glass. Height: 3–3½". Rim diameter: 2¼–2¾".

Locality and Period
The Midwest. c. 1870–1900.

Comment
Most match holders were made as novelties and usually did not match other tableware. Those produced in the 1870s and 1880s were nearly always in whimsical shapes like those illustrated, and were probably intended to hold matches for the parlor coal-stove. They are listed in pressed glass catalogues of the period and were probably not made in cut or mold-blown glass. In the 1890s and slightly later, when it became acceptable to use toothpicks at the table, similar containers may have held toothpicks. Some examples of toothpick holders are found in patterns matching turn-of-the-century pressed tableware.

Hints for Collectors
Match holders have been popular collectibles since the 1930s. A number have been reproduced for sale in gift shops, but reproductions usually show little wear. Most reproductions are blue or amber.

179 New England Peachblow toothpick holder

Description
Cylindrical container with square rim. *Opaque pink near rim shading to opaque white near base.* Thin walls. Pontil mark polished. Matt surface. Silver-plated frame with large rectangular base on 4 feet; figure of 19th-century girl holds glass at rim. *Variations:* may be square or round; pink shading varies; may have glossy finish; rarely "WILD ROSE NEGW" paper label on base.

Type and Dimensions
Free-blown, then tooled into shape. Partially reheated to develop pink shading. Acid-treated after annealing for matt finish. Glass height: 2–2½"; rim diameter: 1¾–2". Stand height: 5–5½".

Locality and Period
New England Glass Works, Cambridge, Massachusetts. c. 1886–88.

Matching Glassware
Tumblers (#68), bowls, and vases. Not made as set.

Comment
When the New England Glass Works introduced a shaded glass called Amberina (#220) in 1883, many other glasshouses tried to imitate it. At one point, the New England Glass Works challenged the use of the name Amberina by its rival, the Mt. Washington Glass Company. Eventually, the Mt. Washington firm abandoned the name Amberina, and New England Glass Works changed the name of its Peachblow glass (illustrated here) to Wild Rose in order to avoid confusion with Mt. Washington's Peachblow (#280).

Hints for Collectors
Beware of reproductions with a slightly grayish cast and a rough pontil mark.

Wild Rose line

Albertine pickle jar

Description
Globe-shaped jar with enameled floral decoration. Pontil mark polished. *Silver-plated frame* and domed cover; elaborate base with 4 feet, handle, *and pickle fork.* Color: opaque white with ivory, pink, or blue enameled background; yellow, blue, or ivory decoration. Rarely paper label marked "ALBERTINE." *Variations:* shapes range from globe to square.

Type and Dimensions
Free-blown, then tooled into shape. Enameled after annealing for background color; added enamel decoration. Applied silver-plated hardware. Jar height: 4–5″; base diameter: 4–5″. Frame height: 9¼″; base diameter: 6″.

Locality and Period
Mt. Washington Glass Company, New Bedford, Massachusetts. c. 1890–1900.

Matching Glassware
Pitchers, bowls, biscuit boxes (#181), cracker jars, marmalade jars, salt and pepper shakers. Not made as set.

Comment
The pickle jar illustrated has a rare paper label with the trademark of the Mt. Washington Glass Company. Albertine glass was made in several enameled colors, but pink and ivory are the most common. Pickle jars in frames were also made in patterned pressed glass. The Pairpoint Manufacturing Company of New Bedford made silver-plated frames for many Mt. Washington pieces, which they sold and advertised in their own catalogues. The frames usually bear the Pairpoint trademark.

Hints for Collectors
It is rare to find a jar complete with the original silver-plated frame and matching fork.

181 Crown Milano and Albertine biscuit boxes

Description
Globe-shaped bowl with enameled floral and leaf-spray decoration. Thin walls. Pontil mark polished. *Silver-plated handle, cover, and rim.* Color: Crown Milano (left) opaque white with ivory or beige enameled background and silver and gold enameled decoration. Albertine (right) opaque white with ivory, pink, or blue enameled background and yellow, blue, or ivory enameled decoration. *Variations:* enameled decoration usually floral, including leaf motif, acorns, or holly. Marked "CM" in reddish-brown (left) or "ALBERTINE" (right).

Type and Dimensions
Free-blown, then tooled into shape. Enameled after annealing for background color; added enameled decoration. Applied silver-plated hardware. Height: 5–6″. Diameter: 5–7″.

Locality and Period
Mt. Washington Glass Company, New Bedford, Massachusetts. c. 1890–1900.

Matching Glassware
Crown Milano: vases, bowls, epergnes, and other decorative pieces (#310); rarely tableware. Not made as set. Albertine: pitchers, bowls, salt and pepper shakers, pickle jars (#180), cracker jars, and marmalade jars. Not made as set.

Comment
Crown Milano almost always has an ivory background, but Albertine, which looks identical in ivory, also comes in pink or blue (#180).

Hints for Collectors
All Mt. Washington art glass is desirable and expensive. Albertine glass is rarer than Crown Milano, but commands about the same price because it is not as well known.

Royal Flemish cracker jar

Description
Barrel-shaped jar with enameled design of colored geometric shapes outlined in gold. Each side has 1 black and 1 gold medallion with classical motifs. Thin walls. Pontil mark polished. Silver-plated rim, handle, and crownlike cover with elaborate finial. Color: opaque white with various shades of brown, red, green, and gold enameling. *Variations:* decorations with gold scroll tracery or birds in flight instead of medallions; rarely enameled trademark on base.

Type and Dimensions
Free-blown, then tooled into shape. Enameled after annealing. Applied gilt trim fired on. Applied silver-plated hardware. Height: 8½–9″. Rim diameter: 3–4″.

Locality and Period
Mt. Washington Glass Company, New Bedford, Massachusetts. c. 1890–1900.

Matching Glassware
Bowls, vases, and other decorative pieces; rarely goblets, pitchers, or other serving pieces. Not made as set.

Comment
Royal Flemish was one of many enameled patterns created by the New Bedford firm. The geometric designs were probably inspired by stained-glass windows, but the origin of the name is unknown. Like Crown Milano and Burmese, this trade name was invented by Frederick Shirley, the firm's manager.

Hints for Collectors
Some Royal Flemish ware bears on the base the red enameled symbol of a backward "R" attached to an "F." Even without this symbol, glass of the type described is authentic; no other company made glass like it and it has never been reproduced.

183 Mold-blown salt shaker

Description
Barrel-shaped shaker with threaded rim. Thin walls. Enameled floral decoration (left) or plain (right). Base with impressed sunburst (right). *Screw-on metal shaker top fits over rim; agitator with 4 prongs* rotated by turning knob. Agitator inscribed "patented December 25, 1877." Color: colorless; transparent or opaque white, blue, or purple. *Variations:* several enameled decorations, mostly flowers or scrolls; agitator may lack inscription.

Type and Dimensions
Blown in full-size mold for pattern and shape. Enameled after annealing. Height: 2¾". Base diameter: 1⅝".

Locality and Period
Boston & Sandwich Glass Company, Sandwich, Massachusetts. c. 1870–88.

Comment
The agitator in this unusual shaker was designed to solve the problem of salt sticking in damp weather. The design probably did not work well, however, after the metal agitator became rusted from the corrosive action of the salt. The variety of decorations suggests that the shakers were popular for 10 years or more. They are often called Christmas salts because of the patent date on the agitator.

Hints for Collectors
With their unique agitators, these salts are among the few glass objects that can be reliably attributed to the Boston & Sandwich firm. Shakers bearing the patent command a slightly higher price. But because they are so common—plain or decorated— these are not as expensive as lacy-pattern pressed salts.

Egg-shaped salt and pepper shakers

Description
Egg-shaped shaker with enameled floral design and push-on pewter shaker top. Thin walls. Color: opaque white, pink, yellow, or red, with multicolored enameling. *Variations:* many floral decorations; occasionally ink-stamped or paper label trademark on base.

Type and Dimensions
Blown in full-size mold for shape. Enameled after annealing. Height: 2½". Base diameter: 2".

Locality and Period
Mt. Washington Glass Company, New Bedford, Massachusetts. c. 1880–95.

Matching Glassware
Large shaker probably used as sugar sifter. Not made as set.

Comment
The Mt. Washington Glass Company made a wide variety of art glass. The firm is the only known manufacturer of these rare egg-shaped salt and pepper shakers. Unlike the pair illustrated, which shows 2 enameled variations, salt and pepper containers usually have identical decoration.

Hints for Collectors
A paper label with "MWGC" or "ALBERTINE" is not necessary for identification, but it will always increase the value of a piece. Occasionally these egg-shaped shakers are found in the characteristic Mt. Washington art-glass styles, such as Burmese (#309) and Crown Milano (#181). These named decorations command a premium price. Shakers are not the most valuable art-glass form, but all glass of this type is popular with collectors and fairly expensive.

Salt and pepper shakers

Description
Rectangular bottle with square base and round threaded neck. *Molded design on 4 sides*, with scallop (left), "s" or "P" (right). Thin walls. Color: opaque purple, yellow, blue, green, pink, or white; frequently marbled as illustrated. *Variations:* may be cylindrical; other designs include shells, fans, flowers, and scrolls; *usually screw-on metal shaker top.*

Type and Dimensions
Blown in full-size mold for pattern and shape. Colored glass mixed with opaque white for marbled effect. Height: 3⅜–3½". Base width: 1½–1⅝".

Locality and Period
West Virginia, Ohio, and other midwestern states. c. 1885–1915.

Comment
Salt has been a valuable trading commodity and a table condiment for centuries. Its importance is reflected in containers made of every conceivable substance, including gold, silver, ceramic, and especially—in early America—glass. It was not until the end of the 19th century, when salt shakers were common, that the use of pepper became popular. Pepper was probably never served in an open container.

Hints for Collectors
Salt shakers, like open salts, come in a variety of patterns and colors. They can be collected singly or paired with pepper shakers. But if their tops are missing, it is often impossible to tell them apart. Shakers without tops are slightly less valuable than complete pieces. Examples like the salts illustrated are quite common and still relatively inexpensive.

Depression salt and pepper shakers

Description
Conical form with flat base and *overall pressed cube pattern around body*. Threaded neck for screw-on metal shaker top. Color: transparent light green, light blue-green, pink, or colorless. *Variations:* many simple geometric designs with circles, squares, or diamonds, occasionally combined.

Type and Dimensions
Machine-pressed in mold for pattern and shape. Height: 3⅛″. Base diameter: 2″.

Locality and Period
Jeannette Glass Company, Jeannette, Pennsylvania. Similar patterns by Federal, Hocking, Indiana, Hazel-Atlas, Macbeth-Evans, and other midwestern firms. c. 1929–33.

Matching Glassware
Set with tumblers, pitcher, bowls, covered sugar bowl, creamer, butter dish, plates, cups and saucers, sherbets, covered candy jar, coasters, tray, and covered powder jar.

Comment
This Cube pattern by the Jeannette Glass Company has the same type of evenly spaced geometric design as their Hex Optic (#48) and Colonial Fluted by Federal Glass Company, as well as Bubble (#251), Block Optic, and Colonial by Hocking. This type of geometric pattern preceded the elaborate pressed patterns such as Mayfair and Patrician (#15).

Hints for Collectors
This is one of the least expensive Depression-glass patterns and is found mostly in pink and green. Be careful not to confuse colorless examples with a contemporary American pattern—similar in design but heavier in weight—by the Fostoria Glass Company, Moundsville, West Virginia.

Cube pattern

Description
5-piece set: 5 cylindrical to barrel-shaped bottles with *pressed geometric pattern of vertical and diagonal ribs, diamonds, waffling, and sunbursts in various combinations.* Each neck has push-on metal shaker top, or flaring rim, small pouring lip, and spherical ground stopper (not shown). Pontil marks rough. Color: colorless; occasionally transparent deep blue with swirled ribs and vertical ribs. Square metal stand on 4 ball feet has 5 loops for 5 bottles and loop handle. *Variations:* stand may have triangular or circular base with 3–6 bottles; may have 1 or 2 pouring lips; usually with solid or hollow spherical stopper.

Type and Dimensions
Each bottle blown in same full-size mold for pattern and shape. Necks tooled into shape. Free-blown stopper. Lead glass. Bottle height: 4–4½″; base diameter: 1½–2″. Stand height: 2½″; width: 5¾″.

Locality and Period
Massachusetts: Boston & Sandwich Glass Company, Sandwich; New England Glass Company, Cambridge. Possibly Kensington Glass Company, Philadelphia. c. 1818–30.

Comment
Castor sets were used in upper-middle-class homes from about the mid-18th century until the end of the 19th century. The bottles contained a variety of condiments, including vinegar, oil, bitters, or pepper sauces. The shaker-topped bottles may have been for sugar or spices. Salt was still served in open containers.

Hints for Collectors
Today it is rare to find a matching castor set. Bottles without frames, however, are readily available in antique shops.

Cut castor set

Description
5-piece set: 5 cylindrical to barrel-shaped bottles with narrow bases. *Cut in overall honeycomb pattern.* Necks ground to fit matching conical stoppers or push-on metal shaker tops. Pontil marks polished. Colorless. Circular silver-plated stand on high stem has 5 circular slots and revolves about center loop handle. *Variations:* with geometric patterns or panels; occasionally brilliant-cut patterns or geometric or floral engraving.

Type and Dimensions
Each bottle and stopper free-blown, then tooled into shape. Neck tooled. Cut after annealing. Ground neck and stopper shaft. Shaker top fitted after annealing. Lead glass. Bottle height: 5–8″; base diameter: 1½–2″. Stand height: 18″; width: 6″.

Locality and Period
The Northeast. c. 1850–80.

Comment
The frame illustrated bears on the base the trademark of the Reed & Barton silver-plating firm of Taunton, Massachusetts. The bottles belonged to the family of Thomas Leighton, superintendent of the New England Glass Company, where they were made. In most cases, silver-plating firms purchased the glass to go in the frames and then sold the unit to retailers.

Hints for Collectors
Because castor sets were often sold by the metal firm that made the frames rather than by the glasshouse, it is seldom possible to identify the manufacturer of these bottles. Many of the frames are marked by the metal factory. Some of the most common trade names are Pairpoint, Reed & Barton, and Meriden Brittania.

Realistic-style pressed castor set

Description
5-piece set: 5 cylindrical bottles with narrow bases. Narrow
vertical ribs and horizontal vine pressed around body of each;
vertical panels on neck. Push-on metal shaker top (front left and
right); plain metal cap (rear center); or wide flaring rim, ground
neck, and pouring lip, with cylindrical stopper in matching rib
pattern (rear left and right). Pontil marks rough. Color:
colorless; rarely opaque blue, white, or green. Silver-plated
stand with 5 round slots revolves around center loop handle.
Variations: patterns with coarse and fine ribs and 1–2 vines.

Type and Dimensions
Each bottle pressed in mold for pattern and shape. Tooled neck
and pouring lip. Free-blown stopper. Ground neck and stopper
shaft. Shaker top fitted after annealing. Lead or nonlead glass.
Bottle height: 6–7½"; base diameter: 1¾–1⅞". Frame height: 9";
width: 8".

Locality and Period
M'Kee & Brothers, Pittsburgh; Boston & Sandwich Glass
Company, Sandwich, Massachusetts; and others. c. 1864–75.

Matching Glassware
Large set with stemware, tumblers, pitcher (#89), decanter,
bowls, sugar bowl, creamer, butter dish, celery vase, spoon
holder (#319), plates, cake stand, and lamp.

Comment
The much-prized pattern illustrated, called Bellflower by
collectors, was introduced by M'Kee & Brothers in 1864 as
Ribbed Leaf. The pattern is also attributed to the Boston &
Sandwich Glass Company and was probably made by other firms.

Hints for Collectors
The Bellflower pattern is expensive, but it is readily available.

Bellflower pattern

Burmese castor set

Description
4-piece set: 2 cylindrical salt and pepper shakers with threading below rims and screw-on metal tops, and 2 globe-shaped cruets with slender necks, high pouring lips, ear-shaped handles, and pointed solid stoppers. *All forms opaque lemon-yellow at base shading to deep pink on upper body,* with narrow vertical rib pattern. Matt finish. Pontil marks polished. Silver-plated stand on 4 feet has 2 larger and 2 smaller circular slots and center loop handle. *Variations:* sometimes glossy finish.

Type and Dimensions
Blown in full-size mold for pattern and shape. Tooled spout. Applied, tooled handle. Reheated to develop pink shading. Acid-treated after annealing for matt finish. Cruet height: 5½–5¾"; base diameter: 3–3¼". Shaker height: 3½–3¾"; base diameter: 1½–1¾". Frame height: 9¼"; diameter: 8½".

Locality and Period
Mt. Washington Glass Company, New Bedford, Massachusetts. Thomas Webb & Sons, Stourbridge, England. c. 1885–95.

Matching Glassware
Bowls, vases (#333), centerpieces (#309), and candlesticks; rarely tumblers. Not made as set.

Comment
The Mt. Washington Glass Company began advertising Burmese glass in the late 1880s. It swiftly became popular after the company presented a tea set of Burmese glass to Queen Victoria.

Hints for Collectors
There is no difference in value between glossy and matt finished Burmese glass. English Burmese usually has a circular mark with the company name on the base. Reproductions look new or have a slight grayish cast.

Agata cruet

Description
Globe-shaped body has slender neck and small ruffled pouring spout. Ear-shaped handle extends from top of neck to below shoulder. Spherical solid stopper. Color: *opaque pink shading to opaque white near base;* pink handle and white stopper. *Entire surface has mottled blackish finish resembling stain. Variations:* amount and intensity of pink color may vary.

Type and Dimensions
Free-blown bottle and stopper, tooled into shape. Applied, tooled handle. Partially reheated to develop shading. Stain sprayed on after annealing. Height: 5½". Base diameter: 3".

Locality and Period
New England Glass Works, Cambridge, Massachusetts. c. 1884–88.

Matching Glassware
Tumblers, pitchers, punch cups, bowls in several shapes, and vases. Not made as set.

Comment
Agata was a further development of New England Glass Works' Wild Rose glassware (#179). The only difference is the mottled blackish stain, which was used to give the glass an agatelike, or mottled, surface. Most Agata ware is small, which suggests that the stain may have been difficult to apply to large pieces.

Hints for Collectors
Agata glass is rarely marked with a paper label, but the mottled dark finish is unmistakable. The glass illustrated was apparently reheated too long. The resulting cruet is entirely pink instead of shading gradually to white at the base. All Agata glass is quite rare and commands a premium price; it has never been reproduced.

Mold-blown molasses can or syrup jug

Description
Pear-shaped pitcher with molded vertical ribs and fruit bowl (left) *or molded drape pattern* (right). Thick walls. Circular base. Ear-shaped handle crimped at base. Metal cap with glass pouring hole or high pouring lip. Color: opaque white; rarely opaque blue or green. *Variations:* decoration within vertical lines, or panels with stylized flowers (#193); rarely with pouring hole.

Type and Dimensions
Each piece blown in full-size mold for pattern and shape. Tooled rim. Applied, tooled handle. Metal cap or spout applied after annealing. Lead or nonlead glass. Height: 6–6¾". Base diameter: 3–3½".

Locality and Period
The Midwest and the East. Ribbed pattern: c. 1850–70; Lincoln Drape: c. 1865–80.

Matching Glassware
Lincoln Drape: set with stemware, pitcher, decanter, sugar bowl, creamer, butter dish, spoon holder, celery vase, footed bowl, covered compote, plates, footed salt, and sauce dish. Ribbed pattern: rarely small pitcher; not made as set.

Comment
The pattern on the right is called Lincoln Drape by collectors since they believe it was made to commemorate President Lincoln following his assassination in 1865. But no evidence supports this. All other pieces in Lincoln Drape are pressed.

Hints for Collectors
Few pressed patterns have a mold-blown counterpart like the syrup jugs. Feel the inside surface. Mold-blown glass is patterned both inside and out.

Lincoln Drape pattern

Mold-blown molasses can or syrup jug

Description
Pear-shaped pitcher with molded vertical ribs and stylized flowers. Thick walls. Circular footlike base. Ear-shaped handle crimped at base. Metal cap. Color: opaque white; rarely opaque blue or green; colorless. *Variations:* a few patterns with vertical ribs or panels. Metal caps and pouring spouts include high pouring lip (left), downward-slanting spout (right), and nozzle-type spout (#192).

Type and Dimensions
Blown in full-size mold for pattern and shape. Tooled neck. Applied, tooled handle. Metal cap applied after annealing. Lead or nonlead glass. Height: 7½–8″. Base diameter: 3–3½″.

Locality and Period
The Midwest and New England. c. 1850–80.

Comment
Molasses cans and syrup jugs are the same form and frequently appear with similar or identical patterns in many catalogues from the 1850s to the 1870s, with different companies using one name or the other. During this period, they were always mold-blown, possibly because of their difficult shape. Their patterns varied little, unlike those of the metal caps and pouring spouts.

Hints for Collectors
The patented metal lids on syrup jugs make an interesting study in themselves. The open one illustrated is more complex than most; its lower part is designed to catch drips, a problem with syrup and molasses. When closed, the lid looks like the head of a hippopotamus. It is marked "Patented November 17, 1857."

Late 19th-century pressed cruet and syrup jug

Description
Both thick-walled pitchers have *overall pressed peacock-feather pattern* and ear-shaped handles. Pear-shaped syrup jug (right) has metal cap; conical cruet (left) has high pouring lip and faceted glass stopper. Colorless.

Type and Dimensions
Pressed from bottom in mold for pattern and shape. Base tooled closed. Metal cap applied after annealing. Nonlead glass. Syrup height: 6¾"; base diameter: 2½". Cruet height: 8¼"; base diameter: 2½".

Locality and Period
United States Glass Company, Pittsburgh. Possibly Ohio. c. 1902–10.

Matching Glassware
Set with mugs (#57), tumblers, pitcher, bowls, sugar bowl, creamer, butter dish, spoon holder, cake plate, and lamp.

Comment
This pattern, called Georgia, is one of many named after states by the United States Glass Company, which was a consortium of tableware factories in the Midwest.

Hints for Collectors
Syrup jugs and cruets like this were made 20 years after the mold-blown jugs (#192, #193). They were pressed from the bottom in an operation called the cut-and-shut method. When first pressed, each piece had a round collar extending down around the open base. A workman reheated the glass and tooled the collar down to make a flat base with a characteristic dimple in the center. This is the only way that a closed piece like a decanter or bottle can be pressed, unless the neck and lip are formed by hand.

Georgia pattern

195 Blown 3-mold cruet

Description
Barrel-shaped bottle with molded vertical ribs from base to neck. Small pouring lip. Thin walls. Ear-shaped handle crimped at base. Pontil mark rough. Color: transparent green or aquamarine. *Variations:* several patterns combine ribs of various widths.

Type and Dimensions
Blown in full-size mold for pattern and shape. Tooled lip. Applied, tooled handle. Nonlead glass. Height: 5–5¼″. Base diameter: 2¼–2½″.

Locality and Period
Mt. Vernon Glass Company, Vernon, New York. c. 1825–35.

Matching Glassware
Mugs, tumblers, bowls, sugar bowls, creamers, bell covers, and inkwells. Not made as set.

Comment
Very few factories made blown 3-mold pieces in nonlead glass. The best-known was the bottle glasshouse at Vernon, New York, owned and operated by Oscar Granger. This factory experimented with making tableware from glass normally used for bottles.

Hints for Collectors
Single nonlead glass cruets are much less common than castor bottles (#187) made of lead glass, which are found in 3- to 6-bottle frames as well as alone. The size and tapered neck of the cruet illustrated indicates that it was probably used for vinegar or oil. It could also have held bitters, pepper sauce, or another liquid seasoning.

196

Late 19th-century pressed ketchup jug or vinegar cruet

Description
Cylindrical jug has pressed hobnail-and-star pattern alternating with X's; row of ovals around shoulder and base. Thick walls. Vertical ribs on neck and square handle. Small pouring spout. Faceted ball stopper. Color: transparent light or dark amber, blue, or colorless. Variations: pattern may have V (Vandyke) instead of X.

Type and Dimensions
Pressed from bottom in mold for pattern and shape. Base tooled closed. Pressed stopper. Ground neck and stopper shaft. Nonlead glass. Height: 9¾″. Base diameter: 3¼″.

Locality and Period
Richards & Hartley Flint Glass Company, Tarentum, Pennsylvania. c. 1885–1900.

Matching Glassware
Set with stemware, mugs, tumblers, pitcher, butter dish, salt and pepper shakers, spoon holder, celery vase, sugar bowl, creamer, covered and uncovered bowls (#242), bread tray, compotes, molasses jug, pickle jar, and toothpick holder.

Comment
Collectors call this popular pattern Daisy and Button with Crossbars, but it was sold originally as the Mikado pattern.

Hints for Collectors
Colored examples in this pattern are hard to find and much more expensive than colorless glass. The Daisy and Button pattern and its many variations are probably the most popular of all 19th-century pressed patterns. This pattern has been in production more or less constantly since the 1880s, especially in blue and amber, but also in other colors and in colorless glass. Except for their new look, reproductions are very difficult to spot.

Daisy and Button with Crossbars pattern

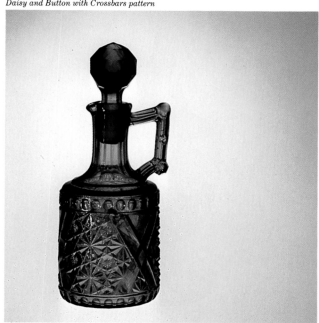

Carnival candy dish

Description
Oval bowl with domed cover has overall pressed tracery pattern resembling cobweb. Pointed knob on domed cover. Disk at base of bowl. Hollow domed foot with radiating panels. Color: transparent orange-amber with *iridescent gold finish.*

Type and Dimensions
Bowl and cover pressed in mold for pattern and shape. Iridescent finish sprayed on before annealing. Height: 7½″. Rim diameter: 3½″.

Locality and Period
Imperial Glass Company, Bellaire, Ohio. Similar patterns by Millersburg, Fenton, and Northwood. c. 1905–20.

Matching Glassware
Large set includes wineglasses, goblets, mugs, tumblers, pitchers in 2 sizes, decanter, bowls in 4 sizes, covered sugar bowl, creamer, covered butter dish, spoon holder, plates in 4 sizes, vase, and toothpick holder.

Comment
The pattern illustrated, patented by the Imperial Glass Company, is a variation of the old pressed Tree-of-Life pattern by the Portland Glass Company, Portland, Maine, and a few Pittsburgh firms of the 1870s and 1880s. Although it has been called Tree-of-Life Variant, Soda Gold, and Spider Web, the pattern is now generally known as Spider Web and Soda Gold, a name that describes both its color and pattern. The pattern only exists in orange-amber, which collectors call marigold.

Hints for Collectors
Candy dishes in this shape first came into fashion about 1905, with the invention of Carnival glass. Depression-glass pieces also come in this shape.

Spider Web and Soda Gold pattern

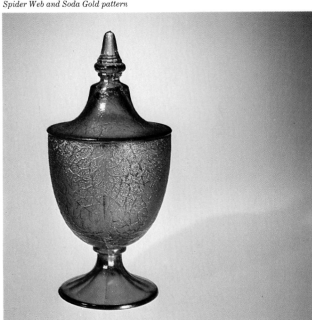

Late 19th-century pressed pickle jar

Description
Cylindrical jar with pressed pattern of marsh scene; long-legged birds standing on 1 side, flying on opposite side. Thick flat base. Cover fits over rim, has pointed knob and floral pattern. Colorless. *Variations:* late 19th-century patterns, including Lion (#315), Westward Ho (#294), Opalescent Hobnail, Daisy and Button with Crossbars (#196), and Ruby Thumbprint.

Type and Dimensions
Bowl and cover pressed in separate molds for pattern and shape. Nonlead glass. Height: 6½–7″. Base diameter: 3–3⅛″.

Locality and Period
The Midwest. c. 1870–1910.

Comment
Pickle jars without frames or serving implements were made in about 50–60 patterns of pressed glass from the 1870s to the 1890s. The poor quality of the glass illustrated indicates that it may have been used originally as a grocery-packing container for pickles or a condiment jar for commercial use in a hotel or restaurant. Jars of this type were also used for jam or marmalade, and similar smaller shapes held mustard, relish, or olives.

Hints for Collectors
These jars are relatively inexpensive and often turn up at flea markets rather than in antique shops, except for those shops specializing in late 19th-century glass. They are useful containers for a variety of things besides pickles.

Plates

Most glass plates are circular, ranging in size from the 3″ cup plate to the 14″ platter. They come in free-blown, mold-blown, cut, and pressed glass, although pressed plates are by far the most common. Free-blown and mold-blown plates, dating from the late 18th and early 19th centuries, are rare and were seldom made to match other plates, let alone other forms. Only in 19th-century pressed glass and the brilliant-cut glass of the turn of the century did sets with plates, bowls, stemware, and serving pieces become popular.

The earliest pressed-glass plates dating from the 1830–60 period are the 6″ tea and 5″ toddy plates, made in lacy patterns (#210). They seldom match other tableware. Slightly larger plates (7″, 8″) also had lacy patterns, featuring floral or geometric designs against the characteristic stippled background (#208). The use of many of these early forms is unknown, however. Most pressed plates are cup plates, a unique 3–4″ form found only in pressed glass (#201–205). Cup plates date from the earliest days of pressed glass in the late 1820s and were made until the early 1860s. According to etiquette books of the period, cup plates were used to hold ceramic teacups. Tea was poured into a handleless teacup and then transferred in small amounts to a deep ceramic saucer. While the teacup rested on the glass cup plate, tea drinkers sipped their beverage from the ceramic saucer. The upper class clearly frowned upon the custom, since cup plates are never found in the more expensive cut glass. Saucer-drinking was also fashionable in England, and manufacturers there made earthenware cup plates expressly for export to America.

In the United States, cup plates were made in a variety of creative designs, although few match the patterns of other tableware. Over 700 pressed patterns were manufactured during the brief 40-year period that these plates were popular. More than half are conventional geometric or floral designs (#203, #205). Many others illustrate historical themes, such as the American Eagle, Bunker Hill Monument (#201), and American ships, or political themes, like the Henry Clay cup plate (#202). With the exception of cup plates, pressed glass manufacturers of the 1850s and 1860s produced fewer plates than bowls and glasses. At the time, most plates were made out of wood, pewter, or clay rather than glass. During the 1870s and 1880s, glass plates regained popularity and manufacturers introduced many unusual shapes, such as rectangles and hexagons (#260). Glass manufacturers of the 1930s and 1940s added even more machine-pressed plate forms, such as the divided grill plate (#219), the handled sandwich server (#216), and the tiered relish dish.

Cut-glass plates achieved their greatest popularity from 1900 to 1915 in the intricate brilliant-cut glass patterns (#206). For the first time, cut-glass plates were made with a wide range of matching forms, from stemware to decanters and bowls. Plates in brilliant-cut glass include principally 6″ underplates, which were placed beneath finger bowls (#29), and large serving platters. Many examples are still found, although identifying the numerous patterns and cutting firms is often a challenge.

199 Ulysses S. Grant memorial plate

Description
Circular plate with *pressed bust of President Ulysses S. Grant at center*, encircled by inscriptions "BORN APRIL 22 1822" and "DIED JULY 23 1885." Heavily veined, overlapping maple-leaf pattern around border inscribed "LET US HAVE PEACE/U. S. GRANT." Serrated leaflike rim. Color: transparent light green, blue, amber, yellow, or colorless. *Variations:* square-shaped, with waffle instead of leaf pattern.

Type and Dimensions
Pressed in mold for pattern and shape. Nonlead glass. Diameter: 10½–10¾".

Locality and Period
Pittsburgh area: Adams & Company and probably other firms. c. 1885–86.

Comment
Grant was not a popular president because of a political scandal that developed between 1869 and 1877. He captured the public's imagination during the last months of his life, however, when he struggled to finish his memoirs in order to pay his debts and leave his family with some financial security. The memorial plate illustrated must have been popular, since it is relatively common. The Adams company advertised a Grant plate in 1885, but since no illustration accompanied this publicity, it may have referred to either the round plate or the square variation.

Hints for Collectors
Unlike the Garfield plate (#200), this Grant plate does not have matching pieces. It attracted little interest from collectors until the Civil War Centennial in the early 1960s, when this type of memorabilia again became popular.

Garfield memorial plate

Description
Circular plate with *pressed bust of President James A. Garfield at center*, encircled by small inscription "BORN NOV. 19, 1831. SHOT JULY 2, 1881. DIED SEPT. 19, 1881" and by border of stars; this encircled by large inscription "WE MOURN OUR NATION'S LOSS." *Stippled drapery pattern with floral design* on border. Scalloped rim. Colorless. *Variations:* plain center.

Type and Dimensions
Pressed in mold for pattern and shape. Nonlead glass. Diameter: 12–12¼".

Locality and Period
Pittsburgh area: possibly Adams & Company. c. 1881–85.

Matching Glassware
Set with drapery pattern only includes goblets, pitcher (#88), bowls, sugar bowl, creamer, butter dish, spoon holder, cake plate, covered and uncovered compotes, and pickle, honey, and sauce dishes.

Comment
The stippled drapery pattern is a typical design of the late 1870s and early 1880s. It may have been in production before 1881, when Garfield's assassination prompted the addition of a memorial plate with the late president's portrait. All of the other shapes in this pattern lack the bust and inscription. Memorial plates and platters were made by a number of firms around this time, including souvenirs for the Centennial, a very different Garfield plate with the inscription "MEMORIAL," and 2 plates commemorating the death of Ulysses S. Grant in 1885 (#199).

Hints for Collectors
The matching glassware in this pattern has not attracted much attention from collectors and is relatively inexpensive.

201 Inscribed cup plate

Description
Circular plate with *scalloped rim and pressed border pattern* of chains (below) or long-stemmed flowers and leaves (opposite). *Center has pressed historical scene,* such as the Bunker Hill Monument illustrated, *or portrait heads;* encircled by inscription, such as "BUNKER HILL BATTLE FOUGHT/JUNE 17 1775" or "THE WEDDING DAY AND THREE WEEKS AFTER." Color: colorless; Bunker Hill pattern also transparent yellow, emerald-green, or opalescent white; Wedding Day pattern rarely with green or pink tint. *Variations:* 13 different Bunker Hill designs, including tassels hanging from junctures of chain pattern (#200); additional inscriptions are "CORNERSTONE LAID BY LAFAYETTE, JUNE 17, 1825/FINISHED BY THE LADIES 1841" and "FROM THE FAIR TO THE BRAVE."

Type and Dimensions
Pressed in mold for pattern and shape. Lead glass. Diameter: 3½–3¾".

Locality and Period
Massachusetts: probably Boston & Sandwich Glass Company, Sandwich, and New England Glass Company, Cambridge. Bunker Hill pattern: c. 1843–50. Wedding Day pattern: c. 1840–60.

Comment
Cup plates were popular from about the 1820s until the Civil War. During this period, it was fashionable to drink tea from a saucer. Tea was poured into a ceramic teacup and then transferred into the matching ceramic saucer for drinking. Meanwhile, the teacup was set aside on a glass cup plate similar to the ones illustrated. Cup plates were made only in pressed glass, never in blown or cut glass. Over 700 different designs

Bunker Hill pattern

have been counted, which indicates their immense popularity. More than half of the designs are relatively conventional, with acorn, leaf, heart, sunburst, and various geometric motifs. Other designs relate to prominent politicians or episodes in American history. George Washington and Henry Clay (#202) each appear on cup plates, as do several American ships.

The Bunker Hill Monument was another subject that inspired cup plate designs. Construction of the monument began in 1825, on the 50th anniversary of the famous battle, but, due to lack of funds, it was not completed and dedicated until 1843. A group of women raised enough money to finish the project, which accounts for the inscription "FROM THE FAIR TO THE BRAVE" on one of the variations. There are over a dozen variations of this design. The Wedding Day plate, by contrast, lacks variations. If the "WEDDING DAY" inscription is upright, the faces are smiling; if "THREE WEEKS AFTER" is upright, the faces are frowning.

Hints for Collectors
Both of the cup plates illustrated were reproduced in the 1930s and 1940s. The lettering on the Bunker Hill reproduction is too large and the letters lack serifs. The monument itself is also somewhat larger in the new plate. Wedding Day reproductions are about ¼" smaller than the original 3½" size. Both reproductions are available in souvenir and gift shops, and are often sold in sets with 2 other plates. Do not confuse cup plates with butter pats, which are much smaller plates (about 1½–2") used in the late 19th century to hold individual servings of butter. Butter pats were made in cut glass, very rarely in pressed glass, and came with a set of matching tableware.

Wedding Day pattern

Henry Clay cup plate

Description
Circular plate with *pressed profile of Henry Clay at center*, encircled by large scrolls. *Alternating shields, fruit baskets, and scrolls around border.* Rim has pairs of small scallops between larger single scallops. Color: colorless; rarely with green or yellow-green tint. *Variations:* may be inscribed "HENRY CLAY" above profile; may have profile of Queen Victoria with "VICTORIA" inscribed above. Rim may have small scallops or alternating scallops and points. Variations in blue or purple.

Type and Dimensions
Pressed in mold for pattern and shape. Lead glass. Diameter: 3⅝–3¾".

Locality and Period
Massachusetts: probably Boston & Sandwich Glass Company, Sandwich. c. 1835–50.

Comment
Henry Clay of Kentucky was a popular politician for nearly 50 years. He served in both the House and Senate and as Secretary of State. It is likely that this plate was made while Clay was campaigning for the presidency between 1832 and 1844. The Queen Victoria plates were probably made by the same firm between 1837 and 1840.

Hints for Collectors
Clay cup plates without inscriptions are common in colorless glass and are among the least expensive of the historical cup plates. Colored glass or inscribed Clay plates are much scarcer, and colored Victoria plates are rare.

Early pressed toddy plate

Description
Circular plate with *pressed diamond-patterned pinwheel at center;* 6-pointed star at center and between each pinwheel arm. Vertical ribs encircle pinwheel. Beaded scalloped rim with fans between scallops. *Thick glass.* Colorless. *Variations:* 6-pointed star or waffle pattern may replace pinwheel.

Type and Dimensions
Pressed in mold for pattern and shape. Lead glass. Diameter: 4⅝–4¾".

Locality and Period
Massachusetts: probably Boston & Sandwich Glass Company, Sandwich; New England Glass Company, Cambridge; and Phoenix Glass Works, Boston. c. 1827–35.

Comment
This is one of the earliest designs used in pressed-glass plates. The plate is quite thick compared to pressed pieces made a few years later, and its designs predate the stippled lacy patterns of the 1835–45 period (#208). At this stage, pressing was still in its infancy, and most designs imitated cut-glass motifs such as diamonds, fans, and pinwheels. The plate illustrated is slightly larger than most cup plates and is probably what collectors call a toddy plate, but its original use is unknown.

Hints for Collectors
These early plates are rare and tend to be quite expensive compared to some of the more common cup plates (#205) and many other toddy plates.

Description
Circular plate with *pressed harp at center*, encircled by grape clusters and leaves. *Border has scroll design against stippled background.* Scalloped rim. Color: transparent light or dark blue, or colorless. *Variations:* plain center or eagle may replace harp.

Type and Dimensions
Pressed in mold for pattern and shape. Lead glass. Diameter: 4¼–4⅜″.

Locality and Period
Massachusetts: possibly Boston & Sandwich Glass Company, Sandwich; New England Glass Company, Cambridge; and American Flint Glass Works, Boston. c. 1830–50.

Comment
Cup plates are generally about 3–4″ in diameter, and anything slightly larger is usually called a toddy plate by collectors, although the exact use of these plates is not really known. They might have been larger cup plates, intended to accommodate a spoon as well as a teacup, or perhaps they were saucers for toddy glasses, which may have been the origin of their name. Between 50 and 100 toddy-plate designs exist, including a range of lacy motifs, some of which match other pieces of lacy-pattern pressed glass. Sizes range between 4¼″ and 5½″; anything larger is usually called a tea plate, which was used to serve refreshments at tea time.

Hints for Collectors
Toddy plates have never been as popular with collectors as cup plates. They are often less expensive, although this depends to some extent on design, color, and rarity. Unlike cup plates, toddy plates have never been reproduced.

Heart-pattern cup plate

Description
Circular plate with *pressed octafoil design at center against stippled background. Stippled hearts around border. Scalloped rim.* Color: transparent blue, green, yellow, or purple; opaque white; opalescent white or bluish-white; colorless. *Variations:* border may have 12–13 hearts; center may lack stippling; rim may have 41, 43, 48, 55, 56, 102, or other even numbers of scallops.

Type and Dimensions
Pressed in mold for pattern and shape. Lead glass. Diameter: 3½–4″.

Locality and Period
Massachusetts: probably Boston & Sandwich Glass Company, Sandwich, and other firms. c. 1835–60.

Comment
The heart-pattern plate was made over a long period and has more variations than any other cup-plate design. Although it is usually attributed to the factory at Sandwich, it seems unlikely that one factory would have bothered to make a number of molds for so many variations. The plate illustrated was made in many colors. It is still relatively common in colorless glass and in the opalescent bluish-white illustrated, but other colors are rare.

Hints for Collectors
The heart pattern was reproduced extensively in the 1930s and other copies are still being made. The hearts on the early reproductions are noticeably smaller than on genuine examples, and the scallops are much more even in size.

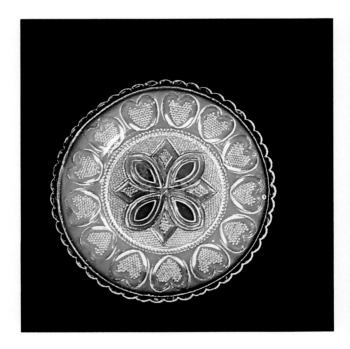

Brilliant-cut plate

Description
Flat plate in form of 8-pointed star. Large 8-pointed cut star covers most of plate; 1 small hobstar at each point and 1 at center. Small hobstars in interstices of design. Scalloped rim. Colorless. *Variations:* many patterns combining brilliant-cut motifs, such as hobstars, diamonds, and fans. May have acid-stamped trademark or paper label.

Type and Dimensions
Free-blown, then tooled into shape. Cut after annealing. Lead glass. Diameter: 13½–13¾″.

Locality and Period
Throughout the United States. c. 1900–15.

Matching Glassware
Set with goblets, wine, cordial, and sherry glasses, tumblers, pitchers, decanters, bowls, plates, and punch bowl with cups.

Comment
The Kensington pattern illustrated appears in several catalogues of T. G. Hawkes & Company of Corning, New York, between 1898 and 1910. This plate also bears Hawkes's acid-stamped trademark, 2 hawks and a shamrock. But other pieces in this pattern may be harder to recognize once the pattern is adapted to the contours of a more 3-dimensional form, such as a decanter or tumbler. To complicate matters further, other glass manufacturers have used the name Kensington for completely different patterns.

Hints for Collectors
Cut-glass plates range in diameter from about 6″ to 20″. Kensington plates were made in 10″, 12″, and 14″ sizes. Large plates are rare and very expensive. Most plates larger than 12″ were probably made as special orders.

Kensington pattern

Brilliant-cut ice cream tray

Description
Oval tray with cut hobstar in center and fan at each side. Row of
hobstars around border, with strawberry-diamonds below.
Scalloped rim. Thick glass. Colorless. *Variations:* sometimes
rectangular with square handle at each end, or oval with pointed
ends; several cut patterns including Russian (#29) and Hobnail
(#111). May have acid-stamped trademark or paper label.

Type and Dimensions
Free-blown, then tooled into shape. Cut after annealing. Lead
glass. Length: 13″. Width: 8¾–9″.

Locality and Period
Throughout the United States. c. 1890–1915.

Matching Glassware
Set with 5″ serving bowls.

Comment
Ice cream sets became fashionable in the 1880s and are another
example of the Victorian desire to create a different bowl or dish
for every purpose. Ice cream trays are rare in art glass (#259)
and are most often found in heavy cut glass like the example
illustrated. They were always sold in sets with 6, 8, or 12 shallow
bowls, sometimes in patterns that matched sets of stemware.

Hints for Collectors
The tray illustrated bears the trademark of J. Hoare & Company
of Corning, New York, yet the pattern is not illustrated in any
known Hoare catalogue. It most closely resembles Hoare's Pluto
pattern, usually shown on deep bowls and decanters. The design
is also similar to the Lotus pattern cut by the O. F. Egginton
Company of Corning but is much more detailed. Probably nearly
every cutting firm of the period had its own version of this
popular brilliant-cut design.

Lacy-pattern pressed plate

Description
Circular plate with *pressed sunflower-and-leaf design at center against stippled background.* 9 stippled panels with thistle, rose, and sunflower designs alternating around border. Flat, finely scalloped rim. Colorless. *Variations:* may be hexagonal; many other designs, including abstract Gothic arch (#166) and zigzag motifs or naturalistic designs, such as thistles and beehives.

Type and Dimensions
Pressed in mold for pattern and shape. Lead glass. Diameter: 7¼–7¾".

Locality and Period
Massachusetts: probably Boston & Sandwich Glass Company, Sandwich, and New England Glass Company, Cambridge. Possibly Providence Flint Glass Company, Providence, Rhode Island, and a Philadelphia firm. c. 1830–50.

Comment
The earliest designs in pressed glass imitated cut-glass patterns. But early glassmakers soon found that the surface of the glass was often cloudy when the mold was not preheated properly. In an effort to disguise this, patterns of the 1830s made great use of stippled backgrounds, a mesh of fine dots which reflected the light and made the glass sparkle. Collectors in the 1920s and 1930s called this style lacy pressed glass because of the lacelike stippling.

Hints for Collectors
Early lacy patterns like the example illustrated were not made in sets. Most of them came in colorless glass, but some examples can also be found in transparent blue, green, purple, and amber —usually in intense hues. Colored pieces are much more expensive than colorless ones.

Early pressed plate

Description
Circular plate with *pressed diamond-patterned 9-pointed star at center. Large pressed chain design of diamond-patterned circles* around border. Arches of 6 scallops alternating with diamond-patterned point around edge. Color: transparent light or dark amber, dark blue, light, medium, or dark purple, reddish-amber, opalescent white, or colorless. *Variations:* star with 11 points.

Type and Dimensions
Pressed in mold for pattern and shape. Lead glass. Diameter: 6–6¼″.

Locality and Period
New England, Pennsylvania, West Virginia, and Ohio. c. 1835–50.

Matching Glassware
Plates, covered and uncovered bowls, sugar bowls, honey dishes (#253), salts, and candlesticks. Not made as set.

Comment
Roman Rosette is the name coined by 1930s collectors for this pattern, one of the most common patterns in early pressed glass. While not exactly a lacy design, it was probably made at the same time, since it appears in the same shapes and colors and is of lead glass. It is found in a greater variety of shapes than any of the other early patterns.

Hints for Collectors
Roman Rosette is one of the least expensive early patterns, especially in colorless glass. It has not been reproduced; however, do not confuse it with the Roman Rosette pattern manufactured by the United States Glass Company of Pittsburgh in the 1890s, which is of nonlead glass (*see* Pressed Pattern Guide).

Roman Rosette pattern

Lacy-pattern pressed toddy plate

Description
Circular plate with *6 interlocking pressed S-scrolls at center, with overall diamond pattern and peacock eyes between scrolls. Peacock-feather pattern* around border. Rim with alternating large and small scallops. Color: transparent purple, blue, yellow, or colorless. *Variations:* rim may have only small scallops or alternating scallops and points; thistles or diamonds may replace scrolls.

Type and Dimensions
Pressed in mold for pattern and shape. Lead glass. Diameter: 5½–5⅝″.

Locality and Period
Massachusetts. Possibly Philadelphia and New York. c. 1835–50.

Matching Glassware
Larger plates, bowls, sugar bowls, creamers, salts (#161), mustard jars, trays (#257), and rare footed compotes. Not made as set.

Comment
The peacock feather is a common motif in early pressed glass and has many variations. It was probably made by all of the glasshouses manufacturing pressed tableware during this period. This small-size plate has been variously referred to as a tea or toddy plate. Catalogues and advertisements did not exist for these early pressed plates, however, and we can only guess at their function.

Hints for Collectors
The purple example illustrated is comparatively rare and commands a much higher price than blue or yellow plates in this pattern. Colorless examples are the most common.

Late pressed plate

Description
Circular plate with *pressed 6-pointed star at center* patterned in closely spaced dots. Vertical ribs surround center. *Overall pressed pattern of closely spaced dots* around wide border. Clusters of circles around scalloped rim. Colorless. *Variations:* many dot patterns, including Dewdrop, Popcorn, Paneled Dewdrop, Beaded Dewdrop, and Loop with Dewdrops.

Type and Dimensions
Pressed in mold for pattern and shape. Nonlead glass. Diameter: 7½–7¾".

Locality and Period
Pittsburgh area: Campbell, Jones & Company; probably also Adams & Company and M'Kee & Brothers. c. 1875–95.

Matching Glassware
Set with goblets, cordials, pitcher, sugar bowl, creamer, butter dish, covered bowls, footed salt, celery vase, spoon holder, cake plate on stand, sauce dish in 2 styles, pickle dish, and lamp.

Comment
The pattern shown is called Dewdrop with Star by collectors. It was patented by Campbell, Jones & Company, although only the lamp is marked with the patent date, August 29, 1876. Plates of the size shown here were probably used as dessert or side plates since glass luncheon or dinner plates did not become popular until the 1920s.

Hints for Collectors
This plate and the matching salt have been reproduced, but both the star and dewdrop dots are slightly larger in reproductions. Although the original pattern came only in colorless glass, reproductions are also transparent pink, green, and purple.

Dewdrop with Star pattern

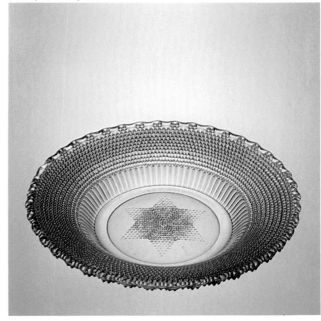

Description
9-piece set: (below, left to right) sherbet, salad plate, bread-and-butter or underplate, cup and saucer; (opposite) cake plate, dinner plate, soup cup on luncheon plate. *All pieces have pressed stylized floral and scroll pattern around border; plates with center sunburst surrounded by diamond pattern.* Color: transparent amber or colorless. *Variations:* similar patterns with alternating flowers and scrolls on stippled background. Colorless examples sometimes with gold or silver trim.

Type and Dimensions
Machine-pressed in mold for pattern and shape. Plate diameters: 6″, 7⅜″, 8⅜″, 9⅜″, 11⅜″. Soup rim diameter: 4⅝″; height: 2¼″. Sherbet rim diameter: 3½″; height: 3″. Cup rim diameter: 3⅝″; height: 2¼″. Saucer diameter: 6″.

Locality and Period
Indiana Glass Company, Dunkirk, Indiana. c. 1933; 1940. Similar patterns by Hocking, Federal, Macbeth-Evans, McKee, Paden City, and other midwestern firms. c. 1925–50.

Matching Glassware
Set with berry bowls (4½″), cereal bowls (6″), serving bowls (#249), oval bowl, sugar bowl, creamer, grill plate (10⅜″), platter (10¾″), 3-part relish dish, and footed tumblers (9 oz., 12 oz.).

Comment
Illustrated are the essential pieces of a Depression-glass place setting, which includes many shapes that were never made in glass before this period. The grill plate (not shown) is divided into 1 large and 2 smaller sections for different foods. The footed sherbet, soup cup, and cup and saucer are still other 20th-century additions. Before this period, hot foods such as soup or

Daisy pattern

coffee were never served in glass dishes because the glass might crack. Depression glass is well annealed, however, and less apt to break as a result of temperature changes. This pattern, originally issued simply as No. 620 by the Indiana Glass Company, is now called Daisy. It was made only in colorless glass in 1933; amber was added in 1940. Gold or silver trim on colorless examples is another characteristic of 1930s glassware. Daisy comes in fewer shapes than most Depression-glass patterns.

Hints for Collectors
Except for its lack of stippling, Daisy resembles 2 other patterns made during the same period. One by the Hocking Glass Company was manufactured from 1939 to 1964, and another pattern by the Indiana Glass Company was made from the 1920s to the 1960s. Both patterns are called Sandwich because of the lacy design resembling earlier lacy-pattern glass attributed to the Boston & Sandwich Glass Company. Each of these Depression-glass Sandwich patterns has a flower in the center instead of the sunburst-and-diamond pattern illustrated here. The Sandwich patterns come in much more vivid colors than Daisy, as well as in the traditional colorless and transparent amber. The Indiana Glass Company reissued Daisy in transparent dark green and opaque white in the 1960s. The 2 Sandwich patterns were reissued about the same time in transparent blue-green, red, dark green, and opaque white. Daisy is one of the least expensive Depression-glass patterns, although amber examples are often nearly twice as expensive as colorless. The later colors, made in the 1960s, are not very popular and are inexpensive.

213 Depression delphite plate

Description
Circular plate with plain center and *pressed swirled ribs around border.* Scalloped rim. Color: opaque light blue; transparent pink, brilliant blue-green, amber, or light blue. *Variations:* may have plain rim; center may have concentric circles.

Type and Dimensions
Machine-pressed in mold for pattern and shape. Diameter: 6¾".

Locality and Period
Jeannette Glass Company, Jeannette, Pennsylvania. c. 1936–38. Similar patterns by Federal, Anchor-Hocking, Macbeth-Evans, Indiana, Hazel-Atlas, and other midwestern firms. c. 1925–40.

Matching Glassware
Set with tumblers, pitcher, cups and saucers, bowls (#277), sugar bowl, creamer, butter dish, salt and pepper shakers, salad and dinner plates, sandwich plate, platter, candy dishes, vases, coasters, ashtrays, and candle holders.

Comment
Opaque light blue, called delphite, is an unusual Depression-glass color made exclusively by the Jeannette Glass Company. Complete delphite tableware sets appear only in the Petal Swirl pattern illustrated and 2 others called Floral and Cherry Blossom. The only similar color in Depression glassware is an opaque powder blue by McKee Glass Company in the Laurel pattern.

Hints for Collectors
In this pattern, delphite pieces are nearly twice as expensive as those in pink, but generally less than those in ultramarine (#277), a vivid blue-green also made by Jeannette. The Westmoreland, Indiana, McKee, and United States Glass companies all made lighter or darker shades of blue-green glass.

Petal Swirl pattern

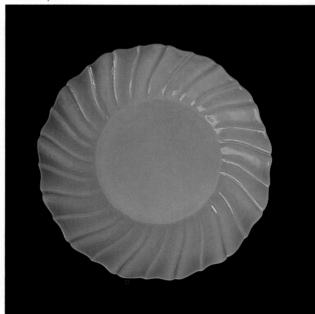

Early midwestern ribbed plate

Description
Circular plate with *molded broken-swirl ribs radiating from
center, swirling to right.* Folded rim. Pontil mark rough. Color:
transparent amber, greenish-aquamarine, or colorless; rarely
transparent purple. *Variations:* may lack second set of ribs;
sometimes molded diamond pattern.

Type and Dimensions
Blown in vertically ribbed mold, then swirled and expanded.
Second set of ribs made by redipping in same mold. Nonlead
glass. Diameter: 6⅛–6⅜″.

Locality and Period
Probably Ohio: Zanesville, Kent, and Mantua. Possibly
Pittsburgh area. c. 1815–35.

Matching Glassware
Tumblers (#44), pitchers (#72), bar bottles (#113), jugs, flasks,
bowls (#274), sugar bowls, creamers, and salts (#176). Not made
as set.

Comment
Plates like this are much rarer than tumblers, pitchers, and
bottles with similar decoration and colors. Plates are inherently
more fragile than closed pieces because of their shape, and
probably fewer have survived. The plate illustrated descended in
the family of a blower employed by the Mantua Glass Works.

Hints for Collectors
Mexican glass plates made in the 1920s and 1930s have very
similar swirled ribs, but the glass is usually more bubbly and in
less brilliant shades of transparent blue, green, and amber. Only
American examples have broken-swirl ribs. It is difficult to
distinguish Mexican plates from Ohio glass that has only 1 set of
ribs; unusual shapes may be Mexican.

Chain-decorated plate

Description
Circular plate with *chain decoration and folded rim*. Pontil mark rough. Colorless.

Type and Dimensions
Free-blown, then tooled into shape. Applied threading pinched together at intervals to form chain. Lead glass. Diameter: 7⅜–7⅝″.

Locality and Period
Boston area: Thomas Cains's South Boston Flint Glass Works and Phoenix Glass Works, c. 1812–35; and New England Glass Company, c. 1818–35.

Matching Glassware
Pitchers, decanters (#104), sugar bowls, creamers (#125), bowls, lamps, and candlesticks. Not made as set.

Comment
This chain decoration is found on both Venetian and English glass of the 16th century. In this country, it seems to have been made chiefly in New England and is usually associated with Thomas Cains's factories. Cains probably became familiar with this decoration in the English glasshouses where he worked before coming to the United States. Other factories, however, may have used this simple decoration as well.

Hints for Collectors
Plates with chain decoration are much less common than decanters and pitchers, but usually are less expensive.

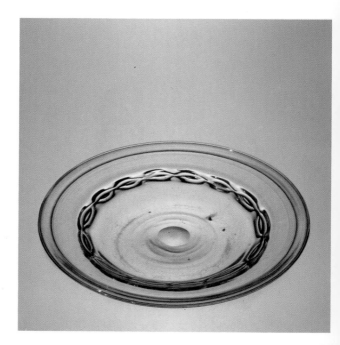

Depression serving tray

Description
Circular tray has *pressed square panels* around border; panels *with abstract floral pattern* alternate with plain panels. Wedge-shaped plain panels radiate from center, which has matching floral design. *C-shaped handle on each side.* Color: transparent pink, green, or yellow; opaque light blue. *Variations:* plain square panels and wedge-shaped panels filled with pansy pattern (Doric and Pansy); this variation in transparent pink, brilliant blue-green, or colorless.

Type and Dimensions
Machine-pressed in mold for pattern and shape. Diameter: 10⅜".

Locality and Period
Jeannette Glass Company, Jeannette, Pennsylvania. c. 1935–38. Similar patterns by Federal, Macbeth-Evans, Hocking, Indiana, and other midwestern firms. c. 1925–40.

Matching Glassware
Set with tumblers, pitchers, bowls, sugar bowl, creamer, salt and pepper shakers, salad, dinner, and grill plates, cups and saucers, sherbets, oval platter, and other serving dishes.

Comment
Pale transparent colors like green and pink are typical of Depression glass. The opaque pale blue, called delphite, comes in only a few shapes in the Doric pattern illustrated and is somewhat higher priced than the transparent pink and green.

Hints for Collectors
The Doric and Pansy variation was made from 1937 to 1938 in fewer forms with different shapes and colors. Prices for both patterns are about the same, except for some very rare pieces in Doric and Pansy that cost more, such as the salt and pepper shakers, sugar bowl, creamer, and covered butter dish.

Doric pattern

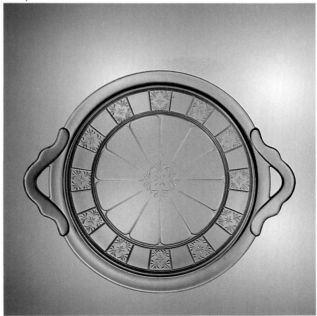

Description
Octagonal, slightly curving plate with pressed heart-shaped handle at center. Plain wedge-shaped panels radiate from center. Color: transparent light or dark green, pink, yellow, amber, light blue, blue-green, dark blue, red, black, or colorless. *Variations:* usually circular; handle may be triangular or oval. Many stylized floral and geometric patterns, including Block Optic, Cameo, Diamond Quilted, Mayfair (#15), and Spiral.

Type and Dimensions
Machine-pressed in mold for pattern and shape. Diameter: 12¼–12½″.

Locality and Period
The Midwest: Jeannette Glass Company, Federal Glass Company, Indiana Glass Company, Macbeth-Evans Glass Company, McKee Glass Company, Paden City Glass Company, and Hocking Glass Company. c. 1925–50.

Comment
These handled serving plates are usually listed as "sandwich servers" in glass catalogues. They were one of the many new shapes created in the 1930s with the advent of the pressing machine. Most were made in patterns that matched other Depression-glass tableware. The plain server illustrated is somewhat unusual not only for its lack of a pattern, but also for its octagonal form and heart-shaped handle. Tidbit servers with 2 and 3 tiers of plates in various sizes were also made with a central rod handle.

Hints for Collectors
Servers like this that do not match any particular pattern are often inexpensive and will go with a variety of different designs if the color is right.

Depression square plate

Description
Square plate with rounded cutout corners, each with central scallop. *Overall pressed delicate scroll pattern;* diamond-shaped ornament encircles cross at center. Color: transparent light green, pink, amber, light blue, or colorless. *Variations:* several scroll patterns including Patrician (#15) and Horseshoe.

Type and Dimensions
Machine-pressed in mold for pattern and shape. Diameter: 10¼".

Locality and Period
Federal Glass Company, Columbus, Ohio. c. 1932–39. Similar patterns by Hocking, Indiana, Jeannette, McKee and Macbeth-Evans. c. 1925–40.

Matching Glassware
Set with tumblers, pitchers, individual and serving bowls, sugar bowl, creamer, butter dish, salt and pepper shakers, cups and saucers, sherbets, grill plates, cake plate, platter, gravy boat and platter, relish plate, cookie jar, wooden lazy Susan with 7 hot-dish coasters, and candlesticks.

Comment
The matching lazy Susan, with a wooden frame and 7 glass inserts, is an example of some of the unique shapes in Depression glass. Tidbit servers with 2 or 3 tiers and relish dishes in metal frames are other novelty items found in just a small number of patterns.

Hints for Collectors
In 1976 the Federal Glass Company reissued the illustrated Madrid pattern in transparent amber and added the number "76" to the design. Examine amber examples carefully to make sure you are not purchasing a 1976 piece. No other colors have been reproduced in this pattern.

Madrid pattern

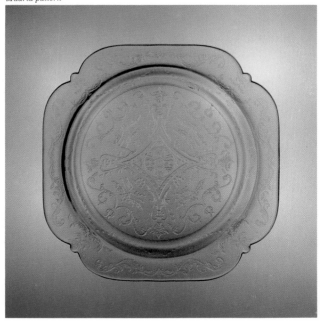

219 Depression place setting

Description
5-piece set: (below) grill plate; (opposite) cup, saucer, bowl, and small plate. *Overall pressed pattern of dogwood blossoms.* Circular grill plate divided into 3 sections, with wide flat rim; cylindrical cup with ear-shaped handle and circular saucer; shallow circular cereal or fruit bowl with slightly flared rim; circular bread-and-butter plate. Color: transparent pink, green, yellow, or colorless; translucent white and cream.

Type and Dimensions
Machine-pressed in mold for pattern and shape. Grill plate diameter: 10½″. Small plate diameters: 5⅞″, 6″. Bowl diameter: 5⅝″; height: 1⅜″. Cup rim diameter: 3⅝″; height: 2½″.

Locality and Period
Macbeth-Evans Glass Company, Charleroi, Pennsylvania. c. 1929–30.

Matching Glassware
Set with tumblers, pitchers, bowls in several sizes, sugar bowl, creamer, salt and pepper shakers, cups and saucers, sherbets, oval platter, cake plate, and tiered trays in several sizes.

Comment
Machine-pressed glass introduced a new range of colors and shapes. Glassware could now be produced more rapidly and inexpensively than ever before. Table settings such as this were made in hundreds of Depression-glass patterns. Goblets and tumblers for iced tea, water, or milk, juice glasses, and smaller bowls could all be added to a basic place setting. Stemware for alcoholic beverages went out of fashion during Prohibition (1919–33), but the new glass, made under controlled temperatures, was less brittle and could be used for hot liquids. The divided grill plate was also introduced during the Depression era. These

Dogwood pattern

divisions not only separated various foods, but also had the effect of making small portions look larger. Transparent pastels, such as pale yellow, blue, or green, became popular, as did rich dark hues like deep red, blue, and black. The pattern illustrated was originally marketed without a name; it is known today as Dogwood or Wild Rose.

Hints for Collectors

Depression glass has only recently achieved collectible status among glass collectors. In the late 1960s and early 1970s, it was sold at house sales and flea markets, but a recent spate of books on the subject, as well as the formation of several collectors' organizations, has elevated machine-pressed glass to a position of greater respectability. Some antique shops now specialize in ware of the 1920s and 1930s. This glass is also available through specialized mail-order dealers who advertise in collectors' publications. Depression glass has several advantages for inexperienced collectors. Many of the companies that made it are still in business, or were until recently, and most of the information needed to identify the patterns is still available. In addition, Depression glass is quite inexpensive since it was made in huge quantities relatively recently. A large collection can be assembled at modest expense.

Covered Bowls and Butter Dishes

Although covered bowls were common tableware in Europe during the 17th and 18th centuries, they did not become fashionable in the United States until at least 1825. The first American covered bowls were made of plain free-blown or mold-blown glass, and occasionally were cut or engraved. As with most tableware, the number and variety of shapes greatly increased after the invention of the pressing machine in the 1820s. Pressed molds insured that the covers and bowls would fit together properly. It is probably for this reason that most covered bowls are pressed.

Some covered bowls were made in the earliest lacy-pattern pressed glass, but few are found today. By the second half of the 19th century, covered bowls were commonly used for serving vegetables and, probably, desserts. About this time, a new form was added, the covered butter dish, called a nappy. The first catalogues of the 1850s advertised pressed-glass table sets with matching sugar bowl, creamer, spoon holder, and covered nappy (#146).

Butter dishes of the 1870s and 1880s were deep bowls with shallow covers. During the 1890s, the form evolved into a plate with a high domed cover, and a greater variety of shapes began to appear, from squares and rectangles (#245) to animal shapes like ducks (#237, #239), roosters (#238), fish (#240), and clam shells (#232). Patriotic themes, such as the Liberty Bell (#227) and the United States shield (#226), as well as helmet- or stove-shaped dishes also enjoyed great popularity. These unusual shapes and realistic animal, floral, and fruit patterns are all characteristic of covered bowls of the last quarter of the 19th century. Opalescent, Carnival, and Depression glass were made in similar shapes, usually with matching sets of tableware. Art-glass and cut-glass butter dishes are rare, however, possibly because they are more fragile and tend to chip easily around the rims of the bowls and covers.

Description
Domed cover with overall pattern of large depressed circles; round faceted knob. Plain circular plate has flaring rim. Pontil mark polished. Color: *cover transparent amber shading to deep red near rim; plate reddish.* Variations: cover sometimes diamond-patterned or plain. May have paper label with "NEGW/ AMBERINA" or acid-stamped "LIBBEY" on base.

Type and Dimensions
Cover blown in mold for pattern, then tooled into shape. Applied, tooled knob cut with facets after annealing. Plate free-blown and tooled into shape. Height: 7⅛–8″. Plate diameter: 9–9½″.

Locality and Period
Massachusetts: New England Glass Works, Cambridge, c. 1883–88; Mt. Washington Glass Company, New Bedford, c. 1883–95. Libbey Glass Company, Toledo, Ohio. c. 1917.

Matching Glassware
Tumblers, punch cups, pitchers, butter dish, sugar bowls and creamers (#150), bowls, toothpick holders, cruets, vase (#332), and centerpieces (#261). Not made as set.

Comment
The cheese dish was a new form that became popular in the 1880s and 1890s. These serving pieces are larger than butter dishes. Most were made in expensive art and cut glass. The cheese dish illustrated is in the typical Amberina colors.

Hints for Collectors
Imitations of Amberina glass made in Europe during the late 19th century are paler than the true Amberina colors and often have enameled decoration. Modern Amberina glass comes in shapes unlike the old ones and in strong harsh colors.

Heisey butter dish

Description
Domed cover with 8 plain flat pressed panels around sides; egg-shaped knob has similar panels. Circular plate with flange has circles around border and scalloped edge. *Plate base has* "H" trademark in diamond. Colorless. *Variations:* usually 6 or 8 panels. Base may lack trademark.

Type and Dimensions
Cover and plate pressed in separate molds for pattern and shape. Nonlead glass. Height: 6½–6¾". Plate diameter: 8½–8¾".

Locality and Period
A. H. Heisey & Company, Newark, Ohio, and other Ohio and West Virginia firms. c. 1900–10.

Matching Glassware
Set with sugar bowl, creamer, spoon holder, and bowls.

Comment
A. H. Heisey & Company was a prolific manufacturer of tableware from the late 19th century to the 1950s. Its pressed patterns are typically midwestern in shape and usually quite plain. In the 1930s and 1940s, Heisey made mold-blown stemware (#34), some with engraved and etched decoration. The company also produced a line of glass animals.

Hints for Collectors
Plain inexpensive designs like the Colonial pattern illustrated were popular around 1900. Since A. H. Heisey was in business until 1958 and did not limit its glassware production, most lines are still available at prices comparable to those for new glassware. The pieces are not always marked, however, and unless one is familiar with the many Heisey patterns, they may be hard to identify. One glass-collectors' organization is devoted entirely to the work of this company.

Colonial pattern

Description
Domed cover with alternating panels of pressed diamonds and upside-down hearts, with circle at center of each heart; faceted knob has circle in each panel and sunburst on top. Matching plate has scalloped edge. Colorless. *Variations:* many brilliant-cut glass motifs, such as diamonds and hobstars. This pattern often with gilt rim (#223).

Type and Dimensions
Cover and plate pressed in separate molds for pattern and shape. Nonlead glass. Height: 6–6¼". Plate diameter: 8–8¼".

Locality and Period
Tarentum Glass Company, Tarentum, Pennsylvania, and other firms in western Pennsylvania, West Virginia, Ohio, and Indiana. c. 1898–1905.

Matching Glassware
Set with wine and cordial glasses, goblets, tumblers, pitcher, bowls (3", 6", 9"), sugar bowl, creamer, salt and pepper shakers, plates (6", 10"), syrup jug, and cruet.

Comment
The Heart with Thumbprint butter dish illustrated was produced by the Tarentum company from 1898 to 1899. It is typical of the heavy pressed patterns of the very end of the 19th century, in contrast to the thinner pressed patterns of the 1870s and 1880s. The butter dish also became larger than it had been in the previous 2 decades.

Hints for Collectors
These late imitation cut-glass patterns have only recently appealed to glass collectors. Most are often very inexpensive, although the popular pattern illustrated commands a somewhat higher price.

Heart with Thumbprint pattern

Gilt-trim pressed butter dish

Description
Domed cover with alternating panels of pressed diamonds and depressed circles; matching pattern on knob with sunburst on top. Plate has central flower and depressed circles around border. *Gilt band around base of knob, rim of cover, and scalloped edge of plate.* Colorless. *Variations:* may lack gilt trim. Many other patterns with naturalistic or abstract motifs in transparent green, blue, purple, amber, or red.

Type and Dimensions
Cover and plate pressed in separate molds for pattern and shape. Gilding applied after annealing and fired on. Nonlead glass. Height: 5½–5¾". Plate diameter: 7¾–8".

Locality and Period
Western Pennsylvania, West Virginia, Ohio, and Indiana. c. 1890–1905.

Matching Glassware
Set with sugar bowl, creamer, salt and pepper shakers, serving bowls in several sizes, spoon holder, water set, and berry set.

Comment
Pressed glass companies began to use gilding at the end of the 19th century, perhaps influenced by the manufacturers of art glass. Gilding most often appears on opaque colored glass, such as custard glass (#230), and on some vividly colored transparent pieces in blue, purple, and green. It is found less often on colorless glass as seen here.

Hints for Collectors
Gilt trim is usually fired on after the glass anneals, and thus it is fairly permanent. Years of washing, however, often leave their mark. If the rim has not been properly fired, the gilt will wear off very easily.

Engraved pressed butter dish

Description

Cylindrical domed cover with engraved flower sprigs around top; *pressed circular knobs around upper edge; spherical faceted knob.* Plate fluted around edge, with circular knobs around base; crosshatches within circle at center. Colorless. *Variations:* row of circular knobs around plate edge may replace fluting; sides of cover may be engraved; sometimes plain cover. Other engravings include more elaborate flowers as well as butterflies or swans; rarely red-stained.

Type and Dimensions

Cover and plate pressed in separate molds for pattern and shape. Plate fluted before annealing. Copper-wheel engraved after annealing. Nonlead glass. Height: 5⅞–6″. Plate diameter: 8–8¼″.

Locality and Period

Western Pennsylvania, West Virginia, Ohio, and Indiana. c. 1885–1900.

Matching Glassware

Large set with stemware, tumblers, mugs, pitcher, covered and uncovered bowls, sugar bowl, creamer, salt and pepper shakers, spoon holder, celery vase, and other serving dishes.

Comment

The pattern illustrated, called Baby Thumbprint by collectors, was originally issued as the Dakota pattern by the Pittsburgh firms Daniel C. Ripley & Company and Doyle & Company. Many similar plain patterns of the 1880s have simple sprig engravings. The butter dish shown here is in hotel-weight glass, which is somewhat heavier than home weight.

Hints for Collectors

Only a few patterns were made in 2 weights. Both types are relatively inexpensive.

Baby Thumbprint pattern

Late 19th-century pressed butter dish

Description
Octagonal form has deep dish with octagonal stippled flange and flat stippled handle at each end; beaded edge on both flange and handles; pressed sunburst on base. Thin walls. Stippled cover has beaded edge and octagonal flange; mushroom-shaped knob with ray pattern and beaded base. Colorless. *Variations:* may have circular foot.

Type and Dimensions
Dish and cover pressed in separate molds for pattern and shape. Nonlead glass. Height: 3¾″. Length: 8″.

Locality and Period
Bryce Brothers, Pittsburgh. c. 1882–91.

Comment
This butter dish appears in an 1882 advertisement of Bryce Brothers as "Albion butter, plain" along with a footed dish called "Albion butter, footed." Both forms apparently were made until Bryce Brothers was absorbed by the United States Glass Company in 1891. No other forms in this pattern were ever issued. Bryce produced a number of individual butter dishes (#226) as well as a farmyard assortment similar to dishes by Challinor, Taylor & Company (#238, #239). The pattern illustrated shows the revival of stippling in midwestern factories during the 1870s and 1880s.

Hints for Collectors
Because this pattern did not come in other shapes, it has not been popular with collectors and is not expensive. The Albion butter, however, would blend well with other stippled patterns of the period and could be substituted if a matching butter dish for a particular set could not be found.

Albion pattern

Banner butter dish

Description
Shield-shaped cover and deep dish with plain sides and shield-shaped flange. Pressed rosette-and-hobnail pattern underneath flange and on base. Cover with plain and rosette-patterned stripes; rosette-and-hobnail pattern covering area perpendicular to stripes. Shield-shaped knob with stars and stripes. Colorless.

Type and Dimensions
Cover and dish pressed in separate molds for pattern and shape. Nonlead glass. Height: 3¾–4″. Length: 8–8¼″.

Locality and Period
Bryce Brothers, Pittsburgh. c. 1882–91.

Comment
At first glance this butter dish looks as if it might have been made for the United States Centennial celebrations in 1876. The design was clearly inspired by the shield on the Great Seal of the United States, with the rosette-and-hobnail design (a version of the popular Daisy and Button pattern) arranged to represent the stripes on the shield. This dish was called the Banner butter in an 1882 advertisement of Bryce Brothers. The same ad included the Albion butter (#225), the Avon and Lorne butters, and several other patterns, but none were made with matching tableware. The Banner dish was probably manufactured until the Bryce glassworks were absorbed into the United States Glass Company in 1891.

Hints for Collectors
Butter dishes in unusual shapes are interesting to collect as novelties. Other popular shapes included a flatiron, a wood-fired cooking stove, and a helmet.

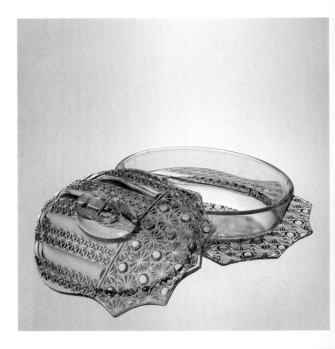

Liberty Bell butter dish

Description
Conical domed cover with pressed bell design, inscribed
"DECLARATION OF INDEPENDENCE," "100 YEARS AGO," and "1776–
1876." Conical knob has flat circular top. Shallow dish has
scalloped flange. Colorless.

Type and Dimensions
Cover and dish pressed in separate molds for pattern and shape.
Nonlead glass. Height: 4½". Plate diameter: 7½".

Locality and Period
Gillinder & Sons, Philadelphia. c. 1875–80.

Matching Glassware
Large set with goblets, pitcher, sugar bowl, creamer, plates,
compotes, pickle and sauce dishes, plates, platters, salt shaker,
celery vase, spoon holder, and toy set.

Comment
Gillinder & Sons of Philadelphia took advantage of their
proximity to the site of the Centennial Exposition to erect a
special glass factory on the exhibition grounds, where they made
and sold souvenirs to visitors. Most pieces in the Liberty Bell
pattern were colorless, except for a platter that occasionally
came in opaque white. Gillinder made many pressed-glass
novelties, including mugs and salt shakers in the shape of the
Liberty Bell, paperweights in the form of the Philadelphia
Memorial Hall, and busts of George Washington and Abraham
Lincoln.

Hints for Collectors
The price of Gillinder's Centennial souvenirs has greatly
increased since the Bicentennial. Reproductions of the Liberty
Bell pattern pieces were marketed, some with "1976" and some
with the original "1876."

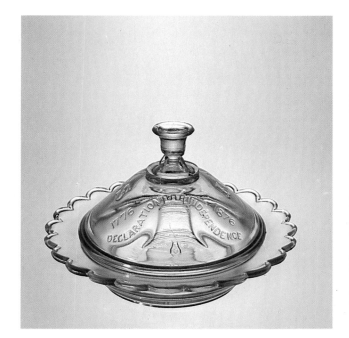

Opalescent pressed butter dish

Description
Conical domed cover has pressed panels with closely spaced ribbing in drapery design separated by vertical ribs. Round knob has similar pattern. Matching plate with scalloped edge and ribbing around flange. Color: *colorless and opalescent* white, blue, yellow, or green. Marked "N" or "N" on base; sometimes "Northwood" in script.

Type and Dimensions
Cover and plate pressed in separate molds for pattern and shape. Partially reheated for opalescent color. Height: 6″. Plate diameter: 8″.

Locality and Period
Northwood Glass Company, Wheeling, West Virginia. c. 1910–19.

Matching Glassware
Set with tumblers, pitcher, sugar bowl, creamer, large and small bowls, covered bowls, spoon holder, rose bowl, and vase.

Comment
Harry Northwood was one of the most innovative glassmakers of the late 19th century, and his factories introduced many new colors and pattern styles. Northwood made iridescent Carnival, opalescent (#85), pink slag (#154), custard (#230), and a variety of transparent colored glasses. Collectors call the pattern illustrated Ribbed Drape.

Hints for Collectors
In the last few years Northwood glass has become a popular collectible and marked pieces are usually quite expensive. The opalescent ware is not as expensive as custard glass and pink slag glass, probably because more opalescent glass was made.

Ribbed Drape pattern

Holly Amber butter dish

Description
Conical domed cover has plain vertical panels alternating with
panels with *pressed meandering holly pattern;* panels outlined in
rows of beads. Plain conical knob on cover. Matching plate has
beaded scalloped flange with matching panels. Color: *plain
panels opalescent white; patterned panels transparent amber;*
rarely completely colorless.

Type and Dimensions
Cover and plate pressed in separate molds for pattern and shape.
Partially reheated for opalescent color. Height: 6¼″. Plate
diameter: 8″.

Locality and Period
Indiana Tumbler & Goblet Company, Greentown, Indiana.
January–June, 1903.

Matching Glassware
Large set with tumblers, mugs, pitcher, plates, bowls, cake
stand, compote, sugar bowl, creamer, pickle jar, salt and pepper
shakers, spoon holder, syrup jar, cruet, toothpick holder, and
tray.

Comment
Glass chemist Jacob Rosenthal introduced this heat-sensitive
Golden Agate glass in 1903. Collectors now call it Holly Amber.
It was an immediate success and would probably have been made
in a variety of patterns, but the factory burned down after only 6
months of production and went out of business.

Hints for Collectors
Holly Amber glass, like pink slag (#154), is very rare and much
more expensive than other glass produced at the same time. A
toothpick holder in Holly Amber was reproduced in the 1970s,
but it is much browner overall than the original examples.

230 Custard-glass butter dish

Description
Domed cover has raised C-scroll pattern interspersed with flower sprigs around sides; scroll handle. Circular plate has 4 scroll feet and scalloped edge. Color: *opaque cream* with gilt-decorated handle, plate edge, and feet. *Variations:* several elaborate designs with shell, floral, or scroll motifs. Some dishes lack gilt decoration.

Type and Dimensions
Cover and plate pressed in separate molds for pattern and shape. Gilt decoration applied after annealing and fixed by firing. Height: 6⅛–6¼″. Plate diameter: 7¾–8″.

Locality and Period
Northwood Glass factories of Indiana, Pennsylvania, and Wheeling, West Virginia. c. 1898–1915.

Matching Glassware
Set with tumblers, pitcher, sugar bowl, creamer, bowls, spoon holder, salt and pepper shakers, compote, cruet, and toothpick holder.

Comment
Harry Northwood, son of a well-known English decorator, came to the United States in the 1880s and worked for several companies before founding factories of his own. It is usually difficult to distinguish the products made at the various factories.

Hints for Collectors
While not as rare as pink slag glass (#154), custard glass is much sought after by collectors. Custard glass came in many more patterns, including the Louis XV pattern illustrated. There are several reproductions, and Fenton Art Glass Company has even copied the "N" trademark. Reproductions are generally lighter in color and have thinner walls.

Louis XV pattern

Simple pressed butter dish

Description
Round form with pressed scroll-like handle on cover. Circular
bowl with 3 scroll feet. Colorless. *Variations:* sometimes
engraved or acid-etched with leafy tendrils.

Type and Dimensions
Cover and bowl pressed in separate molds for pattern and shape.
Nonlead glass. Height: 5″. Diameter: 6¼″.

Locality and Period
King, Son & Company's Cascade Glassworks, Pittsburgh.
c. 1875–85.

Matching Glassware
Set with sugar bowl, creamer, spoon holder, footed plates,
covered plate, and footed bowls in several sizes, uncovered and
covered dishes.

Comment
When King patented this pattern in 1875, the firm called it
Centennial more because of the year than the design. This was
not unusual. Nearly every glass company making tableware
issued a special Centennial pattern, and only a few patterns have
patriotic motifs. The plain design illustrated was particularly
well suited for engraved decoration. Some decorations may have
been acid-etched instead. This relatively new technique was used
by some firms as an inexpensive substitute for engraving.

Hints for Collectors
This pattern is not well known and is one of the least expensive
of all Centennial patterns (#227, #243). Because it was made in a
limited range of shapes, it has not been popular with collectors.

Centennial pattern

Description
Clamshell-shaped bowl and cover with textured clamshell-like surface. *Snail-shell finial on cover and 3 clamshell feet on base.* Colorless.

Type and Dimensions
Cover and bowl pressed in separate molds for pattern and shape. Nonlead glass. Height: 4½–4¾″. Length: 7⅛–7⅜″.

Locality and Period
Western Pennsylvania, West Virginia, Ohio, and Indiana. c. 1885–1900.

Comment
This small covered dish, or nappy, may have been intended as a butter dish since it is about the right size. The cover must have been awkward to use and was probably easily broken. The clamshell shape was part of the wave of animal motifs that became popular in the 1880s, such as the Atterbury duck (#237) and fish (#240), and the Challinor, Taylor & Company hen, rooster (#239), and duck (#239). On some animal dishes, parts of the glass were originally painted in naturalistic colors, but in most cases the paint has worn off. The clamshell shape was probably never painted, however.

Hints for Collectors
The clamshell dish is the least known of the animal dishes, and because its manufacturer has not been identified, it is less expensive than most of the others. Animal dishes were usually sold as novelties and were not made as part of a set.

Realistic-style pressed butter dish

Description
Round bowl and domed cover with *overall stippling. 3 plain oval medallions outlined with beading on bowl and cover.* Acorn-and-oak-leaf finial. Colorless. *Variations:* medallions may enclose pressed grape clusters (Beaded Grape Medallion) or acorn-and-oak-leaf design (Beaded Acorn).

Type and Dimensions
Cover and bowl pressed in separate molds for pattern and shape. Nonlead glass. Height: 4″. Diameter: 6″.

Locality and Period
Boston Silver Glass Company, Cambridge, Massachusetts. c. 1869–71.

Matching Glassware
Large set with stemware, pitcher, sugar bowl, creamer, covered compotes on high and low stems, celery vase, spoon holder, small plates, salts in 3 styles, and relish, sauce, and honey dishes.

Comment
Little is known about the Boston Silver Glass Company, which apparently specialized in mercury, or silvered, glass in the 1850s and 1860s (#171). Alonzo Young, an employee of the firm, patented the mold for the oval compote in this pattern and its variants in 1869. Apparently the firm made pressed glass for only a few years before it closed.

Hints for Collectors
Stippled patterns like the Beaded Mirror illustrated were popular in the 1870s, and are relatively easy to recognize. Unlike the earlier lacy-pattern stippled glass (#246), the later stippled patterns are simpler and not as delicate.

Beaded Mirror pattern

Abstract-style pressed butter dish

Description
Round covered dish with pressed stippled diamond-and-fan design. Round stippled acorn finial. Colorless.

Type and Dimensions
Cover and bowl pressed in separate molds for pattern and shape. Nonlead glass. Height: 4¼–4½″. Diameter: 6⅛–6⅜″.

Locality and Period
Western Pennsylvania, West Virginia, and Ohio. c. 1870–80.

Matching Glassware
Set with cordial glasses, goblets, eggcups, water pitcher, covered and uncovered compotes, creamer, sugar bowl, oval dish, sauce dish, and spoon holder.

Comment
The use of stippling, which had been common in the earliest pressed glass, went out of fashion in the middle of the 19th century. By the late 1860s and early 1870s, glass manufacturers searching for new decorative motifs revived stippling in a variety of patterns. The butter dish illustrated was made by M'Kee & Brothers in Pittsburgh; its production may have resumed after 1889 when the company moved to Jeannette, Pennsylvania. Collectors call this pattern Fan with Diamond.

Hints for Collectors
The late stippled patterns are fairly easy to distinguish from earlier ones. Late stippling occurs in large areas either by itself or combined with 1 or 2 simple motifs as seen here. Early stippled-glass patterns are much busier, combining a variety of motifs, and the glass is heavier.

Fan with Diamond pattern

Late 19th-century pressed butter dish

Description
Round bowl and domed cover with overall pressed double-loop pattern. Row of tiny sawteeth around bowl and rim of cover. Cylindrical knob. Flat base. Colorless. *Variations:* may have plain circular foot.

Type and Dimensions
Cover and bowl pressed in separate molds for pattern and shape. Nonlead glass. Height: 5½–5¾". Diameter: 6½–6¾".

Locality and Period
Pittsburgh: Bryce, Walker & Company, c. 1875–91; United States Glass Company, c. 1891–1900.

Matching Glassware
Large set with wine, claret, and cordial glasses, goblets, tumblers, pitcher, sugar bowl, creamer, plates, footed dishes, salt shaker, celery vase, spoon holder, covered and uncovered compotes, custard cup and saucer, honey and pickle dishes, and cruet.

Comment
This pattern is known by collectors as Ribbon Candy, but it was originally marketed simply as Bryce. Even after the Bryce factory was taken over by the United States Glass Company in 1891, the pattern continued to be issued under the name "Bryce."

Hints for Collectors
Ribbon Candy has never been reproduced. The pattern was made over a long period and comes in a wide variety of tableware shapes. Today it is readily available, inexpensive, and a good choice for pattern glass collectors.

Ribbon Candy pattern

Early geometric-style pressed nappy

Description
Round covered dish with *overall pressed raised diamond
pattern.* Conical acorn finial and flat circular base. *Rims of bowl
and cover serrated to interlock.* Color: opaque white or colorless;
rarely transparent blue. *Variations:* diamonds may be smaller or
with flattened points.

Type and Dimensions
Cover and bowl pressed in separate molds for pattern and shape.
Lead glass; variants nonlead glass. Height: 4⅝–4⅞″. Diameter:
5½–5¾″.

Locality and Period
New England Glass Company, Cambridge, Massachusetts.
c. 1855–75. Bryce Brothers, Pittsburgh; Gillinder & Sons,
Philadelphia; and possibly midwestern firms. c. 1870–85.

Matching Glassware
Large set in colorless glass with stemware, tumblers, pitcher,
decanter, water bottle, covered and uncovered bowls, honey
dish, and cake plate. In opaque white or colorless: set with sugar
bowl, creamer, spoon holder, celery vase, compotes, eggcups,
salts, and sauce dishes.

Comment
Collectors call this popular pattern Sawtooth because of its
serrated edges. The New England Glass Company named it
Mitre Diamond, Bryce called it Deep Diamond, and Gillinder
dubbed it Diamond.

Hints for Collectors
Goblets, tumblers, and wineglasses have been reproduced in
opaque pink glass, a color that was never made originally. Pink
sherbets have also been marketed. Westmoreland reproduced
the dish shown and one on a high stem, but both are marked.

Sawtooth pattern

Atterbury duck dish

Description
Cover and bowl shaped like a duck with sculpted feathers on head, wings, and tail. Marked on base "PAT. MAR. 15, 1887." Color: opaque white with purple head and yellow eyes; also opaque purple, blue, or green, or opaque white with blue-green head. *Variations:* sometimes not marked. Head and body may be the same color or contrasting colors.

Type and Dimensions
Cover and bowl pressed in separate molds for pattern and shape. Purple glass dropped into mold first, followed by opaque white. Eyes glued on after annealing. Height: 4¹⁵⁄₁₆″. Length: 10⅞″.

Locality and Period
Atterbury & Company, Pittsburgh. c. 1887–93.

Comment
The Atterbury duck is one of the most popular of the animal covered dishes that were fashionable on American tables in the 1880s. This particular duck was probably the first animal design and apparently the only bird patented, so it is easily identified. Atterbury & Company manufactured a great number of new designs in the last 3 decades of the 19th century, including dishes shaped like fish (#240), rabbits, foxes, lions, hens, chicks and eggs, owls, cats, and bulls' and boars' heads. Because so much opaque white mold-blown and pressed glass was made there, the Atterbury factory was called the White House.

Hints for Collectors
The Atterbury duck was reproduced in the 1960s, but without a patent date on the base. Reproductions can be found in solid white or purple, with a purple or white head or body, or in marbled purple glass. Not all originals are marked.

Rooster butter dish

Description
Rooster-shaped cover pressed with details of feathers, tail, and comb. Oval bowl has pressed basket-weave design and flat base. Color: opaque white, pale blue, marbled purple, white, or colorless with transparent red eyes. *Variations:* hen figure may replace rooster. Bird may be painted naturalistic colors.

Type and Dimensions
Cover and bowl pressed in separate molds for pattern and shape. Eyes glued on and painted after annealing. Nonlead glass. Height: 6¾–7". Length: 9–9¼".

Locality and Period
Challinor, Taylor & Company, Ltd., Tarentum, Pennsylvania. c. 1885–91. United States Glass Company, Pittsburgh. c. 1891–1900.

Comment
Challinor, Taylor & Company created a large number of opaque white animal covered dishes, which were advertised as a "Farm Yard Assortment." They included this rooster, the variant hen, and an opaque white swan dish and a fish-shaped pickle dish. The company also made pitchers in the shape of a dog, a bull's head, and an owl.

Hints for Collectors
The rooster illustrated has lost its eyes and is therefore worth less than an intact example. Many reproductions of the hen and rooster dishes have been made in opaque white and colored glass since the 1950s. Some are marked "WG" for the Westmoreland Glass Company or "K" for the Kemple Glass Works. Unmarked reproductions are difficult to distinguish from original examples.

Duck butter dish

Description

Duck-shaped cover pressed with details of wings, feathers, and tail. Oval bowl has straight sides and flange with wavy lines simulating water. Pressed sunburst on base. Color: colorless with bluish cast or opaque white. *Variations:* eyes may be painted opaque, naturalistic colors; sometimes made without eyes.

Type and Dimensions

Cover and bowl pressed in separate molds for pattern and shape. Eyes glued on and painted after annealing. Nonlead glass. Height: 5–5¼″. Length: 9–9¼″.

Locality and Period

Challinor, Taylor & Company, Ltd., Tarentum, Pennsylvania. c. 1884–91. United States Glass Company, Pittsburgh. c. 1891–1900.

Comment

Animal-shaped bottles and containers appeared as early as the 1850s and 1860s. The Boston & Sandwich Glass Company, for example, made a bear-shaped jar in the 1860s that was probably used for bear grease. Animal-shaped tableware, however, did not appear in glass until after the Centennial, and the shapes remained popular until about 1905. Covered dishes like this duck and the rooster (#238) were usually sold with extra eyes to replace the originals, which were likely to fall out.

Hints for Collectors

This duck butter dish was reproduced in opaque white glass by the Westmoreland Glass Company of Grapeville, Pennsylvania. The first reproductions made in the 1950s had only paper labels, but recent ones have an impressed "WG" for Westmoreland Glass.

Fish butter dish

Description
Circular covered dish with *pressed pattern of intertwined fish on cover;* shell-shaped finial. Bowl has *lattice edge* and circular base. "PAT. AUG. 1889" pressed underneath base. Color: *opaque white, with transparent red eyes.*

Type and Dimensions
Cover and bowl pressed in separate molds for pattern and shape. Eyes glued on after annealing. Height: 6½". Rim diameter: 7½".

Locality and Period
Atterbury & Company, Pittsburgh. c. 1889–93.

Matching Glassware
Pitcher and relish dish. Not made as set.

Comment
This fish covered dish was made only in opaque white glass and has the lattice edge typical of opaque white ware made in the 1880s and 1890s. Animal motifs were particularly popular in the 1880s, and Atterbury patented more animal covered dishes than any other manufacturer.

Hints for Collectors
The double-fish dish is not nearly as well known as the Atterbury duck (#237) and has never been reproduced. It is considerably less expensive. Like the duck, however, the fish have often lost their original eyes since they were only glued on when they were made. Many have been replaced, often in different colors, and this generally lowers the value of a piece.

Realistic-style butter dish

Description
Round bowl and domed cover with *4 large detailed leaves and tassel pressed on cover;* reclining-dog finial. Bowl has 2 square handles and matching leaf pattern on sides and collarlike base. Colorless. *Variations:* shape may be square with rounded corners and shell-shaped finial; variations rarely transparent blue, amber, or yellow.

Type and Dimensions
Cover and bowl pressed in separate molds for pattern and shape. Nonlead glass. Height: 6⅝". Width: 8".

Locality and Period
George Duncan & Sons, Pittsburgh. c. 1880–91.

Matching Glassware
Set in illustrated shape with creamer, sugar bowl, celery vase, sauce dish, and footed serving dish. Set in square shape with goblets, pitcher, sugar bowl, salt and pepper shakers, celery vase, spoon holder, serving and relish dishes, and tray.

Comment
The square variation was patented in 1881 by Augustus Heisey, an employee of George Duncan & Sons, probably the only firm to make this pattern. The reclining dog or shell on the cover makes it quite distinctive. This pattern appeared in a Duncan catalogue of the 1880s as No. 155, but was renamed Shell and Tassel by collectors in the 1920s. Some pieces, like the creamer and goblet, were probably interchangeable and were meant to be used with tableware sets of either shape.

Hints for Collectors
The goblet in this pattern is quite rare, and most goblets found today are reproductions made in the 1940s. No other pieces in this pattern have been reproduced, however.

Shell and Tassel pattern

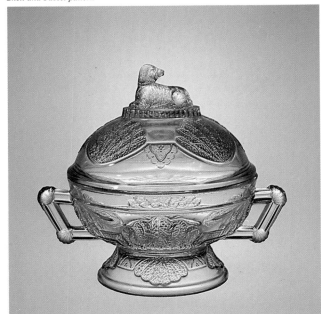

Late 19th-century pressed covered bowl

Description
Cylindrical bowl and domed cover. Pressed pattern of hobnails and stars intersecting X's around sides of bowl and on circular collarlike base. Matching cover has plain sides with pattern and X's at top and hobnails and stars on prominent knob. Color: transparent light or dark amber, blue, or colorless. *Variations:* patterns include plain (Daisy and Button, #261), with V's (Vandyke), and with thumbprint circles (Daisy and Button with Thumbprint).

Type and Dimensions
Cover and bowl pressed in separate molds for pattern and shape. Nonlead glass. Height: 9″. Diameter: 8⅛″.

Locality and Period
Richards & Hartley Company, Tarentum, Pennsylvania. c. 1888–91.

Matching Glassware
Large set with wineglasses, tumblers, mugs, goblets, pitcher, sugar bowl, creamer, butter dish, bowls, bread tray, compotes, jugs, cruet (#196), salt and pepper shakers, celery vase, spoon holder, toothpick holder, pickle jar, and lamps.

Comment
This pattern was originally marketed as Mikado, probably because it made its debut the same year as Gilbert and Sullivan's popular comic operetta. However, it was basically just another variation of the Daisy and Button pattern, and collectors call it Daisy and Button with Crossbars.

Hints for Collectors
Although the plain Daisy and Button pattern has been reproduced by many companies, this variant with crossbars has not. It was made in quantity and is readily available today.

Daisy and Button with Crossbars pattern

Realistic-style pressed covered bowl

Description
Flattened domed cover and bowl on 3 feet, joined to form collarlike base. Cover has scalloped rim and *finial of man's head with 2 faces.* Colorless.

Type and Dimensions
Cover and bowl pressed in separate molds for pattern and shape. Nonlead glass. Height: 9″. Diameter: 8¼″.

Locality and Period
Hobbs, Brockunier & Company, Wheeling, West Virginia. c. 1876–80.

Matching Glassware
Set with goblets, water pitcher, creamer, sugar bowl, covered and uncovered bowls, butter dish, celery vase, spoon holder, salt, pickle and sauce dishes, and platter.

Comment
Hobbs patented this pattern on November 21, 1876, and called the set Centennial. Almost every glass company that year produced a pattern named Centennial, and no 2 designs are alike (#227, #231). Human figures were also popular decorations on glassware (#86).

Hints for Collectors
The Bicentennial inspired new interest in Centennial patterns and prices have risen accordingly. This pattern is one of the least expensive since most collectors do not know that it was originally called Centennial. They refer to it by a variety of names, including Bearded Man and Viking, although it is not certain that the finial faces represent Vikings.

Viking pattern

Realistic-style pressed butter dish

Description
Circular domed cover has pressed *pattern of trailing strawberries and leaves and strawberry finial.* Shallow bowl has flange with matching leaf pattern, plain sides, and circular collarlike base. Color: opaque white or colorless. *Variations:* may lack flange and base.

Type and Dimensions
Cover and bowl pressed in separate molds for pattern and shape. Lead or nonlead glass. Height: 5–5¼". Diameter: 7–7¼".

Locality and Period
Pittsburgh: Bryce, Walker & Company, c. 1870–95; possibly United States Glass Company, c. 1891–95.

Matching Glassware
Set with sugar bowl, creamer, spoon holder, footed salt, goblets, covered compotes on high and low stems, eggcups, and sauce, honey, and pickle dishes.

Comment
This pattern, patented by John Bryce in 1870, was produced for a long period. Although the butter dish matches the other pieces in pattern, its shape—with the collarlike base and wide flange—resembles glassware dating from the 1890s. Probably it is a later reissue, perhaps by the United States Glass Company, which absorbed Bryce in 1891 and reissued many of the 1870 patterns in the 1890s.

Hints for Collectors
The Strawberry pattern is one of the few to come in a full range of shapes in opaque white and colorless glass. Reproductions of the 1960s and 1970s made in both types of glass are virtually indistinguishable from originals, so extreme caution is advised.

Strawberry pattern

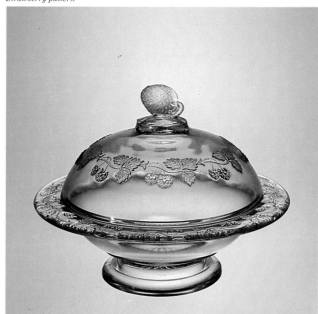

Late 19th-century pressed butter dish

Description
Rectangular dish with flange and arched cover. Cover has pressed scroll pattern on arch and plain sides; 4-lobed knob. Rectangular dish with matching scroll pattern and square pedestal base. Colorless. *Variations:* several scroll patterns.

Type and Dimensions
Cover and dish pressed in separate molds for pattern and shape. Nonlead glass. Height: 7–7¼". Length: 8–8¼".

Locality and Period
Western Pennsylvania, West Virginia, Ohio, and Indiana. c. 1880–90.

Comment
Unusual shapes like this were popular in the 1880s, when competition among midwestern manufacturers was intense and all sorts of new angular shapes were introduced. The pattern illustrated was probably made by the LaBelle Glass Company of Bridgeport, Ohio, since it is similar to several known LaBelle patterns. Many of the patterns produced in this period are anonymous today because they have never been found in catalogues or advertisements. Less than half of the several hundred patterns produced during this prolific decade have been traced to specific firms.

Hints for Collectors
Relatively plain patterns in colorless glass like this are quite inexpensive and still readily available. Except for a few rare colors, most of the pressed patterned glass of the late 19th century cost less than the highest-priced new tableware.

Lacy-pattern pressed covered bowl

Description
Rectangular covered bowl with rounded corners and scalloped flange. *Pressed pattern of S-scrolls and stylized flowers against background of fine stippling* on bowl and matching cover; D-shaped handle. Colorless. *Variations:* may have small pattern of grape clusters around rim.

Type and Dimensions
Bowl and cover pressed in separate molds for pattern and shape. Lead glass. Height: 4¹⁄₁₆″. Length: 10¼″.

Locality and Period
New England: probably Boston & Sandwich Glass Company, Sandwich, Massachusetts. c. 1835–50.

Matching Glassware
Uncovered compotes. Not made as set.

Comment
This pattern is exactly the same as that on porcelain dishes made at the royal factory in Meissen, Germany. Since the porcelain factory had been operating since 1710, it is most likely that the pattern was copied by the American firm.

Hints for Collectors
Very few covered dishes were made in early pressed glass, and consequently they are rare and expensive. The variation with grape clusters on the rim is the rarest and most valuable.

Depression refrigerator butter dish

Description
Rectangular box-shaped bowl and cover with narrow vertical ribs on all 4 sides and ribbed base. Color: transparent pale pink, pale blue, or colorless. *Variations:* S-scroll pattern may replace ribs.

Type and Dimensions
Bowl and cover machine-pressed in separate molds for pattern and shape. Height: 2⅞″. Length: 5⅝″. Width: 3½″.

Locality and Period
Anchor-Hocking Glass Corporation, Lancaster, Ohio; other kitchenware by McKee Glass Company and Jeannette Glass Company, Jeannette, Pennsylvania. c. 1930–49.

Matching Glassware
Mixing bowls, baking dishes, ice-water bottles, custard cups, and other kitchenware. Not made as set.

Comment
Judging from its shape, this covered dish was probably intended to store a pound of butter in the refrigerator. The increasing number of electric refrigerators introduced into homes during the 1930s gave rise to a tremendous number of glass objects specifically designed for use both in the refrigerator and on the table. In their advertisements, glass companies stressed that glass could be kept hygienically clean and sparkling, and therefore was safest for food storage.

Hints for Collectors
Refrigerator dishes such as this one can be found mostly at flea markets and house sales. They are still very inexpensive compared to Depression dinnerware that can be collected in sets.

Bowls

Bowls come in all types of glass—free-blown, mold-blown, cut, engraved, and pressed—and in all shapes and sizes. The simplest form is a circular bowl with low sides (#248), which was popular in the 18th and 19th centuries and is still being made today. With the invention of the pressing machine in the 1820s, bowls took on new rectangular and square shapes and came in a large range of sizes, from the small nappy to the large serving bowl.

The earliest pressed bowls had geometric designs imitating cut glass. Within a few years, lacy patterns unique to pressed glass appeared, with elaborate floral or scroll motifs and stippled backgrounds. By the second half of the 19th century, pressed glass manufacturers were producing bowls with hundreds of different patterns, many in matching sets of tableware. Two specialized forms appear only in 19th-century pressed glass: the 3–4″ bowl, which collectors call a honey dish (#253), and the large bread tray (#258). Honey dishes were made from about 1830 to 1860, but their exact function is unknown. Only a few matched other tableware. Bread trays date from the 1870s and 1880s. Although many bread trays were made to match sets of tableware, a large number were produced in nonmatching designs with mottoes like "Give us this day our daily bread" or "Waste not, want not." This particular motto often appeared with wheat sheaves, a man harvesting, or some other theme related to the production of the staff of life. Oval or rectangular pickle dishes were also introduced in late 19th-century pressed glass and were adopted in Carnival glass and cut glass. Toward the end of the 19th century, art glass manufacturers created several new forms, which were later imitated by cut glass and pressed glass companies. One of these was the rose bowl, a nearly spherical, deep bowl with a turned-in, ruffled edge designed to support the stems of home-grown roses. Popular from around 1890 to 1920, the rose bowl came in numerous Carnival-glass patterns, as well as in a few brilliant-cut glass designs and in specialized art glass in a wide range of colors.

Around the turn of the century, brilliant-cut glass firms introduced the mayonnaise bowl, a small deep bowl with a matching underplate, which was used for serving mayonnaise and salad dressing. Mayonnaise bowls came in a variety of patterns; some matched large sets of cut glass and others were unique. They resemble finger bowls in size and shape, but are usually deeper and often have an elaborately cut rim, while finger bowl rims are usually plain. The 2 forms were probably interchangeable around the turn of the century, when mayonnaise bowls were much more common. Most finger bowls came in expensive cut or engraved glass and art glass, but a few were made in pressed glass. During the same period, brilliant-cut glass manufacturers introduced large oval celery dishes (#263) to replace the upright celery vase (#314). Divided relish dishes with 3 or 4 sections first appeared in the 1880s, although they became most popular in pressed or engraved glassware of the 1920s as well as in Depression glass. Except for these few specialized forms, most bowls cannot be dated on the basis of shape. Rather, the method of manufacture, decorating techniques, and patterns are the best clues for dating.

Early free-blown bowl

Description
Plain circular bowl with folded or plain rim. *Thin walls. Circular foot.* Pontil mark rough. Color: transparent green, brown, amber, or aquamarine; rarely colorless. *Variations:* depth varies greatly in proportion to diameter. Some lack separate foot; many with horizontal threading around rim (#73) or lily-pad decoration (#122, #123).

Type and Dimensions
Free-blown, then tooled into shape. Applied, tooled foot. Colorless lead glass or colored nonlead glass. Rim diameter: 6–7″. Height: 2½–4″.

Locality and Period
Massachusetts, New York, New Jersey, and Pennsylvania. c. 1780–1820.

Comment
This bowl is a standard, classic shape. The example illustrated is made of bottle glass, but other similar bowls can also be found in window glass. Factory glassblowers probably fashioned either type in their spare time to take home or to sell in the company store. Because bowls like this were made over a long period and in many glasshouses, they are difficult to date.

Hints for Collectors
Early simple bowls are rare and always command a high price. Free-blown bowls are virtually impossible to attribute to a specific glasshouse. Do not let an antique dealer convince you that such a piece was definitely made by Wistar, Stiegel, or another early factory because you will pay more for this attribution.

Depression bowl

Description
Circular bowl with slightly flared, smooth rim. *Pressed pattern of stylized flowers and scrolls* around sides; sunburst on base surrounded by geometric spiral pattern. Color: transparent amber or colorless. *Variations:* numerous floral and scroll patterns with stippled backgrounds. Colorless examples may have gold or silver trim.

Type and Dimensions
Machine-pressed in mold for pattern and shape. Rim diameter: 7⅜″. Height: 2⅝″.

Locality and Period
Indiana Glass Company, Dunkirk, Indiana. c. 1933; 1940. Similar patterns by Hocking, Federal, Macbeth-Evans, McKee, Paden City, and other midwestern firms. c. 1925–50.

Matching Glassware
Large set with berry bowls (4½″), cereal bowls (6″), serving bowls (9⅜″, 10″), oval bowl, sugar bowl, creamer, grill plate (10⅜″), platter (10¾″), 3-part relish dish, footed tumblers (9 oz., 12 oz.), and place setting (#212).

Comment
This pattern, originally issued as No. 620 by Indiana Glass Company, is now known as Daisy. The colorless pieces were the first produced in 1933; amber was added in 1940. In 1960 Indiana reissued Daisy in dark transparent green and opaque white glass in a few shapes. Daisy resembles 2 lacy-pattern imitations by Indiana and Anchor-Hocking, but those have stippling.

Hints for Collectors
Most pieces in this pattern are still quite inexpensive, although amber costs more than colorless. Dark green and opaque white reissues are not especially popular.

Daisy pattern

250 Lacy-pattern pressed bowl

Description
Circular *bowl with flat base, slightly flaring sides*, and scalloped edge. *Pressed pattern of 8 tulips* radiating from base, with scrolls, tulips, and leaves on sides; dart pattern on rim. *Overall stippled background.* Color: colorless; rarely transparent blue or yellow. *Variations:* some with oak or acanthus leaves instead of tulips.

Type and Dimensions
Pressed in mold for pattern and shape. Lead glass. Rim diameter: 7½–7¾″. Height: 2–2¼″.

Locality and Period
New England: probably Boston & Sandwich Glass Company, Sandwich, Massachusetts; possibly New England Glass Company, Cambridge, Massachusetts; or Providence Flint Glass Company, Providence, Rhode Island. c. 1830–45.

Matching Glassware
Plates and bowls in several sizes. Not made as set.

Comment
Although it is hard to date the earliest pressed-glass patterns precisely, it seems likely that the stippled lacy patterns with stylized flowers were made after the first wave of imitation cut glass, and before the era of large sets of matching pieces. The stippled background was used to disguise a cloudy surface.

Hints for Collectors
Any colored glassware of this period is considerably rarer than colorless glass. Consequently there is a great difference in price between colored and colorless pieces. A few reproductions of lacy patterns are being made by museums, including The Metropolitan Museum of Art in New York City, which marks "MMA" on the mold.

Depression soup bowl

Description
Shallow circular bowl with scalloped rim. *Overall pressed pattern of protruding circles in concentric rows on outside;* sunburst pattern on base. Color: colorless; transparent pink, light blue, dark green, or dark red. *Variations:* circles may protrude on inside as small bumps (Raindrops) or pear-shaped dots (Pear Optic); both only in colorless or transparent green.

Type and Dimensions
Machine-pressed in mold for pattern and shape. Rim diameter: 7¾". Height: 1⅜".

Locality and Period
Ohio: Hocking Glass Company, Lancaster, c. 1934–37; Anchor-Hocking Glass Corporation, Lancaster, c. 1938–65. Variations by Federal Glass Company, Columbus, Ohio. c. 1929–33.

Matching Glassware
Set with tumblers, pitcher, bowls in 4 sizes, serving bowl, sugar bowl, creamer, bread-and-butter plates, grill and dinner plates, platter, cups and saucers, 2-tiered serving platter, vase (#335), candlesticks, and lamp.

Comment
The pattern illustrated has been marketed under several different names, including Bullseye and Provincial, but Bubble is most often used by collectors today. Examples in dark red are sometimes called Royal Ruby (#335). The transparent pale blue was used for Anchor-Hocking's ovenproof glass called Fire King.

Hints for Collectors
The Bubble pattern is available in more specialized shapes and colors than either Raindrops or Pear Optic, which are found in a limited range of bowls, plates, and tumblers. Prices for all 3 patterns are about the same.

Bubble pattern

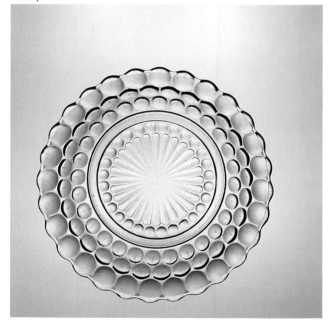

Description
Oval bowl with serrated, scalloped rim. Cut pattern of fine diamonds, strawberry-diamonds, triangles, circles, and fans around sides; sunburst design on base with corner fans. Thick walls. Colorless. *Variations:* several geometric patterns combining diamonds, fans, circles, triangles, and other simple cut motifs.

Type and Dimensions
Free-blown, then tooled into shape. Cut and polished after annealing. Lead glass. Rim at widest: 8–8¼″. Height: 2–2¼″.

Locality and Period
New York City; Jersey City, New Jersey; and Philadelphia; possibly New England. England. c. 1825–50.

Comment
The bowl illustrated descended in the family of Phineas C. Dummer of Dummer's Jersey Glass Company, Jersey City, New Jersey. This company won a silver medal for excellence in glass cutting at the American Institute Fair in New York City in 1843. The same type of glass, however, was probably made by Dummer's competitors in Philadelphia, New York, and Boston.

Hints for Collectors
Cut glass like this is hard to distinguish from its English counterpart made during the same period, since both use the same cut motifs. Blown 3-mold pieces (#254) tried to imitate this type of cut glass. Comparing mold-blown and cut versions of the same pattern can be interesting. Mold-blown pieces are much thinner and the pattern can be felt on the inside surface. Cut pieces have sharper pattern edges and a smooth interior.

Early pressed honey dish

Description
Shallow circular bowl with groups of 6 scallops alternating with diamond-patterned points around rim. *Large pressed chain design with alternating small circles and large diamond-patterned circles* around sides. 9-pointed star at center with diamond pattern. Color: colorless; transparent light, medium, or dark purple, light or dark amber, dark blue; opalescent white. *Variations:* geometric patterns imitating cut motifs.

Type and Dimensions
Pressed in mold for pattern and shape. Lead glass. Rim diameter: 3½–3¾″. Height: ¾–1″.

Locality and Period
New England, Pennsylvania, West Virginia, and Ohio. c. 1835–50.

Matching Glassware
Plates in several sizes (#209), covered and uncovered bowls, oval bowls, sugar bowls, salts, and candlesticks. Not made as set.

Comment
The pattern illustrated, named Roman Rosette by collectors, is relatively common. Although it is not stippled, it dates from the lacy-pattern period of pressed glass. Because it is made in a greater variety of shapes than any of the other early patterns, it probably was made by several factories in the East and Midwest. The shape, which collectors call a honey dish, is seldom found in glass made after 1860.

Hints for Collectors
Honey dishes have never been popular and are consequently inexpensive. They are easily confused with cup plates (#205), which are about the same diameter and often have similar patterns. Honey dishes are slightly deeper, however.

Roman Rosette pattern

Blown 3-mold bowl

Description
Shallow circular bowl with folded rim. Molded pattern of diagonal ribs on base with diamonds around sides. Pontil mark rough. Colorless. *Variations:* many patterns, mostly geometric, combining squares, diamonds, ribs, waffling, and sunbursts.

Type and Dimensions
Blown in full-size mold for pattern, then tooled into shape. Lead glass. Rim diameter: 9⅞–10⅛". Height: 1⅛–1⅜".

Locality and Period
New England; possibly Philadelphia. c. 1820–35.

Matching Glassware
Tumblers, pitchers, decanters, sugar bowls, footed bowls, and celery vases. Not made as set.

Comment
The period of manufacture for blown 3-mold glass was relatively short. It was originally an Anglo-Irish technique, brought to this country after the War of 1812. Probably the first blown 3-mold pieces were made in a New England factory around 1815. The technique proved a successful imitation of cut glass. Shortly afterward, around 1825, the hand press was developed, which offered a faster, cheaper, and more versatile manufacturing method. Glasshouses switched to the production of pressed tableware and abandoned the blown 3-mold process.

Hints for Collectors
So far as is known, blown 3-mold bowls have not been reproduced. The folded rims give bowls like this extra strength. Care must be exercised in washing them, however, because mold-blown glass is sensitive to extremes in temperature and may crack if the water is too hot or too cold.

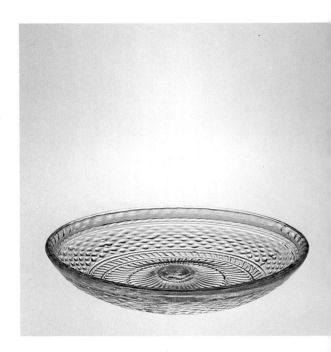

Free-blown bowl

Description
Plain circular bowl with plain rim. Thick walls. *Pontil mark rough.* Color: usually colorless; sometimes transparent amber, green, or aquamarine. *Variations:* some with applied threading. Colored bowls are thinner and may have applied chain or triple-ring decoration.

Type and Dimensions
Free-blown, then tooled into shape. Colorless lead glass or colored nonlead glass. Rim diameter: 10–10¼″. Height: 2½–2¾″.

Locality and Period
The Northeast; probably New York, Philadelphia, and Pittsburgh. c. 1820–50.

Comment
The simplicity and thickness of the bowl illustrated are unusual. It may have been intended as a blank for cutting or engraving (#252), which would explain the unpolished pontil mark at the center of the bowl. The pontil mark was usually polished during the cutting process. As a general rule, blanks were sold by glass factories only to cutting and decorating shops. But businesses were informal in the 19th century, and employees or friends of the management often bought seconds, or unfinished pieces, directly from the factory. That was probably the case with the bowl illustrated. The variation with applied triple-ring or chain decoration has a polished pontil mark.

Hints for Collectors
Plain pieces like this are unpopular with most collectors and fairly inexpensive. The sturdiness of this bowl, however, allows it to be more than just a display piece.

Realistic-style square pressed bowl

Description
Square bowl with slanted sides and cut corners. 2 rows of *pressed diamonds around rim and diamond pattern on base; stylized flowers around sides.* Thin walls. Color: transparent blue, light amber, or colorless; rarely light green. *Variations:* many floral and fruit designs of the period.

Type and Dimensions
Pressed in mold for pattern and shape. Nonlead glass. Rim: 8″ × 8″. Height: 5¾–6″.

Locality and Period
Pittsburgh: Adams & Company, c. 1875–91; United States Glass Company and possibly others, c. 1891–1900.

Matching Glassware
Set with goblets, cordial and champagne glasses, tumblers (#49), pitcher, round bowl, covered bowl, sugar bowl, creamer (#148), butter dish, spoon holder, celery vase, rectangular tray, cake plate, compote, platter, relish dish, and salt and pepper shakers.

Comment
The Wildflower pattern illustrated is typical of the pressed designs of the 1870s. It is made of lime glass, which was a formula for thinner glass developed in the 1860s. Lime glass came in a range of colors not found in earlier pressed glass. When the Adams firm joined the United States Glass Company merger of 1891, the new firm continued to use the same molds. Angular shapes like the one illustrated were not made before 1875 but were common at the end of the century.

Hints for Collectors
Wildflower has been popular with collectors since the 1940s, and has been frequently reproduced, especially in light green, the rarest original color.

Wildflower pattern

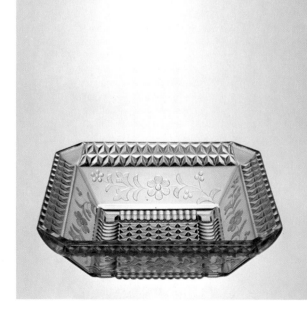

Lacy-pattern pressed tray

Description
Rectangular tray with slanted sides and scalloped and serrated rim. *Pressed peacock feathers and strawberry-diamonds and fans* around sides; strawberry-diamonds surrounded by interlocking peacock feathers on base. Thin walls. Colorless. *Variations:* sometimes oval shape with scrolls on stippled background and open chain around edge.

Type and Dimensions
Pressed in mold for pattern and shape. Lead glass. Length: 10–12″. Width: 8–9″.

Locality and Period
Massachusetts: probably Boston & Sandwich Glass Company, Sandwich, or New England Glass Company, Cambridge. c. 1830–45.

Matching Glassware
Plates, toddy plates (#210), creamers, sugar bowls, bowls, salts (#161), mustard jars, and rare footed compote made from same mold as tray. Not made as set.

Comment
This is the largest lacy-pattern tray known, and is a good example of the later pieces with busy designs. Elaborate patterns, like this one with the peacock-feather motif, give a sparkling effect, although the surface of the glass is really somewhat dull. The tray probably served as a fruit dish or perhaps was meant only for display.

Hints for Collectors
Lacy-pattern trays in this shape are comparatively rare and command a very high price in antique shops. Look for chips on the scalloped rim and on the corners, which are seldom found in very good condition. There are no reproductions in this shape.

Late 19th-century pressed bread tray

Description
Rectangular tray with wavy edge. *Center has pressed representation* of Leonardo da Vinci's "Last Supper"; border with grape clusters and grape leaves. Colorless. *Variations:* usually oval form; patterns with wheat sheaves or harvesting scene at center; sometimes inscribed with "OUR DAILY BREAD," "GIVE US THIS DAY OUR DAILY BREAD," or "BREAD IS THE STAFF OF LIFE" and other mottoes around border.

Type and Dimensions
Pressed in mold for pattern and shape. Nonlead glass. Length: 11″. Width: 7″.

Locality and Period
Pittsburgh area: Atterbury & Company and Bakewell, Pears & Company. Model Flint Glass Company, Findlay, Ohio, and other firms in Ohio and Indiana. c. 1875–1905.

Comment
Bread trays were a new shape in the 1870s, when they began to appear in a few pressed patterns. Today many are still collectible in large sets. Others were sold individually, like the illustrated tray by the Model Flint Glass Company of Findlay, Ohio. Many have religious mottoes, such as "FAITH, HOPE, AND CHARITY" or "ROCK OF AGES," or secular mottoes like "IT IS PLEASANT TO LABOR FOR THOSE WE LOVE." Most bread trays are made of nonlead glass; they were never made in cut or blown glass.

Hints for Collectors
There are probably over 200 different bread tray designs. Unlike butter dishes or goblets, which people have been collecting for a long time, bread trays have only recently become popular and are still inexpensive. The bread plate illustrated was reproduced until 1963 by the Indiana Glass Company of Dunkirk, Indiana.

The Last Supper pattern

Pomona ice cream tray

Description
Rectangular tray with ruffled rim. *Frosted center has naturalistic design* of cornflowers and leaves. Color: colorless, with grayish frosted center; pale yellow or pale blue stained flowers; *yellow rim. Variations:* may have butterflies or meandering vines; sometimes plain.

Type and Dimensions
Free-blown, then tooled into shape. Tooled rim. Acid-frosted after annealing. Metallic stain applied and then fired on. Length: 12½″. Width: 7½″.

Locality and Period
New England Glass Works, Cambridge, Massachusetts. c. 1885–88.

Matching Glassware
Tumblers, goblets, punch cups, pitchers in several sizes, bowls, and vases. Not made as set.

Comment
Pomona was an acid-etched art glass patented by Joseph Locke for the New England Glass Works on April 28, 1885. It is usually free-blown and occasionally mold-blown. Pomona always has stained decoration against a frosted background, achieved either by needle-etching or the less time-consuming plate-etching. A floral pattern usually appears against this frosted ground, and the tray edges are always stained pale yellow.

Hints for Collectors
Like all art glass made by New England Glass Works, Pomona was produced for only a few years, until the company moved to Toledo, Ohio, in 1888. Pomona has not been as popular with collectors as New England Peachblow and is not as expensive, although it often comes in the same shapes.

Late 19th-century pressed serving bowl and platter

Description

2-piece set: oval bowl and oblong platter, both with flat handles on ends and scalloped rim. Bowl has pressed diamond-patterned X on base, rectangular side panels with flowers against stippled background, *and row of triangles below rim. Platter has diamond-patterned panels on ends and flowers against stippled panels on sides. Colorless.* Variations: *sometimes with bars superimposed on flowers (Barred Forget-Me-Not) or with stippled flowers against plain background (Stippled Forget-Me-Not); both variations without diamonds.*

Type and Dimensions

Bowl and platter pressed in separate molds for pattern and shape. Nonlead glass. Bowl length: 10–10¼"; height: 2–2¼". Platter length: 11½–11¾".

Locality and Period

Pittsburgh: Bryce Brothers, M'Kee & Brothers, Adams & Company. c. 1880–90.

Matching Glassware

Set with cordial glasses, goblets, pitcher, creamer, sugar bowl, butter dish, celery vase, spoon holder, covered compote, cake plate, jam jar, and pickle, relish, and sauce dishes.

Comment

The illustrated Regal pattern by Bryce Brothers is called Paneled Forget-Me-Not by collectors. It is somewhat similar to Bryce Brothers' Wreath pattern, known as Willow Oak, which has a sunburst between each panel and lacks diamonds. M'Kee & Brothers and Adams & Company produced similar pressed patterns with slightly different flowers and panels.

Hints for Collectors

It is easy to confuse the various paneled floral patterns.

Paneled Forget-Me-Not pattern

Amberina boat-shaped centerpiece

Description
Boat-shaped bowl with overall pressed pattern of hobnails and stars. Color: *transparent amber shading to red. Variations:* amount of red shading variable.

Type and Dimensions
Pressed in mold for pattern and shape. Partially reheated to develop shading. Length: 14¼″. Width: 4¾″. Height: 2½″.

Locality and Period
Hobbs, Brockunier & Company, Wheeling, West Virginia. c. 1883–90.

Matching Glassware
Full range of tableware in this pattern, but Amberina usually in single decorative pieces, such as vases (#332), bowls, sugar bowl and creamer sets (#150), and cheese dishes (#220).

Comment
This amber-to-red shading, known as Amberina, was patented by the New England Glass Company in 1883. The company produced only free-blown and mold-blown Amberina glass, but licensed Hobbs, Brockunier & Company of West Virginia to use the same formula for pressed glass. Many other companies made this popular Daisy and Button pattern in other transparent, non-shaded colors.

Hints for Collectors
Hobbs, Brockunier & Company called this pattern No. 101, but collectors refer to it as Daisy and Button. It is a pressed imitation of the cut Russian pattern (#29) and has more variations than any other pressed pattern (#242). The pressed piece was much less expensive than the cut version at that time, but is just as costly now.

Daisy and Button pattern

Brilliant-cut canoe-shaped centerpiece

Description
Canoe-shaped bowl with high pointed ends and scalloped rim.
Overall cut pattern forming series of raised squares with crosses.
Thick walls. Colorless. *Variations:* sometimes overall hobnails or
strawberry-diamonds.

Type and Dimensions
Free-blown, then tooled into shape. Cut and polished after
annealing. Lead glass. Length: 12½″. Height: 4″.

Locality and Period
J. Hoare & Company, Corning, New York. c. 1890–1900.

Matching Glassware
Set with wine, champagne, cordial and sherry glasses, goblets,
pitcher, decanter, finger bowls and underplates, and bowls in
several sizes.

Comment
This simple cut pattern, called Quarter Diamond, is typical of the
early period of brilliant-cut glass. Instead of the mixture of
decorative motifs found on later pieces (#226, #267, #268), this
pattern has only one repeating motif. The unusual shape is also
typical of the earlier period. The canoe appeared in an 1895
Hoare & Company catalogue. It may have been used either as a
centerpiece or a celery dish, since horizontal dishes had begun to
replace the vertical celery vase by the 1880s.

Hints for Collectors
On glass with a repeat design like the one illustrated, it is
especially important that the cutting be perfectly even, the lines
parallel, and that all the points of the design meet properly. With
mixed motifs, you may overlook poor cutting, but it will stand
out on a repeat design and lower the piece's value.

Quarter Diamond pattern

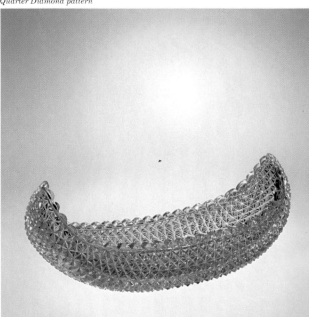

Brilliant-cut celery dish

Description
Shallow oblong dish with sides higher toward middle and lower at ends; serrated rim. *Asymmetrical cut pattern* with fans, hobstars, and sunbursts. Thick walls. Colorless. *Variations:* sides may be same height as ends or lower; many different arrangements of hobstars, fans, diamonds, hobnails, pinwheels, or other brilliant-cut motifs.

Type and Dimensions
Free-blown, then tooled into shape. Cut and polished after annealing. Lead glass. Length: 11–11¾″. Width: 5–5¼″. Height: 1½–2″.

Locality and Period
Throughout the United States. c. 1890–1920.

Comment
Horizontal celery dishes began to replace upright celery vases (#314) on American tables in the 1880s, but the transition was not complete until after the turn of the century. They were popular in brilliant-cut glass, but are found in very few patterns in 19th-century pressed glass, and rarely in Carnival or Depression glass. The twisted shape illustrated is unusual. Celery dishes come in a variety of patterns; some match larger bowls and plates, but many are unique.

Hints for Collectors
Cut-glass celery dishes vary in length from about 8″ to the large size shown here. They are usually reasonably priced unless they are in a very rare pattern. These dishes were a staple of many glass-cutting shops. Many were cut in simple and inexpensive patterns that sold for only a couple of dollars.

Brilliant-cut acorn-shaped nappy

Description
Shallow acorn-shaped bowl with scalloped rim. *Cut pattern* forms 3 groups of parallel lines that cross in center; fan at each of 6 interstices; 6 hobstars around sides. Thick walls. Colorless. *Variations:* different arrangements of hobstars, fans, and prism cutting, possibly with diamonds and hobnails.

Type and Dimensions
Free-blown, then tooled into shape. Cut and polished after annealing. Lead glass. Length: 9½–9¾". Width: 6–6¼". Height: ¾–1½".

Locality and Period
Throughout the United States. c. 1890–1910.

Comment
"Nappy" was a popular term used by glass manufacturers in the 1870s for a small shallow bowl. The piece illustrated appears to be a variant of H. P. Sinclaire & Company's Cumberland pattern. The acorn shape is also illustrated in catalogues of J. Hoare & Company in a different cut pattern. After 1895, when Hoare registered its trademark, most of its pieces were marked "J. HOARE & CO./1853/CORNING." H. P. Sinclaire & Company used the trademark of an "S" in a laurel wreath from its founding in 1904, so it is unusual to find a product of either firm unmarked. Perhaps this example was made by an unknown cutting firm that had bought the blank from the same company that supplied J. Hoare & Company and had copied the Sinclaire pattern. Copying was common in the cut glass industry and makes the identification of unmarked pieces like this one difficult.

Hints for Collectors
Unusual shapes like this always command higher prices than ordinary round nappies.

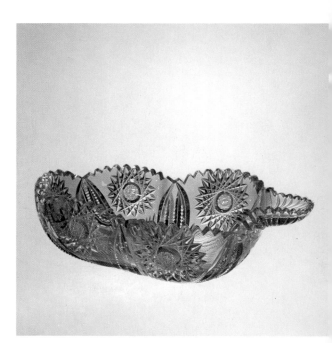

Brilliant-cut leaf-shaped nappy

Description
Shallow leaf-shaped bowl with 7 lobes and stem; scalloped rim.
Cut lines from lobe to lobe intersect in center, forming spaces
filled with hobstars and cane panels; notch cutting on stem. Thick
walls. Colorless. *Variations:* different arrangements of hobstars,
fans, diamonds, and prism or cane cutting.

Type and Dimensions
Free-blown, then tooled into shape. Cut and polished after
annealing. Lead glass. Length: 7⅜–7½". Width: 5¼–5½".
Height: ¾–1½".

Locality and Period
Throughout the United States. c. 1890–1910.

Comment
Makers of both cut and pressed glass used "nappy" as a general
term for shallow bowls in a great variety of sizes and shapes.
Catalogues of the 1870s onward show "covered nappy" and
"footed nappy" for bowls that today's collector might call a butter
dish and a small compote. Fancy-shaped examples, like this leaf-
shaped nappy and the acorn shape (#264), appeared only in cut
glass from the 1890s onward, and were not made in pressed
glass. They came in all kinds of shapes—shells, fans, and, for
those who liked to play cards, diamonds, clubs, hearts, and
spades. The latter were usually sold in sets of 4. Others could be
sold singly, in pairs, or in patterns matching large sets of
tableware.

Hints for Collectors
Nappies are just as useful today as they were when they were
made—for serving mints, candy, fruit, or other finger foods.
Always wash these dishes carefully in tepid water. Cut glass
cracks easily and is very prone to chipping.

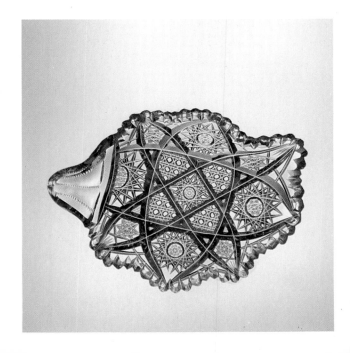

266 Brilliant-cut bowl

Description
Shallow circular bowl with scalloped and serrated rim. *Cut pattern of 8 evenly spaced oval miter cuts;* 6 rows of small hobstars between ovals. Thick walls. Cut hobstar on base. Colorless. *Variations:* different cut motifs including hobstars, fans, and diamonds. Sometimes acid-etched trademark or paper label on base.

Type and Dimensions
Free-blown, then tooled into shape. Cut and polished after annealing. Lead glass. Rim diameter: 8–8¼″. Height: 2¼–2½″.

Locality and Period
Throughout the United States. c. 1900–10.

Comment
This piece is clearly marked with the acid-stamped "J. HOARE & CO./1853/CORNING" trademark, although it does not appear in any of the published Hoare catalogues. The pattern somewhat resembles the Venetian pattern (#9) cut by T. G. Hawkes and Company around the same time. It probably came in a full range of tableware. Although the pattern name cannot be identified, the value of this bowl remains high because of the fine-quality glass and cutting.

Hints for Collectors
Many collectors find the 1853 date in the center of Hoare's trademark confusing since the trademark was adopted in 1895 and used until the firm closed in 1920. The 1853 date was chosen because that was the year that John Hoare came to the United States from England. All of Hoare's pieces are made in the brilliant-cut style that was popular around the turn of the century.

Brilliant-cut bowl

Description
Circular bowl with scalloped and serrated rim. *Cut hobstars alternate with cane panels and other geometric motifs around sides;* large hobstar on base. Thick walls. Color: colorless; rarely cased with red, blue, yellow, or green (#330). *Variations:* many patterns, with hobstars, diamonds, pinwheels, fans, and similar cut motifs in various combinations. Sometimes acid-etched trademark or paper label on base.

Type and Dimensions
Free-blown, then tooled into shape. Cut and polished after annealing. Lead glass. Rim diameter: 8¼–9″. Height: 3½–4″.

Locality and Period
Throughout the United States. c. 1890–1910.

Comment
This is a standard-size bowl and the most common shape found in cut glass, with the possible exception of stemware. It served a variety of ornamental purposes, although it was probably most often used for fruit. Larger and smaller bowls were certainly made in similar cut patterns, but the simple 9″ bowl is the most common.

Hints for Collectors
Because these bowls were popular and cut in so many patterns, they are still low-priced today. The pattern illustrated is an early simple geometric style, probably made in the 1890s, and the cutting is of good quality. Early brilliant-cut patterns like this are likely to increase in value the most in the coming years.

Brilliant-cut bowl

Description
Circular bowl with sloping sides and scalloped and serrated rim. *Cut row of hobstars around sides* with row of fans below. Large hobstar on base. Thick walls. Color: colorless; rarely cased with red, blue, yellow, or green (#330). *Variations:* many patterns, with hobstars, diamonds, pinwheels, fans, and similar cut motifs in various combinations.

Type and Dimensions
Free-blown, then tooled into shape. Cut and polished after annealing. Lead glass. Rim diameter: 8¾–9¼″. Height: 2¾–3″.

Locality and Period
Throughout the United States. c. 1890–1910.

Comment
The original price of these medium-size bowls ranged from about $3 for a simple pattern to about $7 to $8 for a more complicated one. Today this may seem inexpensive, but in a day when $10 to $15 a week could support a small family, this bowl was a luxury. Apprentice glasscutters received $3 to $5 weekly, a journeyman $7 to $15, and even a master cutter only $15 to $25.

Hints for Collectors
The bowl illustrated was cut by L. Straus & Sons of New York City and bears their trademark—a small star within a circle—on the base. Like most of the cut-glass trademarks, it is an acid stamp and is very difficult to see. To find the trademark, you will need a bright light. Only about 10 to 15 trademarks from glass-cutting firms are known. A trademark not only indicates the period and factory, but usually increases the value of the piece.

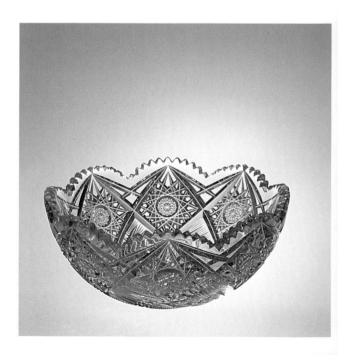

Cut centerpiece

Description
Spherical bowl with incurving, scalloped rim and leaf-shaped panels. *Cut leaf decoration on swirled panels alternates with strawberry-diamond-patterned panels.* Hobstar on base. Thick walls. Colorless. *Variations:* starlike cutting (#29) may replace strawberry-diamonds.

Type and Dimensions
Free-blown, then tooled into shape. Cut into panels after annealing; cut with pattern, then polished. Lead glass. Diameter: 11½–11¾". Height: 5½–5¾".

Locality and Period
J. Hoare & Company, Corning, New York. c. 1885–1900.

Matching Glassware
Set with wineglasses, goblets, decanters, and serving pieces, such as bowls and centerpieces.

Comment
This distinctive pattern is a variation of J. Hoare & Company's Wheat pattern, which appeared in the firm's earliest catalogues about 1895. The original Wheat pattern has leaf panels and starlike panels instead of strawberry-diamonds. A much larger set of tableware was made in the Wheat pattern, indicating that it was probably more popular than the pattern illustrated.

Hints for Collectors
This is an extraordinarily heavy piece; much glass was cut away to make the rounded panels. Its large size is impractical for anything other than a centerpiece. Do not expect to find a trademark on an early piece like this. The simplicity of the pattern and the weight both indicate that it was made before 1900, when acid-stamped trademarks were only beginning to be used.

Wheat pattern variant

270 Simple brilliant-cut bowl

Description
Cylindrical bowl with scalloped rim. *Deeply cut overall diamond-and-rosette design. Thick walls.* Color: colorless; rarely cased with red, blue, green, or yellow (#330).

Type and Dimensions
Free-blown, then tooled into shape. Cut and polished after annealing. Lead glass. Rim diameter: 9–10″. Height: 3–4″.

Locality and Period
Throughout the United States. c. 1905–15.

Matching Glassware
Bowls (7″). Not made as set.

Comment
The bowl illustrated was probably cut by H. P. Sinclaire & Company or O. F. Egginton & Company, both of Corning, New York. The design is similar to the Assyrian pattern, patented by Sinclaire in 1909, and the Trellis pattern by Egginton, patented in 1908. The simple pattern with only 2 repeating motifs and the straight sides of this bowl are unusual in American brilliant-cut glass.

Hints for Collectors
This large bowl originally cost somewhat more than most brilliant-cut bowls (#266, #268), but today it is substantially more expensive. The most important factor to look for in cut glass, however, is quality—like the cutting and the blank on the bowl illustrated. With this kind of simple design, it is easy to see if the cutter has made a mistake. A single error could affect the symmetry of an entire pattern.

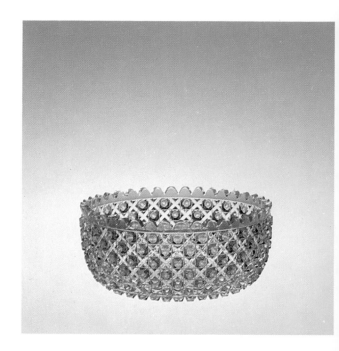

Cut and cased finger bowl

Description
Circular bowl with middle waist, flaring slightly at rim. Row of cut semicircular panels around upper half; oval panels around lower half. Thin walls. Pontil mark polished. Color: colorless; *rarely cased* in red, blue, green, or yellow. *Variations:* shape varies slightly; many are hemispheres; patterns usually hobstars, fans, diamonds, and other brilliant-cut motifs (#29); *usually with matching underplate.*

Type and Dimensions
Free-blown, then tooled into shape. Cased with color after annealing, then pattern cut through. Rim diameter: 4½–5″. Height: 5¼–5½″.

Locality and Period
Throughout the United States. c. 1890–1910.

Matching Glassware
Large set with stemware, tumblers, pitchers, decanters, bowls, and centerpieces.

Comment
Finger bowls are only found in late 19th- and early 20th-century sets and are usually made of expensive cut or engraved glass, rarely in art glass or pressed glass. Fingerbowls were always sold in sets with matching underplates. The bowl illustrated was cut at the Dithridge & Company factory outside of Pittsburgh.

Hints for Collectors
Although finger bowls are seldom used in the modern American home, they are an ideal size for nuts, candy, or table condiments such as salad dressing or pickles. Most colorless finger bowls do not command a high price unless they are cut in a rare or popular pattern. Cased examples like this bowl are unusual and expensive.

Early finger bowl and wine rinser

Description
Cylindrical bowls with vertical ribs around lower body and underneath base. Thin walls. Pouring lip on either side (left) or plain rim (right). Pontil marks smooth. Color: colorless; rarely transparent dark blue. *Variations:* engraved decoration, such as swags and tassels or scattered stars above ribs.

Type and Dimensions
Bowls blown in ribbed molds, then expanded and shaped; or free-blown, then tooled into shape. Tooled pouring lips. Lead glass. Rim diameter: 3¾–4″. Height: 3½–5″.

Locality and Period
England. Ireland: Cork Glass Company, Cork; Penrose Glass Company, Waterford, and others. Widely exported to the United States. Possibly New England. c. 1800–30.

Comment
American collectors are often confused about the function of a wine rinser. It is shaped exactly like a finger bowl except for the 2 pouring lips. Wine rinsers were used extensively in England and to some extent in America by the upper classes to hold, chill, and rinse used wineglasses. They were placed on the table between every other couple and shared by 2 guests. The 2 wineglasses were kept upside down in the wine rinser between courses. Wine rinsers were made only in Europe until the 18th century when the custom went out of fashion.

Hints for Collectors
Early finger bowls like the one illustrated are rare in this country. Late 19th-century finger bowls are more common and usually spherical; they were made in purple, blue, or green.

Depression fruit bowl

Description
Cylindrical lower body with wide flaring scalloped rim. *Pressed pattern of vertical ribs around sides interrupted by 4 broader panels with rose design.* Color: transparent pink, light blue, green, yellow, or colorless. *Variations:* some patterns have floral design in side medallions (Rose Cameo, #15) or arches instead of panels (Rosemary).

Type and Dimensions
Machine-pressed in mold for pattern and shape. Rim diameter: 11¾″. Height: 4⅞″.

Locality and Period
Hocking Glass Company, Lancaster, Ohio. c. 1931–37. Similar patterns by Federal, Jeannette, Macbeth-Evans, Indiana, Paden City, and other midwestern firms. c. 1925–40.

Matching Glassware
Large set with stemware (#15), tumblers, pitchers (#70), decanters, sugar bowl, creamer, cups, butter dish, salt and pepper shakers, soup, cereal, and serving bowls, plates, cake plate, candy dish, celery dish, cookie jar, sandwich server, relish dish, and vases. Not all shapes in all colors.

Comment
Mayfair, or Open Rose, is one of the most popular Depression-glass patterns, partly because it comes in such a wide variety of shapes. The light blue and pink are much more common than green, yellow, or colorless, and are generally less expensive.

Hints for Collectors
Only the whiskey tumbler has been reproduced in this pattern in green and blue shades not used with the original tumbler. Reproductions are also heavier and the rose design has a single, rather than double, stem.

Mayfair pattern

Early midwestern milk bowl

Description
Cylindrical lower body with wide flaring folded rim. *Molded diagonally swirled ribs* around body. Pontil mark rough. Color: transparent amber, aquamarine, or pale green. *Variations:* some bowls less flaring; may have broken-swirl rib pattern (#44).

Type and Dimensions
Blown in vertically ribbed mold, then swirled and expanded. Nonlead glass. Rim diameter: 8½–8¾". Height: 2–3".

Locality and Period
The Midwest, probably Ohio. c. 1800–40.

Matching Glassware
Tumblers (#44), pitchers (#72), bar bottles, (#113), jugs, flasks, salts (#176), plates (#214), sugar bowls, and creamers. Not made as set.

Comment
This shape is usually called a milk bowl, although the example illustrated is rather small for that purpose. Fresh milk was set out in bowls like this to separate; the cream would rise into the flaring top half to be skimmed off and used to make butter. Milk bowls were also made in plain free-blown glass in bottle and window glasshouses, but they do not seem to have been a staple product for tableware factories, since none were advertised.

Hints for Collectors
Do not confuse this type of glass with similar Mexican bowls made in the 1920s and 1930s. Look for signs of wear; a bowl of this kind should have been used a great deal if it is a genuine milk bowl.

Cased and engraved console bowl

Description
Shallow circular bowl with wide flaring rim. Engraved panels of 6 floral sprays separated by dotted lines. Plain circular foot. Pontil mark polished. Color: colorless; rarely cased with transparent pale purple, red, blue, green, or amber. *Variations:* sometimes engraved landscapes or fruit.

Type and Dimensions
Free-blown, then tooled into shape. Cased with color after annealing, then copper-wheel engraved. Lead glass. Rim diameter: 13¾–16″. Height: 4–5″.

Locality and Period
Corning, New York: Steuben Glass Works; H. P. Sinclaire & Company. c. 1920–35.

Matching Glassware
Set with candlesticks. Bowls and vases; not made as set.

Comment
Lightweight engraved glassware was especially popular in the 1920s after many years of the heavy brilliant-cut glass of the turn of the century. Other thin glassware of this period, such as Venetian-style glass (#304), was made with a special formula for lime glass developed during the First World War. Soft pastels, like the lavender illustrated, are typical of this type of glass.

Hints for Collectors
Flaring bowls with engraved decoration were popular only in the 1920s and 1930s, so they are easy to date. Sold in sets with 2 to 4 matching candlesticks, they were often called console bowls because they were placed on console tables—side tables in the living and dining rooms. They could be filled with fruit or flowers or displayed empty. The more elaborate the engraving, the more likely that the bowls were used for display.

276 Pillar-molded bowl

Description
Circular bowl with folded rim and circular domed foot. *Molded vertical ribs from base to rim.* Thick walls. Pontil mark rough. Color: colorless; transparent purple or blue; opaque white.

Type and Dimensions
Bowl blown in ribbed mold, then tooled into shape. Rim folded. Foot applied and tooled. Lead glass. Rim diameter: 5–5¼". Height: 2–2¼".

Locality and Period
Pittsburgh: M'Kee & Brothers, Bakewell, Pears & Company, and James B. Lyon & Company; or other western Pennsylvania firms. c. 1825–50.

Matching Glassware
Punch bowls (#300), pitchers (#84), bar bottles (#110), celery vases, vases (#340), cruets, and syrup jugs. Not made as set.

Comment
Pillar-molded glass like this is exceptionally sturdy. Most of it was probably made for use in taverns and public houses, where wear and tear would be great. The folded rim on the piece illustrated is also a strengthening device—folded rims are almost never found chipped. Pillar molding does not seem to have been fashionable in the eastern factories, although it was well within their technical capabilities. Pillar-molded celery vases and bar bottles appear in an 1859–60 catalogue of M'Kee & Brothers of Pittsburgh, indicating that the technique survived into the second half of the 19th century.

Hints for Collectors
Because of their sturdiness, these bowls survive in large numbers and are comparatively inexpensive. Small-size bowls like this are not as common as celery vases and pitchers.

Depression bowl

Description
Circular bowl with solid handle on each side and scalloped rim. *Pressed swirled ribs extend from bowl base to handles.* Concentric circles on slightly domed circular foot. Color: transparent blue-green, pink, amber, or light blue; opaque light blue. *Variations:* may lack handles and foot; sometimes cover.

Type and Dimensions
Machine-pressed in mold for pattern and shape. Rim diameter: 10⅞". Height: 4⅞".

Locality and Period
Jeannette Glass Company, Jeannette, Pennsylvania. c. 1936–38. Similar patterns by Federal, Anchor-Hocking, Macbeth-Evans, Indiana, and Paden City. c. 1925–40.

Matching Glassware
Large set with tumblers, pitchers, plates (#213), salt and pepper shakers, cups, sherbets, bowls (5¼", 9"), footed bowl without handles, butter dish, candy dishes, creamer, sugar bowl, sandwich plate, vases, and candle holders.

Comment
Jeannette called the blue-green color illustrated ultramarine. This shade is an unusual color in Depression glass, and one that Jeannette used only in the Petal Swirl pattern illustrated and 2 others—Doric and Pansy (#216) and Cube (#186). McKee Glass Company and United States Glass Company, however, made a slightly lighter and darker blue-green in different patterns.

Hints for Collectors
Ultramarine is the most expensive color in this pattern, more than twice the price of pink. The rare water pitcher in ultramarine will fetch one of the highest prices listed for any piece of Depression glass.

Petal Swirl pattern

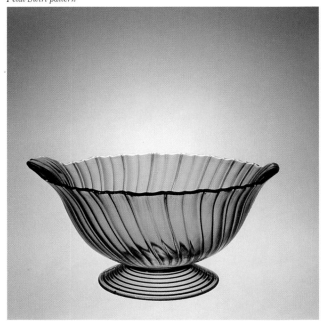

Kew Blas bowl

Description
Cup-shaped bowl with flaring rim and circular domed foot. *Featherlike pattern on sides.* Pontil mark polished. Marked "Kew Blas" in script on base. *Opaque glass with iridescent surface.* Color: exterior opaque white with green feathers; interior and rim enameled reddish-orange. *Variations:* many naturalistic patterns combining opaque blue, cream, yellow, pink, and brown designs and backgrounds.

Type and Dimensions
Free-blown, then tooled into shape. Applied colored threading marvered-in, then pulled with tool to create feather pattern. Iridescent finish sprayed on before annealing. Rim diameter: 5⅛". Height: 3⅞".

Locality and Period
Union Glass Company, Somerville, Massachusetts. c. 1893–1915.

Matching Glassware
Vases and centerpieces. Not made as set.

Comment
The Union Glass Company, founded in the mid-19th century, made pressed-glass tableware until the 1890s. When Julian de Cordova became president and principal stockholder and W. S. Blake became superintendent, the company marketed a line of Art Nouveau pieces inspired by the glass of L. C. Tiffany. The trade name "Kew Blas" is derived from rearranging the letters in the name W. S. Blake.

Hints for Collectors
Most Kew Blas designs are naturalistic, like those of Durand's Vineland Flint Glass Works (#342) and the Quezal Art Glass & Decorating Company, a Brooklyn firm founded by former Tiffany employees. All are marked with the firm name or a trademark.

Carnival bowl

Description
Circular bowl on 3 round feet with *open arches around edge.
Vertical ribs with stippling and pressed pattern of wild rose
blossoms and leaves.* Flat circular base marked "N." Color:
opaque iridescent green, orange-amber, or purple; colorless.
Variations: may lack trademark; may have more flaring shape;
many rose patterns.

Type and Dimensions
Pressed in mold for pattern and shape. Rim flared after removal
from mold. Iridescent finish sprayed on before annealing. Rim
diameter: 5½–5¾". Height: 3½–3¾".

Locality and Period
West Virginia: Northwood Glass Company, Wheeling; Fenton
Art Glass Company, Williamstown. Ohio: Imperial Glass
Company, Bellaire; Millersburg Glass Company, Millersburg.
c. 1905–20.

Matching Glassware
Syrup jugs, vases, baskets, bowls, plates in several shapes, and
lamps. Not made as set.

Comment
The pattern illustrated is Northwood's Wild Rose. Rose patterns
were popular in Carnival glass, and there are almost as many
variations in rose patterns as in grape patterns. Collectors will
find Lustre Rose, Rambler Rose, Rose Show, Captive Rose,
Wine and Roses, Open Rose, and several others.

Hints for Collectors
Not all pieces in this pattern are marked "N." A few Northwood
pieces are marked "Northwood" in script and many others lack a
trademark. Syrup jugs and vases in this pattern are rare.
Openwork bowls, like the one shown, are slightly more common.

Wild Rose pattern

Mt. Washington Peachblow bowl

Description
Circular bowl with ruffled rim; 3 scalloped feet. Color: *opaque pink at rim shading to grayish-white on base and feet.*
Variations: may have raspberrylike blob of glass on top of pontil mark.

Type and Dimensions
Free-blown, then tooled into shape. Tooled lip. Applied, tooled feet and berry. Partially reheated to develop shading. Rim diameter: 4½″. Height: 3″.

Locality and Period
Mt. Washington Glass Company, New Bedford, Massachusetts. c. 1885–90.

Matching Glassware
Bowls, vases, and centerpieces. Not made as set.

Comment
This is the Mt. Washington Glass Company's version of Peachblow, an extremely popular color for glass and cosmetic containers in the 1880s. All of the companies making art glass during this period produced their own varieties of Peachblow.

Hints for Collectors
Mt. Washington Peachblow and New England Peachblow (#68) are similar, since both have a single layer of opaque glass. The New England version is brighter and shaded to white, however, while the Mt. Washington glass is purplish-pink shaded to grayish-white. Wheeling Peachblow (#350) is easy to spot because it has a white lining and a reddish-to-yellow outer surface. Mt. Washington Peachblow is rarer than the New England and Wheeling types and always commands a premium price. Unfortunately, Peachblow has been imitated in Italy over the past 20 years. Be suspicious if the coloring is grayish.

Chocolate-glass dish

Description
Circular bowl with scalloped rim and foot. *Pressed stylized cactus pattern* on bowl, separated by heavy vertical ribs with pressed arrow pattern. Narrow vertical ribs on rim and foot. Color: *opaque light brown exterior, with milky white-brown interior. Variations:* abstract patterns, including leaves and scrolls (Leaf Bracket), geometric designs (Austrian), and narrow vertical ribs (Dewey).

Type and Dimensions
Pressed in mold for pattern and shape. Nonlead glass. Rim diameter: 4½″. Height: 2″.

Locality and Period
Indiana Tumbler & Goblet Company, Greentown, Indiana. c. 1901–03. National Glass Company, Pittsburgh. 1903–04. Fenton Art Glass Company, Williamstown, West Virginia. c. 1908–15.

Matching Glassware
Large tableware set including serving pieces. Tumblers, steins, and novelties; not made as set.

Comment
Jacob Rosenthal, a glass chemist at the Indiana Tumbler & Goblet Company, developed some of the factory's most interesting colors, including Holly Amber (#229), several opaque green and blue glasses, and the chocolate glass illustrated. The formula for chocolate glass was purchased by the National Glass Company in 1902. After the Indiana factory was destroyed by fire in 1903, Rosenthal joined the Fenton company. He produced chocolate glass there, but not in the Cactus pattern shown.

Hints for Collectors
Beware of muddy brown reproductions.

Cactus pattern

Grotesque bowl

Description
Deep flaring bowl with 4 distinct lobes and wavy rim. Molded pattern of widely spaced vertical ribs around bowl. Pontil mark polished. Color: colorless with green, blue, yellow, or red rim. Variations: sides may flare more; may be acid-stamped "STEUBEN" *on base.*

Type and Dimensions
Blown in mold for pattern and shape. Band of colored glass applied before annealing. Rim length: 14½". Height: 6½".

Locality and Period
Steuben Glass Works, Corning, New York. c. 1920–33.

Matching Glassware
Vases, centerpieces, and bowls. Not made as set.

Comment
During World War I, many glass companies were unable to get raw materials from Europe. Most of the factories producing tableware and vases were forced to shut down as nonessential industries. Steuben Glass Works, threatened with closing, was purchased by nearby Corning Glass Works and began to manufacture lighting devices. After 1918, Corning reorganized the Steuben company, and many unpopular or unprofitable designs were discontinued. One of the new ideas was what Steuben called its Grotesque line of colorless ribbed bowls and vases with colored rims like the one illustrated.

Hints for Collectors
Most Steuben glass is acid-stamped "STEUBEN" in a fleur-de-lis on the base. Occasionally, a piece slipped out of the factory unmarked, especially in the case of large sets of tableware. But even without a trademark, the Grotesque design is sufficiently distinctive to be recognized.

Diamond-quilted satin-glass bowl

Description
Circular bowl divided into several lobes; wavy rim. *Overall raised diamond pattern around sides with superimposed gilt floral decoration.* Pontil mark polished. Matt finish. Color: opaque pink, blue, or yellow.

Type and Dimensions
Blown in diamond-pattern mold for pattern, then tooled into shape. Cased with thin layer of opaque colored glass; air trap left between layers. Placed in second mold for vertical lobes. Acid-treated after annealing for matt finish. Gilt decoration applied and fired on. Rim diameter: 8–8¼". Height: 4–4½".

Locality and Period
Phoenix Glass Company, Monaca, Pennsylvania. Mt. Washington Glass Company, New Bedford, Massachusetts. England. c. 1885–1900.

Comment
In the 1880s and 1890s, matt-finished satin glass like this was sometimes advertised as plush or velvet glass. Many bowls were made to fit silver-plated stands (#311), but over the years these stands and bowls have been separated. If the base of the bowl appears quite worn, it may originally have had a stand.

Hints for Collectors
Many reproductions of satin glass have been made recently, especially in Italy. They are very difficult to distinguish from the authentic versions, although reproductions never have gilt decoration. English and American bowls made during the same period are identical because all of the glass companies copied each other to a great extent. Both English and American examples are equally valuable.

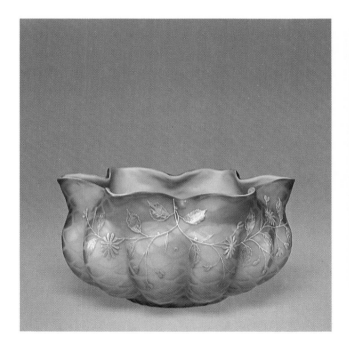

Plated Amberina bowl

Description
Circular bowl with 5 lobes and incurved, scalloped rim. *Molded pattern of widely spaced vertical ribs around sides.* Pontil mark polished. Glossy finish. Color: exterior opaque deep red shading to amber at base; opaque white lining.

Type and Dimensions
Blown in ribbed mold, then tooled into shape. Opaque white glass cased in amber. Partially reheated to develop shading. Rim diameter: 7½″. Height: 3½″.

Locality and Period
New England Glass Works, Cambridge, Massachusetts. c. 1886–88.

Matching Glassware
Tumblers, vases, bowls, punch cups, pitchers. Not made as set.

Comment
This art glass is a further development of the New England Glass Works' popular Amberina glass (#332). It is simply Amberina with an opaque white lining, and is identical to Wheeling Peachblow by Hobbs, Brockunier & Company (#345), except that Wheeling glass is free-blown while Plated Amberina is always made in a ribbed mold and given a glossy finish. "Plated Amberina" was a term used at the factory, but the process is identical to casing. The bowl illustrated has the remains of a paper label that says ". . . RORA/NEGW." It may indicate that the glass was marketed as "Aurora."

Hints for Collectors
Plated Amberina is one of the highest-priced art glasses because of its rarity. Even a small piece will bear a higher price tag than the same shape in Amberina (#332), Pomona (#259), or New England Peachblow (#179).

Carnival bowl

Description
*Round bowl with scalloped rim and circular foot. Pressed
pattern of grape clusters and leaves* below row of arches on
exterior (left) or 12 vertical panels on exterior and grape pattern
on interior (right). Color: *opaque iridescent* bronze, yellow-
orange, green, blue, purple, red, or white.

Type and Dimensions
Pressed in mold for pattern and shape. Iridescent finish sprayed
on before annealing. Rim diameter (left): 4⅞–5″; height: 2–2⅛″.
Rim diameter (right): 5⅛–5¼″; height: 2–2⅛″.

Locality and Period
Ohio: Imperial Glass Company, Bellaire; Millersburg Glass
Company, Millersburg. West Virginia: Northwood Glass
Company, Wheeling; Fenton Art Glass Company, Williamstown.
c. 1905–20.

Matching Glassware
Large tableware set in pattern on left (Helios). Bowls and plates
only in pattern on right (Vintage).

Comment
Designers of Carnival glass often put patterns on both the inside
and outside surfaces of bowls. Because this glass was opaque, the
2 patterns did not compete. The pattern by the Imperial Glass
Company, illustrated on the left, is called Helios. The pattern on
the right is named Vintage by collectors, but its manufacturer is
unknown.

Hints for Collectors
Imperial's Helios pattern is easily distinguished from the many
other Carnival grape patterns since the arches always appear in
combination with the grape design. In the 1970s, Imperial
reissued this pattern and marked new pieces "IG."

Helios and Vintage patterns

Description
Shallow circular dish with scalloped rim. *Interior with raised pattern of cherries, apples, pears, and foliage around rim; cherry spray in center. Exterior plain. Color: opaque iridescent* dark and light orange-amber, dark blue, aquamarine, purple, or green. *Variations:* may be marked "<u>N</u>." Pattern may have stippled background; leaves instead of cherry sprig at center.

Type and Dimensions
Pressed in mold for pattern and shape. Tooled rim. Iridescent finish sprayed on before annealing. Rim diameter: 9–9¼". Height: 1–1½".

Locality and Period
West Virginia: Fenton Art Glass Company, Williamstown; Northwood Glass Company, Wheeling. c. 1905–20.

Matching Glassware
Berry set with serving bowl and individual bowls. Bonbon bowl, 3-footed bowl, dome-footed bowl, and bowl with collarlike base; not made as set.

Comment
Both the Fenton Art Glass Company and the Northwood Glass Company made pieces in the Three Fruit pattern illustrated, which is just one of several fruit designs. It came in fewer shapes than many of the other Carnival patterns.

Hints for Collectors
If a Three Fruit piece is unmarked, like the bowl illustrated, it is difficult to distinguish Northwood from Fenton examples. The background on some Northwood pieces may be stippled, however, and sometimes there are leaves instead of a cherry sprig in the center.

Three Fruit pattern

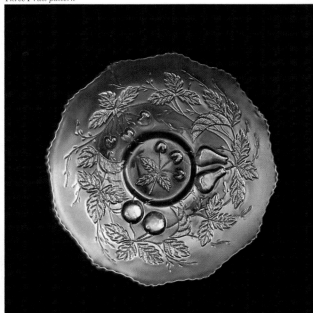

Carnival bowl

Description
Circular bowl with 8 lobes forming scalloped rim. *Interior with pressed pattern of holly stems, leaves, and berries* radiating from center in 8 branches. Exterior plain. Color: *opaque iridescent* orange-amber, bronze, green, blue, purple, red, or white. *Variations:* holly foliage may encircle rim instead of radiating from center (Holly Wreath).

Type and Dimensions
Pressed in mold for pattern and shape. Tooled rim. Iridescent finish sprayed on before annealing. Rim diameter: 9″. Height: 2½″.

Locality and Period
Fenton Art Glass Company, Williamstown, West Virginia. c. 1906–20.

Matching Glassware
Set with decanter, sherbets, bowls in 5 sizes, plates in 3 sizes, compotes in 2 sizes, rose bowl, candy dish, lamp, and hat rack.

Comment
Collectors usually call this pattern Carnival Holly to distinguish it from earlier pressed holly patterns made in transparent glass. It was produced by the Fenton Art Glass Company in all the Carnival-glass colors. Bowls with an interior pattern like the one illustrated could only be used for candy or fresh fruit because cooked food would stick to the patterned surface. Most of the shapes in this pattern are more ornamental than useful and were probably meant for display.

Hints for Collectors
Carnival Holly must have been popular since it is relatively abundant today. It is less expensive than many other Carnival-glass patterns.

Carnival Holly pattern

Description
Circular bowl with scalloped and serrated rim. *Interior with pressed pattern of 4 large grape bunches and 8 grape leaves hanging from cable.* Exterior has pressed basketweave design. "<u>N</u>" pressed on base. Color: *opaque iridescent* orange-amber, purple, light or dark blue, light or dark green, or white; also colorless and cream-white. *Variations:* may lack trademark.

Type and Dimensions
Pressed in mold for pattern and shape. Tooled rim. Iridescent finish sprayed on before annealing. Rim diameter: 8½–8¾". Height: 3¼–3½".

Locality and Period
West Virginia: Northwood Glass Company, Wheeling; Fenton Art Glass Company, Williamstown. Ohio: Imperial Glass Company, Bellaire; Millersburg Glass Company, Millersburg. c. 1905–20.

Matching Glassware
Berry sets, bowls, table set, punch set, breakfast set, water set (#51), lemonade set, whiskey set, and many other pieces. Not all shapes made in all colors.

Comment
Northwood's Grape and Cable with Thumbprint pattern, shown on the inside of this bowl, was probably made in more shapes and colors than any other pattern in Carnival glass.

Hints for Collectors
All Carnival glass companies made at least one grape pattern; both Fenton and Northwood combined the grape and cable motifs. Most Northwood pieces in this pattern are marked, however, and nearly all of the shapes have a row of thumbprints around the outside base (#51), which Fenton pieces do not.

Grape and Cable with Thumbprint pattern

Description
Circular bowl with ruffled and deeply scalloped rim. *Interior with pressed pattern of 4 large grape bunches and 8 stippled grape leaves on cable;* exterior plain. Color: *opaque iridescent* light or dark blue, orange-amber, purple, light or dark green, or white. *Variations:* sometimes marked "<u>N</u>" on base.

Type and Dimensions
Pressed in mold for pattern and shape. Tooled rim. Iridescent finish sprayed on before annealing. Rim diameter: 7½–7¾". Depth: 2¼–2½".

Locality and Period
West Virginia: Northwood Glass Company, Wheeling; Fenton Art Glass Company, Williamstown. Ohio: Imperial Glass Company, Bellaire; Millersburg Glass Company, Millersburg. c. 1905–20.

Matching Glassware
Set with bowls in several sizes, breakfast set, 4-piece table set, covered and uncovered compotes, cookie jar, cups and saucers, plates, punch set, water set, centerpiece, and lemonade and whiskey sets. Not all shapes made in all colors.

Comment
There is a tremendous variety of Carnival grape patterns. Both Northwood and Fenton used the grape and cable combination.

Hints for Collectors
To distinguish Grape and Cable patterns by Northwood and Fenton, remember that Fenton made mostly bowls and plates, while Northwood produced a wide range of matching pieces. On some pieces, Fenton used the Grape and Cable pattern on the exterior and another pattern on the interior. The value is about the same for either company.

Grape and Cable pattern

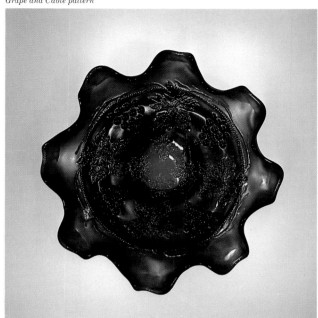

Centerpieces

Centerpieces are large, impressive forms used for serving or to decorate the center of a table or sideboard. They range from simple plates and bowls on high stems to elaborate pieces that fit into silver-plated frames, and magnificent punch bowl sets. Glass manufacturers called the plates and bowls on high stems salvers (#292) and compotes (#290). A salver, or footed plate, was used for serving cake, cookies, or tea sandwiches. A compote, or "comport" (the latter English spelling often appeared in 19th-century American advertisements and catalogues), is a deeper bowl used for fruit or perhaps just for decoration. Both shapes date from 18th-century European free-blown and mold-blown glass. In this country, most compotes and salvers were made in pressed glass in the late 19th century, and their patterns often matched large sets of pressed tableware. A third form on a high stem, called a banana boat by modern collectors, is essentially a flat-topped salver that has been tooled into a U-shape (#291). Covered compotes and covered bowls on high stems also became popular in late 19th-century pressed glass (#296). Listed in catalogues only as "covered compotes" or "covered bowls," they were probably used for candy, fruit, or special desserts; their purpose is not clear. Smaller shapes may have been used for butter.

Punch bowls (#298, #300, #306) with and without matching cups have been made in the United States since the 1820s and 1830s. They were made in all types of glass—free-blown, mold-blown, engraved, pressed, brilliant-cut, art, and Art Nouveau. Around the turn of the century, brilliant-cut glass and pressed-glass punch bowls were especially popular in sets with 12 to 24 cups. Today expensive brilliant-cut glass bowls with matching ladles and cups are still common, as are the more moderately priced pressed-glass imitations that were made about the same time. Carnival-glass punch bowl sets are somewhat less common and early pressed punch bowls of the mid-19th century are rare. Because of their enormous size and weight, most of these punch bowls are impractical for modern use. The cut-glass bowls are especially prone to chipping.

An epergne is a purely decorative centerpiece (#308–309) usually consisting of one or more free-blown or mold-blown trumpet-shaped vases and a supporting frame. A typical epergne has trailing threads and ruffled edges, often combined with colorful enameled or gilt decoration. Another centerpiece form is the art-glass bowl in a silver-plated frame, called a bride's basket by most collectors (#311–312), and undoubtedly a popular wedding present in the 1890s and early 1900s. Like epergnes, bride's baskets were meant for display. Their awkward size and fragile decoration, although impractical for serving, are certainly striking when displayed on a sideboard or étagère. The bowls, or baskets, can be found in American forms of art glass such as Amberina (#332), Burmese (#309), and Crown Milano (#310). Other bowls were imported from England and Bohemia by the American manufacturers of the silver-plated frames and sold as units. Few of these bowls are marked, and unless the type of glass or technique can be associated with a particular factory, identification may be impossible.

Description
Circular bowl with pressed latticelike design around rim. Thin walls. *Draped male figure on stem supporting bowl.* Slightly domed circular foot has scalloped edge and ribs radiating from center. Color: opaque white. *Variations:* rim may be plain; bowl may be shell-shaped. Stem figures in colorless glass include dolphin and biblical figure of Rebecca at the well.

Type and Dimensions
Pressed in mold for pattern and shape. Height: 8¼–8½". Rim diameter: 9–9¼".

Locality and Period
Pennsylvania: probably Atterbury & Company, Pittsburgh; Challinor, Taylor & Company, Ltd., Tarentum; and Westmoreland Specialty Company, Grapeville. c. 1870–90.

Comment
The compote illustrated appeared in an 1870s catalogue of Atterbury & Company, a firm famous for its opaque white glass, which collectors call milk glass. Although no name was indicated for the stem figure, some collectors refer to it as Atlas.

Hints for Collectors
Westmoreland Specialty Company continued to produce milk-glass novelties throughout the early 20th century. Many of its most popular patterns, such as Easter plates, dolphin candlesticks, and covered animal dishes (#237) are still made, often using the original molds. Fortunately, most examples produced after the 1960s are marked with a superimposed "WG" for the renamed Westmoreland Glass Company.

Atlas pattern

The Knopf Collectors' Guides to American Antiques

Also available in this unique full-color format

Chairs, Tables, Sofas & Beds
by Marvin D. Schwartz

Chests, Cupboards, Desks & Other Pieces
by William C. Ketchum, Jr.

Quilts, Coverlets, Rugs & Samplers
by Robert Bishop

Staff

Prepared and produced by Chanticleer Press, Inc.
Publisher: Paul Steiner
Editor-in-Chief: Gudrun Buettner
Managing Editor: Susan Costello
Project Editor: Jane Opper
Assistant Editor: Nancy Hornick
Editorial Assistant: Lori Renn
Art Director: Carol Nehring
Art Assistants: Laurie McBarnette, Ayn Svoboda
Marketing: Carol Robertson
Production: Helga Lose, John Holliday
Visual Key: Carol Nehring, Jane Opper
Symbols: Paul Singer, Alan Singer
Drawings: Dolores R. Santoliquido, Mary Jane Spring
Design: Massimo Vignelli

Early 20th-century pressed fruit server

Description
Upcurving dish with pressed strawberry-diamond and fan pattern on underside; scalloped edge with fan pattern. Thin walls. Hollow cylindrical stem has knop and flat circular foot; both with matching strawberry-diamond and fan pattern. Colorless. *Variations:* a few other pressed patterns, all imitations of geometric brilliant-cut motifs.

Type and Dimensions
Pressed in mold for pattern and shape; dish pressed flat, then curved upward into U-shape. Nonlead glass. Height: 9½–9¾". Length: 10¼–10½".

Locality and Period
McKee Glass Company, Jeannette, Pennsylvania, and other midwestern firms. c. 1903–10.

Matching Glassware
Set with tumblers, pitcher, creamer, sugar bowl, covered and uncovered bowls, butter dish, and spoon holder.

Comment
The fruit server illustrated appeared in a 1903 catalogue as the Majestic pattern. Today collectors refer to these dishes as banana boats, but they were termed fruit bowls at the turn of the century. It seems likely that they were used on a sideboard or table to hold wax fruit, which was popular in the 1890s, or perhaps real fruit. This piece, however, was probably designed for display.

Hints for Collectors
With its strawberry-diamonds and fans, this server is an example of a pressed imitation of the popular brilliant-cut motifs of the period (#78). Look for the mold mark on pressed glass. Cut examples have thicker, heavier glass and sharper edges.

Majestic pattern

Realistic-style pressed salver

Description
Flat circular dish has raised edge with pressed chain pattern.
Thin walls. *Stem has 3 faces of woman* wearing classical Greek
headdress above 1 solid knop. Hollow circular foot has scalloped
edge. Colorless dish with *frosted stem and foot. Variations:* stem
may have 3 baby faces.

Type and Dimensions
Pressed in mold for pattern and shape. Acid-frosted after
annealing for matt finish. Nonlead glass. Height: 8″. Rim
diameter: 10⅝″.

Locality and Period
Woman's face by George Duncan & Sons, Pittsburgh. c. 1873–85.
Baby face by M'Kee & Brothers, Pittsburgh. c. 1880–90.

Matching Glassware
Large set with stemware, pitcher, sugar bowl, creamer, butter
dish, salt dish, salt and pepper shakers, spoon holder, celery
vase, compote, cake plate, and rare biscuit box. Covered pieces
have 3 faces on knob.

Comment
John Miller of Pittsburgh designed this rare pattern for Duncan
in 1873. The classical face is said to have been modeled after his
wife's, although Miller seems also to have been inspired by a
4-faced pattern produced by the Cristalleries de St. Louis in
France before 1870. The baby-face variant by M'Kee was called
Cupid in an 1880 catalogue.

Hints for Collectors
The popular Three Face pattern has been reproduced by various
firms and by The Metropolitan Museum of Art, which marks its
pieces "MMA."

Three Face pattern

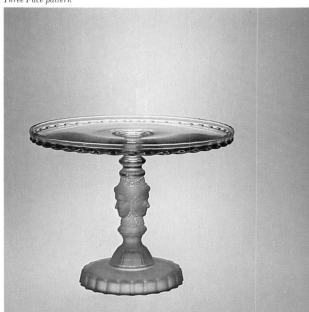

Early geometric-style pressed salver

Description
Flat circular dish with overall pressed swirl pattern of tiny diamonds on underside; slightly raised edge. Thin walls. Hollow paneled stem; hollow circular foot. Color: colorless or opaque white. *Variations:* patterns with large diamonds (Sawtooth, #236), diamonds with sunburst or 8-pointed star at center, or diamonds with rectangular panels (Diamond Point with Panels).

Type and Dimensions
Pressed in mold for pattern and shape. Lead or nonlead glass. Height: 7½–7¾". Rim diameter: 14½–14¾".

Locality and Period
Massachusetts: New England Glass Company, Cambridge; Boston & Sandwich Glass Company, Sandwich. Pittsburgh. c. 1860–70.

Matching Glassware
Large set with stemware (#20), tumblers, mugs, pitcher, decanter, bar bottle, sugar bowl, creamer, covered and uncovered bowls, plates, celery vase, spoon holder, salt, castor bottles, serving dishes, and candlesticks.

Comment
This pattern, known as Diamond Point, has been popular among collectors since the 1920s. It appears as the Sharp Diamond pattern in an 1869 catalogue of the New England Glass Company. Since it is found in nonlead as well as lead glass, it was probably also made by several firms in Pittsburgh.

Hints for Collectors
This pressed diamond pattern is so sharp-edged that beginning collectors may mistake it for cut glass. Look for a mold seam on the foot of stemware or on any plain surface of other pieces. Opaque white glass is more expensive than colorless.

Diamond Point pattern

Realistic-style pressed covered bowl

Description
Cylindrical domed cover with pressed design of charging buffalo, log cabin, and mountain scene around sides; finial of kneeling American Indian. Shallow dish has scalloped edge. Straight stem has concentric rings and 1 buttonlike knop. Flat round foot with sunburst design underneath. Colorless dish with *frosted cover.*

Type and Dimensions
Dish and cover pressed in separate molds for pattern and shape. Acid-frosted after annealing for matt finish. Nonlead glass. Height: 8⅞". Rim diameter: 6⅛".

Locality and Period
Probably Gillinder & Sons, Philadelphia. c. 1876–77.

Matching Glassware
Set with wine and cordial glasses, goblets, pitcher, sugar bowl, creamer, celery vase, spoon holder, compotes on high and low stems, platter, pickle jar and dish, and sauce dish.

Comment
This is probably a butter dish, although its stem makes it more imposing than most butter dishes. The Westward Ho pattern, with its unique Indian motifs, has been attributed to Gillinder & Sons, which made many frosted patterns and Centennial souvenirs (#227). The original name was Pioneer.

Hints for Collectors
Westward Ho has been a popular pattern among collectors for a long time, and consequently there are many reproductions on the market. Goblets and sauce dishes were made in this pattern in the 1930s, but the frosting is usually whiter than on originals. Goblets were also reproduced in blue glass, although this color was never made originally.

Westward Ho pattern

Late 19th-century pressed covered bowl

Description
Cylindrical bowl and cover with *pressed pattern of alternating ribs and coins. Frosted coins with female figure marked "20 cents"* on bowl; matching domed cover has slightly larger 25-cent coins marked "QUARDOL" and frosted knob in the form of a stack of coins. Hollow cylindrical stem has slightly domed hollow foot with scalloped edge. Colorless, with frosted coins and knob. *Variations:* coins stained red or amber.

Type and Dimensions
Bowl and cover pressed in separate molds for pattern and shape. Acid-frosted after annealing for matt finish. Nonlead glass. Height: 7½–7¾". Rim diameter: 6¼–6½".

Locality and Period
Central Glass Company, Wheeling, West Virginia. c. 1891. United States Glass Company, Pittsburgh; possibly others. c. 1893–95.

Matching Glassware
Large set with stemware, tumblers, mugs, pitcher, sugar bowl, creamer, butter dish, salt and pepper shakers, celery vase, spoon holder without foot, berry bowls, compotes, cake plate, bread tray, pickle and sauce dishes, syrup jug, tray, and lamp.

Comment
Depending on the size of the glassware, the coins represent American silver dollars, half dollars, quarters, or dimes. It is rumored that the Treasury Department ordered the molds destroyed, but this is doubtful. Collectors call the pattern Coin.

Hints for Collectors
A toothpick holder and a footed spoon holder have been reproduced, but neither was part of the original set. A similar pattern, which lacks dates on its coins, was sold in the 1950s.

Coin pattern

Late 19th-century pressed covered bowl

Description
Plain conical bowl and cover with *elephant finial* on ribbed
platform. Hollow baluster-shaped stem bulges just before hollow
circular foot. Colorless. *Variations:* elephant usually frosted.

Type and Dimensions
Bowl and cover pressed in separate molds for pattern and shape.
Nonlead glass. Height: 13½–13¾″. Rim diameter: 8–8¼″.

Locality and Period
Ohio: Aetna Glass & Manufacturing Company, Bellaire, and
Canton Glass Company, Canton. c. 1883–85.

Matching Glassware
Set with goblets, butter dishes, sauce dish, sugar bowl, creamer,
covered compotes, and spoon rack.

Comment
P. T. Barnum's elephant Jumbo was highly publicized during his
long circus career, and even after he killed by a train in
1885. Following the accident, Barnum had the elephant stuffed
and continued to exhibit him around the country. The Aetna and
Canton Glass companies both advertised Jumbo souvenirs, but
since no pictures came with the advertisements, it is not known
which company made the covered bowl illustrated. The spoon
rack patented in 1884 by Canton had an elephant on top identical
to the one illustrated, but probably the molds of both factories
were copied from one of the prints of Jumbo circulated by
Barnum.

Hints for Collectors
Jumbo mementos are relatively rare, but so far there has been
little demand for them and their price is still reasonable. Many
collectors of pressed glass prefer patterns that come in large
sets.

Jumbo pattern

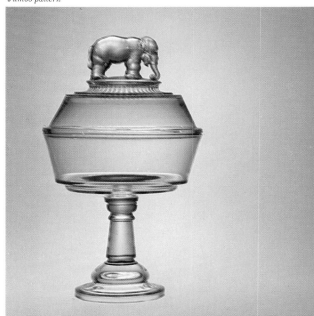

Early geometric-style pressed covered bowl

Description
Bowl and cover form sphere with overall pressed thumbprint pattern. Thick walls. Faceted spherical knob on cover. Hollow stem has narrow vertical ribs. Flat circular foot with thumbprint pattern and scalloped edge. Bowl and cover have scalloped edges that mesh for tight fit. Color: colorless; rarely opaque white. *Variations:* thinner walls and plain stem and foot.

Type and Dimensions
Bowl and cover pressed in separate molds for pattern and shape. Lead or nonlead glass. Height: 14¾–15″. Rim diameter: 8–8¼″.

Locality and Period
Bakewell, Pears & Company, Pittsburgh; other western Pennsylvania and Ohio firms. c. 1850–80.

Matching Glassware
Large set with stemware, tumblers, mugs, pitcher, tumble-up, decanter, sugar bowl, creamer, butter dish, salt, spoon holder, celery vase, punch bowl (#298), compote, plates, cake plate, honey and sauce dishes, pickle dish, syrup jug, paperweight, and lamp.

Comment
This pattern was originally named Argus, after the hundred-eyed creature of Greek mythology, but is known as Thumbprint today. The pattern was introduced by Bakewell, Pears & Company, and subsequently nearly every tableware factory in the Midwest marketed a variation with the name "Argus."

Hints for Collectors
In spite of the popularity of this early pattern, it has never been reproduced. Early pieces made of heavy flint glass have ribbed stems and thumbprinted bases. Later examples made of lime glass have plain stems and feet, and are thinner and lighter.

Thumbprint pattern

Early geometric-style pressed punch bowl

Description
Circular bowl with overall pressed thumbprint pattern and flaring scalloped rim. Thick walls. Hollow stem with narrow vertical ribs. Flat circular foot with thumbprint pattern and scalloped edge. Colorless. *Variations:* thinner walls and plain stem and foot.

Type and Dimensions
Pressed in mold for pattern and shape. Lead or nonlead glass. Height: 12–12¼". Rim diameter: 13¾–14".

Locality and Period
Bakewell, Pears & Company, Pittsburgh; other western Pennsylvania and Ohio firms. c. 1850–80.

Matching Glassware
Large set with stemware, tumblers, mugs, pitcher, tumble-up, decanter, sugar bowl, creamer, butter dish, salt, spoon holder, celery vase, covered bowl (#297), compote, plates, cake plate, honey and sauce dishes, pickle dish, syrup jug, paperweight, and lamp.

Comment
The Argus, or Thumbprint, pattern is one of the most popular early pressed patterns. The large size of the bowl illustrated is rare for any pressed piece, and can only be found in 2 or 3 other early pressed patterns. The heaviness of the glass makes it somewhat impractical.

Hints for Collectors
Earlier lead-glass pieces are usually more expensive as well as heavier than later nonlead examples. The Henry Ford Museum in Dearborn, Michigan, sells a sugar bowl with alternating rows of ovals and thumbprints. These bowls, also called Argus, are impressed "H.F." on the base.

Thumbprint pattern

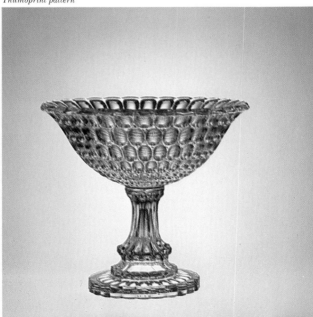

Early geometric-style pressed compote

Description
Circular bowl with overall pressed pattern of circles within diamonds. Deeply scalloped, slightly flaring rim. Thick walls. Paneled stem bulges before flat circular foot. Color: colorless or opaque white. *Variations:* diamond thumbprint pattern on foot. Many geometric patterns, including Ashburton (#20), Honeycomb (#24), Comet (#25), and Horn of Plenty (#56).

Type and Dimensions
Pressed in mold for pattern and shape. Lead glass. Height: 4¾–5″. Rim diameter: 7–7¼″.

Locality and Period
Massachusetts: probably Boston & Sandwich Glass Company, Sandwich; New England Glass Company, Cambridge; and possibly others. c. 1850–75.

Matching Glassware
Large set with wine, champagne, and cordial glasses, goblets, tumblers, mugs, pitcher, decanters, sugar bowl, creamer, butter dish, spoon holder (#321), deep bowl, compotes on high and low stems, honey and sauce dishes, covered jar, and rarely lamp.

Comment
Because this pattern does not appear in any surviving catalogues, its maker and original name are both unknown, but collectors call it Diamond Thumbprint. The fact that all of the known pieces are lead glass suggests that it was made only in New England, for most midwestern firms switched to nonlead glass for their tableware after 1864.

Hints for Collectors
Despite its popularity with collectors, this pattern has never been reproduced. Today it is relatively hard to find, although more examples have been discovered in the East.

Diamond Thumbprint pattern

300 Pillar-molded punch bowl

Description
Spherical bowl with *heavy, wide vertical ribs and folded rim*.
Thick walls. Baluster stem and wide circular foot. Pontil mark
rough. Colorless, with slightly grayish tinge.

Type and Dimensions
Blown in ribbed mold, then expanded and shaped. Applied,
tooled stem and foot. Lead glass. Height: 8–10″. Rim diameter:
10–12″.

Locality and Period
Western Pennsylvania, possibly West Virginia. c. 1840–70.

Matching Glassware
Celery vases, vases (#340), small bowls (#276), bar bottles
(#110), pitchers (#84), cruets, molasses cans, and candlesticks.
Not made as set.

Comment
Most pillar-molded forms were also made in blue, purple, or
amber glass, but large bowls like this one seem to have been
made only in colorless glass. The size of this bowl suggests it was
used for punch, yet no cups have ever been found with this type
of decoration. Given the scarcity of glassware on the frontier in
the 19th century, it is quite possible that plain tumblers or even
ceramic teacups might have been used.

Hints for Collectors
Pillar-molded glassware is still relatively inexpensive,
considering its age. Heavy pieces in this size are awkward to
use, however, and not much in demand.

Engraved compote

Description
Circular bowl with folded rim. Stylized leaves and grapes engraved around sides. Thin walls. Hollow baluster stem. Wide circular foot has rough pontil mark. Colorless. *Variations:* may have applied pressed stem and foot; this is usually a hollow steplike square. Either type of foot sometimes has bowl with engraved swags and tassels, or may be plain.

Type and Dimensions
Free-blown bowl with applied, tooled stem and foot. Copper-wheel engraved after annealing. Lead glass. Height: 6½–8″. Rim diameter: 7–9″.

Locality and Period
Probably New England; possibly western Pennsylvania. c. 1840–60.

Comment
Not all compotes of this type have a folded rim, but its presence indicates a mid-19th-century or earlier date. The folded rim was a strengthening device to prevent chipping around the vulnerable top edge. In the course of everyday use, compotes with a plain edge or a more decorative scalloped or serrated edge are very likely to become chipped, which lessens their value. With heavy pieces, this extra precaution was unnecessary since chipping was less likely to occur.

Hints for Collectors
This kind of compote is relatively inexpensive, possibly costing less than an engraved compote made today. Candlesticks and lamps often have the same kind of pressed hollow base as the variants, but these were not made to match. Today they make an attractive assembled set.

Bakewell-type cut compote

Description
Circular bowl has cut strawberry-diamonds and fans around
sides and serrated rim. Thick walls. Stem with 1 knop. Wide
circular foot with cut sunburst underneath. Colorless.
Variations: cut diamonds and squares with crosshatching, fans,
and circles in various combinations.

Type and Dimensions
Free-blown, then tooled into shape. Applied, tooled stem and
foot. Cut after annealing. Lead glass. Height: 7½–8″. Rim
diameter: 8½–9″.

Locality and Period
Massachusetts, New York, New Jersey, Philadelphia,
Pittsburgh, and western Pennsylvania. c. 1820–45.

Matching Glassware
Small wineglasses, tumblers, mugs, pitchers, decanters, sugar
bowls, creamers, and celery vase. Not made as set.

Comment
Glass in this pattern and its variations is usually attributed to the
Bakewell/Page factory or other firms in the Pittsburgh area. A
nearly identical compote, however, has descended in the family
of Phineas Dummer, a proprietor of the Jersey Glass Company,
Jersey City, New Jersey. Compotes like this may also have been
cut at the Kensington Glass Works, Philadelphia; Brooklyn Flint
Glass Works and New York Glass Works, both of New York; and
New England Glass Company, Cambridge, Massachusetts.

Hints for Collectors
Compotes with this decoration may be confused with English or
Irish pieces, but those examples usually have a turned-over rim
with notched cutting, unlike American compotes.

Free-blown compote

Description
Plain circular bowl has *flaring folded rim. Thin walls.* Stem has
1 round knop. Flat circular foot. Pontil mark rough. Color:
colorless; rarely opaque white, or colorless with red casing cut
with circles and crossed lines. *Variations:* hollow stem and foot
in later examples; early examples may be cased.

Type and Dimensions
Free-blown, then tooled into shape. Applied, tooled stem and
foot. Lead or nonlead glass. Height: 7⅛–8″. Rim diameter:
9–11″.

Locality and Period
Throughout the United States. c. 1850–1900.

Comment
Simple undecorated pieces like this were made by many
glasshouses over a long period, and are consequently impossible
to attribute even to a specific region. The thin walls of the
compote illustrated indicate that it was made after the Civil War.
Unlike this example, compotes made near the end of the 19th
century usually have a hollow stem and foot.

Hints for Collectors
This particular compote is similar in shape to the engraved
compote (#301) and has the same folded rim. It is therefore
likely that both were made around the same time. The bowl on
this compote was evidently made by a less skilled workman,
however, since it sits unevenly on top of its stem and the rim is
not level. Plain compotes are probably less expensive than most
modern examples of free-blown glass. Earlier compotes are made
of lead glass, while later examples from the 1880s and 1890s are
usually made of nonlead glass.

304   Venetian-style centerpiece

Description
Bell-shaped bowl with wide flaring rim. Thin walls. Stem has round ribbed knop and *hollow conical base with folded edge.* Small ear-shaped handle on each side has dangling ring. Circular underplate curves slightly upward. Pontil mark polished. Color: transparent blue, amber, pink, green, or purple, with colorless handles, rings, and upper stem. *Variations:* may lack handles and stem. Upper stem may match bowl color.

Type and Dimensions
Bowl free-blown, then tooled into shape. Applied, tooled handles, rings, stem, and base. Applied knop blown in ribbed mold. Underplate free-blown. Nonlead glass. Bowl height: 9–10″; rim diameter: 12–13″. Underplate diameter: 15–18″.

Locality and Period
Pennsylvania: H. C. Fry Glass Company, Rochester; C. Dorflinger & Sons, White Mills. Pairpoint Corporation, New Bedford, Massachusetts. Corning, New York: Steuben Glass Works; H. P. Sinclaire & Company. c. 1918–35.

Comment
Venetian-style glassware is famous for its brilliant colors and thin, delicate tinted glass. After World War I, in reaction to the waning popularity of heavy cut ware and the rising costs of labor and materials, glassmakers began to produce thinner blown glass like this centerpiece by Dorflinger.

Hints for Collectors
Most Venetian-style glass is unmarked since the Dorflinger and Pairpoint firms, which made most of it, used only paper labels, many of which have disappeared. This style is becoming increasingly popular, a fact reflected in current prices.

Tiffany punch bowl

Description
Round bowl has abstract leaf design around sides; bowl ends in short stem. Disk at base of bowl fits into collar on separate hollow conical base, stem, and foot. Circular foot has folded edge and matching leaf decoration. Pontil mark polished. Paper label beneath foot reads "TIFFANY FAVRILE GLASS REG. TRADEMARK." *Opaque iridescent glass.* Color: gold background with green decoration. *Variations:* may lack decoration; iridescence with reddish or pale bluish tinge.

Type and Dimensions
Bowl and stem with foot free-blown and shaped separately. Applied green glass tooled into leaf shapes and marvered into surface. Iridescent finish sprayed on before annealing. Height: 11¼–16". Rim diameter: 11⅞–16".

Locality and Period
Tiffany Glass & Decorating Company, Corona, New York. c. 1893–1910.

Matching Glassware
Set with punch cups. Vases and bowls; not made as set.

Comment
Two styles of cups match this punch bowl. One has a circular handle; the other lacks the handle but has a stem and foot and resembles a small sherbet glass.

Hints for Collectors
Like most Tiffany glassware, punch bowls and cups are very rare and quite expensive. But they are not nearly as expensive as the famous lamps, even though they seem to be less common. It is unusual to find a paper label, since most were removed or washed off as the bowls were used. On this piece, however, the paper label was placed inside the hollow stem.

Brilliant-cut punch bowl set

Description
Set with punch bowl and 12–24 cups. *Hemispherical bowl with
cut pattern of 8 large hobstars and 8 arches* separated by curved
miter cuts. Deeply scalloped rim has smaller scallops around
edge. Thick walls. Disk at base of bowl fits into collar of separate
hollow, flaring conical base, which has matching pattern and
scalloped edge. Ladle with sterling silver stem and spoon bowl;
"PAIRPOINT" stamped where stem joins glass handle; handle has
pattern matching bowl's. *Circular cup* thicker at base, with cut
hobstar-and-fan pattern around sides and ear-shaped handle; cut
hobstar on base. Color: all pieces colorless; rarely cased in
transparent red, blue, or green. *Variations:* patterns combining
hobstars, strawberry-diamonds, fans, and other motifs.

Type and Dimensions
Bowl, base, cups, and handle free-blown and shaped separately.
Cut after annealing. Lead glass. Bowl height: 12–15″; rim
diameter: 12–16″. Ladle length: 13⅜–14″. Cup height: 1⅞–3″; rim
diameter: 3½–4″.

Locality and Period
Majestic Cut Glass Company, Elmira, New York. c. 1900–10.
Throughout the United States. c. 1900–15.

Matching Glassware
Decanters and tumblers. Not made as set.

Comment
The Majestic Cut Glass Company was founded around the turn of
the century by Saul Spiegel, an Elmira scrap dealer. Its small
staff took over a floor above the junk business for the cutting
shop. The cutters used only the best quality American and
European blanks, and their cut glass was widely distributed
during the company's short life. After 10 years Spiegel closed

Majestic because rising expenses had started to diminish his profits. There were many small firms like Majestic around the United States at the turn of the century, but since most of them did not issue catalogues, use trademarks, or advertise, their products are largely anonymous today. This punch bowl, like the Majestic decanter, has been identified only because it was made for Spiegel and descended in his family. It was exceptionally well cut. The pattern cut on the ladle and cups has been adapted from the bowl pattern, a common practice in sets with different although matching shapes. The ladle illustrated was purchased by Majestic either as a blank or in its complete cut form from the Pairpoint Corporation, a large glass and metal firm in New Bedford, Massachusetts. Pairpoint maintained a cutting shop on its own premises after it took over the nearby Mt. Washington Glass Company in 1899, but it was also a major supplier of glass blanks to cutting firms all over the eastern United States. Majestic imported blanks from other sources as well, including the Val St. Lambert factory in Belgium.

Hints for Collectors
Punch bowl sets were prestige items in a cutting firm's line of products at the turn of the century. They were often sold as wedding or anniversary presents and usually cost several hundred dollars, which was more than the price of a car. In the 1950s and 1960s their status dwindled and many punch bowls were practically given away by their owners. Today the bowls are once more popular among collectors and accordingly expensive. Examples from well-known firms or pieces made in patented patterns command a premium price exceeded only by the price of cut-glass lamps. Patterns from unknown firms, such as this one, are still sold for little more than their original price.

Description
Set with punch bowl and 12–24 cups. *Bell-shaped bowl with deeply engraved design of grape cluster and leaves. Scalloped rim with cut band of alternating hobstars and X-cuts below it.* Disk at base of bowl fits into collar on separate hollow conical base, with square panels above and matching grape design and cut band around edge of foot. *Bell-shaped cup* with delicate flaring rim and matching grape-and-leaf design on bowl and foot; ear-shaped handle; short stem and circular foot; polished pontil mark with "Tuthill" written in script. Colorless. *Variations:* engraved decoration usually floral or fruit design; cut decoration mostly hobstars and a few other brilliant-cut motifs.

Type and Dimensions
Bowl, base, and cups free-blown and shaped separately. Stone-wheel engraved and cut after annealing. Lead glass. Punch bowl height: 16″; diameter: 12–13″. Cup height: 3–3½″; diameter: 2¾–3″.

Locality and Period
Tuthill Cut Glass Company, Middletown, New York. c. 1905–20.

Matching Glassware
Set with goblets, wine and cordial glasses, bowls in several sizes and shapes, decanter, and tumblers.

Comment
The Tuthill Cut Glass Company made brilliant-cut glass from 1900 to about 1923, but was particularly famous for its stone-wheel engraved floral and fruit patterns. The Vintage pattern illustrated, named for its grape motifs, is probably the best known. Stone-wheel engraving came into greatest use at the beginning of the 20th century, when many companies began to substitute it for copper-wheel engraving as a means of cutting

Vintage pattern

costs. The simpler stone-wheel designs took less time and skill to execute, but could be sold for nearly the same price. Many of the larger cutting firms had both types of engravers on their staffs. Stone-wheel and copper-wheel engravings are difficult to distinguish when the motifs are as large as those shown here. The design could have been executed by either technique, although factory records show that most Tuthill engravers worked with stone wheels. Typical stone-wheel engraved patterns depict large flowers, leaves, and fruits, as illustrated. Patterns with much finer details are probably copper-wheel engraved. Stone wheels are also used for cutting, but the technique is quite different from ordinary engraving. In engraving, the glass is held on the far side of the revolving stone so the engraver can see the design as he works. By contrast, the cutter holds the glass between himself and the stone and works by feel. He must look through the glass to see the cut design. Cutting is generally deeper than engraving, but not always.

Hints for Collectors

The punch bowl illustrated has a castellated rim, a combination of evenly spaced squares with cut notches at the top. This cutting design is most unusual and was probably a unique Tuthill decoration. Tuthill was also famous for combining the brilliant-cut style (seen in the band near the rim of this bowl) with naturalistic engraving. Both the Tuthill firm and H. P. Sinclaire & Company of Corning specialized in combined cutting and engraving. All punch bowl sets are expensive today, but those by famous companies like Tuthill are much more expensive than plainer sets or sets that cannot be identified with a particular pattern or firm. A plain or unknown bowl might cost only a tenth as much as the Tuthill punch bowl. Many unsigned punch bowls are underpriced simply because they are not in demand today.

Trumpet-shaped epergne

Description
3-part epergne has trumpet-shaped central vase with inverted baluster stem and hollow slightly domed foot. 2 smaller trumpet-shaped vases fit into rings on either side of stem. Thin walls. Colorless. *Variations:* sometimes spreading dishlike base may replace foot; may have up to 5 vases; occasionally hanging baskets; sometimes engraved with floral or Greek key pattern.

Type and Dimensions
Free-blown and tooled center vase and stem. Applied, tooled foot and rings. Side vases free-blown separately and tooled to fit rings. Lead glass. Height: 13–14″. Foot diameter: 5–5½″.

Locality and Period
Boston & Sandwich Glass Company, Sandwich, Massachusetts. England. c. 1870–88.

Comment
Epergnes are elaborate 18th- and 19th-century centerpieces made of glass, silver, porcelain, or a combination of these materials. They are usually ornate and probably intended for show, although some could be used for flowers or for serving desserts. Epergnes appeared in Europe in the 18th century but were not made in the United States until the 19th. The epergne illustrated, along with more elaborately engraved versions, was shown in an 1875 catalogue of the Boston & Sandwich Glass Company. Similar pieces were made in England during the same period, although most English examples are more complex, with hanging baskets, trailing threads, and ruffled decoration.

Hints for Collectors
Simple epergnes like this have never been reproduced, but recently there have been a number of nonlead reproductions of the more elaborate types associated with English firms.

Double Burmese epergne

Description
Circular bowls with ruffled rims, shading from opaque pink to opaque yellow. Stylized spray of enameled flowers around each bowl. Matt finish. Pontil mark polished. *Silver-plated stand with elaborately decorated central column on 4 feet.* Color: always opaque pink to yellow background; enameled flowers variable colors, such as the red, green, and white shown. *Variations:* sometimes glossy finish; applied floral decoration; intensity of pink color and amount of shading may vary. Bowl may be square.

Type and Dimensions
Free-blown, then tooled into shape. Yellow glass reheated to develop pink shading. Enameled after annealing. Acid-treated after annealing for matt finish. Bowl height: 3–4"; rim diameter: 5½–6½". Stand height: 23½"; width: 23".

Locality and Period
Mt. Washington Glass Company, New Bedford, Massachusetts. Stand by Simpson, Hall, Miller & Co., Wallingford, Connecticut. Thomas Webb & Company, Stourbridge, England. c. 1885–95.

Matching Glassware
Vases (#333), castor set (#190), and some tableware. Not made as set.

Comment
Today Burmese glassware is relatively easy to find, although unusual pieces like this centerpiece are rare.

Hints for Collectors
From 1938 to 1956 Robert M. Gunderson reproduced Burmese at the Pairpoint Corporation in New Bedford, but these pieces are not the original shapes. Italian reproductions have a slight grayish cast. Reproductions by the Fenton Art Glass Company are marked on the base.

310 Crown Milano bride's basket

Description
Square bowl with rounded corners and ruffled rim has enameled flower-and-leaf decoration around sides. Thin walls. Flat base of bowl has "CM" trademark with crown. Pontil mark polished. Color: *opaque white with enameled cream or yellowish finish;* enameled gold, brown, beige, rust, or muted pink or blue decoration. Elaborate silver-plated stand on 4 feet, with birds perched on branchlike handles at sides. *Variations:* enameled decorations, mostly floral. Bowl may lack trademark.

Type and Dimensions
Free-blown, then tooled into shape. Opaque white glass enameled with colored finish after annealing, then enameled decoration added. Bowl height: 4–4¼"; width: 7¾–8". Stand height: 10".

Locality and Period
Mt. Washington Glass Company, New Bedford, Massachusetts. c. 1890–1900.

Matching Glassware
Mostly decorative pieces such as bowls, vases, and biscuit boxes (#181); rarely tableware. Not made as set.

Comment
Glass bowls with silver-plated holders like the one illustrated are called bride's baskets by collectors and were very popular during the 1890s. Sometimes a glass company would purchase the stand for the glassware, and sometimes the silver-plating company would buy the glass to accompany the stand.

Hints for Collectors
It is often difficult to determine whether a stand was originally made for a particular bowl. Examine the base; a bowl that always had a stand will have minute scratches.

Satin-finished bride's basket

Description

Circular bowl with square ruffled rim. Herringbone pattern around sides. Pontil mark polished. Matt finish. Color: exterior opaque blue, pink, yellow, or white; *interior opaque white; rim edge colorless.* Silver-plated frame with basket handle and 4 feet. *Variations:* many patterns and decorations, including diamond-quilting (#283), gilt designs, and enameled flowers. Bowl may be more square.

Type and Dimensions

Bowl blown in mold for herringbone pattern and shape. Cased with thin layer of colored glass; air trap left between layers; cased with third layer of colorless glass. Tooled rim. Acid-treated after annealing for matt finish. Bowl height: 4½–5″; rim diameter: 10¾–11″. Stand height: 10¼–10½″.

Locality and Period

Throughout the United States. England. c. 1890.

Matching Glassware

Vases in several shapes. Not made as set.

Comment

Bowls and vases with a matt, or satin, finish and air traps between layers of glass were made in great quantities in England and in somewhat smaller amounts in the United States. The bowls were never signed, but they were probably made by many firms. It is nearly impossible to tell English from American examples.

Hints for Collectors

The ruffled edges on bowls like this are very likely to chip. Chips, of course, decrease value. Look for small bumps that may form between the 2 layers of glass. These air pockets, or blisters, will adversely affect the value of a piece.

Acid-etched cameo bride's basket

Description
Square-bottomed bowl with ruffles (left) or wavy flaring rim (right). *Cased with colored glass in cameo design* showing eagles (left) or classical profiles (right); both with stylized floral tracery around sides. Thin walls. Pontil mark polished. Stand is silver-plated figure or basket. Color: opaque white glass with pink, blue, or yellow outer casing. *Variations:* slightly varying shapes, as shown. Profile or floral decoration may vary slightly.

Type and Dimensions
Free-blown, then tooled into shape. Cased with thin layer of colored glass after annealing, then acid-etched through. Bowl height: 4–4½″; width: 9½–9¾″. Stand height: 4–12″.

Locality and Period
Mt. Washington Glass Company, New Bedford, Massachusetts. c. 1890–1900.

Matching Glassware
Set with lamp base and shade.

Comment
During the 18th and 19th centuries in England, there was a great revival of interest in ancient Roman cameo glass. Josiah Wedgwood made a fortune in the 18th century with his ceramic copies of the Roman Portland Vase; he also manufactured all kinds of highly successful serving pieces, all with stylized white designs in relief. By the 1880s, English glass manufacturers like Thomas Webb achieved the same effect in glass by carving the design by hand. A similar effect was created with acid by the Mt. Washington firm.

Hints for Collectors
Acid-etched designs are shallower than hand-carved examples and much less expensive.

313 Art-glass centerpiece

Description
Circular bowl with ruffled rim. Decorated with enameled fruit design (left) *or enameled with contrasting color on inside* (right). *Silver-plated stand with winged cherub.* Pontil mark rough or polished. Color: opaque blue, pink, white, purple, or amber glass, with red, yellow, blue, green, purple, or brown enameling. *Variations:* many color combinations, mostly deep colors shading to white or pastel colors; rarely enameled in purple and amber.

Type and Dimensions
Bowl on right blown in mold for size and shape. Bowl on left blown in mold, then cased with thin layer of colored glass. Both bowls have tooled rims. Enameled after annealing. Bowl height: 4–6″; diameter: 12–15″. Stand height: 15–18″.

Locality and Period
Glass: the Northeast; Bohemia. Silver-plated stand: Reed & Barton, Taunton, Massachusetts; Meriden, Britannia & Company, Meriden, Connecticut; Derby Silver Company, Derby, Connecticut. c. 1890–1900.

Comment
Some American silver companies used nearby glasshouses to provide the bowls for their mounts. Still other companies chose to import cheaper glassware, like the bowls illustrated, from Europe.

Hints for Collectors
Because this inexpensive European glass was never signed, it is impossible to determine in which country it was made. Most imports were probably from Bohemia, however.

Celery Vases, Spoon Holders, and Spill Holders

The vaselike forms in this section were common in the 19th century, but are no longer fashionable today. Both celery vases and spoon holders were placed on the table so that diners could help themselves to celery or spoons. Spill holders were designed as containers for spills, twists of paper used to light lamps or candles from the fire. They were probably kept next to oil lamps in the parlor.

Celery vases date back to the late 18th century, when glass and china "celeries" were advertised in England and the United States. Until the 1890s, celery was served in an upright footed vase made of free-blown, mold-blown, or pressed glass. Toward the end of the century, however, these vases became difficult to distinguish from ornamental vases. Some pressed-glass vases may actually have been intended as celery vases (#336).

The first free-blown and mold-blown celery vases of the late 18th and early 19th centuries were cylindrical with a slightly flaring rim and a very short stem, or no stem, and a circular foot (#317). As the 19th century advanced, celery vases became thinner and taller, often with a 2–3″ stem (#314–315). The advent of pressed glass in the 1820s increased the range of shapes and patterns, and by the second half of the 19th century many celery vases were made to match other pressed tableware. New forms, like squares or hexagons, took whatever shape blended best with the pattern design. Only one rare celery vase in the earliest lacy-pattern glass of the 1820s is known; several hundred patterns for celery vases are found in pressed glass of the 1870s and 1880s. Cut celery vases, popular from 1820 to 1850, were much less common after the 1850s. By the end of the 19th century, when brilliant-cut glass motifs became popular, upright celery vases were replaced by flat oval dishes (#263). For this reason, there are no celery vases in either Carnival or Depression glass.

Spill holders and spoon holders, unlike the celery vases which they resemble, were first made in pressed-pattern glass in the late 1840s. Spill holders were probably fashionable for only 15 years, until the early 1860s, while spoon holders were made until World War I. Only the latter form can be found in Carnival glass, mold-blown opalescent glass, and the later pressed glass. Spill holders are cylindrical, with a smooth rim, a flat-bottomed bowl, and usually a foot; sometimes they have a short stem. Because spill holders were made before the era of illustrated catalogues, their function is difficult to document. Advertisements of the period indicate that the containers were also used for cigars. Their patterns and colors often match lamp fonts rather than tableware.

Spoon holders, by contrast, frequently match tableware patterns and appear in many pressed glass catalogues. They are not as cylindrical as spill holders and have a short stem and usually a scalloped rim. Apparently it was a Victorian custom to put knives and forks at each individual table setting, while spoons were placed centrally in a container. Since spoon holders are not found in expensive cut glass, they probably were not used by the upper classes.

Hollow-stem pressed celery vase

Description
Square bowl has 4 pressed vertical corner columns with ends protruding at rim and base. Thin walls. *Hollow square stem contains colored paper bouquet.* Square base on 4 feet has sunburst underneath. Paper label on base reads "PATENTED NOVEMBER 81/JULY 1882." Color: colorless, with green, blue, yellow, and pink paper flowers.

Type and Dimensions
Pressed in mold for pattern and shape. Paper flowers inserted after annealing and fastened with glue or plaster. Nonlead glass. Height: 10″. Base width: 3½″.

Locality and Period
Daniel C. Ripley & Company, Pittsburgh. c. 1882–90.

Matching Glassware
Kerosene lamps. Not made as set.

Comment
The late 19th century was a period of great competition among glass manufacturers, and eye-catching gimmicks like the flowers enclosed in this celery vase and its companion lamp were undoubtedly introduced to make such ordinary low-cost products stand out. The glass of the vase and the lamp is not of good quality, but the sturdy square shape, reinforced by the column at each corner, enables the pieces to withstand heavy use. In many examples, the original paper flowers may be missing, probably having fallen out through the hole at the bottom of the hollow stem.

Hints for Collectors
Late pressed pieces like this celery vase are still quite plentiful and relatively inexpensive.

Realistic-style pressed celery vase

Description
Cylindrical bowl with plain sides and panels at bottom. *Flaring scalloped rim.* Thin walls. *Frosted stem has 3 lions' heads forming knop.* Circular frosted foot has scalloped edge. Colorless.

Type and Dimensions
Pressed in mold for pattern and shape. Acid-frosted after annealing for matt finish. Nonlead glass. Height: 9–9¼". Rim diameter: 4½–4¾".

Locality and Period
Pennsylvania: probably Gillinder & Sons, Philadelphia; Pittsburgh area; Richards & Hartley Flint Glass Company, Tarentum. c. 1876–80.

Matching Glassware
Large set with stemware, tumblers, pitchers, bowls, sugar bowl, creamer, butter dish, salt, relish dish, platter, and compotes. Lamp and bread plate; not made as set.

Comment
Frosted-glass patterns were popular from the mid-1870s until the 1880s. Patterns like Classic (#86), Three Face (#292), and Westward Ho (#294)—made during this period—have similar realistic motifs of people and animals on partially frosted glass. The Gillinder attribution is based on the company's similar Westward Ho pattern and also on a lion paperweight sold as a Centennial souvenir. Most glassware in the pattern illustrated has a lion's-head stem or a lion finial, inspiring its name "Lion."

Hints for Collectors
The many reproductions generally have whiter frosted stems that are rougher, but these differences are subtle.

Lion pattern

316 Engraved celery vase

Description
Cylindrical bowl with flaring rim and molded gadrooning around lower body. *Engraved decoration* of draped garlands around upper body. Thin walls. Short stem has flat buttonlike knop. Circular foot. Pontil mark rough. Colorless. *Variations:* usually floral engraving; rarely pictorial. May lack gadrooning or engraving.

Type and Dimensions
Free-blown bowl, with extra pattern-mold gather of glass, applied and tooled on lower body. Applied, tooled stem and foot. Copper-wheel engraved after annealing. Lead glass. Height: 8–8½". Rim diameter: 4½–5".

Locality and Period
Probably Pittsburgh, Philadelphia, New York City, and Baltimore. c. 1820–50.

Comment
Celery vases like the one illustrated are commonly associated with Pennsylvania, New York, and Maryland rather than New England. Judging from their individuality, the vases were probably factory-blown, then engraved to order by self-employed glass engravers. Several engravers advertised regularly in the local papers of large cities such as New York, Baltimore, and Philadelphia during this period.

Hints for Collectors
These celery vases are very expensive, but they have not been reproduced and are therefore a safe buy. They are fragile, however, so examine each piece carefully. In general, the more detailed the engraving, the higher the price.

Bakewell-type cut celery vase

Description
Conical bowl has *cut strawberry-diamond and fan pattern* above vertical panels. *Serrated rim* with cut fans below. Thick walls. Short stem with round knop. Circular foot has cut sunburst underneath. Colorless. *Variations:* many patterns combine strawberry-diamonds with polished circles, ovals, and rays.

Type and Dimensions
Free-blown bowl tooled into shape. Applied, tooled stem and foot. Cut after annealing. Lead glass. Height: 7½–8″. Rim diameter: 5–5½″.

Locality and Period
Pittsburgh, and Wheeling, West Virginia. c. 1825–45.

Matching Glassware
Wineglasses, tumblers, compotes, and decanters; rarely sugar bowls and creamers. Not made as set.

Comment
Cut celery vases of this type are traditionally attributed to the Midwest, although the pattern was cut in the East as well. The vase illustrated was made in Pittsburgh at Bakewell, Page & Bakewell and descended in the Bakewell family. Similar vases were probably also made in Pittsburgh at the Robinson and Curling factories and in Wheeling by the Ritchie and Sweeney firms. Because records are incomplete, however, attributions are tentative.

Hints for Collectors
Cut celery vases are more common than engraved ones. Although they were made about the same time, cut examples are usually less expensive since the engraved pieces generally required more labor. The chipped rim on the vase illustrated should lower its value only slightly.

318 Realistic-style pressed spoon holder

Description
Bell-shaped bowl with pressed stippled floral pattern. Thin walls. Large scalloped rim and circular foot. Colorless. *Variations:* many realistic-style patterns (#319) as well as early geometric-style patterns, such as Ashburton (#126) and Thumbprint (#297).

Type and Dimensions
Pressed in mold for pattern and shape. Tooled rim. Nonlead glass. Height: 4½–4¾". Rim diameter: 3⅞–4⅛".

Locality and Period
Pittsburgh: King, Son & Company's Cascade Glass Works, c. 1870–90; United States Glass Company, c. 1891–1900.

Matching Glassware
Large set with stemware (#31), mugs, tumblers, large pitcher, sugar bowl, creamer, bowls, butter dish, celery vase, covered compotes, salt, relish dish, plates, platter, and cake plate.

Comment
This pattern was called Floral Ware when originally issued, but is now referred to by collectors as Bleeding Heart. The stippled effect was popular in floral and fruit patterns of the 1870s and is reminiscent of the early 19th-century lacy-pattern glass. Like cup plates and butter dishes, spoon holders were made mostly in pressed glass, including opalescent and Carnival glass. They are never found in Depression glass. Occasionally, spoon holders are included in large sets of blown and engraved glass.

Hints for Collectors
Spoon holders do not appear before 1850 and lasted only until the end of the 19th century, when they gradually went out of use. Earlier examples usually have a scalloped rim; those made after 1891 have plain rims.

Bleeding Heart pattern

Realistic-style pressed spoon holder

Description
Bell-shaped bowl with pressed pattern of 2 horizontal flowering vines superimposed on fine vertical ribs. Thin walls. Flaring rim has 6 scallops. Circular foot has sunburst underneath. Color: colorless; rarely transparent amber or blue, opaque white, or opalescent white. *Variations:* sometimes only 1 flowering vine.

Type and Dimensions
Pressed in mold for pattern and shape. Tooled rim. Lead or nonlead glass. Height: 5½–5¾". Rim diameter: 3¼–3½".

Locality and Period
M'Kee & Brothers, Pittsburgh; Boston & Sandwich Glass Company, Sandwich, Massachusetts; and others. c. 1864–75.

Matching Glassware
Large set with stemware, mugs, tumblers, pitcher (#89), decanter, bar bottle, sugar bowl, creamer, butter dish, salt, bowls, castor set (#189), celery vase, plates, cake stand, and lamp.

Comment
This pattern, now called Bellflower by collectors, was listed as the Ribbed Leaf pattern in an 1864 M'Kee catalogue. It was probably made by several companies, since it has more variations than any other pattern except Daisy and Button (#242). Other shapes in this pattern can be found in lead or nonlead glass, with fine or coarse ribs, or single or double vines.

Hints for Collectors
In the 19th century, only knives and forks were placed at each table setting. Spoons were kept in spoon holders located in the center of the table along with celery vases. The scalloped rim on this example was tooled by hand, but the lack of a pontil mark indicates that the piece was probably held in a snap case.

Bellflower pattern

Blown 3-mold celery vase

Description
Cylindrical bowl has *flaring folded rim and molded pattern of vertical ribs and diamonds.* Thick walls. Hollow domed foot with similar pattern. Pontil mark rough. Colorless. *Variations:* several geometric patterns combine ribs, diamonds, squares, waffling, and sunbursts. Foot may be flat, with a short stem.

Type and Dimensions
Bowl blown in full-size mold, then tooled into shape. Foot applied and tooled. Lead glass. Height: 6–6½″. Rim diameter: 4–4½″.

Locality and Period
New England. c. 1820–35.

Matching Glassware
Bowls, plates, pitchers, tumblers, decanters, serving platters, and sugar bowls. Not made as set.

Comment
Blown 3-mold celeries are rare. Because of their wide mouths, celery vases are especially fragile. As a result, relatively few examples have survived, while blown 3-mold decanters and bar bottles are somewhat more common.

Hints for Collectors
Blown 3-mold celery vases were reproduced in the 1930s, usually in colored glass, although originals were made only in colorless glass. The reproduction colors include several unusual shades of bluish- and reddish-purple that were never made in the 19th century. Reproductions of the celery vase made for The Metropolitan Museum of Art in New York City are sea-green in color and are marked "MMA" on the base.

321 Early geometric-style pressed spoon holder

Description
Cylindrical bowl with pressed overall pattern of thumbprints and diamonds. Thick walls. Scalloped rim. Paneled stem bulges at circular foot, which has matching pattern underneath. Colorless. *Variations:* foot sometimes plain; rim sometimes flaring.

Type and Dimensions
Pressed in mold for pattern and shape. Lead glass. Height: 6¼–6½". Base diameter: 3–3⅛".

Locality and Period
Massachusetts: probably New England Glass Company, Cambridge; Boston & Sandwich Glass Company, Sandwich. Possibly other New England firms. c. 1850–75.

Matching Glassware
Set with goblets, cordial and champagne glasses, tumblers, mugs, pitcher, decanter, bowls, butter dish, compote (#299), sugar bowl, creamer, honey and sauce dishes, cake stand, covered jar, and rarely lamp.

Comment
The scalloped rim on this Diamond Thumbprint spoon holder was created by pressing alone, unlike the flaring rim of the Bellflower spoon holder (#319), which was tooled in addition to being pressed. Flaring the scalloped rim by hand was more common, although it required extra labor.

Hints for Collectors
The scalloped rim on this early form indicates that it was used as a spoon holder rather than as a spill holder. Both types of containers were made chiefly in pressed glass and probably were never made in ceramic or silver.

Diamond Thumbprint pattern

322 Early geometric-style pressed spill holder

Description
Hexagonal bowl with overall pressed star pattern. Thick walls. Smooth hexagonal rim. Short thick stem and hexagonal foot. Color: colorless; rarely transparent blue, green, or purple. *Variations:* sometimes stars within ovals (#323).

Type and Dimensions
Pressed in mold for pattern and shape. Lead glass. Height: 5⅛–5⅜". Rim diameter: 3–3¼".

Locality and Period
Massachusetts: Boston & Sandwich Glass Company, Sandwich; possibly New England Glass Company, Cambridge. c. 1850–60.

Matching Glassware
Set with goblets, wine and cordial glasses, compotes, oblong bowl, decanter, lamp, and rare compote with triple-dolphin base.

Comment
Spill holders like this one probably were kept on the mantel of a fireplace to hold spills, twists of paper that were used to light a candle, lamp, or pipe. The pattern illustrated is one of the very few thought to have been made only at the Boston & Sandwich Glass Company. The attribution is based on fragments found at the factory site and also on a wooden model of the mold used for this pattern, which is believed to be from the Sandwich factory. It is likely, however, that the pattern was also made in nearby Cambridge. Collectors call this pattern Sandwich Star.

Hints for Collectors
The thicker, heavier glass used for this pattern indicates that it is probably an early design. All shapes made in this pattern are rare and expensive, especially the colored examples.

Sandwich Star pattern

Early geometric-style pressed spill holder

Description
Hexagonal bowl has 6 pressed panels of stars within ovals and circles around sides. Thick walls. Flat hexagonal rim. Short thick stem and circular foot. Color: opaque jade-green, transparent purple, cobalt-blue, yellow, or colorless. *Variations:* patterns with stars, diamonds, diamonds and circled stars, and ovals and harps.

Type and Dimensions
Pressed in mold for pattern and shape. Lead glass. Height: 5¼–5½". Rim diameter: 3–3½".

Locality and Period
New England. c. 1850–60.

Matching Glassware
Perfume bottle, lamp font, and hand lamp made with same mold. Not made as set.

Comment
Most collectors refer to this pattern as Star and Punty. Although often called spill holders, these forms actually may be early spoon holders (#318, #319). By the time glass-factory catalogues were first printed in the 1850s, the form was listed as a spoon holder. Still, the patterns on these containers match those on lamp fonts more often than those on tableware forms, which suggests that they may have been used for spills.

Hints for Collectors
Spill holders and spoon holders are easily confused, but the rim of spill holders is always smooth, never scalloped. They were made only in lead glass in a limited number of patterns and mostly by New England glasshouses. Spill holders are usually made of very sturdy thick glass that is not easily damaged.

Star and Punty pattern

Vases

Vases have been made since ancient times in all types of
materials, including ceramic, metal, and glass. Most vases are
upright containers meant for flowers. More than any other form,
glass vases come in a tremendous variety of shapes, colors, and
sizes, ranging from a few inches to several feet tall.

Early 19th-century vases are usually free-blown or blown and
cut. They were probably always expensive, since these objects
were basically decorative rather than functional. Unlike pitchers,
vases were seldom made in bottle glass, but were usually
produced by glasshouses specializing in tableware (#324–325).
In this early period, the upright celery vase (#316–317) meant
for the table was often also used for show. By mid-century, the
number of shapes and types had greatly increased, so that
neither criterion can be used to date examples. Middle 19th-
century pressed-glass vases usually display simple patterns and
striking colors (#336). Although these patterns match lamp
fonts, they seldom match sets of pressed-glass tableware. These
early colored pressed vases, like their free-blown counterparts,
may have been intended for celery; in pressed glass catalogues of
the 1860s and 1870s, the only vases shown are listed as "celery
stands."

In the late 19th century, manufacturers of brilliant-cut glass and
art glass introduced the corset-shaped vase with a distinct waist
(#327). But cut vases also came in baluster, pear, and trumpet
shapes as well as irregular forms. The trumpet shape is probably
the most common, adopted in glass of nearly every type,
including Depression glass of the 1930s. Near the turn of the
century, elongated vases known as "swing vases" became
fashionable in both Carnival glass (#329) and opalescent pressed
glass. The name comes from the unusual method of manufacture.
The cylindrical shape was pressed in a pattern mold; then a
workman "swung" the vase on the end of a tool, thus using the
vase's own weight to elongate it. Finally, the top of the vase was
ruffled for the characteristic rim.

Because only a few firms made the most popular art glass, the
different patented colors often come in the same vase shapes,
including Wild Rose (#68), Agata (#191), Amberina (#332), and
Plated Amberina (#284)—all made by the New England Glass
Works—and Burmese (#333) and the Peachblow (#280) made by
the Mt. Washington Glass Company. Most of these are quite
simple shapes, relying on the bright colors for decorative effect.

324 Paneled vase

Description
Pear-shaped vase with arched vertical panels around lower body and flaring folded rim. Thin walls. Slightly depressed base. Pontil mark rough. Color: transparent purple, green, blue, colorless, or opaque white. *Variations:* rim rarely ruffled or folded.

Type and Dimensions
Blown in mold for pattern, then expanded and shaped. Lead glass. Height: 7¾–9″. Base diameter: 3⅜–4″.

Locality and Period
Massachusetts: probably Boston & Sandwich Glass Company, Sandwich, and New England Glass Company, Cambridge. c. 1825–50.

Comment
In 1914 Frederick Hunter, a glass collector, attributed vases of this type to the glasshouse of Henry W. Stiegel in Manheim, Pennsylvania. The attribution was based on a single fragment found at the Stiegel factory site. During the 1940s, however, American glass researchers George and Helen McKearin disputed the Stiegel origin, based on the 19th-century shape and panels of this vase. Most pieces of this type have been found in New England, but sometimes collectors still erroneously call them Stiegel-type paneled vases.

Hints for Collectors
While vases of this type are rare compared to most pressed vases, they turn up occasionally in New England in antique shops and at auctions, or in other parts of the country at sales of older collections. Any example will command a premium price.

New England coin loving cup

Description
Baluster-shaped vase with folded rim and rings around waist and lower bowl. Hollow stem with *bulbous knop containing 1819 English silver coin.* 2 large ear-shaped handles crimped at bases. Heavy circular foot. Pontil mark rough. Colorless. *Variations:* rarely with matching cover.

Type and Dimensions
Free-blown, then tooled into shape. Coin inserted during blowing. Applied horizontal rings. Applied knop, handles, and foot. Lead glass. Height: 9–10″. Foot diameter: 5½–6″.

Locality and Period
Massachusetts: probably New England Glass Company, Cambridge; Thomas Cains's South Boston Flint Glass Works, Boston; and Boston & Sandwich Glass Company, Sandwich. c. 1815–30.

Matching Glassware
Coins in knops of large goblets, footed mugs, sugar bowls, vases, and banks. Not made as set.

Comment
Commemorating a special occasion with an object containing a coin was an old tradition popular in 18th-century England and also sometimes on the Continent. In this country, it seems mainly to have been done by English glassblowers.

Hints for Collectors
Do not assume that the date on the enclosed coin is the year that a piece was made. The coin may have commemorated a date 10, 25, or 50 years earlier. When dating objects, it is best to rely on the usual criteria of decorative technique and form.

Dorflinger cut vase

Description
Urn-shaped vase has spreading scalloped rim with cut fan on each scallop. Square panels around neck. *Cut strawberry-diamonds alternating with waffled diamonds* on body; step cutting and row of fans above. 2 ear-shaped handles with notched cutting. Cut sunburst on base. Colorless. *Variations:* sometimes has Dorflinger paper label on base.

Type and Dimensions
Free-blown, then tooled into shape. Applied handles. Cut after annealing. Lead glass. Height: 12½–13″. Rim diameter: 6–7″.

Locality and Period
C. Dorflinger & Sons, White Mills, Pennsylvania. c. 1880–90.

Matching Glassware
Stemware, tumblers, pitchers, decanters, and bowls. Not made as set.

Comment
C. Dorflinger & Sons was one of the largest and best glass-cutting establishments in the United States. It operated from the early 1850s until 1863 in Brooklyn, New York, and from 1868 until 1921 in White Mills, Pennsylvania. Both a blowing factory and a cutting shop, Dorflinger supplied uncut blanks to many of the small cutting shops around the country. The vase illustrated is cut in the standard strawberry-diamond pattern of the 1880s, but it is unusual for its elegantly cut rim. This pattern was replaced by patterns with curvilinear designs soon afterward. The vase was a gift made for one of Christian Dorflinger's sons.

Hints for Collectors
Special items like this vase do not come on the market often. They always command a premium price, even without a company trademark or paper label.

Corset-shaped brilliant-cut vase

Description
Corset-shaped vase with scalloped rim. *Cut pattern of large hobstars* between 2 miter cuts, alternating with smaller hobstars and fine diamonds, and circular bands of stars. Cut hobstar on base. Colorless. *Variations:* many cut patterns include various combinations of hobstars, diamonds, fans, pinwheels, or cut starlike motifs. Sometimes with paper label or acid-etched trademark on base.

Type and Dimensions
Free-blown, then tooled into shape. Cut after annealing. Lead glass. Height: 12–12½″. Base diameter: 3–3½″.

Locality and Period
Throughout the United States. c. 1895–1915.

Comment
Corset-shaped vases were probably the most common vases made during the brilliant-cut period. The type of cutting ranges from relatively simple motifs to the elaborate pattern illustrated. Original prices depended largely on the amount of cutting and the skill of the cutter. The vase illustrated was cut at the Wright Rich Cut Glass Company of Anderson, Indiana, which operated from 1904 to 1914. This vase was one of a pair made specially for the firm's owner. According to the cutter, the vase was worth $200 when new. This special-order piece is not marked, unlike most pieces from the Wright cutting shop, which may be acid-stamped "Wright" in script on the base.

Hints for Collectors
Today even a trademark is no guarantee of authenticity. The popularity of cut glass has risen dramatically in the last 10 years and forged trademarks have become more common.

Description
Cylindrical vase flares slightly at rim and base. *Gilt decoration* with flowers and leaves and wavy band on upper and lower body. Pontil mark polished. Colorless. *Variations:* gilt decoration may be scrolls and vertical lines. Inscribed "Honesdale" or with "P" in keystone near pontil.

Type and Dimensions
Free-blown, then tooled into shape. Gilt decoration applied after annealing and fired on. Height: 12–14″. Base diameter: 5½–6″.

Locality and Period
Honesdale Decorating Company, Honesdale, Pennsylvania. c. 1900–32.

Matching Glassware
Bowls and vases in several shapes, tumblers, stemware, and pitcher. Not made as set.

Comment
Austrian Carl Prosch was working for a glass-importing firm in New York City around 1900 when Christian Dorflinger helped him to finance a small decorating shop in Pennsylvania that specialized in gold work. Prosch decorated glass from Dorflinger's factory in nearby White Mills, as well as the glass of other firms. In 1915, Prosch bought the decorating shop from the Dorflingers and continued to operate it until 1932. Prosch's gilt decoration resembles the European Art Nouveau style and reflects his Austrian training.

Hints for Collectors
Prosch's firm is not yet well known and its glass is still very reasonably priced, although its value will probably increase in the future.

Carnival vase

Description
Narrow cylindrical vase flares slightly at rim and at flat base. Rim ruffled or scalloped. Narrow vertical ribs (left) or panels (right) around body. Color: *opaque iridescent* purple, amber, or orange. *Variations:* several patterns, mostly vertical ribs, flutes, or horizontal ribs in various combinations.

Type and Dimensions
Pressed in mold for pattern and basic shape; vase on left elongated. Tooled rim. Iridescent finish sprayed on before annealing. Height (left): 16–16¼"; rim diameter: 4¾–5". Height (right): 8¼–8½"; rim diameter: 4¼–4½".

Locality and Period
Ohio: Millersburg Glass Company, Millersburg, and Imperial Glass Company, Bellaire. West Virginia: Fenton Art Glass Company, Williamstown, and Northwood Glass Company, Wheeling. c. 1905–20.

Comment
Carnival-glass vases like this were very popular during the first decades of the 20th century. Elongated shapes, called swing vases, were often made with an iridescent finish and are seldom found in colorless or colored pressed glass of the same period. Base colors in Carnival glass range from amber, red, and blue-green to purple. These were sprayed with iridescent orange, blue, green, or purple for a tremendous color range.

Hints for Collectors
Because this type of vase was made by several companies and was seldom marked, it is impossible to identify positively the origin of given examples. This has not, however, affected their value, because the shape is popular.

Cased and cut vase

Description
Trumpet-shaped vase with scalloped serrated rim. *Cut pattern of strawberry-diamonds, fans, and sunbursts* around sides. Thick walls. Large and small vertical panels on upper stem; notches on lower stem. Circular foot has cut sunburst. Color: *usually colorless with red casing;* rarely green, purple, blue, turquoise, or yellow casing. *Variations:* several hundred patterns, mostly combining strawberry-diamonds, fans, hobnails, and panels; may lack casing. Sometimes with paper label or acid-etched trademark underneath foot.

Type and Dimensions
Free-blown, then tooled into shape. Drawn stem and applied, tooled foot. Cased with color, then pattern cut through after annealing. Lead glass. Height: 15–16″. Rim diameter: 4½–5″.

Locality and Period
Throughout the United States. c. 1882–1915.

Matching Glassware
Large tableware set with stemware, platters, and serving bowls; only select pieces cased.

Comment
Collectors often call this relatively rare cased glass "colored cut to clear." Most pieces of this type were specially ordered and required thicker blanks. Cased white-wine glasses were nearly always available in the most expensive patterns (#29); most other colored pieces were not listed in trade catalogues. The piece illustrated was cut by C. Dorflinger & Sons of White Mills, Pennsylvania.

Hints for Collectors
Cased and cut glassware commands a premium price, regardless of color or pattern.

Sinclaire cut and engraved vase

Description
Trumpet-shaped vase with wide flaring rim. *Cut vertical panels narrow at base, becoming wider at rim; cut Greek key design below rim interlaced with engraved leaves.* Circular foot with same engraved leaf design. Pontil mark polished. Colorless. *Variations:* sometimes engraved floral design below rim; engraved floral designs may replace cut panels. Sometimes "s" within laurel wreath acid-stamped underneath foot.

Type and Dimensions
Free-blown bowl, tooled into shape. Drawn stem and applied, tooled foot. Cut and copper-wheel engraved after annealing. Lead glass. Height: 12¼–13″. Rim diameter: 5–6″.

Locality and Period
H. P. Sinclaire & Company, Corning, New York. c. 1915–28.

Matching Glassware
Vases, bowls, trays, and jars. Not made as set.

Comment
H. P. Sinclaire & Company was one of Corning's largest cutting and engraving firms, operating from 1904 to 1929. Although the firm made brilliant-cut glass (#78), it was best known for its quality copper-wheel engraving and for its simple cut glassware like the vase illustrated. Panels were a favorite Sinclaire motif, combined with a simple cut design like the Greek key or a more complex copper-wheel-engraved design.

Hints for Collectors
Until just a few years ago, the Sinclaire company was much less well known by collectors than T. G. Hawkes & Company and J. Hoare & Company, both of Corning, New York. Sinclaire's trademark, an "s" in a laurel wreath, was often mistaken for that of Steuben Glass Works of Corning.

Description
Trumpet-shaped vase has vertical ribs and wavy flaring rim. Narrow stem ends in circular foot. Pontil mark polished. Color: *transparent amber at base shading to deep red at rim.* *Variations:* sometimes paper label with "NEGW/AMBERINA" or acid-stamped "LIBBEY" on base.

Type and Dimensions
Blown in ribbed mold, then expanded and shaped. Drawn stem and applied, tooled foot. Partially reheated to develop shading. Height: 6–7½". Rim diameter: 3½–4".

Locality and Period
Massachusetts: New England Glass Works, Cambridge, c. 1883–88; Mt. Washington Glass Company, New Bedford, c. 1883–95. Libbey Glass Company, Toledo, Ohio. c. 1917.

Matching Glassware
Vases, bowls, centerpieces (#261), sugar bowls and creamers (#150), pitchers, tumblers, butter and cheese dishes (#220), toothpick holders, and spoon holders. Not made as set.

Comment
Amberina was developed and patented at the New England Glass Works in 1883. It was immediately popular and is said to have saved the company from bankruptcy. After the New England Glass Works moved to Toledo, Ohio, in 1888 and changed its name to the Libbey Glass Company, Amberina was revived in 1917 for only a year.

Hints for Collectors
The Mt. Washington Glass Company of New Bedford, Massachusetts, marketed an identical glass called Rose Amber. European copies of Amberina are often paler and have enameled decoration.

Burmese trumpet-shaped vase

Description
Trumpet-shaped vase with wavy flaring rim. Enameled fern
design on sides. Circular foot has enameled decoration around
edge. Pontil mark polished. Matt finish. Color: *opaque salmon
rim shading to lemon-yellow base;* enameled brown and green.
Variations: glossy finish; many enameled decorations. May be
acid-stamped "THOS. WEBB & SONS/PATENTED QUEEN'S BURMESE
WARE" on base.

Type and Dimensions
Free-blown or mold-blown bowl. Drawn stem and applied, tooled
foot. Acid-treated after annealing for matt finish. Enameled
decoration added after annealing. Height: 17½–17¾". Rim
diameter: 5⅛–5⅜".

Locality and Period
Mt. Washington Glass Company, New Bedford, Massachusetts.
Thomas Webb & Sons, Stourbridge, England. c. 1885–95.

Matching Glassware
Decorative objects, such as bowls, castor sets (#190),
centerpieces (#309), and candlesticks; rarely tumblers. Not made
as set.

Comment
Burmese was introduced in 1885 by the Mt. Washington Glass
Company's manager, Frederick Shirley. He presented Queen
Victoria with a tea set and, when she liked it, the success of
Burmese was assured. Thomas Webb & Sons was licensed to
produce the glass in England in 1885.

Hints for Collectors
Burmese was reproduced by the Pairpoint Corporation from 1938
until 1956, but these pieces are heavier, modern shapes. This
glass, called Gunderson Burmese, is now a collectible.

Depression hobnail vase

Description
Conical vase with ruffled rim. Overall pressed hobnail pattern.
Flat circular foot with sunburst underneath. Color: colorless with
opalescent white rim as shown; also colorless, transparent pink,
green, or amber with no difference in rim color. *Variations:*
hobnails may be more closely spaced.

Type and Dimensions
Machine-pressed in mold for pattern and shape. Height: 5⅝–5⅞″.
Rim diameter: 3–3¼″.

Locality and Period
Ohio: Anchor-Hocking Glass Corporation, Lancaster, and
Imperial Glass Company, Bellaire. Fenton Art Glass Company,
Williamstown, West Virginia. Macbeth-Evans Glass Company,
Charleroi, Pennsylvania. Liberty Glass Company, Egg Harbor,
New Jersey. c. 1925–46.

Matching Glassware
Large set with goblets, sherbet glasses, plates, creamer, sugar
bowl, cups and saucers, divided relish dish, candy dishes, candle
holders, and miscellaneous jars. Vases sold singly.

Comment
Anchor-Hocking called the pattern illustrated Moonstone, after
the opalescent color rather than the design. Except for the
opalescent rim, it is quite similar to hobnail patterns produced by
other companies in the 1930s and 1940s. The more closely spaced
hobnail pattern, called American Pioneer by Liberty Works,
came in the widest range of colors—transparent pink, green,
amber, and colorless.

Hints for Collectors
Hobnail vases made in the 1880s (#347) are of heavier, thicker
glass than Depression examples like the one seen here.

Moonstone pattern

Depression vase

Description
Globe- to trumpet-shaped vase with ruffled rim. Pressed bubblelike pattern (left) on globe-shaped lower body; conical upper body with vertical ribs. Squat globe-shaped vase (center) has short neck. Trumpet-shaped vase (right) has round knop on short stem and square foot. Color: (left) transparent pink, light blue, dark green, dark red, or colorless; (center) transparent blue and forest-green; (right) transparent medium blue. *Variations:* vase on left may be plain.

Type and Dimensions
Machine-pressed in mold for pattern and shape. Height (left): 8¾"; rim diameter: 6½". Height (center): 3⅝"; rim diameter: 2½". Height (right): 7⅜"; rim diameter: 4".

Locality and Period
Left and center at Anchor-Hocking Glass Corporation, Lancaster, Ohio. c. 1938–65. Right at L. E. Smith Company, Mt. Pleasant, Pennsylvania. c. 1930–40.

Matching Glassware
Vases on left and center in full range of tableware, including serving bowls, soup bowls (#251), plates, platters, and cups (#66).

Comment
The red vase is from the Royal Ruby line marketed by Anchor-Hocking. It was made in a variety of shapes and patterns, including the Bubble pattern illustrated. The green vase is from Anchor-Hocking's Forest Green line. Much of this glass was given away by filling stations during the 1950s.

Hints for Collectors
Anchor-Hocking reissued Royal Ruby in 1977. All reissues are slightly lighter in weight and color than the originals.

Bubble pattern and Forest Green line

Description
Trumpet-shaped vase with vertical panels around sides. Panels rectangular, hexagonal, arched, or heart-shaped. Rim plain (opposite left), scalloped (below left and right), or ruffled (below center, opposite right). *Flat disk at base joins bowl to stem.* Conical stem (below left and right) with panels or ridges; or baluster stem (below center, opposite) with hollow hexagonal foot, or square foot. Color: transparent purple, blue, green, amber, or yellow; rarely colorless or opaque white. *Variations:* about 20 bowl designs and 14 base designs in a variety of combinations.

Type and Dimensions
Base and bowl pressed in separate molds for pattern and shape, then joined with glass disk before annealing. Tooled rim. Lead glass. Height: 7–12″. Base width: 3–5″.

Locality and Period
Massachusetts: probably Boston & Sandwich Glass Company, Sandwich, and New England Glass Company, Cambridge. c. 1845–65.

Matching Glassware
Whale oil and fluid-burning lamps. Not made as set.

Comment
The shape of this type of glass suggests that it may have been intended as a celery vase. These pieces, however, are taller than most celeries, and it may be that they were used in pairs to decorate a mantel or sideboard—possibly with flowers. In the early stage of pressed glass, technology had not advanced sufficiently to produce a complete vase from a single mold. Many earlier pieces are a combination of pressed bowl and blown base, or vice versa. A few early compotes, as well as lamps,

candlesticks, and vases, are found joined in this way, with bowls and bases in different patterns. Around mid-century, New England glass manufacturers discovered that new variations could be achieved with a limited number of molds by mixing and matching different molds for base and bowl. During the same period, there was much greater use of colored glass than during the earlier experimental phases of pressed-glass production. Unfortunately, these vases are not marked. Since they never appeared in the catalogues of midwestern firms, New England seems a likely place of origin, and most vases of this type are found in New England.

Hints for Collectors
Around 1875, the Atterbury factory in Pittsburgh perfected a method of pressing pieces like this in a single mold. Early examples will always have vertical mold marks on the bowl and base that are interrupted where both pieces are joined at the disk. If the mold mark runs from bottom to top and there is no disk, the piece probably was made in the 1870s or 1880s in Pittsburgh. If it runs through the disk, the vase is a reproduction made in the 1920s or 1930s. Both early and late 19th-century pieces are equally sought after for their bright colors, and many collectors are not even aware of the difference.

337 Midwestern looped coin vase

Description
Trumpet-shaped bowl with flaring rim; loop decoration around body; transparent layer of glass around spherical base. Stem has rings and *hollow spherical knop containing American coin dated 1849.* Heavy circular foot. Pontil mark rough. Color: transparent gray with opaque white loops.

Type and Dimensions
Free-blown bowl, tooled into shape. Applied threading dragged to form loops, then marvered into surface before annealing. Extra gather of glass applied and tooled around base. Applied, tooled stem, knop, and foot; coin added to knop during blowing process. Lead glass. Height: 10½–10¾". Base diameter: 4⅛–4⅜".

Locality and Period
The Midwest: probably Pittsburgh. c. 1820–50.

Matching Glassware
Mugs, pitchers, flasks, creamers (#124), sugar bowls, compotes, and vases (#338). Not made as set.

Comment
Glassware with a coin enclosed in the stem is more common in New England than in the Midwest (#325). The swirled decoration (#338), weight, and color of this piece, however, all suggest a midwestern origin. Coins are very rarely found in colored examples.

Hints for Collectors
Any glass with an enclosed coin is rare, but the unusual loop decoration on the vase illustrated makes it even more desirable. Enclosed coins are most often American or English; rarely has a Spanish, French, or even Japanese coin been found.

Looped vase

Description
Trumpet-shaped bowl with flaring ruffled rim and spherical base. Loop decoration around body. Plain straight stem and round foot. Pontil mark rough. Color: colorless with opaque red, white, and blue loops. *Variations:* colors of loops vary, with 1 color most common; rarely 2 or 3 combined as illustrated; sometimes horizontal rings around lower body.

Type and Dimensions
Free-blown bowl, tooled into shape. Tooled rim. Applied threading dragged to form loops, then marvered into surface before annealing. Applied, tooled stem and foot. Lead glass. Height: 9⅝–9⅞″. Base diameter: 4½–4¾″.

Locality and Period
Western Pennsylvania, probably Pittsburgh; possibly southern New Jersey. c. 1860–70.

Matching Glassware
Mugs, pitchers, flasks, creamers (#124), sugar bowls, compotes, and vases (#337). Not made as set.

Comment
Both opaque white blown pieces (#340) and those with multicolored decoration such as these were very popular in the Pittsburgh area during the mid-19th century. Looped decoration of this type, however, is also found on pieces made in southern New Jersey (#124). Decoration and shape vary markedly from piece to piece.

Hints for Collectors
Free-blown pieces like this are understandably rarer and more expensive than the mass-produced pressed glass of the period. A matching pair like the one illustrated is especially valuable.

Description
Conical bowl with scalloped rim, short stem, and circular foot. Widely spaced pressed vertical ribs around body. Color: *marbled opaque purple and white;* rarely marbled white and gray, green, amber, blue, or turquoise. *Variations:* colors may be relatively separate or nearly blended. Peacock or lion's-head trademark.

Type and Dimensions
Pressed in mold for pattern and shape. Height: 7⅞–8⅛". Rim diameter: 4½–4¾".

Locality and Period
Challinor, Taylor & Company, Ltd., Tarentum, Pennsylvania; possibly another western Pennsylvania firm. c. 1886–1900. England: George Davidson & Sons, Gateshead, Tyne; Sowerby & Company, Newcastle. c. 1880–1900.

Matching Glassware
Set with goblets, sugar bowl, creamer, butter dish, and spoon holder. Bowls, vases, and animal dishes; not made as set.

Comment
Marbled glassware probably originated in England, where both Davidson and Sowerby produced large quantities in an extensive range of colors. Davidson was originally thought to have produced the effect by adding slag, or waste material from iron-working, to his glass mixture. The marbled effect, however, was obtained by careful mixing. In this country, Challinor, Taylor & Company patented the glass in 1886, and several other glasshouses probably also produced marbled glass.

Hints for Collectors
The English pieces are far more varied in color and shape than American ones, and are usually marked. Most American examples are purple and white or amber and white.

Pillar-molded vase

Description
Baluster-shaped bowl with flaring rim. Heavy, molded vertical ribs from rim to base. Baluster-shaped stem. Circular foot. Pontil mark rough. Color: opaque white, transparent purple, blue, amber, or colorless. *Variations:* shape often more cylindrical; ribs sometimes swirled to right or left; rarely, colored vertical thread, plain or twisted, on each rib (#84); ribs sometimes twisted together.

Type and Dimensions
Blown in ribbed mold, then expanded and tooled into shape. Applied, tooled stem and foot. Lead glass. Height: 8½–8¾″. Foot diameter: 3⅞–4⅛″.

Locality and Period
Pittsburgh area. c. 1850–70.

Matching Glassware
Decanters, bar bottles (#110), pitchers (#84), punch bowls (#300), and footed bowls (#276). Not made as set.

Comment
The size of this piece indicates that it may have been used originally as a celery vase. The narrow waist would limit its capacity, however, which means that, unlike the cylindrical variation, it was probably used for purely decorative purposes. Pillar-molded pieces always have a great sculptural effect. Because of their weight and sturdiness, many have survived.

Hints for Collectors
A distinctive shape like the vase illustrated commands a higher price than a cylindrical pillar-molded vase in colorless glass. Purple or white are rare in pillar-molded glass. Plain examples without added colored threads are usually less expensive.

341 Art Nouveau engraved vase

Description
Urn-shaped vase with slight swelling at base and serrated rim. *Engraved stylized tulips around shoulder; engraved leaves around base; overall fish-scale pattern.* Pontil mark polished. Colorless.

Type and Dimensions
Free-blown, then tooled into shape. Copper-wheel engraved after annealing. Lead glass. Height: 11–12″. Base diameter: 3–3½″.

Locality and Period
Engraved by J. F. Haselbauer & Sons, Corning, New York; also others in the Northeast. Blank made throughout the United States. c. 1910–15.

Comment
This is one of the few engraved pieces that seems to have been influenced by the floral designs and the curving shapes of the Art Nouveau style popular in Europe. American engraved designs are much more conventional—engraved floral motifs scarcely changed from the 18th through the 19th centuries (#30, #107, #119, #316). The flowers on this vase, however, are similar to those found on some engraved Tiffany pieces and to the enameled flower designs on some Art Nouveau glass.

Hints for Collectors
Although this vase is not signed, it has been identified because it was inherited by a daughter of the engraver George Haselbauer. Even if the engraver is not known, however, it is usually possible to date a piece like this to the first decades of the 20th century on the basis of its Art Nouveau style. The value of such a vase derives from quality and design, not from its maker.

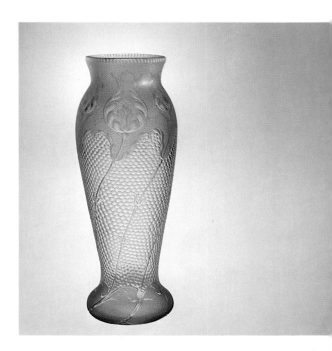

Durand vase

Description
Urn-shaped vase with slightly flaring rim and flat circular base. *Feather pattern overlaid with horizontal gold threading.* Pontil mark polished. "V DURAND" scratched under base. *Iridescent finish.* Color: opaque white with gold, blue, green, white, or red decoration.

Type and Dimensions
Free-blown, then tooled into shape. Threading applied before annealing; marvered into surface, then dragged with tool for feather decoration; second layer of threading applied horizontally in random fashion. Iridescent finish sprayed on before annealing. Height: 9–9¼". Rim diameter: 4–4¼".

Locality and Period
Victor Durand's Vineland Flint Glass Works, Vineland, New Jersey. c. 1924–31.

Matching Glassware
Bowls and vases in several shapes. Not made as set.

Comment
The Vineland Flint Glass Works manufactured tubing and chemical ware from 1900 until 1924, when its owner, Victor Durand, started producing fine glassware in the Art Nouveau style popularized by L. C. Tiffany. The design and production of these glasses was supervised by Martin Bach, a former employee of the Quezal Art Glass & Decorating Company in Brooklyn, New York. Durand was killed in an automobile accident in 1931; production ceased abruptly and the factory was sold.

Hints for Collectors
Durand glassware looks very much like Art Nouveau glass by Tiffany, Steuben, and Quezal. But Durand glass does not yet command the high price of Tiffany glass.

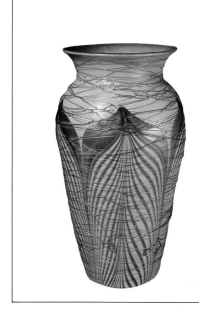

343 Tiffany paperweight vase

Description
Urn-shaped vase with *multicolored floral design encased in sides. Very thick walls.* Pontil mark polished. Marked "L.C.T. US099" on flat base. Color: colorless with green, blue, yellow, red, purple, or brown decoration. *Variations:* variety of shapes and naturalistic designs.

Type and Dimensions
Free-blown, then tooled into shape. Applied layers of colored decoration, each cased between layers of colorless glass. Height: 4–4¼". Base diameter: 2½–2¾".

Locality and Period
Tiffany Glass & Decorating Company, Corona, New York. c. 1895–1915.

Matching Glassware
Bowls and vases in variety of decorative shapes. Not made as set.

Comment
L. C. Tiffany was a leader in the Art Nouveau style of glassware. Although his iridescent glasses were copied by many other companies, paperweight pieces were not, perhaps because they took a great deal of time and skill to make. The paperweight decoration was applied gradually; the piece was redipped several times in different layers of colorless glass until the desired effect was achieved. By the time a design was completed, it was usually impossible to tell how many layers were used. The paperweight vase derives its name from this layering technique, which is also used to make paperweights.

Hints for Collectors
Like all Tiffany glass, paperweight vases are always marked, sometimes with a design number as here.

Aurene vase

Description
Urn-shaped vase with narrow neck and flaring rim. Circular slightly domed foot. Pontil mark polished. Color: *iridescent blue or gold. Variations:* occasionally, feather decoration in white, blue, or gold; sometimes iridescent white background with red or green feathers. Usually signed "AURENE" near pontil mark or with "STEUBEN" superimposed on fleur-de-lis.

Type and Dimensions
Free-blown, then tooled into shape. Applied, tooled foot. Iridescent finish sprayed on before annealing. Height: 16½–16¾". Rim diameter: 6½–6¾".

Locality and Period
Steuben Glass Works, Corning, New York. c. 1903–33.

Matching Glassware
Bowls, plates, compotes, vases, covered jars, perfume bottles, candlesticks. Not made as set.

Comment
Aurene is the trade name for this iridescent glass. The name derives from Au, the chemical symbol for gold. Aurene was created by Frederick Carder, the first director of Steuben Glass Works. Tiffany later sued Carder and Steuben for allegedly infringing on his patented Favrile glass, but Carder was able to prove that iridescent glass had been on the market in Europe before Tiffany's company was founded.

Hints for Collectors
Although Steuben made about the same quantity of blue and gold Aurene, blue has always been more popular with collectors and costs more than the gold. Since the 1960s, a number of reproductions have appeared with faked Steuben trademarks; usually the "STEUBEN" and fleur-de-lis trademark is too large.

Wheeling Peachblow vase

Description
Slender oval vase with narrow neck and flat base. Pontil mark polished. *Separate glass stand* has hollow base and 5 griffin figures around sides; stand is hollow or open in center. Color: *outside transparent amber shading to deep red; inside opaque white;* glossy finish. Stand is transparent amber with matt finish. *Variations:* sometimes matt finish on vase.

Type and Dimensions
Free-blown and cased with amber glass, then shaped. Partially reheated to develop shading. Pressed stand; acid-treated after annealing for matt finish. Vase height: 7⅞–8″; rim diameter: 1–1½″. Stand height: 2–2¼″; width: 3–3¼″.

Locality and Period
Hobbs, Brockunier & Company, Wheeling, West Virginia. c. 1886–90.

Matching Glassware
Decorative pieces, cruets, and punch cups (#67). Not made as set.

Comment
This vase, called the Morgan Vase by collectors, is a copy of a Chinese porcelain vase from the collection of Mrs. Mary Morgan that sold for $18,000 at a public auction in 1886. The rare Chinese piece made nationwide headlines twice—first for its record-breaking price, and later when it was suspected as a fraud. Hobbs, Brockunier & Company had just begun to market Coral glass, now called Peachblow, when the auction took place. The firm quickly added a similar vase to its Peachblow line.

Hints for Collectors
Most of these vases were probably originally sold with stands, although few stands are likely to have survived.

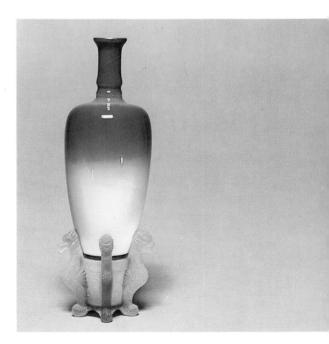

Onyx vase

Description
Globe-shaped vase with cylindrical neck and flat base. *6 lobes around neck and raised flowers on body.* Thin walls. Color: opaque cream-colored background with silver, reddish, amber, orange, purple, or green raised design. *Variations:* floral design varies slightly.

Type and Dimensions
Blown in small mold for pattern, then in larger mold for shape. Reheated to color raised design. Stain for decoration applied after annealing. Rim roughly ground. Height: 6⅜–6½". Rim diameter: 3¼–3½".

Locality and Period
Dalzell, Gilmore & Leighton Company, Findlay, Ohio. c. 1889–90.

Matching Glassware
Set with tumblers, sugar bowl, creamer, small bowls, and compotes.

Comment
This successful product was patented by George Leighton in 1889. Unfortunately, it proved difficult to manufacture since the glass was brittle and prone to breakage during shipping. Newspapers of the period reported that the factory went bankrupt only months after Onyx was first marketed. Onyx ware was never made after the firm reopened in 1890, although the company remained in business until 1898.

Hints for Collectors
Onyx glass is rare and therefore expensive. Like Holly Amber glass (#229), Onyx was intended to be a mass-produced version of art glass. Because both were in production for such a short period, they are rare and command a high price.

347 Opalescent hobnail vase

Description
Cylindrical vase with fluted rim. *Overall raised hobnail pattern on body and base.* Color: opalescent pink, amber, or blue with opalescent white, amber, or blue hobnails. Rarely paper label on base marked "PATENTED 1886."

Type and Dimensions
Pressed in mold for pattern and shape. Partially reheated to develop opalescent color. Height: 6¾–7″. Base diameter: 3⅞–4⅛″.

Locality and Period
Hobbs, Brockunier & Company, Wheeling, West Virginia, and other firms in West Virginia and Ohio. c. 1885–1900.

Matching Glassware
Set with tumblers, pitcher, barber bottles, vases, and bowls in several shapes.

Comment
Opalescent hobnail glassware was produced almost continuously from the 1890s until the 1940s. The glass could be pressed, as in the vase illustrated, or mold-blown (#77). A few hobnail items were also made in transparent glass. The label on the vase illustrated probably refers to the year William Leighton patented the Hobbs, Brockunier & Company mold. The pattern appeared in a Hobbs catalogue as Dewdrop. Hobnail glass is usually not marked and is difficult to identify with a particular firm since its manufacture was widespread.

Hints for Collectors
Most opalescent hobnail glass is relatively inexpensive because so much of it was made and is still available. With a little practice, it is possible to tell the modern pressed versions from earlier mold-blown examples. Older pieces are usually heavier.

Dewdrop pattern

Description
Cylindrical or conical vase with flat base. Thin walls. *Enameled design of birds in greenery around sides* against beige enameled background with enameled gold and white rings above and below. Color: opaque white with pink or white enameled background and blue, red, yellow, green, white, and brown enameled decoration. *Variations:* sometimes signed "Smith Bros." in enameled script below design; enameled decoration mostly flowers or birds.

Type and Dimensions
Blown in mold for shape and ring pattern. Background enameled first, then enameled decoration applied after annealing. Height: 5¼–6″. Base diameter: 1¾–2¼″.

Locality and Period
New Bedford, Massachusetts: blanks and enameling by Mt. Washington Glass Company; enameling only by Smith Brothers Decorating Shop. c. 1889–1900.

Comment
Englishmen Harry and Alfred Smith decorated vases like this one for about 10 years for the Mt. Washington firm before opening their own decorating shop in New Bedford in 1894. Their work for the Mt. Washington factory, however, is virtually indistinguishable from their later pieces, and in both instances blanks from Mt. Washington were used.

Hints for Collectors
The Smith Brothers' work is not well known. The pieces are often undervalued by dealers who are not familiar with art glass. A signed piece is always more valuable, but unsigned ones are just as attractive and much less expensive.

349 Opaque white vase

Description
Globe-shaped vase (left) with slender neck and flat base or conical vase (right) with flaring rim and 3–4 scrolled feet. Thin walls. *Enameled floral decoration on sides and simple gilt decoration around rim, base, or feet.* Pontil mark polished. Color: *opaque white glass* with red, green, white, black, or gold enameling. *Variations:* enameled coloring varies; usually fruit or floral decoration. Some lack gilt decoration. May be urn-shaped.

Type and Dimensions
Free-blown, then tooled into shape. Enameled and gilt decoration applied after annealing. Lead glass. Height: 9–9¼″. Base diameter: 3–3¼″.

Locality and Period
Massachusetts: Boston & Sandwich Glass Company, Sandwich; New England Glass Company, Cambridge; Mt. Washington Glass Company, New Bedford. c. 1870–90.

Comment
Many vases of this type in several shapes were exhibited at the Centennial Exposition in Philadelphia in 1876 by the New England Glass Company. The 3-legged vase (right) is exactly like those appearing in a Boston & Sandwich Glass Company catalogue of about 1875.

Hints for Collectors
These vases were also made in England, France, Bohemia, and possibly other European countries from about 1850 until about 1890. Nonlead examples are probably Continental and should not cost as much as English or American ones. English examples are occasionally marked, but are otherwise difficult to distinguish from American vases.

Description
Egg-shaped vase with boat-shaped, flaring ruffled rim. *Overall raised branching-coral decoration.* Thin walls. Flat circular base. Pontil mark polished. Matt finish. Color: exterior opaque pastel blue, white, pink, yellow, or green; *interior always opaque white. Variations:* several types of coral designs; occasionally trefoil or quatrefoil decoration instead of coral.

Type and Dimensions
Blown in mold, then tooled into shape. Crimped rim. Acid-treated after annealing for matt finish. Tiny glass beads glued on and then fired for branching pattern. Height: 8½–8¾″. Base diameter: 3–3¼″.

Locality and Period
England and Continental Europe; possibly the United States. c. 1885–1900.

Matching Glassware
Vases and bowls in several shapes. Not made as set.

Comment
Coralene is similar to many other forms of art glass made in the last quarter of the 19th century. Coral decoration is often found on diamond-quilted satin glassware (#283) made in the United States, England, and Bohemia. Unfortunately, this glass does not appear in any advertisements or catalogues of American art glass, so it is not possible to make a definite attribution. The coral-branch decoration is the most common and has given the glassware its name.

Hints for Collectors
Coralene is a rare art glass but not exceptionally expensive. Imitations sometimes have the beads simply glued in place. Genuine Coralene glass beads are glued and fired.

Pressed Pattern Guide

During the 19th century, pressed glass companies manufactured more than 1500 different patterns. At least 600 to 700 were made in large sets. To help you learn to recognize and date the most common patterns, over 60 are illustrated here, including 22 that are not shown elsewhere in this guide. They are divided into 4 groups, based on chronological period and style. The dates given for each group indicate the period during which the patterns were introduced, except for Garfield Drape, which was widely produced as a reissue after 1881.

Early Geometric Patterns (c. 1849–75)

Huber

Honeycomb, #24, #102

Thumbprint, #297, #298

Excelsior

Victoria, #17

Divided Diamond, #23

Waffle and Thumbprint, #23

Horn of Plenty, #56, #146

New England Pineapple, #26

Tulip

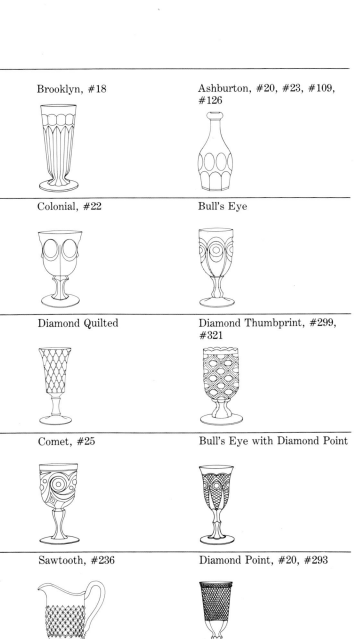

Brooklyn, #18

Ashburton, #20, #23, #109, #126

Colonial, #22

Bull's Eye

Diamond Quilted

Diamond Thumbprint, #299, #321

Comet, #25

Bull's Eye with Diamond Point

Sawtooth, #236

Diamond Point, #20, #293

Realistic and Abstract Patterns (c. 1865–80)

Thousand-eye

Jacob's Ladder or Maltese Cross, #147

Princess Feather

Lincoln Drape, #192

Wildflower, #49, #148, #256

Bleeding Heart, #31, #318

Blackberry, #138

Strawberry, #244

Shell and Tassel, #241

Viking, #243

Ribbon

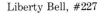

Fan with Diamond, #234

Roman Rosette

Bellflower, #89, #189, #319

Tree-of-Life

Beaded Mirror, #233

Lion, #315

Westward Ho, #294

Three Face, #292

Late 19th-century Patterns (c. 1880–95)

Ruby Thumbprint

Coin, #295

Daisy and Button with
Crossbars, #196, #242

Deer and Pine Tree

Paneled Daisy

Lily-of-the-Valley

Beaded Grape

Rose-in-Snow

Special Color Techniques (c. 1900)

Heart Band, #145

New Jersey, #52

Inverted Fan and Feather,
#154

Louis XV, #230

Red Block

Heart with Thumbprint, #222

Classic, #86

Garfield Drape, #88

Baltimore Pear

Paneled Grape

Wheat and Barley

Stippled Forget-Me-Not

Ribbed Drape, #228

Holly Amber, #229

Carnival Holly, #287

Grape and Cable with
Thumbprint, #51, #288

Cut Motif Guide

Cut glass often uses combinations of standard motifs. The individual motifs can be difficult to recognize, especially when several appear in complex brilliant-cut patterns. This table will familiarize you with 16 basic cut designs.

bull's eye	convex diamond or honeycomb
sunburst	prism cut
miter cut	pinwheel
block cut	cane

step cut	notched cut
fan	strawberry-diamond
hobstar	hobnail
relief diamond	crosscut-diamond

Cut Glass by Period

American Glass Manufacturers by Type

Most glass companies manufactured more than one type of glass. In the following list, the companies are grouped according to the type of glass for which they are best known.

Art Glass
Boston & Sandwich Glass Company
Dalzell, Gilmore & Leighton Company
Hobbs, Brockunier & Company
Honesdale Decorating Company
Imperial Glass Company
Indiana Tumbler & Goblet Company
Locke Art Company
Mt. Washington Glass Company
New England Glass Company
New England Glass Works
Pairpoint Corporation
Phoenix Glass Company
Smith Brothers Decorating Shop

Art Nouveau Glass
Victor Durand's Vineland Flint Glass Works
J. F. Haselbauer & Sons
Honesdale Decorating Company
Imperial Glass Company
Libbey Glass Company
Pairpoint Corporation
Quezal Art Glass & Decorating Company
H. P. Sinclaire & Company
Steuben Glass Works
Tiffany Glass & Decorating Company
Union Glass Company

Blown Glass *(free-blown and/or mold-blown)*
John Frederick Amelung's New Bremen Glassmanufactory
American Flint Glass Works, Boston
Bakewell companies
Boston & Sandwich Glass Company
Boston Crown Glass Manufactory
Boston Silver Glass Company
Bridgeton Glassworks
Bryce Brothers
Thomas Cains's glasshouses
Cambridge Glass Company
Corning Glass Works
Dorflinger companies
Fostoria Glass Company
H. C. Fry Glass Company
Libbey Glass Company
Mantua Glass Works
Mt. Vernon Glass Company
Mt. Washington Glass Company
Mt. Washington Glass Works
New England Glass Company
New York Glass Works
Pairpoint Corporation
Saratoga Glass Works

H. P. Sinclaire & Company

Steuben Glass Works
Henry William Stiegel's American Flint Glass Works
Weeks & Gilson Glass Works, Stoddard, New Hampshire
Caspar Wistar's Wistarburgh Glassworks

Carnival Glass
Fenton Art Glass Company
Imperial Glass Company
Millersburg Glass Company
Northwood Glass Company

Cut and Engraved Glass
John Frederick Amelung's New Bremen Glassmanufactory
Bakewell companies
A. L. Blackmer Company
Boston & Sandwich Glass Company
Brooklyn Flint Glass Works
Cambridge Glass Company
Dithridge & Company
Dorflinger companies
O. F. Egginton Company
Fostoria Glass Company
H. C. Fry Glass Company
T. G. Hawkes & Company
J. Hoare & Company
Hunt Glass Company
Ideal Cut Glass Company
Jersey Glass Company
Kensington Glass Company
Libbey Glass Company
Majestic Cut Glass Company
Mt. Washington Glass Company
New England Glass Company
New York Glass Works
Pairpoint Corporation
Ritchie & Wheat Company
H. P. Sinclaire & Company
L. Straus & Sons
M. & R. H. Sweeney
Tiffin Glass Company
Tuthill Cut Glass Company
Union Glass Company, Somerville, Massachusetts
Wright Rich Cut Glass Company

Depression Glass
Anchor-Hocking Glass Corporation
Belmont Tumbler Company
Cambridge Glass Company
Consolidated Lamp & Glass Company
Duncan & Miller Glass Company
Federal Glass Company
Fenton Art Glass Company
Fostoria Glass Company
Hazel-Atlas Glass Company
Hocking Glass Company

Imperial Glass Company

Indiana Glass Company
Jeannette Glass Company
Liberty Glass Company
Macbeth-Evans Glass Company
McKee Glass Company
New Martinsville Glass Manufacturing Company
Paden City Glass Manufacturing Company
L. E. Smith Company
United States Glass Company

Pressed Glass
Adams & Company
Aetna Glass & Manufacturing Company
American Flint Glass Works, Boston
Atterbury & Company
Bakewell, Pears & Company
Beatty-Brady Glass Company
Boston & Sandwich Glass Company
Boston Silver Glass Company
Bryce companies
Thomas Cains's Phoenix Glass Works
Campbell, Jones & Company
Canton Glass Company
Cape Cod Glass Company
Central Glass Company
Challinor, Taylor & Company, Ltd.
R. B. Curling & Sons
Curling, Robertson & Company
Dithridge & Company
Doyle & Company
George Duncan & Sons
Fostoria Glass Company
Gillinder & Sons
A. H. Heisey & Company
Hobbs, Barnes & Company
Hobbs, Brockunier & Company
Hocking Glass Company
Indiana Tumbler & Goblet Company
Jersey Glass Company
Kemple Glass Works
King, Son & Company's Cascade Glass Works
LaBelle Glass Company
James B. Lyon & Company
M'Kee & Brothers
McKee Glass Company
Model Flint Glass Company
Mt. Washington Glass Works
National Glass Company
New England Glass Company
Northwood Glass Company
Portland Glass Company
Providence Flint Glass Company
Richards & Hartley Flint Glass Company
Daniel C. Ripley & Company
John Robinson & Sons
Tarentum Glass Company
United States Glass Company
Westmoreland companies

American Glass Manufacturers

This table lists the major manufacturers of glass tableware and vases operating in the United States between 1739 and the 1940s. It includes the company name, factory location, and dates of operation for manufacturers of all types of glass—blown, cut, engraved, pressed, Carnival, Depression, art, and Art Nouveau. A few of the early companies are listed under the names of their famous owners, such as Stiegel or Amelung. Many firms used more than one name over the years, as partnerships and owners changed; these are listed in chronological order. Major reorganizations and mergers involving several companies are listed under the new name, such as United States Glass Company and Pairpoint Corporation. Important trademarks are

Company
Adams & Company
Aetna Glass & Manufacturing Company
John Frederick Amelung's New Bremen Glassmanufactory
American Flint Glass Works
Atterbury & Company
Bakewell companies Bakewell & Ensell Benjamin Bakewell & Company Bakewell, Page & Bakewell Bakewell & Anderson Bakewell, Pears & Company
Beatty-Brady Glass Company
Belmont Tumbler Company
A. L. Blackmer Company
Boston & Sandwich Glass Company
Boston Crown Glass Manufactory
Boston Silver Glass Company
Bridgeton Glassworks
Brooklyn Flint Glass Works
Bryce, Walker & Company Bryce Brothers
Thomas Cains's South Boston Flint Glass Works Thomas Cains's Phoenix Glass Works
Cambridge Glass Company
Campbell, Jones & Company
Canton Glass Company
Cape Cod Glass Company
Central Glass Company
Challinor, Taylor & Company, Ltd.
Consolidated Lamp & Glass Company
Corning Glass Works

included. In most cases, the trademarks are pressed or acid-stamped and are permanent, but some firms used only paper labels. Since few paper labels from the 19th century have survived, they are described only in the entries. Many Depression glass companies used paper labels that are still found today, and these are included here. Some trademarks consist solely of the company name; since these are easy to identify, no trademark is reproduced. To help you associate glass manufacturers with the type of glass they made, we also group the manufacturers according to glass types in the section "American Glass Manufacturers by Type."

Location	Dates of Operation
Pittsburgh, Pennsylvania	1861–91
Bellaire, Ohio	1880–c. 1890
New Bremen, Maryland	1784–95
Boston, Massachusetts	1843–58
Pittsburgh, Pennsylvania	c. 1867–93
Pittsburgh, Pennsylvania	1808–09
Pittsburgh, Pennsylvania	1809–24
Pittsburgh, Pennsylvania	1824–32
Pittsburgh, Pennsylvania	1832–36
Pittsburgh, Pennsylvania	1836–82
Dunkirk, Indiana	1898–1900
Bellaire, Ohio	c. 1925–35
New Bedford, Massachusetts	1894–1916
Sandwich, Massachusetts	1825–88
Boston, Massachusetts	1787–1827
Cambridge, Massachusetts	1857–71
Bridgeton, New Jersey	1836–76
Brooklyn, New York	1823–c. 1855
Pittsburgh, Pennsylvania	1865–82
Pittsburgh, Pennsylvania	1882–91
Mt. Pleasant, Pennsylvania	1896–1965
Boston, Massachusetts	c. 1812–20
Boston, Massachusetts	c. 1819–70
Cambridge, Ohio	1901–58
Pittsburgh, Pennsylvania	1865–86
Canton, Ohio	1883–94
Marion, Indiana	1894–99
Sandwich, Massachusetts	1858–82
Wheeling, West Virginia	1863–91
Tarentum, Pennsylvania	1884–91
Coraopolis, Pennsylvania	1894–1967
Corning, New York	1868–present

Company

R. B. Curling & Sons
Curling, Robertson & Company

Dalzell, Gilmore & Leighton Company

Dithridge & Company

Dorflinger Glass Company
C. Dorflinger & Sons

Doyle & Company

George Duncan & Sons
Duncan & Miller Glass Company

Victor Durand's Vineland Flint Glass Works

O. F. Egginton Company

Federal Glass Company

Fenton Art Glass Company

Fostoria Glass Company

H. C. Fry Glass Company

Gillinder & Sons

J. F. Haselbauer & Sons

T. G. Hawkes & Company

Hazel-Atlas Glass Company

A. H. Heisey & Company

J. Hoare & Company

Hobbs, Barnes & Company
Hobbs, Brockunier & Company

Hocking Glass Company
Anchor-Hocking Glass Corporation

Honesdale Decorating Company

Hunt Glass Company

	Location	Dates of Operation
	Pittsburgh, Pennsylvania	1828–34
	Pittsburgh, Pennsylvania	1834–57
	Findlay, Ohio	1888–98
	New Brighton, Pennsylvania	1887–c. 1900
	White Mills, Pennsylvania	1867–81
	White Mills, Pennsylvania	1881–c. 1920
	Pittsburgh, Pennsylvania	1866–91
	Pittsburgh, Pennsylvania	1874–91
	Washington, Pennsylvania	1895–1955
	Vineland, New Jersey	1897–1931
	Corning, New York	1896–c. 1918
	Columbus, Ohio	1901–present
	Williamstown, West Virginia	1906–present
	Moundsville, West Virginia	1887–present
	Rochester, Pennsylvania	1901–34
	Philadelphia, Pennsylvania	1867–c. 1930
	Corning, New York	c. 1910–38
	Corning, New York	1880–1962
	Wheeling, West Virginia	1902–present
	Newark, Ohio	1895–1958
	Corning, New York	1868–1920
	Wheeling, West Virginia	1845–63
	Wheeling, West Virginia	1863–c. 1890
	Lancaster, Ohio	1905–38
	Lancaster, Ohio	1938–present
	Honesdale, Pennsylvania	1900–32
	Corning, New York	1895–1972

Company

Ideal Cut Glass Company

Imperial Glass Company

Indiana Glass Company

Indiana Tumbler & Goblet Company

Jeannette Glass Company

Jersey Glass Company

Kemple Glass Works

Kensington Glass Company

King, Son & Company's Cascade Glass Works

LaBelle Glass Company

Libbey Glass Company
(now Owens Illinois, Inc.)

Liberty Glass Company

Locke Art Company

James B. Lyon & Company

Macbeth-Evans Glass Company

M'Kee & Brothers

McKee Glass Company

Majestic Cut Glass Company

Mantua Glass Works

Millersburg Glass Company

Model Flint Glass Company

Mt. Vernon Glass Company

Mt. Washington Glass Works
Mt. Washington Glass Company

National Glass Company

New England Glass Company
New England Glass Works

New Martinsville Glass Manufacturing Company
(now Viking Glass Company)

New York Glass Works
(Bloomingdale Flint Glass Works)

Northwood Glass Company

Paden City Glass Manufacturing Company

Pairpoint Manufacturing Company
Pairpoint Corporation

Location	Dates of Operation
Canastota, New York	1904–33
Bellaire, Ohio	1901–present
Dunkirk, Indiana	1907–present
Greentown, Indiana	1894–1903
Jeannette, Pennsylvania	c. 1900–present

Jersey City, New Jersey	1824–c. 1860
East Palestine, Ohio	c. 1945–60
Kenova, West Virginia	c. 1960–present
Philadelphia, Pennsylvania	1826–74
Pittsburgh, Pennsylvania	1869–91
Bridgeport, Ohio	1872–88
Toledo, Ohio	1888–present

Egg Harbor, New Jersey	1903–32
Mount Oliver, Pennsylvania	1900–20
Pittsburgh, Pennsylvania	1853–91
Charleroi, Pennsylvania	1899–1936
Pittsburgh, Pennsylvania	1856–89
Jeannette, Pennsylvania	1889–99
Jeannette, Pennsylvania	1903–51

Elmira, New York	c. 1900–10
Mantua, Ohio	c. 1821–29
Millersburg, Ohio	1909–11
Findlay, Ohio	1888–1902
Vernon, New York	1810–44
New Bedford, Massachusetts	1869–71
New Bedford, Massachusetts	1871–1900
Pittsburgh, Pennsylvania	1899–1904
Cambridge, Massachusetts	1818–80
Cambridge, Massachusetts	1880–88
New Martinsville, West Virginia	c. 1901–present

New York, New York	1820–40

Indiana, Pennsylvania	1895–98
Wheeling, West Virginia	1901–20

Paden City, West Virginia	1916–51

New Bedford, Massachusetts	1880–1900
New Bedford, Massachusetts	1900–29

Company

Phoenix Glass Company

Portland Glass Company

Providence Flint Glass Company

Quezal Art Glass & Decorating Company

Richards & Hartley Flint Glass Company

Daniel C. Ripley & Company

Ritchie & Wheat Company

John Robinson & Sons

Saratoga Glass Works

H. P. Sinclaire & Company

Smith Brothers Decorating Shop

L. E. Smith Company

Steuben Glass Works

Henry William Stiegel's American Flint Glass Works

L. Straus & Sons
(now Straus-Duparquet)

M. & R. H. Sweeney

Tarentum Glass Company

Tiffany Glass & Decorating Company

Tiffin Glass Company
(formerly United States Glass Company; now Towle Sterling, Inc.

Tuthill Cut Glass Company

Union Glass Company

United States Glass Company

Weeks & Gilson Glass Works

Westmoreland Specialty Company
Westmoreland Glass Company

Caspar Wistar's Wistarburgh Glassworks

Wright Rich Cut Glass Company

Location	Dates of Operation
Monaca, Pennsylvania	c. 1875–95
Portland, Maine	1865–75
Providence, Rhode Island	1830–33
Brooklyn, New York	1901–c. 1924
Pittsburgh, Pennsylvania Tarentum, Pennsylvania	1866–84 1884–91
Pittsburgh, Pennsylvania	1866–91
Wheeling, West Virginia	1829–36
Pittsburgh, Pennsylvania	1823–45
Saratoga, New York	1844–90
Corning, New York	1904–28
New Bedford, Massachusetts	1878–c. 1900
Mt. Pleasant, Pennsylvania	1907–present
Corning, New York	1903–present
Manheim, Pennsylvania	1763–74
New York, New York	1888–present
Wheeling, West Virginia	1831–68
Tarentum, Pennsylvania	1898–99
Corona, New York	1893–1924
Tiffin, Ohio	c. 1900–present
Middletown, New York	c. 1900–20
Somerville, Massachusetts	1851–1924
Pittsburgh, Pennsylvania	1891–1938
Stoddard, New Hampshire	1850–73
Grapeville, Pennsylvania Grapeville, Pennsylvania	1889–1923 1923–present
Alloway, New Jersey	1739–c. 1776
Anderson, Indiana	c. 1904–14

Tips for Recognizing Glass Types and Styles

Acid-etched Glass
Acid-etched designs often appear on glassware made in the 1890s, 1920s, and 1930s. Look for grayish lines resembling engraving but with sharper edges.

If examined under a magnifying glass, acid-etched lines cut perpendicularly into the surface of the glass, while engraved lines curve.

Art Glass
Look for free-blown or mold-blown glass with subtle color shading and/or enameled decoration.

Agata
This type of glassware is opaque pink shading to white, with a mottled blackish finish that resembles stain. (No known reproductions.)

Albertine
This type of glassware has an enameled ivory, pink, or blue background with enameled decoration. (No known reproductions.)

Amberina
Authentic pieces are transparent red shading to amber. Glass made after 1917 will have an acid-etched Libbey trademark. Reproductions have harsher or paler colors than the originals. European Amberina is often decorated.

Burmese
Authentic pieces are opaque salmon-pink shading to yellow. Gunderson Burmese is in modern shapes. Fenton reproductions are marked on the base. Italian copies are grayish.

Crown Milano
This type of glassware has an enameled ivory or beige background. (No known reproductions.)

Frances Ware
This type of glassware is frosted colorless glass with amber decoration. (No known reproductions.)

Peachblow, Mt. Washington
Authentic pieces are opaque grayish-white shading to purplish-pink. Often, but not always, there is a raspberrylike blob of glass on top of the pontil mark. Reproductions have a slightly grayish cast and a rough pontil mark.

Peachblow, New England (Wild Rose)
Authentic pieces are opaque white shading to bright pink. Look for a polished pontil mark. Reproductions have a slightly grayish cast and a rough pontil mark.

Peachblow, Wheeling
Authentic pieces are opaque yellow shading to red on the outside and opaque white on the inside. Avoid examples with very white linings, which are probably reproductions.

Pomona
This type of glassware is frosted and transparent with etched patterns and a stained yellow rim. (No known reproductions.)

Royal Flemish
This type of glassware is in earthy colors with designs resembling stained glass. (No known reproductions.)

Art Nouveau Glass

Look for free-blown or mold-blown glass in iridescent colors and unusual shapes, sometimes combining opaque and transparent glass. Tiffany, Steuben, and Durand are among the best-known American Art Nouveau glassmakers.

Only buy this glass from a reputable antique dealer because there are numerous fakes on the market.

Aurene

Authentic pieces are iridescent blue or gold and usually signed "AURENE" near the pontil mark or "STEUBEN" with a fleur-de-lis. Note that pieces with an unusually large "STEUBEN" or fleur-de-lis are fakes.

Coralene

Authentic pieces are opaque pastel on the outside, with overall beaded, branching coral decoration; the inside is opaque white. Check to see if the beads are glued in place. Genuine Coralene beads are fired on and will not loosen.

Carnival Glass

Look for pressed glass in opaque iridescent colors, such as bronze, orange-amber, green, dark blue, purple, or red.

Check the base for a trademark. Most reproductions made in the 1950s have an impressed "IG" for Imperial Glass or "F" for Fenton Art Glass. A smooth area on the base may indicate that the trademark was ground off to disguise a reproduction.

Cut Glass

Look for a polished pontil mark or a cut design, such as a sunburst or a hobstar, beneath the foot or base.

Feel the cut lines for sharp edges. Check the quality of the cutting. Parallel lines should be straight, and all lines should meet exactly at each point in the design. Lines that do not meet, an asymmetric design, or rough edges are signs of poor quality.

Simple designs involving only a few motifs in a repeat pattern are typical of the early and mid-19th century.

Brilliant-cut patterns of the 1880–1915 period cover almost the entire surface with combinations of many cut motifs, especially hobstars and pinwheels. Many pieces made after about 1895 have an acid-stamped trademark or signature. Check beneath the foot of stemware, on the inside or uncut surface of a bowl or a plate, around the handle of a pitcher, or on the stopper of a decanter. In most cases, acid-stamped trademarks are difficult to see without strong light. Try turning the piece slowly to allow the light to catch the smooth surface and penetrate the transparent glass. A trademark increases the value of an object, especially if it belongs to a well-known firm.

Feel the edges of the pattern to make sure that it is not pressed. Pressed patterns have blunt edges and may have mold lines; cut glass has sharp edges and never has mold lines.

Depression Glass

Look for relatively thin pressed glass with mold lines. Many Depression-glass pieces are in characteristic 20th-century shapes, such as uncovered sugar bowls, sandwich servers, handled soup bowls, and cups and saucers.

Check beneath the foot or base for a pressed trademark. Companies making reissues of Depression-glass patterns often use a trademark different from the original.

Beware of reissues made with the same molds as the original examples. Look for unusual colors. Check the pattern for subtle differences—sketchier designs, sharper ridges, changes in pattern details.

Engraved Glass
An engraved design is usually grayish and stands out against a colorless background; occasionally the design is polished to look transparent. Look for monograms or realistic representations of flowers, leaves, or scenes.

Avoid crudely engraved, greenish bubbly glassware. These examples may be 20th-century imports from Czechoslovakia.

On red-stained glass, beware of reproductions with shallow engraving that lacks detail and a thin stain that scratches off easily.

Free-blown Glass
Look for a rough or polished pontil mark beneath the foot or base. (If there is a cut design, see Cut Glass.)

Check beneath the foot or base for minute scratches where the object touches the table. If the base or foot lacks signs of wear, this example may be a reproduction.

Make sure the rim and foot have not been ground down to eliminate chips. Tampering with the original proportions decreases value.

Very bubbly colored glass may be Mexican.

Only buy pieces with lily-pad decoration from a reputable antique dealer. The many lily-pad reproductions are difficult to spot, even for experienced collectors.

Do not be fooled into thinking that you can tell an old glass by its ring when tapped. This simply indicates whether or not it contains lead. Only open shapes, like goblets or wineglasses, will produce a sound; closed forms, such as some vases, cannot ring no matter what their lead content.

Mold-blown Glass
Feel the contours of the pattern on the inside of the piece. Look for mold lines on the outside surface of the body, foot, or cover.

Blown 3-mold patterns combine vertical ribs, squares, sunbursts, diamonds, and waffling. Most examples are colorless, rarely transparent blue or purple, and very rarely green. Colored blown 3-mold glassware, especially in green or amber, is probably not authentic.

Swirled ribs and simple diamond patterns are typical of early mold-blown examples from western Pennsylvania and Ohio. Most pieces are colored, rarely colorless. Beware of very bubbly colored glass with swirled ribs; this glass is probably Mexican. Diamond-patterned reproductions are more difficult to recognize, *438* unless they are unusual modern shapes.

Pressed Glass
Feel the inside of the object; it should be completely smooth. The pattern appears on the outside, but, unlike cut glass, the edges of the design are blunt. Look for mold lines on the body or foot.

Some early pressed glass may have a polished pontil mark because it was fire-polished to remove mold marks, or because a handle was added or a lip tooled.

Check the original colors and shapes. Many reproductions are in shapes or colors that were not made originally. Depression-glass imitations of older pressed patterns are usually lighter in weight.

Special Types of Pressed Glass

Chocolate Glass
Authentic pieces are opaque light brown on the outside and milky brown on the inside. Reproductions are muddy brown.

Custard Glass
Authentic pieces are opaque cream-white. Beware of bright white or thin glass, which may be a reproduction.

Holly Amber Glass
Authentic pieces are opalescent white and transparent amber. Reproductions are browner overall.

Marble or Slag Glass
Look for glassware that is marbled opaque purple and white, amber and white, gray and white, green and white, blue and white, or turquoise and white. Avoid pieces with harsh colors; these may be reproductions.

Milk Glass
This type of glass is opaque milk-white. Beware of reissues and reproductions. Some are marked "WG" for the Westmoreland Glass Works, a major source of milk-glass reproductions.

Glossary

Acid-etching A method of decorating glass using hydrofluoric acid to eat away an exposed surface, while the remainder of the surface is covered with a protective coating. Acid-etched glass superficially resembles engraved glass, but the design is flatter.

Acid-polishing The polishing of a glass surface using concentrated hydrofluoric and sulfuric acids.

Annealing The controlled cooling of a glass object to remove tensions in the glass that might lead to breakage.

Applied glass Glass added from a separate gather and attached to the main gather during blowing and shaping or just after pressing.

Art glass Decorative glassware of the late 19th century, frequently brightly colored or shaded, such as Amberina or Peachblow.

Art Nouveau An art style originating in France in the 1870s, brought to this country in the 1890s. Glass objects in this style by L. C. Tiffany and others are free-blown, often iridescent, and frequently use floral motifs.

Baluster-shaped stem A stem shape that curves inward at the top and outward at the bottom.

Batch A mixture of the unmelted raw materials used to make glass, such as sand, cullet, and chemicals.

Berry set A large bowl with matching smaller bowls used for serving fruit and other desserts.

Blank Any preliminary shape of glass that requires further decoration, such as cutting.

Blown glass Glassware shaped by blowing air into a gather of molten glass using a blowpipe.

Blown 3-mold glass A collector's term used to describe glassware made from about 1815 to 1835 that was blown in a full-size mold. The patterns are mostly geometric, but some have hearts, chains, flowers, and other motifs.

Blowpipe A hollow iron rod 4–6 feet in length, used to make blown glass.

Bottle glass Inexpensive glass made from sand with iron impurities that impart an amber, aquamarine, green, or brown color.

Breakfast set A small sugar bowl and creamer, made only in Carnival glass.

Bride's basket A collector's term for an art-glass bowl in a silver-plated stand or frame, used for display around 1900.

Broken-swirl ribbing A decoration on mold-blown glass that has 2 sets of ribs. After a gather is blown in a vertically ribbed mold, it is twisted for a swirled effect, then redipped in the same or another ribbed mold to superimpose a second set of ribbing.

Cameo glass Cased glass in which the outer layer or layers have been carved with ornamental designs.

Camphor glass A collector's term for frosted glass.

Carnival glass Pressed glass with a colorful iridescent finish, made from around 1905 to 1920.

Cased glass   Glassware completely covered with one or more layers of colored glass. The inner layer of glass may be blown into each succeeding outer layer while hot, or the gather may be dipped into molten glass of another color.

Castor set   A set of 3–6 bottles in a metal frame, made to contain a variety of condiments.

Celery vase   An upright container used to serve celery.

Compote   A bowl on a high footed stem.

Cracking off   The process of severing a glass article from the blowpipe or pontil rod.

Crackle glass   Glassware with a surface resembling cracked ice; the surface has been intentionally cracked by immersing hot glass in cold water, then reheating it partially before the final shaping, or by covering and marvering a warm surface with broken bits of glass. Crackle, or craquelle, glass was popular in the late 19th century.

Crimp   To finish the end of a handle by pinching it with a special tool.

Crizzled glass   Glassware with a multitude of surface fractures, often caused by an imbalance in glass composition; found on glass made before the 20th century.

Crystal glass   Colorless glass containing a high percentage of lead oxide. Crystal glass is very transparent and has a high index of refraction and considerable sparkle. It is frequently used for fine tableware.

Cullet   Broken glass added to a batch to speed melting and to improve quality.

Cup plate   A 3–4″ plate made in pressed glass from the 1820s to the 1860s. It was used to hold ceramic teacups.

Custard glass   Pressed glass in an opaque cream color.

Cutting   A method of decorating glass using a rapidly rotating stone or cast-iron wheel, fed with an abrasive mixture, such as sand. The cuts are usually polished with a fine abrasive or an acid bath.

Depression glass   Machine-pressed glassware of the 1920s, 1930s, and 1940s.

Drawn stem   A stem that is taken from the main gather rather than from a separate, applied gather.

Dresser set   A set of 3–7 matching pieces for a woman's dresser, including perfume bottles, powder jars, and similar containers.

Engraving   A method of decorating glass using a rapidly rotating stone or copper wheel, fed with an abrasive mixture, such as sand. Engraving is performed in much the same way as cutting, but the abrasions are shallower, allowing greater freedom of manipulation and detail.

Epergne   An elaborate tiered centerpiece consisting of a metal frame with dishes, vases, or candleholders made of glass, silver, or porcelain.

Finishing   The process of cracking off, grinding, or polishing glass after it has been blown and shaped.

Fire-polishing   Reheating a glass for a smoother and glossier finish.

Flashed glass   A term incorrectly used to describe cased or stained glass.

Flint glass   A 19th-century term for glass with a high lead content. Also a trade designation for fine tableware.

Fluting   Narrow vertical panels or grooves, made by cutting or with a mold.

Folded rim   A rim that has been doubled over for added strength, usually found on the edge of a foot or a bowl.

Free-blown glass   Glass blown and shaped completely by hand without the use of molds.

Frosted glass   Colorless glass with a gray matt finish, created by exposing the object to acid fumes, which remove the surface layer of glass and leave a nonglossy finish.

Gadrooning   An applied decoration that is tooled to form a ribbed or swirled band usually on a foot or the base of a bowl.

Galleried rim   A wide rim that somewhat resembles a gallery or balcony; often appears on a covered bowl.

Gather   The gob of molten glass before it is blown or tooled.

Green glass   Inexpensive glass used for bottles or windows, made from sand with iron impurities that impart an amber, aquamarine, green, or brown color.

Grill plate   A divided plate introduced during the 1930s.

Hand press   A small hand-operated metal press shaped like an old-fashioned lemon squeezer, used to make lamp bases, bowls, goblets, decanter stoppers, and decorative prisms for light fixtures in the mid-18th and early 19th centuries.

Humidor   An airtight container for cigars that protects them from drying out.

Iridescent finish   A rainbowlike colored finish found on Art Nouveau glass and Carnival glass. The finish is sprayed on while the piece is still warm.

Lacy-pattern glass   Pressed glass of the mid-1820s to the mid-1840s, usually characterized by a stippled background and a complex scroll-and-flower design.

Lapidary cutting   A decorative technique in which the glass is cut into facets, as a gemstone is cut. This technique is often used on knife rests and on stoppers of decanters or perfume bottles.

Lead glass   Glass containing a substantial amount of lead oxide. The addition of lead increases the density of glass and enhances its ability to refract and disperse light. Lead is principally used in decorative and luxury tableware, ornaments, and optical glass.

Lehr   A tunnel-shaped oven in which glass in annealed.

Lime glass   The most widely used nonlead glass formula, made with lime. This glass is thin enough to be melted in mass quantities in large tanks.

Marbled glass   Pressed glass of the 1880s and 1890s with a marblelike coloring, made by melting opaque white glass and a

colored glass in the same pot. Also called mosaic glass or slag glass.

Marver   To roll a gather on a smooth stone or metal surface in order to make it symmetrical or to center it on the blowpipe. This term also refers to the stone or metal surface.

Matt finish   A nonglossy finish created by exposing glass to acid fumes or by grinding. Also called satin finish by collectors.

Metal   A term used for glass in the molten state.

Milk glass   A collector's term for opaque white pressed glass made from about 1860 to the present.

Mold-blown glass   Glassware made by blowing a partly expanded gather of molten glass into a full-size or part-size pattern mold.

Molded glass   Glass formed in a mold, as distinct from cast, rolled, drawn, or free-blown ware.

Mold mark   A seam or mark resulting from a mold joint.

Mosaic glass   A 19th-century term for marbled glass. Also called slag glass by collectors.

Nappy   A manufacturer's term used in the 19th century to describe a small bowl in any shape. Some nappies are covered, while others look like small compotes.

Off-hand process   The blowing and shaping of glass without the use of molds; the resulting glass is also called free-blown.

Opalescent glass   Glass that resembles an opal in color; it is usually bluish-white and translucent unless held to a strong light, when it will show red highlights.

Pattern mold   A multipartite mold with a decorative pattern; glass blown into this type of mold picks up the pattern on its exterior.

Pillar-molded glass   Glassware decorated with protruding vertical ribs formed by placing the gather in a mold.

Pontil mark or scar   A rough place on a blown piece where the pontil rod has been broken away. May be ground or ground and polished to form a smooth, circular depression.

Pontil rod   A solid iron rod that supports a glass object during the finishing process. After the object is blown, it is transferred from the blowpipe to the pontil rod for final shaping and decorating.

Pressed glass   Glassware made by dropping molten glass into a mold and using the pressure of a plunger for shaping.

Punty   A workmen's term for a pontil rod. This term also refers to circular facets cut on the glass for decoration.

Rock-crystal engraving   A style of engraving in which the glass has been polished after engraving to restore its former gloss and transparency. This style, named after genuine rock crystal made from quartz in Europe in the 16th century, was popular from about 1885 until 1940.

Salver   A round tray or platter on a high stem, used for serving desserts or tea sandwiches or for the presentation of visiting cards in the 18th and 19th centuries.

Satin finish   A 19th-century term for glass with a matt finish; also advertised as plush glass or velvet glass.

Slag glass   A collector's term for marbled glass. Also called mosaic glass by collectors.

Spill holder   A vaselike container for twists of paper, or "spills," used to light a candle or a lamp. Spill holders were made in pressed glass only during the mid-19th century.

Spoon holder   A vaselike container used to hold spoons on the dining table from the mid-19th century to World War I.

Stones   Pieces of unmelted raw material left in the molten glass.

String holder   A cylindrical, bell-shaped or dome-shaped container for a ball of string, with a hole through which the string is fed. String holders were made in blown or pressed glass from the 1860s to the 1920s.

Swirled ribbing   A decoration made on mold-blown glass by expanding and twisting a ribbed gather after it is removed from the mold.

Table set   Matching sugar bowl, creamer, spoon holder, and butter dish.

Threading   Applied strands of glass on an object as decoration.

Toddy plate   A collector's term for a 4¼–5½″ plate made in pressed glass from the 1830s to the 1860s. It may have been used under a toddy glass or as a large saucer.

Tooling   The process of shaping the molten glass after the bubble is formed, using pincers, paddle, shears, and other tools to make such features as the handle, rim, foot, stem, knop, and applied decoration.

Toy set   Miniature pressed-glass set usually with matching sugar bowl, creamer, spoon holder, and butter dish.

Venetian-style glass   A type of blown glass popular in the 1920s and 1930s, characterized by thin walls, graceful shapes, and bright colors.

Water set   A pitcher with matching tumblers and, sometimes, a matching tray; made primarily in pressed or cut glass.

Whiskey set   A decanter with matching small tumblers; made primarily in pressed or cut glass.

Window glass   Inexpensive glass made from sand containing iron impurities that impart an amber, aquamarine, green, or brown color.

Wine set   A decanter with matching wineglasses and, sometimes, a matching tray; made primarily in pressed or cut glass.

Organizations for Collectors

Few clubs have permanent headquarters. In most cases, the addresses given are those of the current secretary or president.

American Cut Glass Association
P.O. Box 7095, Shreveport, LA 71107

Fenton Art Glass Collectors of America, Inc.
P.O. Box 2441, Appleton, WI 54911

Fostoria Glass Society of America
Box 826, Moundsville, WV 26041

Heart of America Carnival Glass Association
7809 Arlington, Raytown, MO 64138

Heisey Collectors of America
P.O. Box 27, Newark, OH 43055

International Carnival Glass Association
RR 2, Warren, IN 46792

National Cambridge Collectors, Inc.
P.O. Box 416, Cambridge, OH 43725

National Depression Glass Association
Box 556, Milford, NJ 08848

National Duncan Glass Society
Box 965, Washington, PA 15301

National Early American Glass Club
Park Street Church, Boston, MA 02108
(This organization has 33 branches throughout the country. The Boston area club can refer you to the nearest branch.)

National Toothpick Holder Collectors Society
8320 Old Courthouse Road, Suite 305, Vienna, VA 22180

Permanent Antique Glass Collections

Most large city art museums contain some antique American glass. The sources listed below include those museums with significant permanent collections on view.

In New England
Connecticut: Wadsworth Atheneum, Hartford.
Maine: The Jones Gallery of Glass and Ceramics (June-October), Sebago; Portland Museum of Art, Portland.
Massachusetts: New Bedford Glass Museum, New Bedford; Old Sturbridge Village, Sturbridge; Sandwich Glass Museum (April-November), Sandwich.
New Hampshire: The Currier Gallery of Art, Manchester.
Vermont: Bennington Museum (March-November), Bennington.

In the Mid-Atlantic Region
Delaware: Henry Francis du Pont Winterthur Museum, Winterthur.
New Jersey: The Wheaton Museum of American Glass, Millville.
New York: The Corning Museum of Glass, Corning. Cooper-Hewitt Museum, Smithsonian Institutions, National Museum of Design (by appointment); The Metropolitan Museum of Art; and The New-York Historical Society; all New York.
Pennsylvania: Historical Society of Western Pennsylvania, Pittsburgh; Philadelphia Museum of Art, Philadelphia.
West Virginia: The Huntington Galleries, Inc., Huntington; Oglebay Institute-Mansion Museum, Wheeling.

In the Southeast
Florida: The Morse Gallery of Art (Tiffany glass), Winter Park.
Louisiana: New Orleans Museum of Art, New Orleans.
Tennessee: Houston Antique Museum, Chattanooga.
Virginia: Chrysler Museum at Norfolk, Norfolk.
Washington, D.C.: National Museum of American History, Smithsonian Institution.

In the Midwest
Indiana: Greentown Glass Museum, Inc., Greentown.
Michigan: Henry Ford Museum, Dearborn.
Ohio: The Cambridge Glass Museum, Cambridge; Milan Historical Museum, Inc., Milan; National Heisey Glass Museum, Newark; The Toledo Museum of Art, Toledo.
Wisconsin: John Nelson Bergstrom Art Center and Mahler Glass Museum, Neenah.

On the West Coast
California: Los Angeles County Museum of Art, Los Angeles; The Wine Museum of San Francisco and M. H. de Young Museum, San Francisco.

Where to Find Glass

Many people start glass collections more or less by accident: they acquire a piece of glass and, finding that they enjoy having it, look for more. Once you know the particular type of glassware that most interests you, there are specific places to look. General antique shops usually contain a sampling of mid-19th-century pressed glass and blown glass, as well as some late 19th-century art glass and cut glass. Dealers who carry Depression glass or Carnival glass tend to specialize in glass of that type. Depression glass and stemware of the 1930s and 1940s are often available at tag sales and flea markets. Although cut glass is also found at tag sales, most of these pieces tend to be ordinary. Nevertheless, in recent years a few lucky collectors have been known to stumble on museum-quality glass worth hundreds of dollars at garage sales!

Early blown glass and pressed glass can be found through specialized dealers in the East and Midwest, and at auctions in New York City, New England, and the Midwest. Glass is most often available near its place of origin: New England shops will carry a selection of early pressed glass, while midwestern antique stores are more likely to have glass from the Pittsburgh area. Since no 19th-century factories were located in the South or on the West Coast, the supply of early glass tends to be smaller in those areas. Mid-19th-century cut glass and brilliant-cut glass of the turn of the century, however, are sometimes available in the South, where heirloom pieces have been sold to antique dealers. Every fall in Silver Springs, Maryland, and every spring in White Plains, New York, large antique shows devoted solely to glass are sponsored by local glass clubs. Large Depression glass shows are held annually at several cities around the country. Joining collectors' clubs, reading the many collectors' magazines and newspapers, and attending lectures and seminars on glass will enable the beginner to meet other collectors with similar interests. Check the Organizations for Collectors section in this guide for names and mailing addresses.

Stemware

Stemware prices reflect an extensive range, from $3 to $7 for a plain late 19th-century wineglass to $250 to $325 for a signed Tiffany example. Many types of stemware included here cost less than $25, however, and a substantial number are under $50. Date is seldom a factor in determining value; rather, the glass type and its popularity influence stemware prices. Generally, the best buys are plain blown wineglasses and goblets (#4, #5) or simple cut (#7) or engraved (#30) pieces. Early pressed stemware (#22, #25, #26), which is extremely popular and relatively scarce, commands a higher price.

1 **Late blown wineglass** $3–7
2 **Early blown wineglass** $35–50
3 **Early midwestern ribbed wineglass** $150–200
4 **Trumpet-shaped wineglass** $15–25
5 **Button-stem wineglass** $15–25
6 **Decorated button-stem wineglass** $30–40
  Matching decanter $65–80
7 **Cut button-stem wineglass** $20–30
  Matching glassware $50–100
8 **Engraved Gravic wineglass** $40–50
  Matching glassware $30–200
9 **Cut water goblet**
  With engraving $300–375
  Without engraving $25–40
  Matching glassware, without engraving $20–50
10 **Blown 3-mold wineglass** $100–150
11 **Depression goblet** $4–9
  Matching glassware $2–75
12 **Rummer** $25–40
13 **Flute champagne glass**
  Plain $20–30
  Cut $25–35
14 **Firing glass**
  With engraving $175–275
  Without engraving $100–200
15 **Depression stemware**
  Rose Cameo $6–8
  Matching glassware in Rose Cameo $2–10
  Mayfair $20–23
  Matching glassware in Mayfair $5–125 (more for rarities)
  Patrician $22–25
  Matching glassware in Patrician $3–75
16 **Trumpet-shaped jelly glass** $50–60
17 **Early geometric-style pressed tumbler** $20–30
  Matching glassware $16–150
18 **Early geometric-style pressed ale glass** $35–45
  Matching glassware $35–100
19 **Centennial pilsner** $50–75
  Centennial beer mug $50–75
20 **Early geometric-style pressed jelly glass** $30–45
  Matching glassware in Diamond Point $25–200 (more for rarities)
  Matching glassware in Ashburton $15–265
21 **Red-stained and engraved goblet** $85–135
22 **Early geometric-style pressed goblet** $35–45
  Matching glassware $30–240

23 **Early geometric-style pressed eggcup** $30–50
   Matching glassware in Waffle and Thumbprint $35–165
   Matching glassware in Ashburton $15–265
24 **Early geometric-style pressed eggcup or wineglass** $20–40
   Matching glassware $15–135
25 **Early geometric-style pressed goblet** $60–80
   Matching glassware $35–100
26 **Early geometric-style pressed wineglass** $50–60
   Matching glassware $15–250
27 **Brilliant-cut cordial or liqueur glass** $15–20
   Matching glassware $15–300
28 **Brilliant-cut saucer champagne glass** $25–40
   Matching glassware $15–300
29 **Brilliant-cut place setting** $750–1000
   Individual pieces $75–100
   Matching glassware $35–500 (more for rarities)
30 **Engraved goblet** $20–35
   Matching glassware $15–75
31 **Realistic-style pressed goblet** $30–45
   Matching glassware $12–105
32 **Locke Art wineglass** $65–80
33 **Engraved goblet and wineglass** $8–18
   Matching glassware $5–25
34 **Mold-blown 1930s stemware** $20–26
   Matching glassware $5–40
35 **Spanish threaded wineglass** $25–30
   Matching glassware $20–45
36 **Cased goblet and wineglass** $85–135
   Matching glassware $60–150
37 **Tiffany white-wine glass** $250–325
   Matching stemware $200–400

Tumblers, Mugs, Tankards, and Cups

Many glasses in this category are priced between $25 and $50. A 1940s mug (#69)—a glass type that is just beginning to interest collectors—costs as little as $1, while Depression-glass tumblers (#48) are only $4 to $7. Because tumblers and mugs are among the first glassware made in this country, several early pieces command extremely high prices, ranging from $150 for an early 19th-century Pennsylvania Dutch tumbler (#43) to $5000 or more for a rare 18th-century engraved tumbler by Amelung (#41). But date does not always determine price. An early midwestern ribbed tumbler (#44) made in 1820 may cost substantially less than a currently fashionable turn-of-the-century art-glass tumbler (#68).

38 **Blown bottle-glass tumbler** $90–175
39 **Blown tumbler** $100–200
40 **Stiegel-type tumbler** $1200–1500 +
41 **Amelung tumbler** $5000 +
42 **Paneled bar tumbler** $40–65
43 **Pennsylvania Dutch engraved tumbler** $150–250
44 **Early midwestern ribbed tumbler** $30–40
45 **Blown 3-mold tumbler** $50–125
46 **Blown 3-mold tumbler** $50–125
47 **Rock-crystal whiskey glass** $15–25

48 **Depression tumbler**
Hex Optic $4–6
Matching glassware in Hex Optic $1–25
New Century $5–7
Matching glassware in New Century $1–45
49 **Realistic-style pressed tumbler** $20–35
Matching glassware $7–50
50 **Pressed whiskey taster** $185–235
51 **Carnival water and whiskey tumblers** $30–40
Matching glassware $15–400 (more for rarities)
52 **Gold-decorated pressed tumbler** $13–15
Matching glassware $10–65
53 **Brilliant-cut highball tumbler**
Marked $50–60
Unmarked $40–50
Matching glassware in both types $15–300
54 **Bakewell-type cut mug** $275–335
Sulphide base tumbler $750–1200
55 **Blown 3-mold mug** $250–350
56 **Early geometric-style pressed tumbler and mug** $75–120
Matching glassware $15–350 (more for rarities)
57 **Late 19th-century pressed tumbler and mug** $18–35
Matching glassware $20–90
58 **Lemonade glass** $25–45
Matching pitcher $50–75
59 **Double-handled mug** $300–350
60 **Early tankard** $700–1000
61 **Free-blown mug** $200–350
62 **Free-blown lemonade or punch cup** $15–20
63 **Beer mug** $450–600
64 **Blown 3-mold punch cup** $250–350
65 **Carnival punch cup** $12–15
Matching glassware $25–145
66 **Depression punch cup** $1–2
Matching glassware $1–30
67 **Wheeling Peachblow punch cup** $275–375
68 **New England Peachblow tumbler** $380–520
69 **Depression mug**
Plain $2–3
Tom & Jerry $1–2
Matching punch bowl in Tom & Jerry $60–70

Pitchers, Jugs, Decanters, and Bar Bottles
All of these objects are extremely popular forms to collect. Most
cost between $100 and $300. Pitchers of all types and cut-glass
decanters are generally more expensive than bar bottles. But
early pressed decanters (#102) and bar bottles (#109)—unlike
other early pressed shapes—are among the least expensive
objects in this group, ranging from $40 to $75. A Depression-
glass decanter (#112) may cost $5. Pitchers with lily-pad
decoration (#74, #75) command the highest prices, soaring over
$1000. Most of these rare examples of glass folk art belong to
museums or are in long-established private collections. Even
damaged pieces are purchased for $200 to $300.

70 **Depression pitcher** $24–28
Matching glassware $5–125
71 **Engraved pitcher** $175–275

72 **Early midwestern ribbed pitcher** $100–200
73 **Free-blown pitcher** $150–200
74 **Lily-pad pitcher** $850–1000 +
75 **Johnson lily-pad pitcher** $1000 +
76 **Spanish Lace pitcher** $250–300
   Matching glassware $25–350
77 **Frances Ware pitcher** $200–250
   Matching glassware $25–350
78 **Brilliant-cut water set**
   Tumbler $25–35
   Pitcher $200–250
   Matching glassware $15–300
79 **Brilliant-cut pitcher** $225–275
   Matching glassware $15–300
80 **Early 19th-century cut pitcher** $350–550
81 **Blown 3-mold pitcher** $350–400
82 **Mold-blown pitcher** $100–125
83 **Beehive pitcher** $70–130
84 **Pillar-molded pitcher** $550–750
85 **Early 20th-century pressed water set**
   Tumbler $7–13
   Pitcher $180–240
   Matching glassware $15–325
86 **Late 19th-century pressed pitcher** $275–350
   Matching glassware $35–400
87 **Late 19th-century pressed pitcher** $125–150
   Matching tumbler $20–25
88 **Late 19th-century pressed pitcher** $45–65
   Matching glassware $15–100
89 **Realistic-style pressed pitcher** $160–210
   Matching glassware $10–300
90 **Depression water pitcher** $22–27
   Matching glassware $5–35
91 **Carnival pitcher** $25–35
   Matching tumbler $10–15
92 **Corset-shaped brilliant-cut pitcher** $200–250
   Matching tumbler $15–25
93 **Pitcher-form brilliant-cut vase** $475–600
94 **Brilliant-cut pitcher** $300–350
   Matching glassware $15–350
95 **Crackle-glass champagne pitcher** $125–175
96 **Silver-decorated 1930s decanter** $75–100
   Matching glassware $2–100 (more for rarities)
97 **Rock-crystal claret jug** $600–950
   Matching glassware $50–1000
98 **Rock-crystal decanter** $250–300
99 **Locking jug** $100–125
100 **Brilliant-cut 20th-century decanter** $175–235
101 **Early cut and engraved decanter** $225–300
   Matching glassware $40–300
102 **Early geometric-style pressed decanter and bitters bottle**
   Decanter $50–75
   Bitters bottle $45–50
   Matching glassware $15–135
103 **Blown 3-mold labeled decanter** $250–350
104 **Chain-decorated decanter** $350–400
105 **Triple-ring decanter** $125–225
106 **Bakewell-type cut decanter** $280–330
   Matching glassware $100–500

107 **Engraved and cut decanter** $360–430
Matching glassware $50–450
108 **Engraved bar bottle** $350–450
109 **Early geometric-style pressed bar bottle** $40–75
Matching glassware $15–265
110 **Pillar-molded bar bottle** $75–150
111 **Brilliant-cut water bottle and tumbler**
Water bottle $200–225
Tumbler $15–25
Matching glassware $15–300
112 **Depression decanter** $5–6
Matching glassware $1–15
113 **Early midwestern ribbed bar bottle** $450–500

Sugar Bowls and Creamers
Early midwestern sugar-bowl-and-creamer sets are especially
expensive since this type of glass is rare and has been in great
demand since the 1950s. Midwestern sugar bowls and creamers
made in a 10-diamond mold or a 24-rib mold command the highest
prices; fragments of these molds have been excavated at a
glasshouse in Zanesville, Ohio. These prices have increased only
at about the same rate as inflation, however. Although early
pressed patterns and rare pieces are also costly, late pressed
glass is relatively moderately priced, ranging from $20 to $30
apiece. Only Depression-glass sets can be purchased for under
$25.

114 **Early midwestern ribbed creamer** $320–430
Matching sugar bowl $350–500
115 **Simple creamer** $50–60
116 **Early midwestern sugar bowl and creamer** $450–500 (pair)
117 **Early midwestern ribbed sugar bowl** $5000 +
118 **Simple sugar bowl** $125–175
119 **Engraved sugar bowl** $75–100
Matching glassware $35–200
120 **Triple-ring sugar bowl** $275–375
121 **Gadrooned sugar bowl and creamer** $400–500 (pair)
122 **Lily-pad sugar bowl** $750–1000
123 **South Jersey creamer** $500–850
124 **Looped creamer** $600–750
125 **Chain-decorated creamer**
Blue $750–1000
Colorless $300–400
126 **Early geometric-style pressed creamer** $135–185
Matching glassware $15–265
127 **Cut sugar bowl** $250–350
128 **Bakewell-type cut creamer** $125–150
Matching sugar bowl $150–200
Matching glassware $50–350
129 **Bakewell-type cut sugar bowl** $225–275
Matching creamer $100–150
130 **Engraved sugar bowl** $250–350
131 **Blown 3-mold sugar bowl** $600–900
132 **Midwestern blown 3-mold sugar bowl and
creamer** $5000 (pair)
133 **Stiegel-type creamer** $200–250
134 **Stiegel-type sugar bowl** $3700 +

135 **Midwestern diamond-patterned sugar bowl and creamer** $3200+ (pair)
136 **Blown 3-mold creamer** $300–375
137 **Late lacy-pattern pressed creamer** $200–225
138 **Realistic-style pressed sugar bowl and creamer** $300–350 (pair)
Matching glassware $20–200
139 **Enameled art-glass creamer** $35–75
Matching sugar bowl $50–85
140 **Late lacy-pattern pressed sugar bowl** $400–600
141 **Late lacy-pattern pressed sugar bowl and creamer** $225–325 (pair)
142 **Lacy-pattern pressed sugar bowl and creamer** $500–800 (pair)
143 **Lacy-pattern pressed creamer** $200–250
144 **Carnival milk pitcher** $25–28
Matching glassware $20–75
145 **Red-stained milk pitcher** $25–30
Matching glassware $15–75
146 **Early geometric-style pressed table set** $800–1000
Spoon holder $30–50
Washington finial butter dish $500–600
Plain butter dish $50–75
Sugar bowl $40–60
Creamer $40–60
Matching glassware $15–350
147 **Abstract-style pressed creamer** $22–26
Rare compote $350
Matching glassware $15–140
148 **Realistic-style pressed creamer** $17–32
Matching glassware $7–50
149 **Brilliant-cut sugar bowl and creamer** $65–135 (pair)
150 **Amberina sugar bowl and creamer** $1200–2000 (pair)
151 **Depression sugar bowl and creamer** $10–12 (pair)
Matching glassware $3–75
152 **Depression sugar bowl and creamer** $7–9 (pair)
Matching glassware $2–25 (more for rarities)
153 **Enameled sugar bowl and creamer** $75–135 (pair)
154 **Pink slag creamer** $300–600
Matching glassware $200–750

Salt Dishes, Condiment Servers, and Small Table Accessories
Color and rarity of pattern are the 2 determining factors in pricing salt dishes. All types of glass salts have been collected for at least 50 years, and although prices have kept pace with inflation, they have not outstripped it. The most expensive salts are blown 3-mold, lacy-pattern, and 18th- and 19th-century pattern-molded salts. All 3 types often range from $100 to $500. Individual pressed or cut salts are still widely available for under $15. There are probably fewer collectors of salt dishes today than there were in the 1950s, while the number of people collecting salt shakers has increased.
Napkin rings, knife rests, syrup jugs, and pickle jars are not much in demand. Price is determined by color and decoration. An art-glass piece (#180, #181, #182) always brings a high price regardless of its function as a cracker barrel or a pickle jar. Collectors of toothpick holders are becoming increasingly

numerous; they have formed their own club and hold regular conventions. Undoubtedly this new popularity will cause prices for toothpick holders to rise in the near future.

155 **Pressed napkin ring** $8–15
156 **Brilliant-cut knife rest** $30–60
157 **Pressed individual salt** $3–8
   Cut individual salt $5–10
158 **Blown 3-mold salt** $50–75
159 **Brilliant-cut salt** $35–50
   Matching glassware $35–500 (more for rarities)
160 **Bakewell-type cut salt** $15–30
161 **Lacy-pattern pressed salt** $175–225
162 **Rectangular pressed salt** $25–75
163 **Stag's-head pressed salt** $135–185
164 **Scallop-shell pressed salt** $115–145
165 **Boat-shaped pressed salt** $350–400
166 **Lacy-pattern pressed salt** $90–125
167 **Lacy-pattern pressed salt** $115–140
168 **Floral-pattern pressed salt** $110–165
169 **Crown pressed salt** $40–65
170 **Tiffany salt dip** $100–150
171 **Mercury-glass salt** $100–150
172 **Goblet pressed salt** $15–25
173 **Blown 3-mold salt** $150–225
174 **Free-blown salt** $200–250
175 **Stiegel-type salt** $300–400
176 **Early midwestern ribbed salt** $225–300
177 **Pressed toothpick and match holders**
   Match holder $30–40
   S-repeat toothpick holder $12–18
   Matching glassware in S-repeat $5–75
178 **Pressed match holder** $30–40
179 **New England Peachblow toothpick holder** $500–550
180 **Albertine pickle jar** $550–650
181 **Crown Milano and Albertine biscuit boxes** $425–675 (apiece)
182 **Royal Flemish cracker jar** $1600–2200
183 **Mold-blown salt shaker** $50–75
184 **Egg-shaped salt and pepper shakers** $325–375 (pair)
185 **Salt and pepper shakers** $25–35 (pair)
186 **Depression salt and pepper shakers** $18–25 (pair)
   Matching glassware $2–40
187 **Blown 3-mold castor set** $200–300
188 **Cut castor set** $175–275
189 **Realistic-style pressed castor set** $165–265
   Matching glassware $10–300
190 **Burmese castor set** $1500–2000
191 **Agata cruet** $1350–1800
192 **Mold-blown molasses can or syrup jug**
   Unnamed pattern $50–100
   Lincoln Drape $75–125
   Matching glassware in Lincoln Drape $15–175
193 **Mold-blown molasses can or syrup jug**
   Left $40–65
   Right $90–135
194 **Late 19th-century pressed cruet and syrup jug** $20–40 (apiece)
   Matching glassware $18–90
195 **Blown 3-mold cruet** $150–200

196 **Late 19th-century pressed ketchup jug or vinegar cruet** $25–40
Matching glassware $15–75
197 **Carnival candy dish** $14–17
Matching glassware $15–100
198 **Late 19th-century pressed pickle jar** $30–45

Plates
Glass plates are far rarer than tumblers and bowls, yet they are among the least expensive types of American glass tableware. Except for cup plates, they have never been great favorites with collectors, which has kept prices down and makes plates an excellent area for collecting today. Depression-glass plates have the lowest prices—only $5 to $10. The highest prices for early 19th-century free-blown or mold-blown plates are only a few hundred dollars. Brilliant-cut plates in an intricate pattern tend to be high, however, especially if cut by a well-known firm. But an unidentified cut piece often costs little more than $100. Cup plates, unlike other glass plates, have been widely collected for over 50 years, perhaps because they are small, easily displayed, and come in so many variations. Rarity of pattern, color, and condition determine price. A rare colored cup plate in good condition may bring up to $400, but many common cup plates cost only $20 to $40.

199 **Ulysses S. Grant memorial plate** $50–75
200 **Garfield memorial plate** $80–100
Matching glassware $15–75
201 **Inscribed cup plate**
Bunker Hill $20–80
Wedding Day $20–30
202 **Henry Clay cup plate** $17–28
203 **Early pressed toddy plate** $75–100
204 **Lacy-pattern toddy plate**
Blue $75–100
Colorless $50–75
205 **Heart-pattern cup plate** $20–35
206 **Brilliant-cut plate** $1000 +
Matching glassware $100–1000
207 **Brilliant-cut ice cream tray** $300–1000
Matching bowl $50–60
208 **Lacy-pattern pressed plate** $100–200
209 **Early pressed plate** $150–200
210 **Lacy-pattern pressed toddy plate** $120–150
211 **Late pressed plate** $25–35
Matching glassware $12–90
212 **Depression place setting**
Sherbet $4–5
Salad plate $3–4
Bread-and-butter plate $1–2
Cup and saucer $5–6
Cake plate $7–8
Dinner plate $4–5
Soup cup $4–5
Luncheon plate $3–4
Matching glassware $1–20
213 **Depression delphite plate** $10–12
Matching glassware $1–25

214 **Early midwestern ribbed plate** $135–200
215 **Chain-decorated plate** $150–250
216 **Depression serving tray** $6–8
Matching glassware $2–30
217 **Depression sandwich server** $6–7
218 **Depression square plate** $20–25
Matching glassware $2–90
219 **Depression place setting** $20–26
Matching glassware $3–100

Covered Bowls and Butter Dishes
Most of the covered bowls and butter dishes illustrated were
made after 1860 and retail for under $50. A few are in the $100–
200 range. The lacy-pattern covered bowl (#246) is a great rarity
and has one of the highest prices of any piece of lacy-pattern
glass. Yet it is not as expensive as some art glass and signed cut
glass. The rare Holly Amber butter dish (#229) also commands
an exceptionally high price.

220 **Amberina cheese dish** $400–450
221 **Heisey butter dish** $25–50
Matching glassware $15–75
222 **Late 19th-century pressed butter dish** $40–60
Matching glassware $10–75
223 **Gilt-trim pressed butter dish** $50–65
Matching glassware $10–75
224 **Engraved pressed butter dish** $45–60
Matching glassware $30–250
225 **Late 19th-century pressed butter dish** $40–60
226 **Banner butter dish** $125–165
227 **Liberty Bell butter dish** $175
Matching glassware $10–200
228 **Opalescent pressed butter dish** $50–100
Matching glassware $40–200
229 **Holly Amber butter dish** $1000–1650
Matching glassware $200–2000
230 **Custard-glass butter dish** $125–165
Matching glassware $40–225
231 **Simple pressed butter dish** $40–60
Matching glassware $10–200
232 **Clamshell nappy** $25–35
233 **Realistic-style pressed butter dish** $55–65
Matching glassware $15–150
234 **Abstract-style pressed butter dish** $40–50
Matching glassware $15–75
235 **Late 19th-century pressed butter dish** $40–50
Matching glassware $20–100
236 **Early geometric-style pressed nappy** $75–100
Matching glassware $15–300
237 **Atterbury duck dish** $300–350
238 **Rooster butter dish** $35–50
239 **Duck butter dish** $65–75
240 **Fish butter dish** $150–175
241 **Realistic-style butter dish** $60–75
Matching glassware $25–150
242 **Late 19th-century pressed covered bowl** $50–75
Matching glassware $15–75

243 **Realistic-style pressed covered bowl** $50–75
Matching glassware $10–125
244 **Realistic-style pressed butter dish** $55–70
Matching glassware $20–100
245 **Late 19th-century pressed butter dish** $35–50
246 **Lacy-pattern pressed covered bowl** $800–1000
247 **Depression refrigerator butter dish** $5–8

Bowls

Bowls, like tumblers and mugs, were made over a long period in every type of glass and consequently have a wide price range. Cut bowls and art-glass pieces command the highest prices. In cut glass, prices vary greatly, based on the quality of the glass, whether it is cut in a well-known pattern, bears a trademark, or is a rare shape. For example, the canoe-shaped bowl (#262) is a rarer form than the celery dish (#263) and thus would probably be in greater demand and bring a higher price. Art glass prices are determined by the color and type of decoration. Carnival-glass bowls, which are fashionable collectibles today, usually range from $25 to $60, but rare colors and patterns may cost more than $150. As in other categories, Depression-glass bowls are low-priced, often less than $30.

248 **Early free-blown bowl** $200–350
249 **Depression bowl** $8–12
Matching glassware $1–20
250 **Lacy-pattern pressed bowl** $45–100
251 **Depression soup bowl** $3–4
Matching glassware $1–15
252 **Simple cut bowl** $200–250
253 **Early pressed honey dish** $15–25
254 **Blown 3-mold bowl** $75–125
255 **Free-blown bowl** $30–50
256 **Realistic-style square pressed bowl** $75–100
Matching glassware $7–50
257 **Lacy-pattern pressed tray** $300–375
258 **Late 19th-century pressed bread tray** $25–35
259 **Pomona ice cream tray** $450–600
260 **Late 19th-century pressed serving bowl and platter** $50–75 (pair)
Matching glassware $12–100
261 **Amberina boat-shaped centerpiece** $350–400
262 **Brilliant-cut canoe-shaped centerpiece** $500–750
Matching glassware $25–1000
263 **Brilliant-cut celery dish** $475–575
264 **Brilliant-cut acorn-shaped nappy** $325–400
265 **Brilliant-cut leaf-shaped nappy** $175–250
266 **Brilliant-cut bowl** $300–450
267 **Brilliant-cut bowl** $150–200
268 **Brilliant-cut bowl** $150–200
269 **Cut centerpiece** $750–850
Matching glassware $50–1000
270 **Simple brilliant-cut bowl** $750–850
271 **Cut and cased finger bowl** $150–200
Matching glassware $100–1000
272 **Early finger bowl and wine rinser** $30–50 (apiece)
273 **Depression fruit bowl** $28–30
Matching glassware $5–125 (more for rarities)

274 **Early midwestern milk bowl** $1000–1750
275 **Cased and engraved console bowl** $225–325
276 **Pillar-molded bowl** $150–200
277 **Depression bowl** $20–23
    Matching glassware $1–20
278 **Kew Blas bowl** $200–300
279 **Carnival bowl** $45–50
280 **Mt. Washington Peachblow bowl** $750–900
281 **Chocolate-glass dish** $40–60
    Matching glassware $30–250
282 **Grotesque bowl** $165–265
283 **Diamond-quilted satin-glass bowl** $200–300
284 **Plated Amberina bowl** $3500–4000
285 **Carnival bowl** $40–55
    Matching glassware $20–150
286 **Carnival dish** $55–60
    Matching berry set $20–175
287 **Carnival bowl** $22–25
    Matching glassware $20–75
288 **Carnival bowl** $80–90
    Matching glassware $15–400 (more for rarities)
289 **Carnival bowl** $45–55
    Matching glassware $25–650

Centerpieces

Centerpieces and punch bowl sets have always been among the most expensive glass forms. Very few pressed fruit servers, compotes, and free-blown pieces can be purchased today for less than $100. Many centerpieces and bride's baskets range from $200 to $500, and punch bowl sets may bring thousands of dollars. The punch bowl set engraved by Tuthill (#307) is worth more than the set cut by Majestic (#306), primarily because Tuthill is a much better-known name. A similar but more simply cut punch bowl without a trademark or signature would cost considerably less, perhaps only $500 to $1000. Carnival-glass punch bowl sets are now in great demand and tend to be as high-priced as cut or engraved sets.

In art glass, the products of the Mt. Washington Glass Company (#309, #310, #312), the New England Glass Works, and Hobbs, Brockunier & Company are worth significantly more than pieces by unknown art glass firms (#311, #313). Tiffany glassware (#305) commands some of the highest prices in American glass. Over the last 15 years, these prices have risen at a rate far greater than that of inflation, largely because many of the people now buying Tiffany are investors, rather than collectors, who are buying regardless of price.

290 **Milk-glass compote** $65–100
291 **Early 20th-century pressed fruit server** $50–100
    Matching glassware $10–100
292 **Realistic-style pressed salver** $130–150
    Matching glassware $25–350
293 **Early geometric-style pressed salver** $215–400
    Matching glassware $25–200
294 **Realistic-style pressed covered bowl** $145–165
    Matching glassware $15–250
295 **Late 19th-century pressed covered bowl** $350–475
    Matching glassware $100–650

296 **Late 19th-century pressed covered bowl** $260–320
   Matching glassware $85–360
297 **Early geometric-style pressed covered bowl** $200–300
   Matching glassware $20–350 (more for rarities)
298 **Early geometric-style pressed punch bowl** $300–450
   Matching glassware $20–350
299 **Early geometric-style pressed compote** $65–100
   Matching glassware $15–350
300 **Pillar-molded punch bowl** $200–250
301 **Engraved compote** $125–175
302 **Bakewell-type cut compote** $250–300
303 **Free-blown compote** $75–100
304 **Venetian-style centerpiece** $200–275
305 **Tiffany punch bowl** $10,000–15,000
   Matching punch cup $150–175
306 **Brilliant-cut punch bowl set** $3000–4000
307 **Engraved punch bowl set** $4000–6000
   Matching glassware $50–500
308 **Trumpet-shaped epergne** $175–225
309 **Double Burmese epergne** $2000–2500
310 **Crown Milano bride's basket** $400–600
311 **Satin-finished bride's basket** $175–275
312 **Acid-etched cameo bride's basket** $750–1000
313 **Art-glass centerpiece** $200–300

Celery Vases, Spoon Holders, and Spill Holders
Pieces in this category are very reasonably priced, since all are
relatively common types of 19th-century glass. This is an
excellent area for beginning collectors. In recent years there has
not been much interest in some of these forms and the market is
very stable. Most pressed pieces cost between $25 and $70.

314 **Hollow-stem pressed celery vase** $25–35
315 **Realistic-style pressed celery vase** $90–120
   Matching glassware $15–300
316 **Engraved celery vase** $135–215
317 **Bakewell-type cut celery vase** $150–250
318 **Realistic-style pressed spoon holder** $35–50
   Matching glassware $12–105
319 **Realistic-style pressed spoon holder** $40–70
   Matching glassware $10–300
320 **Blown 3-mold celery vase** $750–1000
321 **Early geometric-style pressed spoon holder** $65–85
   Matching glassware $15–350
322 **Early geometric-style pressed spill holder** $100–150
   Matching glassware $55–350
323 **Early geometric-style pressed spill holder** $200–300

Vases
The price of a vase, like that of a centerpiece, is determined by
the type of decoration and its rarity rather than by shape or
function. Here again, the highest price is for a Tiffany vase
(#343), followed by the art-glass vases (#333, #345). In cut
glass, a cased vase (#330) will always bring a significantly higher
price than a similar colorless example. Some of the best buys in
this category are in Carnival glass and Depression glass.

324 **Paneled vase** $900–1400
325 **New England coin loving cup** $1000–1500
326 **Dorflinger cut vase** $800–1000
327 **Corset-shaped brilliant-cut vase** $750–800
328 **Honesdale vase** $200–300
329 **Carnival vase**
Left $25–30
Right $20–30
330 **Cased and cut vase** $1700–2200
Matching glassware, not cased $50–500
331 **Sinclaire cut and engraved vase** $200–275
332 **Amberina trumpet-shaped vase** $375–450
333 **Burmese trumpet-shaped vase** $1200–1400
334 **Depression hobnail vase** $6–8
Matching glassware $2–15
335 **Depression vase** $7–8
Matching glassware in Bubble pattern $1–15
Matching glassware in Forest Green line $1–15
336 **New England pressed vase** $375–550
337 **Midwestern looped coin vase** $300–400
338 **Looped vase** $375–500
339 **Marble or slag vase** $50–75
Matching glassware $25–200
340 **Pillar-molded vase** $900–1100
341 **Art Nouveau engraved vase** $275–400
342 **Durand vase** $350–650
343 **Tiffany paperweight vase** $3000 +
344 **Aurene vase** $800–1000
345 **Wheeling Peachblow vase** $1500 +
346 **Onyx vase** $275–300
Matching glassware $200–500
347 **Opalescent hobnail vase** $200–275
Matching glassware $25–300
348 **Ring vase** $35–100
349 **Opaque white vase** $175–225
350 **Coralene vase** $200–250

The Price Guide was written by William C. Ketchum, Jr.

Bibliography

General
Archer, Margaret and Douglas
Imperial Glass
Paducah, Kentucky: Collector Books, 1978.

Bickenhauser, Fred
Tiffin Glassmasters. 2 vols.
Marietta, Ohio: Antique Publishers, 1979, 1981.

Fauster, Carl U., ed.
Libbey Glass Since 1818: Pictorial History and Collectors Guide
Toledo: Len Beach Press, 1979.

Hammond, Dorothy
Confusing Collectibles: A Guide to the Identification of Contemporary Objects
Rev. ed. Des Moines: Wallace-Homestead Book Co., 1979.

Heacock, William
Fenton Glass: The First Twenty-five Years
Marietta, Ohio: O-Val Advertising Corp., 1978.
Fenton Glass: The Second Twenty-five Years
Marietta, Ohio: O-Val Advertising Corp., 1980.

Innes, Lowell
Pittsburgh Glass, 1797–1891: A History and Guide for Collectors
Boston: Houghton Mifflin Co., 1976.

McKearin, George S. and Helen
American Glass
Reprint of 1941 ed. New York: Crown Publishers, 1948.
Two Hundred Years of American Blown Glass
New York: Crown Publishers, Bonanza Books, 1950.

Padgett, Leonard
Pairpoint Glass
Des Moines: Wallace-Homestead Book Co., 1978.

Pepper, Adeline
The Glass Gaffers of New Jersey and Their Creations from 1739 to the Present
New York: Charles Scribner's Sons, 1971.

Peterson, Arthur G.
Glass Salt Shakers: 1000 Patterns
Des Moines: Wallace-Homestead Book Co., 1970.

Spillman, Jane Shadel
Glassmaking: America's First Industry
Corning, New York: The Corning Museum of Glass, 1976.

Toledo Museum of Art
Libbey Glass: A Tradition of 150 Years, 1818–1968
Toledo, 1968.
New England Glass Company, 1818–1888
Toledo, 1963.

Weatherman, Hazel Marie
Fostoria: Its First Fifty Years
Springfield, Missouri: published by author, 1972.

Wilson, Kenneth M.
New England Glass and Glassmaking
New York: Thomas Y. Crowell Co., 1972.

Art Glass
Revi, Albert Christian
Nineteenth Century Glass: Its Genesis and Development
Rev. ed. New York: Thomas Nelson, 1965.

Art Nouveau Glass
Gardner, Paul
The Glass of Frederick Carder
New York: Crown Publishers, 1971.

Koch, Robert
Louis C. Tiffany: Rebel in Glass
New York: Crown Publishers, 1964.
Louis C. Tiffany's Glass, Bronzes & Lamps: A Complete Collector's Guide
New York: Crown Publishers, 1971.

McKean, Hugh F.
The "Lost" Treasures of Louis Comfort Tiffany
New York: Doubleday & Co., 1980.

Perrot, Paul, and Paul Gardner and James S. Plaut
Steuben: Seventy Years of American Glassmaking
New York: Praeger Publishers, 1974.

Revi, Albert Christian
American Art Nouveau Glass
Reprint of 1968 ed. Exton, Pennsylvania: Schiffer Publishing, 1981.

Carnival Glass
Hartung, Marion T.
Book of Carnival Glass, 1–10
Emporia, Kansas: published by author, 1960–1973.

Klamkin, Marian
The Collector's Guide to Carnival Glass
New York: E. P. Dutton, Hawthorn Books, 1976.

Cut and Engraved Glass
Farrar, Estelle Sinclaire
H. P. Sinclaire, Jr., Glassmaker. 2 vols.
Garden City, New York: Farrar Books, 1974, 1975.

Farrar, Estelle Sinclaire, and Jane Shadel Spillman
The Complete Cut & Engraved Glass of Corning
New York: Crown Publishers, 1979.

Pearson, J. Michael
Encyclopedia of American Cut and Engraved Glass, 1880–1917. 3 vols.
Miami Beach, Florida: published by author, 1975, 1977, 1979.

Revi, Albert Christian
American Cut and Engraved Glass
New York: Thomas Nelson, 1965.

Spillman, Jane Shadel, and Estelle Sinclaire Farrar
The Cut & Engraved Glass of Corning, 1898–1940
Corning, New York: The Corning Museum of Glass, 1977.

Depression Glass
Florence, Gene
The Collector's Encyclopedia of Depression Glass
5th ed. Paducah, Kentucky: Collector Books, 1981.

Klamkin, Marian
The Collector's Guide to Depression Glass
New York: E. P. Dutton, Hawthorn Books, 1973.

Krause, Gail
The Encyclopedia of Duncan Glass
Hicksville, New York: Exposition Press, 1976.
A Pictorial History of Duncan & Miller Glass
Hicksville, New York: Exposition Press, 1976.
The Years of Duncan, 1865–1955
Heyworth, Illinois: Heyworth Star, 1980.

National Cambridge Collectors
The Cambridge Glass Company
Reprint of 1930–1934 catalogues. Cambridge, Ohio, 1976.

Weatherman, Hazel Marie
Colored Glassware of the Depression Era. 2 bks.
Springfield, Missouri: published by author, 1970, 1974.

Pressed Glass

Ferson, Regis R. and Mary F.
Yesterday's Milk Glass Today
Pittsburgh: published by authors, 1981.

Hartung, Marion T.
Northwood Pattern Glass in Color: Clear, Custard, Colored and Carnival
Emporia, Kansas: published by author, 1969.
Opalescent Pattern Glass
Des Moines: Wallace-Homestead Book Co., 1971.

Heacock, William
The Encyclopedia of Victorian Colored Pattern Glass
Bks. 1–4, *Toothpick Holders; Opalescent Glass; Syrups, Sugar Shakers and Cruets; Custard Glass*
Marietta, Ohio: Antique Publishers, 1974–1977.

Heacock, William, and Fred Bickenhauser
Encyclopedia of Victorian Colored Pattern Glass
Bk. 5, *U.S. Glass from A to Z*
Marietta, Ohio: Antique Publishers, 1978.

Kamm, Minnie Watson
Pattern Glass Pitchers. 8 vols.
Grosse Pointe, Michigan: Kamm Publications, 1939–1954.

Lee, Ruth Webb
Early American Pressed Glass
Rev. ed. Wellesley Hills, Massachusetts: Lee Publications, 1960.
Victorian Glass Specialties of the Nineteenth Century
4th ed. Northboro, Massachusetts: published by author, 1944.

Lee, Ruth Webb, and James H. Rose
American Glass Cup Plates
Reprint of 1948 ed. Wellesley Hills, Massachusetts: Lee Publications, 1971.

Lindsey, Bessie M.
American Historical Glass
Reprint of 1948 ed. Rutland, Vermont: Charles E. Tuttle Co., 1967.

M'Kee and Brothers
M'Kee Victorian Glass: Five Complete Glass Catalogs from 1859/60 to 1871. Introductions by Lowell Innes and Jane Shadel Spillman
New York: Dover Publications, 1981.

Measell, James
Greentown Glass: The Indiana Tumbler and Goblet Company
Grand Rapids: Grand Rapids Public Museum, 1979.

Neal, Logan W. and Dorothy B.
Pressed Glass Salt Dishes of the Lacy Period, 1825–1850
Philadelphia: published by authors, 1962.

Pears, Thomas C.
Bakewell, Pears & Company Glass Catalogue
Reprint of c. 1875 catalogue. Pittsburgh: Davis and Warde, 1977.

Revi, Albert Christian
American Pressed Glass and Figure Bottles
New York: Thomas Nelson, 1963.

Spillman, Jane Shadel
American and European Pressed Glass in The Corning Museum of Glass
Corning, New York: The Corning Museum of Glass, 1982.

Stout, Sandra McPhee
The Complete Book of McKee Glass
North Kansas City, Missouri: Trojan Press, 1972.

Index

Numbers in boldface type refer to entries. Numbers in italics refer to pages.